BOMBS AND BARBED WIRE

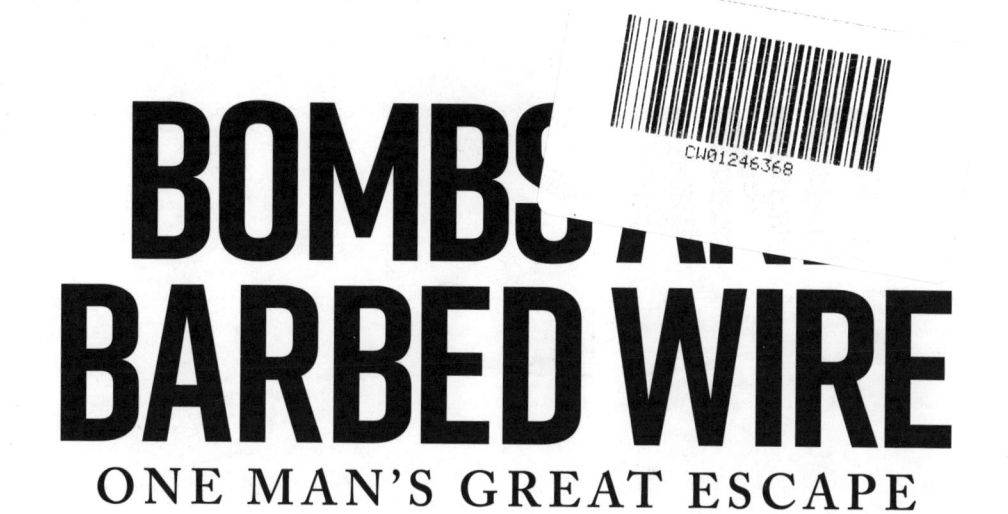

ONE MAN'S GREAT ESCAPE

JEFF STEEL and
MICHAEL ADLAM

Disclaimer: Every effort has been made to source copyright holders of images within, in some cases ownership could not be determined.

Copyright © Jeffrey Scott Steel and Michael John Adlam

First published 2021

This book is copyright. Apart from any fair dealing for the purposes of private study, research, criticism or review as permitted under the Copyright Act, no part may be reproduced, stored in a retrieval system or transmitted in any form or by any means, electronic, mechanical, photocopying, recording or otherwise, without written permission.

All inquiries should be made to the publishers.

Big Sky Publishing Pty Ltd
PO Box 303, Newport, NSW 2106, Australia
Phone: 1300 364 611
Fax: (61 2) 9918 2396
Email: info@bigskypublishing.com.au
Web: www.bigskypublishing.com.au

Cover design and typesetting: Think Productions

Title: Bombs and Barbed Wire: One man's great escape
Creators: Jeff Steel and Michael Adlam
First published 2021
ISBN: 978-1-922488-24-4

 A catalogue record for this book is available from the National Library of Australia

Cover images of Ambrose and Miranda Adlam are courtesy of the Adlam family. The image of the RCAF 405 Squadron Halifax bomber is supplied with thanks to the Royal Canadian Air Force History and Heritage Office, with the assistance of the Royal Australian Air Force History and Heritage Branch.

BOMBS AND BARBED WIRE

ONE MAN'S GREAT ESCAPE

www.bigskypublishing.com.au

JEFF STEEL and MICHAEL ADLAM

Dedicated to Norman Moss 1929 – 2020
of Whitehaven County Grammar School, UK
Teacher, Mentor, Friend

Und wenn Du meinst, es geht nicht mehr,
kommt von irgendwo ein Lichtlein her.

Just when you think there's no hope,
from somewhere comes a little light.

CONTENTS

Chapter 1: Dawn 4

Chapter 2: The Balloon Goes Up 12

Chapter 3: 38 Squadron and Vivian Rosewarne 17

Chapter 4: The Shiny Ten 31

Chapter 5: Mr and Mrs Adlam Return from South Africa..... 41

Chapter 6: Johnny Lennox and the Crew Come Together 56

Chapter 7: A Walk on the Wet Side – Leeming Revisited 70

Chapter 8: Ambrose's Raids – St Nazaire 76

Chapter 9: The Raid on Kiel 88

Chapter 10: The Raid on Stuttgart... 98

Chapter 11: Welcome to Gransden 110

Chapter 12: The Raid on Duisburg...................................... 119

Chapter 13: Target for Tonight: Dortmund 130

Chapter 14: Enemy Coast Ahead! 142

Chapter 15: Hauptmann Thimmig Boosts His Tally 149

Chapter 16: Imprisonment – The First Days 158

Chapter 17: Dulag Luft – The Subtle Oppressors................ 170

Chapter 18: Dulag Luft – The Unsubtle Oppressors 185
Chapter 19: Ambrose in Wonderland 196
Chapter 20: Welcome to Stalag Luft III! 217
Chapter 21: A Penguin Once Again 232
Chapter 22: That Bitter Sweet Winter of '43 248
Chapter 23: Extortion and Two Earthquakes 261
Chapter 24: I See You Stand Like Greyhounds in the Slips 279
Chapter 25: The Great Escape – The Moment of Truth 294
Chapter 26: Reality Dawns 303
Chapter 27: Fallingbostel: The Three Realities and W/O Deans 315
Chapter 28: The Long March 326
Chapter 29: The 1219 from Paddington to loucester (Central) 339
Appendix 1: What Became of the People in the Story? 349
Appendix 2: Ambrose's Odyssey 353
Select Bibliography 355
Acknowledgements 358
About the Authors 360

SERGEANT AMBROSE ADLAM, 405 SQUADRON, RCAF

And could a man do good?
There was one way that he could
In a world descended into filth and mire
So, his name went on the form
For a light blue uniform
He signed for Bomber Command... and barbed wire.

Each night in hostile air
Stuttgart, Duisburg, St Nazaire,
He chose to fly into the way of harm
'Bombing Nazis' was the aim
With high explosive, shrapnel, flame
Nightfighter bastards came for him in swarms.

Dortmund was 'target for tonight'
And there never was a fight
But a 110 made his Halifax a pyre
Four only got away
Those he never saw again
No more bomber command... just barbed wire.

To Stalag Luft he came
With escape the greatest game
What part he might have played? Of that he never said
He was never the kind of bloke
To sit it out and light a smoke
No bloody fear, he'd sooner have been shot down and very dead.

But that game it went awry
With fifty men condemned to die
His unspoken memory unsaid, locked in but dire
But would he do it all again?
He would have signed that dotted line
To sign for Bomber Command... and barbed wire.

PROLOGUE

My own dear wife, I am out of hospital and at a camp at last and my address is Kriegsgefangenenlager No 3.

Ambrose Adlam wrote those words on 5 October 1943. The place in which he had found himself was Stalag Luft III. When he wrote them he had no idea that that place would become famous, or infamous, across a whole world of military history. After the war he never mentioned the camp or his time there. As a product of the English working class and from the back streets of an industrial town, he would have had no expectation to touch the hem of history. Touch it he did but, having touched it, he just wanted it out of his mind forever.

Miranda, his wife, his children and his six siblings had no idea that he had ever been there. His letters had indeed been marked 'Kriegsfangenlager III' but the significance was not apparent. There was only one glimpse of the story and that flickered and died with Ambrose who, himself, died in 1962. The clue lay in a hand-drawn map which Ambrose drew of his war-time journey for his children. He indicated that he had been held prisoner in Stalag Luft III but the reader had to look for that fact. No one did and, indeed, in 1962 few people in the world had ever heard of Stalag Luft III. In a fit of irony, fate had decreed that the famous film The Great Escape was already in production when he died. The map is added as an appendix to this book.

Half a century later, his son Mike in Gloucestershire talked with researcher and writer Jeff Steel in Melbourne, Australia. Mike had inherited a pile of letters after his mother's death. She had asked that he burn them. Instinct told him not to.

BOMBS AND BARBED WIRE

Given that Ambrose had taken part in a number of raids, Jeff thought that the story might well be interesting: 'No promises, mind!'. The letters might hold valuable information; sometimes they do in these cases. He took the job on.

What Jeff found was evidence of a dramatic story, one which Ambrose clearly did not want to tell during his lifetime.

Among the letters was one postmarked Stalag Luft III on 25 March 1944. Ambrose had written it at the exact time that the camp was in an uproar as the Luftwaffe guards had discovered the tunnels and the Great Escape.

Regarding Ambrose's career in different squadrons, it was relatively easy to find out what Royal Air Force (RAF) units he had served in and which raids he had been involved in.

From his letters and historical information, it was possible to reconstruct life on an operational bomber station: Ambrose was at RAF Leeming and Marham as an 'erk' – technical ground crew. This was not enough for him. A mixture of pride, bravado, competition with his brother Bill and a dislike of the Third Reich made him volunteer for air combat duty. He was later at RAF Leeming and RAF Gransden Lodge as a flight engineer, whose technical expertise helped the pilot, Johnny Lennox, fly their heavy Halifax bombers.

Ambrose's story charts the perils of training: some 5,000 Bomber Command crew members died in training without ever flying on operations. It also charts the perils of flying on those missions – Ambrose would have known perfectly well that he would be unlikely to complete a 'tour' of 30; *all aircrews did. But he had* made a commitment to risk his life dropping bombs on Hitler's Third Reich.

It was also possible to reconstruct the life and death struggle of the actual raids, how he was shot down and life in the POW camps. Ambrose was held in several different camps; the key ones were Dulag Luft, near Frankfurt; Stalag Luft III; and Fallingbostel near Hannover.

Jeff was fortunate enough to be helped by Tony Casson of Melbourne, whose father, John Casson, was in the first two camps. As will become evident in the story, John Casson would have known

PROLOGUE

Ambrose. Tony gave Jeff key insights into the Great Escape, some of which have not been published in other works.

Ambrose's son Mike is in no doubt that, as a 'get-go' type, Ambrose would have involved himself in the work of the Great Escape. With his bullet and shrapnel wounds he could not have done digging or heavy lifting work, but there were plenty of other roles to help the escapers for which he was admirably suited.

The events such as raids, conditions in prison camps and historically significant events depicted in this book are all true. There is ample source material from published works (see Select Bibliography) and especially from the UK National Archive, which allows us to track Ambrose's journey through World War II.

Mike described his father's personality, attitudes and bias for action to Jeff. He also gave insights into his dad's general view of the world, the war and the Nazis, which enabled Jeff to develop dialogue to bring the character of Ambrose to life for readers. If Ambrose were to read this biography what would be his comment? Mike believes he'd say wryly, 'You got it about right, you buggers! But I wanted to forget it – all of it.'

CHAPTER 1
DAWN

AUGUST 1936

Ambrose Adlam was destined for a high stakes game. At the start he did not know it. *He would find out.* It is 1936; it is either the best time for a male to be approaching manhood or it is the worst.

This year is the seminal year of the 20th century. Adolf Hitler has been in power for three years and is gaining in confidence, daring and muscle. He sends troops to kick out the French and Belgian occupation troops from the Rheinland. He reclaims it for Germany. Hitler dabbles in the Spanish Civil War. Hitler's Olympic Games in Berlin show a vision of a new dynamic Germany. Hitler announces to the world the Volkswagen: each German family is to have a car. Hitler opens the first concentration camp, albeit quietly, at Oranienburg. Hitler forms a special relationship with the Italian dictator Mussolini, and signs a pact with Japan against the Soviet Union.

It is not clear at this stage where the world is headed. On the streets of Ambrose's native Gloucester in the English heartland, there is trepidation, uncertainty and fear. As in Gloucester it is the same in Paris, in London, in Melbourne, Australia and across the entire globe.

If Ambrose Adlam had wanted a life without drama, Adolf Hitler's various strategies, plans and aspirations were to put paid to that pretty darned smartish. On that evening in the middle of the year, in Gloucester, Ambrose was faced with the dawning of a new world. It was not merely one dawn, it was several. Each of those dawns would, in its own unique way, interplay with his life. Each would take him where fate had decreed he should go. It would take him to places

CHAPTER 1

he never expected to go; some of these were fascinating and without doubt became major highlights of his life. Finally, fate would take him somewhere that he did not want to go: Stalag Luft III. It would be important, later, to suppress that memory and never talk of it. The family might think that all had been well. They would be quite at liberty to do so but they would be badly in error. All had not been well. Ambrose was destined to soar into the clouds. He was destined to descend into the lower intestines of hell. Afterwards, he could not allow those memories into his mind.

Few survivors could.

However, on this night in 1936 he would go to the pictures in Gloucester with his brother, Bill.

'What a bloody flick, eh, Bill?'

'You could see why they banned it,' said Bill expansively. 'Mr Baldwin wanted us to be nice to the Germans when he was in power last time. Now he's back in power again he's perfectly happy for us not to be nice to the Germans. Bloody politicians, eh?'

'Tell you what, Bill, I think things are going to get very nasty with Germany in the next couple of years. I don't know, mind, but I reckon his taking the ban off this film is just one way of softening us all up.'

'You reckon?'

'Well, the whole film makes the Germans look bloody uncivilised for a start; I mean, it takes a special kind of monster to shoot nurses.'

They walked away from the crowds at the Picturedrome Theatre and headed into town. The film which they had seen was *Dawn* starring Dame Sybil Thorndike. It was a powerful piece. It told the story of Nurse Edith Cavell, who had been shot by the Germans in World War I. She had helped hundreds of British soldiers escape from German captivity. They put her against a wall in her underclothes and shot her. It was not merely the narrative, the superb storytelling and charismatic acting which were of note. 'Bill, you know lots of people in the army… did we do that to German nurses in the Great War?'

'Not in the Gloucestershire Regiment, I can tell you that. Some of the old-timers have got some nasty stories about the German troops, though. There was one place where they were dragging prisoners behind trucks for fun. They shot an awful lot of civvies as well.'

'I see Germany's backing Spain now in the civil war down there. Do you reckon that can lead to war in Europe?'

'I really don't know, Ad, but with that bloke Hitler in power any bloody thing can happen. If the Spanish Civil War does really get going, there's a couple of blokes in our works say they will volunteer to fight on the republican side against the Fascists.'

'Would you go with them?'

'Not a chance. That Franco bloke is a nasty piece of work, but he has a proper army and that means disciplines, drill and training. These blokes in our factory are just rank amateurs; they won't last beyond the first skirmish. How much money would you put on Gloucester City against the Arsenal?'

'Not much.'

'Well, that's what it would be like, Ad: slaughter.'

'She was fantastic in that film, though, didn't you think? Dame Sybil, I mean.'

'She's fantastic in everything; do you remember we went to see her in *Macbeth* and the *Merchant of Venice*? They're big Labour Party supporters, you know, she and Sir Lewis, her husband.' In the general run of events men of the working class are not given to enthusiasm for Shakespeare. Such was Dame Sybil's following as an actress that she attracted a vastly wider audience to his plays. Some said that they would pay to see her read the Gloucester telephone directory, not that there were many entries in it in those days. In one of those flukes of fate which are stranger than fiction, a family member of Dame Sybil was to play a key role in Ambrose's story at the lowest point of his life.

'Hang on, Ad, what have we here?'

They were walking down Eastgate Street in the centre of Gloucester.

'Leaflet, gents? British Union of Fascists! Read it and come and join us!'

An earnest young man in black trousers and a tight, black, rolled-neck pullover walked over to them. His accent was from London; this had to be one of Mosley's henchmen trying to drum up support.

CHAPTER 1

There was little doubt in any British person's mind at that time that Sir Oswald Mosley had a long-term plan to take over parliament, take over the army and take over the country. It would then become a vassal state to Hitler's Germany. There was no doubt whatsoever that a vast majority of British people did not want Mosley at any price.

'Fight against the communists and the Jewboys, protect the British Empire. One per cent of the population are Jewish and 25 per cent of them are millionaires. There has to be something wrong with that, doesn't there?'

'Look, mate, it would do us all a favour if you would take your anti-Semitism and stick it where the sun doesn't shine.' It was Bill who spoke.

'Come on, gents, Karl Marx was Jewish; the Rothschilds; in Germany there was Eisener, Luxemburg and Liebknecht. The Jews winkle their way in everywhere; we have to winkle them out again like Herr Hitler is doing to protect Germany.'

'Yeah, we saw how your lot tried to protect us with your battle in Cable Street in London. You are a bloody disgrace to this country, that's all you are.'

'You look like a couple of likely lads who could look after yourselves. Come to one of our meetings. We've got William Joyce coming in a couple of weeks' time. You should hear what he has to say.'

William Joyce was a brilliant scholar of English, a very charming man and a dyed-in-the-wool fascist. He will come into the story later as the evil 'Lord Haw Haw'.

'If I came to your meeting, I would bloody show you if I can take care of myself or not.' Ad joined the conversation.

'Oh, come on, Ad, we don't really want a punch-up on the way home.'

'Come on, lads, Sir Oswald Mosley is the future for this country. We should be in alliance with Herr Hitler and protecting this country from the Stalinists and the Jewish menace.'

'Listen, matey, if you peddle that stuff around here you are going to finish up in the river and there will be no bugger to pull you out.'

'Now then, now then, what's all this?'

A tall figure in a helmet emerged from the shadows.

'You shouldn't be protecting this scum, Constable, you should be kicking his head in. We're going to be fighting them in a couple of years' time.'

'My job is to protect the King's peace, lad, and these blokes are not disobeying any laws as far as my inspector can see.'

'Yeah! That's another thing, MATEY!' said the earnest young man, very paramilitary in his tight black sweater. 'We have got the King on our side.'

'Like bloody hell you have. Why would King Edward have anything to do with scum like you?'

'That's enough! Go on, lads, off home; we don't want any trouble, do we?'

From his tone, the policeman found Mosleyites as unpalatable as did most of the rest of the population of Great Britain. But a policeman's lot is sometimes not a happy one and he had a duty to perform. That meant protecting the buggers.

The young man backed away.

'Ad! Come on, let's go home. You are going to have plenty of time to deal with the likes of this creature and it will be soon enough.'

They walked on and were both calm by the time they got back to the family home.

'It's going to get nasty, you know, Bill, you can just bloody smell it in the air.'

It was not a good time to be 20-something in that seminal year of 1936. The world stood at a crossroads. Everyone alive at that time reported that you could smell it in the air. Only the most optimistic could hold any hope that the world would remain as sane, reasonable and benign as it was in Britain's sceptred isle.

'I was talking with Dad a couple of days ago, Ad; he reckons the world is going daft.'

'Why was that, then?'

'Well, in his day, King Edward was on the throne – Edward VII that is, not Edward VIII – and the world ran properly. Everyone had a place and they got on with what they had to get on with. It was a nicer place. We hadn't had a war that killed millions. We didn't have

CHAPTER 1

communists or fascists or any of these scum regimes around Europe. There was no general strike. God! Wasn't that just awful? We didn't have unemployment…'

Unemployment – there was the rub! Both Bill and Ad were fortunate enough to be in employment: Bill as a machinist in the England's Glory match factory; Ad as a cooper, a barrel maker, at the Gloucester Oil Mills. Neither man was in a job which matched his personality or capability. In those hard times, being in the wrong job was not an issue. Even though the pay was meagre they were consciously grateful for the simple ability to pay their bills.

Many were reduced to eating in soup kitchens or taking soul-destroying charity. The Gloucestershire collieries of Foxes Bridge, Bilson and Lightmoor were laying men off by the hundreds. Families stayed in bed all day to conserve energy. There was nothing to eat. Similar stories came in from nearby South Wales, and the industrial heartlands of Staffordshire, Lancashire, Yorkshire, Durham and Northumberland. It felt as though Britain was dying.

'I see Hitler's army has invaded the Rheinland now and no-one did anything to stop him,' said Ad.

'How could he invade it? The Rheinland is in Germany.'

'Oh, I don't know. It was something to do with the Treaty of Versailles.'

'I see his henchmen are rounding up communists now and sending them to prison camps.'

'Did you ever work out what the difference is between the communists and the fascists?'

'There's a bloke at the factory says he knows what the difference is. Fascism is the exploitation of one man by another and communism is the complete opposite.'

They both laughed.

'Do you think the King will abdicate, Bill?'

Oh God! It did not matter where you looked, there was turmoil, uncertainty and anxiety.

'It's starting to look like it. It won't go down well in the country, though, Ad, I can tell you that. He visited those people in the East

End when the unemployment was at its worst and that went down very well. Even the *Daily Mirror*, which supports the socialist Labour Party, gave him a good write-up. The King is a very popular man. And Prince Albert, I mean he's a nice bloke, but he's not exactly a leader of men. England's Glory, eh? England's bloody glory! If the Moreland family started the factory what would they call it now? "England's bugger's muddle", I would think. Come on, get the kettle on, I want a cup of char before I go home. Have you got any of those elvers left?'

'For God's sake, let's cheer up a bit. Think about something else. What's on at the pictures next week?'

'Oh, there's that new picture *Things to Come*.'

'Isn't that about Britain getting bombed into ruins? That's just what we bloody need,' said Ad, sighing.

'Oh, come on, Ad, it's got Ralph Richardson in it, he's always very good.'

'I'd rather find a nice comedy.'

Twenty-year-olds are supposed to be like Labrador dogs: happy, optimistic and finding something to love in everyone and everything.

In a perfect world, 20-somethings would not have to agonise about whether the country was going to descend into chaos. They should not have to worry about whether the whole of Europe was going to war again. The horrors would now be much worse than those of 20 years previously. Now there were bombers which could reduce a city to ashes. Twenty-year-olds should not have to worry about whether their entire civilisation, which had ruled the waves (if not the world), now showed cracks in the edifice, which, unchecked would fall into some kind of civil strife or even civil war.

Nevertheless, to those who were of adult age in those dark days a series of challenging questions could not be ignored.

Was the regime of Adolf Hitler in Germany taking Europe back into a second tragic war within a half-century?

CHAPTER 1

It was.

Was the Spanish Civil War about to break out and Hitler use it as a proving ground for his massively increased army and air force?

It was.

Was the other unpalatable face of Europe, as embodied in Stalin's Union of Soviet Socialist Republics, plotting day and night to undermine and overthrow every other government in Europe?

It was.

Was King Edward VIII really on the side of the fascists, as the young man in the street had claimed?

He was, although knowledge of this was to be officially managed for over half a century.

Was Britain's war machine on a par with that of Nazi Germany in the event of war breaking out?

It was not.

Everyone alive at that time understood quite clearly that the old certainties of Bill and Ambrose's dad's time were gone. That age of certainty, stability and accepted truth and normality had gone. The dark night that occurred after World War I had come and gone. Now was the dawn of a new age.

What they did not know was what kind of age it would be. They were not in a state of optimism. They had seen the Depression descend on Gloucester as it descended on the rest of Britain and America and Germany and Australia and all of Western Europe. They had seen the Spanish Civil War begin. The fascist dictator Mussolini had increased his empire in Abyssinia. He had gassed tribesmen on horseback. Was there no limit to the disgusting behaviour of these people? Over in Hungary and Rumania more fascist dictatorships sprouted like fountains of evil.

Hitler annexed Austria, which, in all honesty, wanted to be annexed but it represented yet another victory for fascism. Then Hitler annexed the Sudetenland of Czechoslovakia. Then he annexed the rest of Czechoslovakia. Where was this all going? No-one had any answers. Everyone was frightened.

CHAPTER 2
THE BALLOON GOES UP

25 AUGUST 1939

'They're coming! They're coming!'

The policeman in his tall, authoritative helmet held out his arms widely and smiled indulgently and paternally at the crowd on College Street. The worst thing in the world was just about to happen. Britain was now very nearly at war with Germany again. You heard it over and over that 'you could smell it in the air'. Gloucester still showed the results of World War I 20 years before: men with missing limbs, nervous tics, and those who woke up screaming late at night. It was also full of those who had not come back, who only existed as memories. Few families escaped the sadness left from World War I. Now it was all going to start again. The 5th Battalion of the Gloucestershire Regiment had been mobilised to go to France 'just in case'.

The threat of war had at least given Ambrose Adlam a direction beyond the soul-destroying task of making barrels; he had volunteered to join the RAF as an aircraftman: a technician repairing aircraft engines. He was grateful that the commanding officer had given him a leave pass. He wanted to turn out on the Gloucester streets as did most of the rest of the population of that medieval city. They filled the pavements and crowded onto the road. There was no question about it: hearts were heavy going into this new war. Even so, they were going to give 'their lads' a rousing cheer. The British prided themselves on

CHAPTER 2

their stiff upper lip and, heavy heart or not, they were going to give their boys a good send-off.

'Come on, everyone, step back onto the pavement and let the lads pass. Thank you, madam. A bit further back if you would, sir.'

From around the corner in Westgate Street they could hear the soldiers already. They could hear the thumping of the bass drum. They heard the staccato clatter of 800 pairs of hobnailed boots 'clacking' in strict unison. They heard the band playing the regimental song 'Where Be that Blackbird Be?'

Around the corner they could hear the waves of applause. The first of the parade swung around smartly to the right and into College Street. The band music was closer now. The troops marched with the expected military precision and 'bags of swank'. Ambrose looked for the massive primrose-coloured regimental flag: that flag with the Union Jack in its top left-hand corner – there it was!

The regimental flag was en route from the barracks and coming nearer now. In the procession were several hundred soldiers led by a colonel on horseback. The flag was to be placed in Gloucester Cathedral for the duration of hostilities. It was now understood with crystal transparency from the inner sanctums of Downing Street to the roughest pub in London's east end that war with Germany, yet again, was inescapable. The crowd were supportive but sombre. You could almost hear their thoughts: 'What sort of world will we have when all of this is over? Which of these soldiers will not come back? Who do I know that will die? But we still have to show that we support them and that every bullet they fire is for us.'

The huge regimental flag flapped and fluttered its magnificent way past Ambrose, borne by a colour guard of six who clattered by with a hail of hobnailed boots and operatic military pomp.

A junior officer carried the flag with military pomp, gravitas and ceremony. Behind him marched the colour sergeant with no less authority, certainty and self-confidence. Behind the colour sergeant, with their red sashes, rifles and fixed bayonets, marched the colour guard with great pomp and ceremony. *There he was!* That was the man that Ambrose was looking for: his brother Bill. Bill had been selected for this party, which was an astonishing honour for a man who had not yet been a sergeant for six months. Ambrose would have to say, though, that Bill was every inch the soldier and was going to do his duty whether Mr Hitler and his massive army stood in the way or not. Heck! Bill looked so military, so proud and so determined that Mr Hitler and his hordes stood no chance. 'There wasn't a Nazi who could kill an Adlam!'. The brothers had said it time and time again. They really believed it. They had to believe it! The trouble was that the German army was known to be very, very good at what they did. Ad hoped he was not looking at Bill for the last time.

Something else was placed at Gloucester Cathedral for the duration of hostilities: the Coronation Throne from Westminster Abbey. The only time in 800 years that the Coronation Throne had been moved previously was for the investiture of Oliver Cromwell as Lord Protector in 1653. It was all so relentless! Everywhere you looked, every small fact that you learned, behind every corner of existence there was something which said, 'war is just around the corner'.

The 5th Battalion now went off by special train to join the 2nd Battalion in Northern France. Gloucester was left in silence, foreboding and fear. *What would happen next?*

Less than a week later, Hitler's armies had attacked Poland. He was not going to pull them back. Hearts sank in Gloucester and across the whole of the United Kingdom. Eight days later, back now at RAF Locking, near Bristol, Ambrose listened to Neville Chamberlain's radio speech.

It was 11:15 on Sunday, 3 September 1939. Ambrose would never forget that speech, nor would anyone else who heard it.

> *This morning the British Ambassador in Berlin handed the German Government a final note stating that, unless we heard from them by 11 o'clock that they were prepared at once to withdraw their troops from Poland, a state of war would exist between us.*
>
> *I have to tell you now that no such undertaking has been received, and that consequently this country is at war with Germany.*

CHAPTER 2

Those words 'and that consequently this country is at war with Germany' resounded and reverberated and replayed through their minds. The last lot had been bad enough with God knows how many dead. This lot was likely to be worse. The words stopped reverberating as Mr Chamberlain ended his speech.

Now may God bless you all. May He defend the right. It is the evil things that we shall be fighting against – brute force, bad faith, injustice, oppression and persecution – and against them I am certain that the right will prevail.

Ad was glad he was in the RAF. At least he had volunteered to join up. At least he was in a position to do something about the evil German bastards. So far, however, his RAF career had been less than glorious. After volunteering he had been posted to RAF Cardington in Bedfordshire, which was probably the least glamorous posting in the world: a balloon station. Facing a war in which bombers were going to be the main form of attack he was stuck in balloons, which were a failed technology even during World War I. His unit was known as the 'balloonatics'. Funny though it was, it was also an accurate title. That was depressing.

He had applied for a transfer to a technician's role and was now aircraftman Grade 2 in training. He was, at least, training for a ground crew role in which he would 'maintain airframes, engines and rigging' on aircraft on an operational station. Eight weeks after the war had been declared, he passed his course and was duly posted to 38 Squadron at RAF Marham near Norwich, which had recently been equipped with the new and rather natty Vickers Wellington twin-engined bombers.

And so now, in November 1939, the developments in the war were… none. Nothing whatsoever had happened. Hitler had swallowed up one half of Poland; Stalin had swallowed up the other half. What was happening there did not bear thinking about but

BOMBS AND BARBED WIRE

over here, in rural East Anglia, the main atrocity of the war was life in freezing Nissen huts. Letters from his brother Bill said the same. The papers were now calling this 'World War II', but this war was a complete and total non-event.

Nevertheless, a strict blackout was enforced by pompous, self-important and generally hated air raid wardens. They would shout in a very rude and un-British voice at any family letting the slightest chink of light sneak out of their parlour. Rationing of food came in. The management of the family ration book rapidly became a central part of the civilian ecosystem. By law, everyone had to carry a gas mask when they left their house in case of a gas attack from the Luftwaffe. The lessons of the bomber threat from 'Things to Come' were being taken seriously in high places.

CHAPTER 3
38 SQUADRON AND VIVIAN ROSEWARNE

3 NOVEMBER 1939

'Hallo! You're the new erk are you? I'm Vivian Rosewarne. How's my kite looking?'

Aircraftmen were always called 'erks' after the London cockney pronunciation of 'erkcraftmen'.

'Pleased to meet you, Vivian, I'm Ambrose Adlam, but everyone calls me Ad. We found out why it was overheating and it's as good as new now.'

So, on this day Ad did indeed join the ranks of the erks. The relationship of erks to aircrews was of a special and rarified nature. The aircrews flew the aeroplane, but it was the erks who did the engineering work and the maintenance work. It was they who were to patch up the bullet holes, removed the shrapnel and scrubbed the inside of an aeroplane, after a raid, with petrol. At least they would if there were any meaningful raids. 'Not like last time,' said the old-timers. 'After we declared war, we was off to France. After three weeks we was sticking bayonets into Jerry at Mons. It's been eight weeks now and nothing's happened. Not much of a war, this one.'

BOMBS AND BARBED WIRE

No. 38 Squadron flew sweeps and sorties and reconnaissance operations over the North Sea. No-one was dropping any bombs on any German positions, shipping or armed formations. In fact, there were no armed formations within range of RAF Marham. Could it just be that the war was going to fizzle out and come to nothing at all? Some people in the pubs, church halls and byways of middle England were starting to ask just that question.

It was with some comfort, therefore, that Ad was able to bring his feet under the table in his first operational squadron. He was in the odd situation of doing a war-time job during an official war but where no war time activity was happening. The pilots would report any faults to 'Chiefie', typically a flight sergeant who would allocate jobs among the erks. A day or so later the pilot would look into the hangar to see how repairs were progressing. The pilots were quite clear that they depended on the erks if their aeroplane was to stay in the air and bought them lots of beer to cement that relationship.

In the pubs of that Norfolk village – The Jolly Brewers, The Crown and Mitre and The Globe – aircrews and erks frequently drank together. The pubs were much better places to fight a war than the bloody trenches of Flanders that the old boys, irritatingly, kept telling them about. Old-timers were outraged that RAF officers and 'other ranks' would not only drink together but were on first name terms. This was a daring development in class-obsessed Britain. 'This lot will never beat 'Itler,' you might have heard them say. 'This behaviour is just not done among real military men. Not done at all!'

And so, the war progressed, or indeed did not progress because nothing kept on happening throughout November, all through the winter and into spring. Over in Alsace somewhere, Bill had won a Military Medal in a skirmish with a German armed patrol. He had retrieved a machine gun from being captured at some risk to his own life. Risky though Bill's adventure was, it was all a long way short of the butchery of the Somme, Ypres and the Marne. Oh well, there were always card games, and Ad was becoming very proficient at maintaining the very impressive Vickers Wellington heavy bombers.

CHAPTER 3

'Honestly, though,' said Rosewarne, 'you should have seen what we had here a few weeks before you got here.'

'Before we had these magnificent brand-new kites?'

'Yeah, we had Fairey Hendons and Handley Page Heyfords.'

'Crikey, I haven't even heard of those, let alone worked on them.'

'Oh, we didn't need erks on those. If anything went wrong the pilots used to stick them together with chewing gum and string. It terrified us flying those bloody contraptions, but I don't know if they would have terrified Jerry too much.'

On 3 December events became more serious.

After breakfast, Ad went to hitch a lift into Kings Lynn to do a bit of shopping.

'No you don't, mate, the station's closed,' said the RAF police sergeant.

'It's what?'

'Everyone has to stay on the station, mate, that includes you. You weren't going to meet a young lady were you?'

'Just to buy some boot polish and toothpaste, really.'

'Well, those boots will just have to stay dirty. Anyway, those are our orders.'

'What about officers, then?'

'Group Captain Keith is allowed out but no-one else; not wing commanders not no-one else.'

It was just as well that Ad had not made it to Kings Lynn. Rosewarne and a couple of the other pilots came to see Chiefie.

'Well, Chiefie, it looks like this is it. There's a "do" on this afternoon.'

'What? We're going to go and bomb someone? So that was why the station's cordoned off.'

'Yes. It very much looks like it. The reason we came down is just to make sure that our kites are in tip-top order. We don't want any Germans getting the drop on us if we can help it.'

BOMBS AND BARBED WIRE

After exactly a month on the station, the level of urgency increased suddenly and dramatically.

An hour later the pilots came back from their pre-operation test flight.

'Right, chaps, that's as good as we can get them. If you get shot down it's down to Mr Barnes Wallis who designed the bloody things and not us because we have tuned them like a fiddle in the Halle Orchestra.'

'Thanks, Chiefie, we're just off for the briefing with Wing Commander Adams.'

An hour later the pilots were back. 'There's three of us on an op together with some kites from 115 and 149 squadrons to bomb some German warships in the Heligoland Bight.'

The selected crews were in a state of great excitement. The whole station was energised, enthused and entranced at the idea of giving old Hitler a punch 'up the throat'. All aircrews, not only the selected three but the whole station, were bubbling with the thought of it. They looked avidly at atlases and found that Heligoland was off the West Coast of Germany, north of Cuxhafen. That meant about an hour and a bit flying time from Marham and they would be back in time for dinner and a few pints of best bitter in the Jolly Brewers afterwards.

After the early afternoon takeoff, the station was quiet, tense and on edge. They wanted to hear that the bomber fleet (well, it almost was) had sunk a battleship or two or at least a cruiser. Some three and bit hours later they were back: all three.

As his aeroplane taxied back to the hangar, Ad could see through the Perspex canopy that Rosewarne's demeanour was a mixture of elation tempered with disappointment.

'We saw them and we dropped bombs but we didn't hit a bloody thing.'

So, even if they had not actually sunk the massive German battleships the squadron had, at least, broken its duck and was off to a start in the war.

A second aeroplane taxied back. The pilot was in a state of extreme elation.

CHAPTER 3

'We got attacked by a Messerschmitt, Leading Aircraftman Copley, the rear gunner, shot the bugger down.' This meant that he was likely to be awarded a Distinguished Flying Medal (which turned out to be true) and this, in turn, meant that the 'quiet celebratory drinks' in the Jolly Brewers turned into a right old Royal Air Force booze-up, of which the erks were an integral part.

Then nothing happened again.

Kings Lynn was a major centre for the evacuation of children from London. The assumption was that London was likely to be bombed. Rural Kings Lynn was not. Thousands of London children were therefore billeted with families around Kings Lynn and Norfolk. Now they were starting to drift home. Ever since the declaration of war there had been a governmental edict: all British people were to carry their gas masks at all times. Failure meant possible prosecution. Now the British people were starting not to carry their gas masks as they went about their business. In theory the Norfolk Constabulary should have charged them, but the police were as fed up with the non-war as much as anyone else.

Both in RAF Marham and in Kings Lynn people still grudgingly observed the blackout but the enthusiasm was clearly waning. When the air raid warden shouted, 'Turn off that bloody light!' he was likely to get a reply that was equally as raucous and completely unprintable. For the whole United Kingdom, the war seemed to be running out of steam. Rationing of food, clothes, furniture and all necessities of life had rapidly become an integral but irritating part of the tapestry of life. As a member of an operational squadron Ad was largely exempt from this but resentment across the country was growing; you could see it in the carping editorials in the daily newspapers.

Christmas came and went as did Pancake Day, Valentine's Day and Easter. People were openly complaining about the rationing. What the hell was it all for? 'In the first lot we had lost a million men by now,' said the old-timers. 'This isn't much of a bloody war.'

Rosewarne's crew drew a commendation from Wing Commander Adams for spotting a stricken lighthouse ship in the North Sea, which led to the crew being taken off and saved from a very nasty situation.

'Well done, Viv!' said the gang in the Jolly Brewers.

'Not exactly war, though, is it?' Rosewarne shrugged apologetically.

On 9 April, the war finally began to hot up. British forces, for some inscrutable reason, invaded Norway. This was decidedly odd because Norway was a declared neutral country like Switzerland. No. 38 Squadron was given reconnaissance work reporting on German Naval movements in the North Sea. It was not exactly hot war work but it was, at least, war work of some sort. The Germans took Denmark.

The Norway campaign was shorted lived, grotesquely unsuccessful and demonstrated that whatever was happening in the war, Britain was not winning it. On 10 May, the newspaper headlines screamed that Chamberlain had resigned and Winston Churchill had taken over. This was a highly controversial appointment because many saw Churchill as a megalomaniac, self-deluded war monger. Others thought he was just the right man to stand up to Hitler.

As it transpired, the United Kingdom was not afforded any time whatsoever to debate the controversy. With no prior ceremony the German forces came pouring through the Ardennes mountains and into Holland and Belgium. No-one saw it coming. No-one could believe the suddenness. No-one anticipated the size of the attack. No-one was prepared. It was though a massive dam had burst and the floodwaters were rising by the minute. The flow of brotherly letters from Bill to Ad ceased immediately.

The mood on RAF Marham changed. Holland fell to the Germans; Belgium fell to the Germans. By the end of May the huge British Expeditionary Force in France had been pushed into a small pocket

CHAPTER 3

around Dunkirk. Britain and her French allies were losing everything. Germany was winning everything.

On 27 May, the vast evacuation at Dunkirk had begun. Where the hell was Bill? There had been no letter now for three weeks. Was he alive or was he dead? He was unlikely to be a prisoner, he would have charged the Germans with bayonet, broken bottles and half bricks, if need be, but would have gone down fighting. On 30 May RAF Marham was again closed off: this meant an 'op' – an operation.

'Mornin', Viv, where you off to today?'

'Mornin', Ad, we've got to go to a place called Veurne in Belgium to drop as much ordnance as possible on the Germans. There's no particular aiming point; it's just "hit anything that is coloured grey". Roads, railways, tanks, gentlemen in square helmets, our orders are to hit anything that we can. They're pressing onto the northern approaches to Dunkirk. Apparently, there are hundreds of thousands trying to get out through the port.'

'Hell!' Ad thought. 'Bill is probably in that lot if he is still alive. Let him be safe, oh, let him be safe.'

Chiefie demanded the erks do a perfect, perfect job that morning: better than perfect.

RAF Marham waved off the 17 Wellingtons of the squadron. Later that afternoon they came back; at least, most of them did. Rosewarne's crew was not among them. So, this was it then: this was what the war was going to be like.

The disappearance of Rosewarne was the first sign of a procedure with which Ad would become only too familiar. At around 4 a.m. he would be woken by the clatter of boots as the men from the Committee of Adjustments entered the Nissen hut to remove the personal effects of Rosewarne and his crew. Their small van drove away taking all traces of the man with him. The next morning over breakfast someone would say, 'Rosewarne's crew have had the chop.'

'Poor buggers' would be the answer. No-one would refer to the crew again. It was as if it were tempting fate.

A new crew would take over the beds of the missing crew and life went on. It was as though ripples had gone across a surface of water but now it was smooth again.

In the normal run of events, Rosewarne's crew would have been forgotten. In the case of Rosewarne something else happened.

A week later, Group Captain Keith summoned all ranks for an address in one of the empty hangars. Wing commanders were present as was the adjutant. This was clearly something of importance.

'Maybe Hitler's thrown the towel in.'

'Bet you half a crown?'

'No, not really.'

'Parade! Parade, attention! Quiet everyone!' shouted the authoritative warrant officer.

The Group Captain jumped up onto an empty packing case as the squadron, erks and aircrew sprang to attention.

'At ease, gentlemen. The reason for calling you here this morning is to bring to your attention to something which I have discovered and which may be of some importance to all of us. Now, firstly, you are all aware that Flying Officer Rosewarne and his crew have not returned from an operation just north of Dunkirk. We have no information that he has put in at a different airfield or that he has crashed. His crew is posted as missing and it will be some time before we know precisely what has happened. You are all aware that aircrews write letters to next of kin, which are to be sent in this kind of contingency.'

The squadron nodded. A murmur rang out.

'Thank you, gentlemen!' The warrant officer flexed his authority.

'Before he left on his last operation, Flying Officer Rosewarne left his letter unsealed. The adjutant has brought it to my attention. It appears that Flying Officer Rosewarne intended Wing Commander Adams and myself to read it in the event of his non-return.'

'Reading a chap's private letters?' whispered a voice. 'Dashed bad form!'

'Shush you lot!' hissed the warrant officer.

CHAPTER 3

'As you are all aware, last week's evacuation of Dunkirk has been a resounding success. I do not know how many men we have extricated but it would fill the Empire Stadium at Wembley several times over. This squadron has played its part in this and none moreso than Flying Officer Rosewarne.

'I have now contacted Flying Officer Rosewarne's mother in Brentwood in Essex and requested her permission to make his letter public. She has graciously consented to do so. I therefore propose to read it out to you. I trust that you will find it as moving as I do.'

Dearest Mother:

Though I feel no premonition at all, events are moving rapidly and I have instructed that this letter be forwarded to you should I fail to return from one of the raids that we shall shortly be called upon to undertake. You must hope on for a month, but at the end of that time you must accept the fact that I have handed my task over to the extremely capable hands of my comrades of the Royal Air Force, as so many splendid fellows have already done.

First, it will comfort you to know that my role in this war has been of the greatest importance. Our patrols far out over the North Sea have helped to keep the trade routes clear for our convoys and supply ships, and on one occasion our information was instrumental in saving the lives of the men in a crippled lighthouse relief ship. Though it will be difficult for you, you will disappoint me if you do not at least try to accept the facts dispassionately, for I shall have done my duty to the utmost of my ability. No man can do more, and no-one calling himself a man could do less.

I have always admired your amazing courage in the face of continual setbacks; in the way you have given me as good an education and background as anyone in the country: and always kept up appearances without ever losing faith in the future. My death would not mean that your struggle has been in vain. Far from it. It means that your sacrifice is as great as mine. Those who serve England must expect nothing from her; we debase ourselves if we regard our country as merely a place in which to eat and sleep.

BOMBS AND BARBED WIRE

History resounds with illustrious names who have given all; yet their sacrifice has resulted in the British Empire where there is a measure of peace, justice and freedom for all, and where a higher standard of civilisation has evolved, and is still evolving, than anywhere else. But this is not only concerning our own land. Today we are faced with the greatest organised challenge to Christianity and civilisation that the world has ever seen, and I count myself lucky and honoured to be the right age and fully trained to throw my full weight into the scale. For this I have to thank you. Yet there is more work for you to do. The home front will still have to stand united for years after the war is won. For all that can be said against it, I still maintain that this war is a very good thing: every individual is having the chance to give and dare all for his principle like the martyrs of old. However long the time may be, one thing can never be altered – I shall have lived and died an Englishman. Nothing else matters one jot nor can anything ever change it.

You must not grieve for me, for if you really believe in religion and all that it entails that would be hypocrisy. I have no fear of death; only a queer elation... I would have it no other way. The universe is so vast and so ageless that the life of one man can only be justified by the measure of his sacrifice. We are sent to this world to acquire a personality and a character to take with us that can never be taken from us. Those who just eat and sleep, prosper and procreate, are no better than animals if all their lives they are at peace.

I firmly believe that evil things are sent into the world to try us; they are sent deliberately by our Creator to test our mettle because He knows what is good for us. The Bible is full of cases where the easy way out has been discarded for moral principles.

I count myself fortunate in that I have seen the whole country and known men of every calling. But with the final test of war I consider my character fully developed. Thus at my early age my earthly mission is already fulfilled and I am prepared to die with just one regret: that I could not devote myself to making your declining

CHAPTER 3

years more happy by being with you; but you will live in peace and freedom and I shall have directly contributed to that, so here again my life will not have been in vain.

Your loving son

The ranks of 38 Squadron at RAF Marham were silent. The warrant officer did not have to air his breezy authority.

'Parade! Parade, dis-miss.'

The Rosewarne letter did not end its career at Marham on that bright June morning.

On 18 June, Ad was stopped by one of his mates.

'Oy, Ad! Have you seen *The Times* today?'

'Oh, I'm a *Daily Mirror* man myself; I don't have much truck with those posh papers.'

'You might have truck with this one: Rosewarne's letter is published in it!'

'What?'

Opening the unfamiliar and vast expanse of *The Times*, authoritative and magisterial even in its form of cheap, thin wartime paper he found it.

'Good God!'

There, in black and white, was the letter, exactly as Group Captain Keith had read it out. 'Hey, it doesn't actually mention his name and goodness knows how it got in the paper; there's no clue as to where it came from.' It was now called, very simply, 'An Airman's Letter to His Mother'.

'Good old Viv. Well, if he has gone down, he has certainly gone down in glory.' It was an uplifting detail against a backdrop of utter gloom in every other respect.

On this day Winston Churchill was to make one his famous speeches to the House of Commons. Part of that speech was broadcast to the British nation. Those who heard it said that the hairs stood up on the backs of their necks. The last paragraph, and especially the last sentence, was to become part of the fabric of British consciousness for decades.

> *What General Weygand called the Battle of France is over. I expect that the Battle of Britain is about to begin. Upon this battle depends the survival of Christian civilisation. Upon it depends our own British life, and the long continuity of our institutions and our Empire. The whole fury and might of the enemy must very soon be turned on us. Hitler knows that he will have to break us in this Island or lose the war. If we can stand up to him, all Europe may be free and the life of the world may move forward into broad, sunlit uplands. But if we fail, then the whole world, including the United States, including all that we have known and cared for, will sink into the abyss of a new Dark Age made more sinister, and perhaps more protracted, by the lights of perverted science. Let us therefore brace ourselves to our duties, and so bear ourselves that, if the British Empire and its Commonwealth last for a thousand years, men will still say, 'This was their finest hour'.*

Even despite this tour de force from the Prime Minister the Rosewarne letter continued to hold the nation's attention. *The Times* received upwards of 10,000 requests for copies of Rosewarne's letter. This, in turn led The Times Publishing Company to publish the letter in a short monograph. The first print ran out, as did the second print, as did the third print. While the Battle of Britain was raging, Vivian Rosewarne, improbably, had hit the nerve of the nation like a dentist's drill applied without an anaesthetic.

Once France fell, 38 Squadron was drawn quickly and irrevocably into the war. Too many aeroplanes and men did not return. Daylight raids were quickly abandoned. To the amazement of the men who flew and the men who serviced the aircraft, higher command had actually practised common sense and recognised that daylight raids were suicidal. Night raids became the norm. Ad's task now was to keep Wellingtons in the air, which were engaged several times each week on bombing the Channel Ports, Essen and other targets in the Ruhr and

CHAPTER 3

even as far as Berlin. The impetus behind the Rosewarne letter kept increasing. By the end of 1940 the letter had sold half a million copies. It had come to the attention of King George VI, who wrote personally to Rosewarne's mother.

The letter had become such a topic of conversation that there were claims from sceptics that the letter had been written by a paid propagandist in some shadowy government agency. Shortly before Christmas, Rosewarne's identity was revealed. This led to the letter crossing the Atlantic and being published by E.P. Dutton and Co. This ran to 12 editions and became a major text among the many Americans who felt that their country should be fighting Hitler and not maintaining neutrality.

In 1941 the film producer Michael Powell made a short film entitled *An Airman's Letter to his Mother* to be shown before the main features through the United Kingdom.

We could only imagine that Ad and the other members of 38 Squadron were in a state of total amazement that one of their pilots, a 23-year-old, had written a letter to his mother which had taken the world by storm. Someone is bound to have said, 'The pen is mightier...' etc.

By the time that the Rosewarne letter achieved its eventual international status Ad was long gone from 38 Squadron. The squadron had been alerted that it was about to transfer to Egypt and was due to leave in November. There is bound to have been banter such as 'you'd look great in a fez!'. A matter of days before the squadron departed Ad was surprised to discover a transfer order posting him to 10 Squadron at RAF Leeming in Yorkshire.

'How the hell did you pull that off?' some of his fellow erks must have asked.

How indeed? The Royal Air Force worked in mysterious ways.

During his time at 38 Squadron there was one piece of information which Ambrose Adlam would have found interesting. Vivian Rosewarne had been killed on 30 May 1940 at Veurne on the northern coast of France. Ad's prayer to the Cosmos was answered: his brother Bill was still alive, although he had had some very close calls with a grisly death from German machine guns. He had escaped the German clutches and embarked a friendly British ship to take him 'back to Blighty'. He was picked up from the beach at Bray Dunes. Bray Dunes and Veurne are within walking distance of each other. It is highly likely that Bill Adlam actually saw Rosewarne's aircraft being shot down.

Such are the ironies of war.

CHAPTER 4
THE SHINY TEN

11 OCTOBER 1940

The train chugged and strained up the long embankment out of Manchester Victoria on its way to York. Thank goodness! He had a compartment to himself. He would be able to read the paper and maybe even indulge in forty winks.

The compartment door ground open. 'These seats aren't taken are they?' He grudgingly smiled and shook his head with politeness rather than enthusiasm.

His head still felt a bit thick, if he was honest with himself, after that last boozey night on leave at home in Gloucester. A family – dad, mum and 12-year-old boy entered the compartment, arranged luggage and coats on the rack and sat down, smiling.

'God! What a bloody mess!' said the dad looking out of the window.

The ugly industrial factory-scapes of Miles Platting and Newton Heath were showing the signs of the war. Hitler's Luftwaffe had reduced large factories to smoke blackened empty shells. They had reduced complete terraced streets of houses to piles of rubble. God knows how many people had lost their homes, been injured or died. Those factories that were still operating were now decked out in camouflage paint which made them look like the deranged imaginings of a deeply troubled surrealist painter.

Ad was on his way from Gloucester to Northallerton in Yorkshire to join 10 Squadron, 'The Shiny Ten', at RAF Leeming. No-one had explained why he had been transferred from 38 Squadron, especially as that squadron was bound immediately to go to Africa. 'Oh well,' as someone had so aptly said, 'military intelligence is a contradiction in terms.' That had not saved him from friendly ribbing in the mess.

There had been a lot of predictable gibes about 'dodging the column', 'having it easy in Blighty' and 'don't worry, we'll sort out the Afrika Korps for you' but it was all good natured and it hadn't stopped them buying him a pint – actually a lot of pints – before he left for a week's leave. Then there was the other gibe. It had not been uttered in his presence, but he knew it did the rounds among the aircrews. The gibe was 'penguin': airmen who did not fly. It did not cause him to lose sleep, but it gnawed in the background. It worried him.

'Fag?' asked the dad, proffering a vivid red cigarette packet.

'Oh, Du Maurier, very nice, I'm afraid I've only got Capstans to offer back.'

'Oh, don't worry about that.'

'It doesn't sound like you're from around these parts,' said Ad good-naturedly.

'No, we're from London, got bombed out two weeks ago.'

'Oh, I'm sorry to hear that. Did you manage to salvage anything?'

'Oh yes, we got back from the air raid shelter in the morning. There was a big mirror left that was on the chimney breast and there were half a dozen eggs left in the larder.'

'What?'

'Actually, we had to laugh, our next-door neighbour came around and asked if she make us a cup of tea, so we said, "We can all have an omelette as well!"'

They all laughed.

The man continued. 'Actually, I'm glad to be out of London. I travelled a lot in my job…'

'He works for an engineering firm…' butted in the woman. Ad had to smile internally; civvies always had to be so quick to prove that they were playing their part.

'It's a reserved occupation,' said the boy. Even schoolboys knew that 'doing your bit' was the most vital attribute of life in this whole sorry mess of a war.

'Thank you, Eric,' said his mum.

CHAPTER 4

'Well,' the man continued, 'you can travel from Wanstead in the east to Ealing in the west and you can smell fires and smouldering everywhere. There's bombed-out houses all over the place…'

'They're great fun to play in,' added Eric jovially.

'What did I tell you about keeping out of those?' said his mother sternly.

'Anyway,' his dad persisted, 'the East End is in ruins, all the buildings around St Paul's have gone, they've hit Buckingham Palace, Big Ben, half the shops on Oxford Street have been hit, and we don't know how many dead there are but there's a lot, a real lot. They're using the Spurs' football ground at White Hart Lane as a huge mortuary. We're not supposed to know about it, but the word gets around.'

'So, we came to Manchester to live with my sister-in-law until we get on our feet again. We're all right, though, aren't we Eric?'

'Yes, I got given a new Meccano set and it was better than the old one that I lost.'

This was a different perspective on the war from that which Ad had been living under for the last year or so. Once hostilities had started, he had seen men go out and not come back. He had heard of men who had ended up in prisoner of war camps. He had heard of a few seriously wounded men who had been repatriated. Now he was seeing what it was like for civvies.

'Mind you, though, I had a worse experience than that last week. I was on my bike in Wilmslow Road in Withington and a couple of Jerry planes appeared in the sky out of no-where, there was no air raid siren or anything. I heard the ack-ack guns starting up. Then there was this whistling sound. I knew what it was, so I jumped off my bike and into a ditch.'

'You must have been terrified.'

'Didn't have time to think about being terrified. Anyway, there was this great big bloody bang…'

'Harry, don't swear in front of the lad.'

'Sorry, there was this great big bang and I kept my head down while all the debris was falling around me and on me and chunks of roadside and bits of kerb and bits of wood… oh, it was everywhere.'

BOMBS AND BARBED WIRE

'Were you hurt?'

'Only my pride. But when I stuck my head up there was a great big hole in the road and my bike had disappeared.'

'He never found it, did you?'

They all dragged back the smoke from their Du Maurier cigarettes in silent contemplation.

'Are you an aviator, sir?' asked the boy.

'No, I'm ground crew. I make sure the aeroplanes fly properly.'

'That's a pity!' said the boy petulantly.

'Eric!' said his mother. 'Manners, young man! I'm so sorry, he's only 12.'

'Why is it a pity?' asked Ad in that kindly but indulgent manner that grown-ups reserve for children who have come close to overstepping the mark of propriety.

'Well, if you were an aviator you could drop bombs on Germans and kill the lot of them.'

'Eric!' hissed his mother. 'That's not nice!'

'I don't know,' said his dad. 'Look at what's happened in Liverpool, Birmingham, Weymouth, Southampton and London are getting bombed every night now. Every flippin' night and there just isn't an end to it.'

'Gloucester too,' was added to his list.

'What happened in Gloucester?' asked the dad.

'About five squadrons of Dorniers were on a daylight raid after the industrial factories. There were about 90 dead. A couple of my parents' friends were killed when a stray bomb hit their house.'

They dragged on their cigarettes again. The train was grinding its way up into the Pennines now. The black, bomb scarred industrial heartland was behind them now. As they passed and into the higher country the first dustings of snow could just be seen on the mountain tops. They had left the 'dark satanic mills' and had entered 'England's green and pleasant land'.

'You know, up here the war could be a million miles away,' said the dad.

'No, it couldn't,' said Eric. 'Look over there. There's a convoy of lorries going up into the hills. That'll be the men back from Dunkirk, training to re-invade Europe.'

CHAPTER 4

No-one said the obvious. There was no chance of an invasion in the near future, the middle future or, perhaps, in any future.

Ad disagreed with the man profoundly on another count as well. He had noticed something. It was something that it would have been a profound discourtesy to have noticed at all. It was Mum's legs. They were stained with tea to make it look as though she were wearing stockings. She had pencilled a stocking 'seam' onto the back to complete the illusion. The war was stained in tea all over Mum's calves.

'Oh no! We're stopping. What for this time?'

A feature of wartime railway journeys was for a passenger train to be stopped for a war supplies freight train to be given priority. After a couple of minutes, they heard the rush of a steam locomotive rapidly approaching in the opposite direction. It passed them with a great clatter.

'Anti-aircraft guns!' said Eric in triumph. 'I hope they shoot down every German who flies into British air space!'

Ad waited for his mother to admonish him. She did not do so. Dad was wrong. The lad was right: even up here in the Pennines there was no escape from the war. Britain might not be able to invade Europe, but the war invaded every facet of life. Your very existence only had relevance in terms of what part you played. Even a 12-year-old schoolboy felt it necessary to justify to a total stranger that his dad was playing his part, albeit from the cosy backwater of a reserved occupation.

He looked out of the window at the Pennines as the train chugged relentlessly on. Ad's war had not been a bad war, at least not yet. Losing good friends in 38 Squadron had been a blow but within the bounds of expectation. The destruction from the bombing was awful and there was always the nagging feeling that bloody Hitler might win anyway. On the other hand, he had seen more of the country than he would have seen otherwise. There was a good camaraderie in the 'other ranks' mess. They had had some epic booze ups and high jinks in the local pubs in Norfolk.

His train of thought was halted.

'Well, we have to get out at the next stop; we're only going as far as Huddersfield, but it's been nice talking to you,' said the mum.

The dad passed over the red Du Maurier packet.

'We're really grateful for what you lads are doing for us. There's the best part of a packet of 20 there so enjoy them. They're nicer than flippin' Capstans.'

They both laughed.

'Just before you get off can I just ask you a question?'

'Yes, of course.'

'You're from London and London is being bombed every night?'

'Yes.'

'Are there some people who say, "Let's pack it in and surrender or have an armistice or a ceasefire with Hitler" or anything like that?'

A cloud came over the dad's face. The affability vanished.

'Not one! We lived in the Blitz from the time it started in September to two weeks ago: that's eight weeks and we were hammered every night, every flippin' night. No, you won't find anyone, not one person who wants to throw in the towel, not to that bloody dictator.'

The mum did not admonish him for using bad language this time.

'Not one,' she said. He waved at them as the train pulled out of Huddersfield station.

'Penguin?' 'Pity he wasn't aircrew?' Ad was still doing his bit and the aircrews valued what he did.

Oh well, then, he would go on to play his part in Hitler's downfall at No. 10 Squadron at RAF Leeming.

It was to be a time of intense frustration.

At first glance RAF Leeming proved not to be too bad. It was a newly established station, only a few months old. Before the war it had been the base for the Londonderry Flying Club until the land had been compulsorily purchased by the War Office from the Duke of Cleveland. It was nice to see 'the nobs' doing their bit for the war effort.

The commanding officer of the station was a huge man, Group Captain 'King Kong' Staton. Ad looked at his medal ribbons: DSO MC DFC ADC. This was an airman's airman! Things were looking up.

CHAPTER 4

The aircraft on which he had to work at Leeming were Armstrong Whitworth Whitleys: two-engined bombers. These were very modern machines although not quite thoroughbreds like the Wellingtons at Marham. He learned that his new squadron had had a very interesting raid when Italy had come into the war.

They had been on detached duty in the Channel Islands and flown over the Alps to hit the Fiat Works in Turin. 'The searchlights and the flak were only working until we got there then the searchlights stopped moving and the flak stopped. All the gunners had gone down the air raid shelters.' This story always provoked gales of laughter. 'They just left us to our bombing runs and we had the easiest raid you could possibly imagine.'

'Tell him about the ice cream cone.'

This provoked further gales of laughter.

'Well, you know how we paint a bomb on a plane's fuselage after they come back from a raid?'

'Yes.'

'Well, here, if you do a raid over Italy, they paint an ice cream cone.'

The very few Italians in pre-war Britain were famous for being sellers of excellent ice cream.

'Tell you what, though, the sight of the Alps in the moonlight was something you would never forget in the whole of your life.'

It occurred to Ad that there was something about aircrews that was to be envied; not least because they were doing something at the sharp end in this awful bloody war.

Then the Channel Islands had fallen and the exotic side of life in No.10 Squadron had taken a downward turn. Two days after his arrival at Leeming the news came through on the radio of the massive raid on Coventry. How many dead? Five hundred? He saw the pictures in the paper: the charred shell of the cathedral; the façade of Owen and Owens department store where some 200 had been trapped in a basement. The bombs had fractured a water main. They had all drowned. The bombing of London carried on unabated for week after week.

As Ad was to discover further, there were three factors which would now prevent him carrying out his desired maiming of Hitler's Reich.

Firstly, the year was rapidly closing in. Cloud was low. Navigation was difficult. Leeming was far to the north of the country. The number of operations against Nazi-held territory was decreasing by the week. The squadron's motto was *rem acu tangere*: 'to hit the mark'. It was a squadron joke that they could be reported to the fraud squad at Scotland Yard. 'Hitting the mark' was something that they were manifestly not doing.

Over the next four months the squadron did take part in raids, but only sporadically. There would be eight Whitleys, perhaps, sent off to join a raid in Hamburg, Bremen, Düsseldorf or Cologne or perhaps half a dozen sent to Calais, Dieppe, Brest or Dunkirk.

On their return the reports usually said that because of the cloud cover the results of the bombing were unknown. Sometimes they would report that they had seen another port facility which seemed to have German boats in it and they had dropped the bombload there in the hope of doing some sort of damage. On other occasions they would report that they had totally failed to find the intended target, or any target whatsoever.

While No. 10 Squadron was hobbled, hampered and hapless, it was extremely frustrating that the Luftwaffe had no similar difficulty. The bombing of London still carried on, unabated, for week after week.

The second frustration factor was the serviceability of the aircraft. From an 'A' flight of 22 it was relatively common to have 30 per cent or even 40 per cent of the Whitleys 'u/s' (unserviceable). The causes for this ranged from faulty gauges to dead radios to leaky fuel pumps to iced-up hydraulics. Ad was working on the aeroplanes. He and all the other erks were putting in long hours and working in extreme cold in the hangars but the faults in the Whitley bombers were at epidemic level. Even when an aeroplane took off, too many turned back before even passing over the British coastline because of a crisis with some component or other. Even when they got back there were crashes at the airfield because an undercarriage collapsed or a vital component stuck at a vital moment. After three months the squadron had lost more aircraft and men through faulty equipment than it had through

CHAPTER 4

the combined efforts of the Luftwaffe and the German flak.

And the bombing of London carried on unabated.

The third source of frustration was that RAF Leeming became so waterlogged that aeroplanes could not take off from its grass runways. This meant that the squadron, aircrews and erks were sent out on detached duty to the nearby RAF stations at Dishforth and Linton on Ouse. This improved matters only slightly. The crews still failed to find their targets too often because of the cloud, fog and rain. On one night seven aircraft went out. One got back to Linton; the others put down variously at Langham, Kirton, Bircham-Newton and Honnington.

And the bombing of London carried on unabated.

The aircrews, the erks and the powers that be must all have asked the question 'how the heck do the Luftwaffe continue to fly and mount large-scale raids of 200 to 300 bombers when the RAF can hardly get off the ground?' Of answer there was none, at least none in public.

After all of that came the cold. That year was one of the worst ever for snow, ice and freezing fog. In the Nissen huts of RAF Leeming, the chilly residents went to bed wearing full uniform and two or three shirts in an attempt to keep warm. The occasional evening rat hunts were, nevertheless, a rousing way of keeping warm, having fun and bonding together as a team.

On top of all of that, Ad was a still a penguin, a non-flying airman. Was he playing his part? Was he doing his bit? Was he answering the call to arms? Was he buggery! He was getting frozen stiff day after day on a dysfunctional squadron which had all the willingness in the world to bomb Hitler and all his works and very little ability to do so.

In the first week of March in that dreadful year of 1941 the newspapers reported a rare, uplifting event. There had been a Commando raid in the north of Norway at some islands called the Lofotens, wherever they might be. British Commandos and Norwegian soldiers had taken over the islands, destroyed a number of German ships and taken a lot of prisoners. A camera team had taken joyous footage of exploding oil tanks, captured Nazi flags and – even better – downhearted German sailors and airmen being brought back to Blighty as prisoners for the duration.

A couple of weeks later came the confirmation that Ad had thought highly possible: his brother Bill was on the raid.

The raid was portrayed in the press as a propaganda and logistical victory, albeit of a tactical nature but at least someone was doing something somewhere. There was somebody giving the Germans a bloody nose.

Frustration won its four-month battle. There was nothing for it.

'I'd like to see the adjutant please.'

'Certainly, Aircraftman Adlam, just go in please.'

'Adlam, isn't it? What can I do for you?'

'I'd like to apply for aircrew, sir.'

'Fill this form in and bring it back to me tomorrow morning. With your technical knowledge you'd be best off as a flight engineer would you not?'

'Sounds good to me, sir.'

'Good man. See you in the morning with the forms completed. Dismissed.'

He had worked on two bomber stations. He knew that few were destined to complete their tours of duty. He was quite clear that he could be shot down or finish up as a prisoner of war. Well, there was a war on and he did not want to be a bloody 'erk' anymore, or a 'penguin'. He did not want 12-year-old boys looking disappointed when he said he was not aircrew. He wanted wings on his tunic and to be able to look Bill in the eye when he met him next in Gloucester.

He completed and signed the forms.

That felt good; in fact, it felt very good.

CHAPTER 5

MR AND MRS ADLAM RETURN FROM SOUTH AFRICA

11 AUGUST 1942

'Oh God! It is so bloody cold!'

He didn't speak the words, but they rattled inside his head like ice cubes in the drinks at his wedding just a few short weeks ago. The sea off Mozambique hissed by as His Majesty's Transport *Britannic* slugged along in the middle of a convoy headed for Liverpool. Now, Liverpool you would expect to be cold and miserable, but this was in the bloody tropics! He huddled inside his greatcoat. It was 0425 in the morning and on his watch no-one was around, nothing was happening. He had never seen anything like those stars at sea. People talked of the Milky Way and, for the first time ever, he really understood what it meant. It was a sight of primaeval, incomprehensible beauty.

In the bright, theatrical light from a million stars he could clearly see the other couple of dozen ships in the convoy and, further out, the dark menacing shapes of the escort vessels. That was comforting, although they were assured that the German navy was not active (or at least not very active) in the Indian Ocean. Ah! He had to admit that the light of a million brilliant stars was not something that you would see in Gloucester. In accordance with wartime regulations, no ship showed any lights: it did not matter. The Indian Ocean was lit as brightly as if it were day.

He was on the mistitled 'morning watch'; his position was on the port quarter. 'Just stay there and keep watch' the officer of the watch had said at the briefing. Miranda had also volunteered and was on the port bow somewhere up ahead, although he couldn't see her. Every time he had craned forward to catch sight of her, a splattering of spray drenched his coat from the lively swell beneath the gunwale. That coat was going to reek of seawater. He looked at the stripes on the sleeves and smiled. Hell! He was a sergeant now and really liked the way that everyone addressed him as 'Sergeant'. It was gratifying to notice that slight but palpable deference which had not been there before. On the front of his tunic, however, was the flight engineer's brevet. That 'E' and the half-wing about it said more than the sergeant's stripes. That meant he had committed to fly and to drop bombs on Nazis, which everyone agreed was a very good thing to do. It also meant that he was unlikely to see the war out. The RAF boys all knew that. They gave him much more respect than when he had been a mere 'aircraftman'. A pang of sibling rivalry reminded him that even this was not great competition to his brother Bill's 'lieutenant' status, not to mention his 'No 4 Commando' shoulder patch. Nevertheless, Ad was still in the game when it came to intra-family prestige.

Oh bollocks! He was bored stiff. He decided to go forward and see what Miranda was doing.

He rolled in his walk to tension himself against the rolling of the ship.

'Anne! Is that you?' Miranda she was but always to him 'Anne'.

'Ad, for God's sake come and give me a cuddle; I'm absolutely freezing out here.'

'Well, before I do I have something to say.'

'What, darling?'

'Right! Are you ready?'

'Oh no, you're going to tell me you are already married in Blighty?'

'No, better than that.'

'What then, you silly man?'

'*Ek kan nie sien 'n wors daar buite.*'

CHAPTER 5

'Ambrose, what on earth are you talking about?'

'Well, it's Afrikaans; I've spent hours putting that together.'

'I know it's Afrikaans but what on earth are you talking about sausages for?'

'Well, it means I can't see a sausage out there.'

'What have sausages got to do with anything? Oh, look, you can say that in English but in Afrikaans it doesn't make any sense.'

'*Ek is lief vir jou baie.*'

'Yes, that makes complete sense. Come and give me a cuddle.'

He folded her into his arms and pulled her towards him.

'I love the way the steam from our breath mingles together,' he said.

'You can kiss me if you want to, you know, I'm a respectable married woman, now.'

'I don't remember it stopping you when you weren't a respectable married woman. I've just had the most incredible thought, you know,' he blurted out giggling.

'Kiss me quick.' He did so.

'Well, you know how I've just trained as a flight engineer to drop as many bombs as possible on as many Nazis as possible?'

'Yes.'

'If it hadn't been for that nice Mr Hitler and his Nazi henchmen I would never have found you. I might add that but for him I would have been bored stiff in some awful civvy job in Gloucester and I would never have been to Gibraltar, Sierra Leone, South Africa or lots of other places.'

'So that nice Mr Hitler is a good man, then?' she said, giggling up at him.

'It's thanks to him that the Empire Air Training Scheme is in existence. I know blokes who have gone to Canada and Australia, some went to Rhodesia and I got a buckshee trip to South Africa. So he's not all bad.'

He pulled her to him and kissed her lightly on the cheek.

'Not all bad, just mainly bad,' he said breathlessly.

'Sergeant Adlam!' said a voice of authority behind him. It was the officer of the watch. 'Why are you not at your post?' Ad noticed there was a steward with him carrying a tray of drinks, so possibly this conversation was not going to be too bad.

'Oh, sorry, sir, I just came forward to see how Miranda was.'

'You don't have to "Sir" me; I'm a civvy, Sergeant, not a group captain.'

'Well, what should I call you?'

'McCarten is my name, so that will have to do. Now, are you two feeling a bit cold?'

'Oh, we're freezing,' said Miranda. God! How Ad loved that South African accent.

'Steward, gunpowder tea for two if you please.'

'Right, sir, piping hot and Bristol fashion.' He proffered the tray.

'Better just let it cool off just a bit, darling.' He thought for a moment and asked, 'Mr McCarten, what exactly is gunpowder tea?'

'Tea with no milk but laced with navy rum; the good stuff, not that witch piss you can buy in Civvy Street.'

'Mr McCarten…'

'Oh, sorry, Sergeant, sorry, ma'am. I didn't mean any lack of respect to you.'

'No offence taken, Mr McCarten,' she said in her soft, rather clipped voice from inside the shadows.

'So, you've just got married, have you?' said McCarten changing the subject quickly. 'How did your parents feel about you marrying a Brylcreem Boy?'

'Hey! Don't you call my husband a Brylcreem Boy!'

They all laughed. 'Brylcreem' was a men's hair styling product made of water, mineral oil and beeswax and highly perfumed. Most men used it, or something like it. According to popular gossip it was especially popular among the RAF as part of their debonair, devil-may-care, swashbuckling image. While the RAF boys scoffed at the notion of 'Brylcreem Boy' in public, privately they rather liked the notion.

'Gosh!' Miranda blurted out involuntarily. 'This is tea? This stuff is lethal.'

'It'll warm you up, though, madam. Nothing like it on the morning watch!'

CHAPTER 5

'Anyway,' Miranda continued, 'to answer your question, my mum is sorry to see me go and so will my brothers and sisters: I'm one of eight girls and two boys. Don't know about my stepdad, but I won't miss him either. He's what they call a "hartnakkiger Afrikaaner".

Anyway, when this is over, we're coming back to live in South Africa. From what Ad tells me Gloucester is a nice place. It's not as nice as East London, though, darling, is it?'

McCarten looked at Ad but said nothing. Ad held his gaze for a moment and looked away. Both men knew that the chances of his surviving even a single tour in Bomber Command were slight.

It was Ad's turn to change the subject.

'Mr McCarten, your man put us on watch here but didn't really tell us what we are watching for. What exactly are we looking out for?'

McCarten laughed. 'Sometimes seamen forget that not everyone is a seaman. Well, what you are looking out for is anything that might be a danger to the ship.'

'Like a U-boat?'

'Precisely, although the chance of seeing one of those buggers – oh, sorry about the language, ma'am – in the dark is well on nigh impossible. Anyway, there are no intelligence reports of any of those in the Indian Ocean. You'd be looking out for any other ships getting too close, any sudden fogbanks, any rocks breaking surface where they shouldn't be... Oh, and if you see any other ships sending messages on the signal lamps you should report those.'

'Can't the man in the wheelhouse see those?'

'Oh yes, but the more pairs of eyes the better. Anyway, once we get to Aden we'll break away from the convoy because there is no danger at all in those waters and we'll re-form up again once we get to Alexandria. Once we're in the Med you won't be on watch; we'll have seamen on watch all the time.'

'Can't beat the professionals, hey?'

'Well, once we are in the Med we have to worry about Italian subs and then once we're past Gib we have to worry about the Jerries. Oh! And there is one thing to look out for. Don't look at the stars through the ship's rigging or you'll start to get seasick.

BOMBS AND BARBED WIRE

'Ooh! said Miranda. 'I started doing that and I thought I was going to be ill so I looked away quickly. It's very hypnotic, though.'

'Right, let's get moving. Sergeant, I'll be back around here in 20 minutes and I do want to see you at your proper station, please.'

'Point taken.'

'Oh, and one other thing, don't go around by the stern, some of those nurses are meeting with some of you Brylcreem Boys and I don't think they want to be disturbed, if you get my drift. The captain says to leave them to it because it's the last chance most of the poor buggers will get.'

He froze at the enormity of his own gaffe.

'Twenty minutes, Mister McCarten,' said Ad forcefully, grabbing the agenda again.

'What the heck did he mean by that? Last chance for what?' asked Miranda in a voice which betrayed as much concern as curiosity.

'Oh, just some silly jack-tar joke, I imagine. I'd better get back to my station or he'll probably have me keel-hauled in the morning.'

Britannic, Ad and Miranda and several hundred other trained RAF crews plugged on through the tropical night. It plugged on past the Horn of Africa. It plugged on through the Suez Canal where Ad and Miranda were charmed to see tribesmen riding camels.

'Best not hang around on deck too long,' said a passing seaman. 'Sometimes they take pot shots with the rifles they inherited from World War I.'

After passing the vast British naval base at Alexandria they were into the Mediterranean. The watches were doubled now due to the threat of Italian submarines. The small fact that the watches were for sailors indicated that matters were becoming more serious. The captain was not trusting his ship to amateurs.

The trip down the Mediterranean was attended by a new seriousness. There were boat drills, fire drills and standing orders to keep valuables with you at all times. There was a distinct possibly of a sudden explosion and jumping over the side.

'You'd better keep beside me, just in case,' Ad said to Miranda.

'That's no hardship. I want to be beside my big strong man,' she replied.

CHAPTER 5

If there were a sudden explosion and they had to jump for it, he wondered how much a big strong man he might be. He hoped he would not find out.

Putting in to Gibraltar gave them a respite from the sea, a trip up the rock and a view of the monkeys that lived there.

'Ambrose, that one looks like he is going to jump on me, make him go away.'

'Go on! Get out of it, you scabby looking animal! It's OK, he's gone.'

A day later they saw a different-coloured horizon. The blue of the Mediterranean had given way to the dark grey of the Bay of Biscay and the North Sea. The tension mounted. The threat from German U-boats was greater than that of the Italian submarines. Ad and Miranda looked at the corvettes and destroyers busily scampering around the convoy like sheep dogs. It was comforting.

They slept now in their clothes with life jackets at the ready 'just in case'. To their relief an extra escort of two destroyers picked them up at the approaches to the Irish Sea. Now they could see North Cornwall to the right, the southern coast of County Wexford in Ireland was to the left and Liverpool was somewhere just ahead. They had been on the ship for… how long? Perhaps four weeks but they were so habituated to the strictures of shipboard life it felt as though they had been on the *Britannic* forever.

'Not a bad honeymoon, though,' said Ad cheerfully.

'Well, not if you don't mind the threat of getting blown up, the dreadful rough weather and the monotonous food,' she replied and kissed him on the cheek.

'Oh dear,' he thought, 'wait until she sees what passes for a food ration when she gets to Gloucester.' He decided not to say anything.

At last they pulled up the River Mersey. The busy dockyard cranes, the plumes of steam from a hundred railway locomotives and the urgent traffic going up and down the estuary and from one side to the other showed a port city of dynamism, importance and energy.

'Oh, but, Ad, it is so dirty. I cannot believe that people live in those tiny little houses.'

As they found their way to Birkenhead Woodside station, he could see her looking at the poor conditions of the houses, the people's clothing, the paucity of goods in shop windows. At least Gloucester was not this bad. Nor, she would find, was it very good, either.

'The train now standing on platform five is the 11.31 to Cardiff General calling at Birmingham Snow Hill, Stratford on Avon, Cheltenham Spa, Gloucester Central and…'

'Right, love, that's us, drink up your tea and let's get over there.'

Once Ad had hoiked her cases, his kitbag and their gas mask bags onto the luggage racks, Miranda said, 'Did he say Stratford on Avon?'

Ad smiled. 'Second stop; shall we pop in and see if Mr Shakespeare's in?'

They giggled as newlyweds are prone to do.

'I can't believe it, you know. I can't believe I'm in England, the mother country.'

The sea journey had been mercifully uneventful, which in wartime days meant that no ship in the convoy had been sunk. Their married quarters on the *Britannic* had been cramped but private. Ad reflected that those quarters were a far cry from the journey out to South Africa where he had slept in a hammock on a deck with several hundred other airmen and the combined never-ending miasma of unwashed bodies, cigarettes and seasick buckets.

He was growing tense now. The threat which loomed before him was worse than that of German U-boats last week. Without putting too fine a point on it, it was all of his own making. He had 'shot her a line' as the saying went in the Royal Air Force. His family were not the well-to-do pillars of society that he had portrayed. He had not been to private school. His family did not live in a desirable residence; they lived in a 19th century terraced street, built cheaply, cramped and grimy. Charles Dickens could well have used it as a backdrop to *Hard Times*. This 'desirable residence' had been built to house the victims

CHAPTER 5

of the Industrial Revolution as they flooded into towns full of hope and devoid of prospect. Several people had said, 'You know, if 'Itler dropped a bomb on this lot he would be doing us all a favour.' This was not a joke.

Now she was going to see for herself. The train jolted forward southwards, through industrial town after industrial town and eventually into the tunnels which led from Snow Hill station into Birmingham's vast rail yards.

He knew that she had already been horrified at what she had seen. As the tugs had guided them through the murk and steam and fog into the Mersey, the slums on the shore around Liverpool's Brunswick Dock had appalled her. 'Even the blacks don't live like that in South Africa.' There had been little that he could say.

She had been affronted by the paranoid atmosphere which reigned in Britain in those dark days. She had been unaccustomed to seeing people – in fact everyone – walking around with a gas mask bag over their shoulder in case of a surprise attack by the Luftwaffe. She had seen the ruins left by the bombing raids in Liverpool. The great railway junction at Wolverhampton was festooned with barrage balloons to ward off the attentions of the Luftwaffe, should they decide to attack. Passing by an engine shed she said, 'Look at those locomotives; everything is filthy, absolutely filthy.'

'It wasn't like that two years ago,' he said. 'The engines used to be very posh; some were dark red and some were green. Now they're all just black – all the cleaners are off to the war.'

Without asking, he knew what she was thinking. Where were the intense blue skies that she had been accustomed to in South Africa? In Britain the skies were the same battleship grey as the escort vessels which had shepherded them from South Africa. Where were the large detached houses that people lived in: at least the white people? Why were there signs everywhere telling you not to discuss anything that could help the enemy? Why did you need a ration book to buy the most meagre amount of food, clothing or even confectionary? Where were the black people to carry your bag and undertake other menial tasks? He also knew that she was thinking about the family. Would they like her? She hoped that they would. He also hoped that she would like them. That was more problematical. There was no way back for her. Would she resent it?

He picked up the *Daily Mirror* as the train gathered speed.

'What's happening?' she asked, cuddling into him.

'The Germans are into Stalingrad; they've been attacking it for a month and it looks as though they're going to take it.'

'Is that bad?'

'It will be *next stop Moscow* if they win. Anyway, on the bright side, we've done heavy raids with the new Lancaster Bombers on Hamburg, Karlsruhe, Nuremberg and Duisburg.'

'Oh, just think of all those poor people,' said Miranda.

'Poor people! What do you mean poor people?' A voice from the corner of the compartment arose from a magazine and chimed in suddenly and without introduction. They had hardly noticed the old lady, stern in her Queen-Mother-type hat and pearls.

'How long have you been in this country, dear?'

'About six hours,' said Miranda in her lilting South African accent. 'We've just come off the ship at Liverpool.'

'Flight engineer are you, love?' she asked Ad.

He smiled and nodded. He was really enjoying this new-found status that his brevet gave him.

'Well, you go over there and drop as many great big bombs on those bloody evil Germans as you possibly can. Poor people? They voted him in! There's no complaining if they get their just desserts. You just drop as many bombs on them as you can.'

She went back to reading her *Church Times*.

Miranda was speechless.

The woman looked up again and smiled beneficently.

'Would you like a cigarette, dear?'

'Oh!' said Ad, 'Passing Cloud; I don't run to those on airman's pay.' They all laughed.

'Thank you.'

'I'll stick with Players' thanks,' said Ad and offered lights all round.

'If you don't mind me asking, how old are you, dear?'

CHAPTER 5

'Eighteen,' replied Miranda.

The women fell into conversation. It was one of those conversations which women, even total strangers, are good at. Women have a conspiratorial way of sharing feelings, important family matters, relationships and deep emotion. The unwritten law is that men are excluded from these deliberations. For Ambrose Adlam that was good. He could think.

Ad had to think about his great risk and how it was all going to come to a head in about – he looked at his watch – 90 minutes time. Miranda was telling the women how all the ladies had black 'help' in South Africa.

She would not have black 'help' in Beaufort Road. When he grew up it had been a cosy place of emotional warmth and family living. His time in South Africa meant that he could now view it as Anne would view it: a slum. In that poky, tiny, smoky, miserable house there would be Mum, Dad, his younger brother Ray, sisters Iris and Myra. There would be seven of them in the house and only two bedrooms. There was no bathroom. How would Anne cope with having her once-a-week bath in a large tin vessel in front of the fire? Oh God! This could go wrong!

Miranda was telling the woman about having a 'braai' in the back garden. There was always lots of meat, wine was very cheap even for a family of ten, and friends would come around and join in.

The concrete backyard at Beaufort Road would only accommodate the family if you moved the tin bath out to the back lane and, even then, it might disappear if you didn't chain it to the wall. No-one would have heard of such a thing as a barbecue and, in all probability, no-one would ever have drunk wine. That was for posh people. Hell! If she used the word 'wine' they would think she was posh and above herself, or, even worse, above them. Oh, why did he have to shoot a line and tell complete bloody lies when he didn't have to? She loved him and it was clear for all to see.

Miranda was telling the woman how many houses in South Africa were made of wood but were painted in bright colours and how, in the sunshine, the green lawns and trees made a lovely environment.

BOMBS AND BARBED WIRE

She said she had never seen the 'joined-up' houses of Liverpool and Wolverhampton and Birmingham as she was seeing on that rail journey for the first time. She didn't actually say 'scruffy, miserable, impoverished joined-up houses' but that is what she was thinking.

Beaufort Road! Oh hell! What was he going to do? Time was running out.

He could blurt out now that he had shot a line and throw himself on her mercy. How would she react? Disappointment? Rage? Indignation?

He could just let matters take their course. The family were going to meet them at Gloucester Central station and they would take the bus to Beaufort Road. He decided on the latter.

And there they were! As Ad and Miranda climbed down from the train, a rush of Mum, Dad, Ray, Iris and Myra rushed towards them with arms outstretched.

The family greeted Miranda warmly at the station but the flat hats of the men, 'costume' jewellery of the women and ill-fitting hand-me-down clothes of the children made a clear announcement. They did not fit the well-to-do mercantile picture that Ad had painted. He introduced her to everyone and looked for any sign of discomfort. There was nothing obvious yet. He slung his kitbag and her suitcase under the bus stairs and ushered her into the bottom level of the bus.

The bus ride from the station was characterised by the normal conversations: 'How was the journey?' 'How did you two meet?' 'Have you brought us some wedding photos?'

Walking down the confines of grimy Beaufort Road, Ad managed not to look at Miranda. He had thought a thousand times how she might react. She could scold him very bitterly for his exaggerations. She might withdraw into a quiet but seething sulk. The one thing that she might not do (and which would have been her first-choice option) was to go back to South Africa.

In the house he knew what she was thinking: 'It's like a telephone box.'

'I'll just pop upstairs a moment and powder my nose,' she had said.

Quite why women have to spend so much time adjusting their make-up is as much a mystery to most men as why, in a public house,

CHAPTER 5

women always go the ladies' room in a formed-up troop. He knew that when she came down it would be the most critical point of their marriage and, potentially, of his entire life. If this went wrong, he could lose her before their life together had even started.

'How was South Africa?' 'Did you meet any black people?' 'What planes did you fly?' 'Did you see any zebras?' The family's questions were relentless but there was definite warmth in their welcome and Ad hoped that would have come across to Miranda.

Her footsteps were audible as she was coming down the stairs.

His heart was in his mouth as much as when the crew had lost an engine over Buffalo Flats, just outside of East London. The pilot had got the engine started again but what was going to happen now to the engine of his marriage?

The door opened. He looked toward it in stark apprehension.

She looked at him and smiled. He looked at her pointedly in the eyes. She met his gaze firmly and kept smiling. It was all right. Her love for him had trumped his desperate and rather silly 'line shoot'. He made an instant decision not to do that again; the sticky moment which he had just experienced was something that he did not wish to experience again in the whole of his life.

'I expect you would like a nice cup of tea, dear?' said Rose, her new mother-in-law.

And so, they proceeded to all the questions that a new mother might ask an unexpected but nevertheless welcome daughter-in-law.

'Where did you two meet?'

Miranda had been in the South African Air Force; Ad had been on training and that is how they had met.

'How long had you known each other before you got married?'

The answer was a few weeks, barely into months.

In wartime this passed for normality. Ad's brother Bill had been with number 4 Commando based in Troon in Scotland for some months. During that time no fewer than 28 marriages had taken place. The reality was that someone on the front line did not know if they would be alive next year or even next week. They had to grab life and enjoy it while they could.

Ad then told the family that he was only home for a couple of days and had to report to No 24 Operational Training Unit at Honeybourne in three days' time. This was only an hour or so from Gloucester, so home visits would be relatively easy. He expected to be at Honeybourne for the best part of a year and after that he could be posted anywhere where Bomber Command operated.

'I am so proud of you with your flight engineer's brevet,' said Rose. He could get used to the adulation showered on aircrews. He could also get used to the fact that an airman with an aircrew brevet could walk into a pub and never have to buy a drink.

'Why can't I come to Honeybourne with you as it's so close?' Miranda asked.

'King's regulations, I'm afraid. Apparently, some of the air stations built before the war even had married quarters but now the war's on the regulation is "no wives". I don't know why that is.'

He could guess, though. Ad was shrewd enough to realise that if wives were able to join husbands at operational air stations then when a few dozen had failed to return there would be embarrassing demonstrations outside of the gates, which would inevitably make the headlines in the press. This threatened a massive loss of public morale. If Vivian Rosewarne had been married and his wife had been there it would have made life difficult for everyone on the station. Fortunately for those for whom Rosewarne was a propaganda godsend, he was not married. There was no teenage bride to hit the front page of the *Daily Mirror* inconveniently. That was always assuming that wartime censorship did not make the story disappear first.

This also applied to Operational Training Units. The figures were top-secret but deaths in training were running at scandalously high rates. The heady cocktail of inexperienced crewmen, clapped-out aircraft and lesser-skilled ground staff was leading to a death rate hidden by censorship from the newspapers of the day. Anyone who had worked on an operational station, as Ad had, would have heard the stories, known the realities and, with some thought, have guessed at the numbers. A thousand a year were being killed in training.

CHAPTER 5

'So, there's nothing for it but to stay here and find a job, Anne, love.' In wartime Britain, finding a job would not be difficult.

After three days of tourist visits to Gloucester Cathedral, catching a bus out into the country and a quick visit to yet more distant relatives, Anne and Ad parted; she and the family saw him off to Honeybourne for his final bout of training to drop bombs on Hitler's Germany. He had wanted to drop bombs on Nazis for some time.

Now, Ad's assignation with the Third Reich was edging closer.

CHAPTER 6
JOHNNY LENNOX AND THE CREW COME TOGETHER

21 SEPTEMBER 1942

The carriage doors banged, the guard's whistle sounded down the packed platform, and Ad leant through the train window and kissed Anne one last time.

'Love you,' he said.

'Write to me and come back every leave.'

The train jolted forward.

'I will. I'll try and be back next week. They'll have to let us have some leave.'

'Course they will.' She smiled at him and he mouthed 'love you' again.

His hand reached out to touch hers, the accelerating train pulled his hand out of reach. He smiled and waved. As the train gathered ever more speed and the platform was filled with the locomotive's smoke, he leant out to wave to her; she was still there on the platform waving to him. Her handbag was in her left hand as her right arm waved more and more as the train pulled him away from her.

'Oy!' said a gruff but kindly voice behind him.

'Better get your head in, Sergeant, or one of those signal posts will knock your block off.'

CHAPTER 6

The ticket collector smiled at him.

'Wish I had a quid for every airman I've seen waving goodbye to his lady out of those windows.'

'That's no lady, that's my wife!'

They both laughed. He took his seat in the carriage. He had already travelled in dozens of trains during wartime. It seemed that every one of them was packed and two thirds of everyone was wearing military uniforms of one sort or another. Now there was something that he hadn't seen before: American uniforms. He had left for South Africa in May of 1941 when America had not even been in the war. Now it was 21 September 1942; America had joined the war and here were the first of their soldiers that he had seen.

They were different to British servicemen. Their uniforms were made out of much better material and cut so much better than the rough khaki of the British army. They held themselves in a more confident manner and chewed gum. They spoke in curiously loud voices which rather grated on British ears, but their demeanour was friendly and they had an unmistakable courtesy to everyone around them. Those Yanks certainly had a 'Hollywood' air about them. They had none of the British reserve but struck up conversations easily, addressing people as 'sir' and 'ma'am'. He felt that if he approached them they would be friendly. His thoughts were more about missing Anne, however. The war had brought her to him and the war was taking her away. He had to think of something else.

He buried himself in the *Daily Mirror* and noted that the German attack on Stalingrad was building. 'Oh bugger! Not another German success!'

Honeybourne railway station was situated in the picturesque, idyllic and very English Vale of Evesham. In different times it might be a place where Ad and Anne might spend a private and very loving weekend. As Ad's train pulled into the station it displayed all the frantic busy turmoil typical of small railway stations beside large airfields.

'Honeybourne station!' roared a voice of authority. 'All ranks for Operational Training Unit 24 get off now.' Ad, with his kitbag, his gas mask bag and his carrier bag with potted meat sandwiches which

BOMBS AND BARBED WIRE

Anne had made, jumped to the platform. As he did so, several hundred others alighted behind him. It seemed that almost all of the train had been packed with airman volunteers on their way for the final leg of training before operations over Germany.

A large commanding figure, badges of office on his sleeve, was acting as master of ceremonies. This was the 'Tate and Lyle': the station warrant officer. His nickname came from the resplendent crowns of office on his sleeve which resembled the trade mark of a popular brand of syrup which was to be found in every larder in the land. At least they did if the food coupons would run to it. The wing commander might be the titular head of the squadron, but the station warrant officer was the person to stay on the right side of, or else!

'All ranks through the arch, if you would, and assemble in the station yard. There are lorries to take you to the OTU. All ranks through the arch, if you would.'

The lorries ferried the hundreds of airmen past the delightful village, past the sign saying 'Authorised personnel only beyond this point', past the twin-engined bombers, Wellingtons and the slightly odd-looking Whitleys, silent and dormant, at their dispersals. As an experienced aircraftman and fitter his spirits drooped. One glance told him that those aeroplanes were clapped out and fit only for the scrap heap. No wonder there were so many accidents at operation training units. There were also some Lockheed Hudsons and Bristol Beauforts. That was interesting! He wouldn't mind a spin in one of those if he could wangle it.

The truck forged on past the rifle-carrying provosts – the RAF police – with their grim faces, immaculate uniforms and white-covered caps. The same warrant officer now walked along the line of lorries.

'All ranks into the aircraft hangar if you would. All ranks into the hangar. Leave your kitbags by the door and pick them up on the way out.'

It struck Ad as rather strange that, in the middle of a war, an aircraft hangar would be empty. That was decidedly odd. At Marham and even the wretched Leeming, hangars had always been places packed with aircraft, the smell of aviation fuel and the feverish activity of erks busying themselves around the aircraft.

CHAPTER 6

The warrant officer formed them up into lines.

'That man there, what the bloody hell do you think you're doing?'

'Just having a fag, sir.'

All heads turned to the miscreant.

'Will someone tell this bloke what he's doing wrong?'

'There's no smoking in aircraft hangars, mate.'

'YES!' roared the warrant officer; 'there's no smoking in aircraft hangars, mate. This place is full of petrol and liable to blow up if you do that. Do we take it you're from Civvy Street?'

'Yes, sir,' said the man dolefully.

'Sir?' repeated the warrant officer with a tone between mock-horror and mock-amusement. 'We are from Civvy Street aren't we? Tell him someone, how do you address a warrant officer?'

'Mister,' chorused a few voices.

'You address me as "Mr Davies" because that is what it says in King's Regulations. Oh God! I can only hope the Luftwaffe are this bad. That is my only hope to win this war.'

A few laughed nervously. Most did not. They were not sure if he was joking.

The warrant officer cast his eyes to heaven; the man stubbed out the cigarette.

'Parade, parade, ATTENSHUN!' roared the warrant officer as the wing commander and his entourage of squadron leaders and a sergeant WAAF entered and stepped up onto a low temporary platform made up of packing cases.

'Stand easy, my name is Wing Commander Smith and it is my pleasure to welcome you to number 24 Operational Training Unit. You have all attained a satisfactory performance in previous training. Some of you, I know, have had the joys of South Africa and Canada. Others of you have had the joys of the Orkney Islands.'

He paused for a ripple of laughter to go through the ranks.

'You can expect to be here for some six months and you will be required to pass out, preferably with flying colours, before being posted to an operational station. There are a couple of things that you will need to know. Firstly, all of your instructors are "expired airmen".

Before some clever Harry asks the question, that does not mean they are dead.'

Again, muffled laughter passed through the throng.

'It means that they have undertaken a tour of 30 operations and have come to Honeybourne to share their experience with you. You will find that there are chaps here who can tell you both the theory of flying on ops and, and more importantly, the practice.'

The wing commander looked around to ensure that the message had got home.

'Secondly, this is a training airfield but some of our more advanced crews are called upon from time to time for operational work. This is sometimes called "nickelling" or "gardening" (RAF slang for dropping leaflets or sea mines) but they also take part in dropping bombs on the Hun, which, I can assure you, is jolly good fun.'

Everyone present would be very aware of the blue-and-white-striped ribbon on his uniform: the Distinguished Flying Cross. This man had credibility.

'We are therefore subject to the highest security standards. Do not invite civvies onto the station, be very careful what you say when you are in public and, most of all, if any civvy starts to ask you questions about the station you are to obtain their name and address and report them immediately to the provosts, or, if more convenient, to the civil police. Is that clearly understood?'

'Yes, sir,' muttered the serried lines.

'Now, the third item on the agenda is to form you into crews. Mr Davies, take over if you would. Well, welcome to Honeybourne and I hope that we see all of you pass out in six months from now.'

Ad felt a pang of vulnerability. He hoped he would pass out with flying colours but was quite aware of what would happen if he did not. He would officially be a 'wash-out' and would be posted as an erk at Leeming or possibly the dreaded Orkneys, which was so awful that there was even a song about it, or possibly even somewhere worse. No! In the RAF world even German prison camps were reputed to be not as bad as the Orkneys. He had to pass out, he had to!

CHAPTER 6

'Atten-SHUN!' barked Warrant Officer Davies and the wing commander departed with the squadron leaders and WAAF sergeant.

'Right, everyone, this is what will happen next. The WAAF girls will bring in some char and a wad [tea and sandwiches] for everyone. The hangar doors will close. You will have two hours. At that point the hangar doors will reopen. The wing commander and I will return and, by that time, you will have formed yourselves into crews. Any questions?'

'Yes, Mr Davies, how do we do it? I mean how do we form ourselves into crews?' asked a nervous voice with the timbre of the valleys of South Wales.

'Well, lad, you and your crew are going to be making decisions a few months from now with a Focke Wulf on your tail and whatever decision you make will mean life or death for you and your crew. Now, that being the case, it should not be too difficult to make a decision like "crewing up" should it?'

'No, Mr Davies.'

'No, Mr Davies, indeed! Right, you lot, I will be back at 1230 sharp, with you lot formed up into crews.'

They lined up for 'char and a wad' each. Ad reflected that his family back in Gloucester would have killed to get a well-filled cheese sandwich like that, but the coupons always had to be spent on more urgent items.

'What on earth do I do now?' thought Ad.

As flight engineer, Ad knew that pilots would approach him and others with the 'E' brevet, first.

'Hello,' said a pilot officer, beaming, 'my name is Owen. I'm looking for an engineer. I want to form a Christian crew who can pray together, worship our Lord together and drop bombs together.'

'Well, thanks, but I'm not really religious...'

'Oh, don't mind that, the Presbyterian Church is here for the likes of you. If you join my crew—'

'Many thanks, I'll keep looking.'

Another pilot approached him in the middle of the blue/grey maelstrom which was starting to circulate and recirculate throughout the hangar as the volume of noise grew louder.

'Hello, my name is Nicholson, what's yours?'

Oh no! This man had the mark of death about him. From his time at Marham and Leeming, Ad was able to recognise this in a man. If he had been asked, he would not have been able to describe it. An experienced RAF man still knew that peculiar quality. It was a quality which said 'this man will not last more than two operations'. Especially at Marham, which had been the more active station, some pilots and some crews had the reputation of being 'death crews'. He had even seen one crew appear at breakfast one morning, go on an operation that night and not return. No-one on the station had even known their names. Over breakfast the next morning he had heard the comment 'thought so'.

He moved quickly on.

'Hi!' A tall, slightly built pilot officer with the shoulder-flash 'Canada' came towards him.

'I'm John Lennox and I'm looking for an engineer. First up, would you mind if I asked you a couple of questions about yourself?'

'No, not at all. I'm Ambrose Adlam but everyone calls me Ad. Fire away.'

There was already a connection.

'Well, Ad, can you tell me, before you went on flight engineer training, where were you?'

'Oh, I was a fitter at Marham with 38 Squadron and then later at Leeming with No. 10 Squadron.'

'Thirty-eight Squadron, isn't that where the guy wrote the Rosewarne letter?'

'That's right. I knew Viv Rosewarne, although he was in a different mess. He was an officer and I was a sergeant.'

'Ah! That old British class distinction.' They both laughed.

'What aircraft did you work on?'

'Wellingtons and Whitleys.'

'How well do you know them?'

'Well. After working on them for a couple of years and with the training in South Africa, I know them both backwards.'

'Could you find all the equipment in the dark?'

CHAPTER 6

'Well, yes, and I have done.'

'Do you want to be my flight engineer?'

'Love to!' They shook hands.

'Honestly, Ad, I'm just so relieved to find a flight engineer who knows what's what. I talked to that guy who got pulled up for smoking in the hangar. He's just a civvy in uniform and I don't feel lucky with guys like that.'

Ad noted that John had an accent very similar to the Americans on the train but with a slight, almost Scottish tang in the accent.

The two forged on together.

'Right, John, what's next?'

'Well, I guess we're going to need a navigator.'

'Ah! Here's one. What's your name, Sergeant?' Johnny asked.

'Well, first off, can I ask if you chaps play cricket? I want to join with some cricketers if at all possible.'

'I'm afraid we don't play much cricket in Canada,' said Johnny with mock misery.

'Nor in Gloucester,' said Ad bursting into involuntary laughter.

'Yes, you do. W.G. Grace played for Gloucestershire!'

'Well, I'm afraid I don't. Hope you find a silly mid-off.'

'Hope you find a WHAT?' asked Johnny incredulously.

'Take too long to explain.'

He did feel, though, that he and Johnny were bonding rather quickly.

After cursory discussions with a couple of men that neither of them really fancied, and they could probably not say why, they came across Sergeant A.T. Knight. No sooner was he taken on than he was dubbed 'Knighty'.

'How about a wireless operator?'

The same process took the three to Sergeant Roberts, instantly called Robbie.

The maelstrom in the hangar had changed. Instead of tentative approaches of one man to another they had snowballed into clusters of men. The next crew member aboard was bomb aimer Graham (Grahamie), and finally a gunner: two gunners: the French Canadian Jacques Priert and Bernard Moody, instantly named Bunny.

BOMBS AND BARBED WIRE

The RAF method of crew selection was, indeed, interesting. At face value it was haphazard and had that very British quality of 'muddling through'. The reality hid a deeper significance. The men had chosen themselves for better or worse. Each would depend on the other for their life. In the months to come the crew would not be fighting for Churchill or against Hitler. They would not fight for Britain against Germany. Each man was fighting for the continued survival of the crew. The bond between aircrew members forged itself quickly, profoundly and irrevocably. The bond which this forged would last until death. Some seven decades later an aircrew survivor, who was to die of natural causes, had written on his gravestone 'together again at last'. He spoke for all of them.

At Honeybourne, events sped by quickly, orders came rapidly: 'be here', 'be somewhere else', 'see the MO', 'assemble at 0800 hours'. Feet did not touch the ground. It seemed only minutes until the newly formed crew were allocated a billet in a standard Nissen hut; they had drawn flying gear and parachutes and were airborne and training for operations.

Ad knew that Johnny was watching him more than the others. Ad's position in the aircraft was on a seat on Johnny's right. Johnny flew the aeroplane. Ad's job was to react immediately to all of Johnny's orders. A really good flight engineer would anticipate the order before it arrived. Johnny and Ad were close. They had to be.

'Start engines. Throttle back. Throttle forward. Wheels up. Trim flaps.' It was also Ad's job to watch all the dials on the console. Was the heat of the engines as per the textbook? If not, what immediate advice did he give the pilot? Was the oil pressure within acceptable limits? How was the fuel consumption? How far could the aircraft fly with this much fuel left? Ad had to anticipate the question and give an accurate answer without hesitation. When Johnny gave an order, Ad had to flick the correct switch immediately, without thinking and even without looking at it. In some months they would be on operations. An incorrect response by Ad to one of Johnny's orders could kill them.

Horror stories abounded in the mess. At 44 Squadron, at Waddington, a Lancaster had been on a cross-country flight. As it

CHAPTER 6

passed Lincoln Cathedral and came back to base, the starboard inner engine burst into flames. The pilot ordered the flight engineer to operate the fire extinguisher and feather the engine. In his panic the flight engineer made a fatal mistake and feathered the starboard outer engine. The Lancaster stalled and went into a yaw. It crashed on a pig farm, broke into two and immediately burst into flames. Some unfortunate pigs were trapped underneath the burning plane. Their squeals were terrible to hear. The wireless operator survived the crash, having been pulled clear by two local farmers who had gone into the burning wreck at terrible risk to their own lives. The wireless operator was lying on the ground helpless and coughing blood. Then in a moment of utter surrealism, a nice old lady appeared with a tray. 'You'll be ready for a cup of tea, luv,' she said as .303 ordnance exploded, cracked and ricocheted all around them.

The job of a flight engineer was not to be underestimated.

As soon as he could find five minutes, Ad wrote a letter to Anne. He needed very badly to tell her that he was missing her. He needed her reply to get the comfort of knowing that she was not mortally upset with him for 'shooting a line' about his well-to-do-family. He needed to know that she was settling down in that tiny and overcrowded 'joined-up' house in the backstreets of Gloucester.

At exactly the same moment, 600 miles to the east, another RAF man thought about his love life. He sat in a dark, silent room alone as he had for the previous ten days. He had no human contact apart from the Luftwaffe guards who brought his food.

His love life was somewhat more colourful than Ad's. His first love, Lady Georgiana Curzon of Belgravia, had married a naval officer who proved to be a rotter and shortly afterwards, eloped with her mother. His second love was Marguerite Hamilton of Sloane Square. In captivity he had made over his RAF pay to her, but she had been beastly enough to give up on him and married a toff to become Lady

Petre. His third love, Blaža Zeithammelová of Přístavni Street, Prague, had ceased to exist. A Gestapo operative had put a bullet in the back of her head. The fate of her remains was not known.

Ad was destined to meet this man, which would not be the most pleasant of meetings. He would, however, find him one of the most – if not the most – impressive person that he was ever to encounter. Destiny had also laid down that Ad would work for him – long, hard hours with little thanks and no recognition but without stint. Destiny had further laid down that after it was all over he would never mention him.

His name was Roger Bushell.

Bushell had been born into a wealthy family in South Africa and migrated to England at the age of 13. Not for him the gritty backstreets of industrial Gloucester. Roger Bushell had won a scholarship to Wellington College, Crowthorne in the affluent Thames Valley. This was in stark contrast to Ad, who was expelled from grammar school for fighting when the other boys had taunted him because of his dilapidated shoes. Roger Bushell followed his privileged existence in the leafy realms of Berkshire by going up to Pembroke College, Cambridge and being offered captaincy of the joint Oxbridge skiing team. This was followed by being called to the bar via the Chambers of Lincoln's Inn. At this stage, 1932, he was invited, as 'the right sort of chap', into the RAF Volunteer Reserve's 601 Squadron: the Millionaires' Squadron. As war broke out he had joined the RAF as a flying officer with rapid promotion to squadron leader of 'B' Flight in 92 Squadron flying Spitfires and was promptly shot down over Dunkirk on his first operation.

This had led to incarceration at Dulag Luft, the transit camp for shot-down airman from which he had made his first escape attempt. He was tall, well built, charismatic, ebullient and completely self-confident. He had made it to the Swiss border only to be apprehended by an alert policeman. On Bushell's progression from Dulag Luft he was to be taken by train to Stalag Luft 1 at Barth in the far east of the Reich. The German commanding officer at Dulag Luft, Oberst Rumpel, would present Bushell and the other escapers with a

CHAPTER 6

complimentary case of Champagne for the journey with a gift tag bearing the words 'nice try'. There was still some gallantry and chivalry at play in the war in those early stages.

On that morning of 21 September 1942, Bushell was again in solitary confinement, this time at Barth. He had made another escape attempt but this time there was less chivalry. The German commanding officer warned him that if he were to escape again the SS would arrest him and we would be taken to a concentration camp for summary execution.

The talk at Honeybourne that morning was of the previous night's raid over Munich.

'It says here, in the Daily Mirror, that they bombed the Oktoberfest,' laughed Bunny.

'What the heck is that?' asked Ad.

'It's a load of Germans dressing up in leather shorts and listening to oompah bands and getting pissed out of their minds,' said Johnny with a smile. 'They have it once a year back home in Toronto.' Ad noticed how he pronounced it as 'Torronno'. The crew picked up the same affectation when talking to Johnny about 'home'.

They were airmen and young. They were infinitely proud of the new brevets on their uniform. They loved it when they walked into the charming town of Honeybourne and passed an officer. Regulations said that they had to salute the uniform. They dutifully did this, but their great joy was to pass an officer who had not got wings: a bird that did not fly, a 'penguin'. Their aircrew brevet trumped an officer's cap. They just felt so bloody and wonderfully superior.

Then there was the serious business of writing to and receiving letters from Anne. He would write every day if he could. Despite the endless catalogue of privations in wartime Britain the General Post Office maintained standards impeccably. A letter from Monday would be received on Tuesday.

BOMBS AND BARBED WIRE

There was only a single telephone box on the station at Honeybourne. The Adlams did not have a telephone at home nor did they know anyone who had. The station phone box was, however, of the utmost importance to all of them in a very unexpected and unforeseen way. Ad would find this out after being posted to ops.

Fortunately, on quiet days, Ad could hitchhike over to Gloucester to see Anne or she could take the train to Honeybourne for a couple of stolen but precious hours. It would be typical of those days that neither would bemoan the long days of separation and the sensation of missing the other. There was a war on.

Ad received a letter from Anne. She had got herself a job as a timekeeper in a local factory. It did not pay very high wages but did grant her the great good fortune of independence. She had also found a bed sitting room with a nice old lady in Gloucester, which meant that she was out of the overcrowded terraced house in Beaufort Road. She was free, mistress of her own destiny and was settling down. That was utterly wonderful. Now he could get on with the business of winning the war.

He loved the camaraderie and the high jinks in the local pubs. The Gate, The Fleece and The Seagrave were all places where the crews would gather at night for a pint and a song around the piano. Many of the airmen in 1942 could play the piano. 'Roll Me Over in the Clover', 'White Cliffs of Dover' and 'Run Rabbit Run' would belt out with unabashed enthusiasm against a backdrop of the cigarette smoke, smell of stale beer slops and the closing-time shout of the publican: 'Time, gentlemen, please. Haven't you lot got any homes to go to?' To which the answer was a chorus of 'NO!'

Then there were the pub games. A pyramid of drunken airmen would assemble itself. The one on top would carry a flying boot whose sole was covered in soot. This would be planted firmly on the ceiling as a prank, a merrymaking gesture and a sign that 'we all know we are going to die but can still laugh'.

The gunners in the crews had the best of it in some ways: they got close and personal access to the girls in the armoury. One of the vital jobs was the loading of .303 bullets into the belts for the guns

CHAPTER 6

to fire. This had to be done carefully, painstakingly and by hand. An incorrectly inserted bullet could cause a jam. If that jam occurred when a Messerschmitt 110 was on your tail, then your life expectancy was measured in seconds. Many gunners elected to join the armoury girls in inserting the bullets. Many a joyful romance blossomed from the dour confines of the armoury.

Unfortunately, the station senior officers found this threatening and very worrying. Too-close relationships between an armoury girl and a shot-down airman spelt tears, tantrums and a corrosive loss of morale. If an armoury girl was seen to be too close to an airman she was likely to find herself posted 'this minute' to another station many miles away.

This brought the crew to thinking about the other aspect of the war. Operational Training Units were exceptionally dangerous places. Despite the best efforts of officialdom to stifle it, the word was going around that a couple of weeks ago, No. 27 Operational Training Unit at Lichfield had lost five aircraft in one week with some 30 dead. Some did not believe the rumour.

It was true.

Best not to think about it, eh?

The crew lived together, ate together, trained together, drank together, sang together and formed into a team to the point where each could depend on the others for their life. They bonded. They did well. They passed out. They awaited their posting to ops with great anticipation.

CHAPTER 7
A WALK ON THE WET SIDE - LEEMING REVISITED

17 FEBRUARY 1943

He saw the posting orders. To be sent to 405 Squadron, Royal Canadian Air Force was good. Then he saw the home station. Ad was not happy; in fact, he was furious. In early 1941 he had spent several frustrating months at RAF Leeming, wet, depressed and ineffective. Now, in early 1943 he had been to South Africa to learn the job of flight engineer, passed through an Operational Training Unit and a Heavy Conversion Unit to be back once again – after two years of very expensive training – at bloody Leeming. That cold, wet, soggy outpost was to be his operational station.

He had arrived with Johnny earlier that afternoon after arriving at Northallerton station. His train journey, after a week's very welcome leave with Anne in Gloucester, had taken him to Birmingham, Sheffield, Leeds and, finally, on a very slow stopping train to his final, totally unwanted destination. Was the Royal Air Force completely off its head? There was a bloody big air station at Upper Heyford not half an hour from where he lived. Why could they not post him there instead of this awful bloody place up in bloody Yorkshire which he never wanted to see bloody well again in the whole of his life?

CHAPTER 7

'Oh, come on,' said Johnny, 'it doesn't look that bad. Come and show me around.'

'Good God!' said Ad as they stepped outside of the Nissen hut and onto the grass that led to the runway.

'What's that?'

'It's concrete! When I was here last time it was all grass runways. The whole place was totally useless, in wet weather this place was completely out of action.'

Johnny walked over to the side of the runway.

'Well, I can tell you one thing, Ad, if I'm taking off or taxiing I do not want to go off the runway; this is like a bog. A Halifax would just sink into it. God knows how long it would take to pull out.'

They availed themselves of two 'issue bicycles' which lay ready for use beside the Nissen hut wall.

They watched as a huge Halifax four engine bomber landed after a test flight. The massive Rolls Royce Merlin engines drowned out their conversation as it touched down with a piercing shriek of tyres.

'That's another thing – when I was here all we had was bloody Whitleys. They were completely and totally useless. We had anything up to a third of them out of action with endless faults and things that didn't work. They must have sent flight engineers mad. Look at these Halifaxes – now they can do some real damage to Mr Hitler.'

They cycled over to the hangars. Erks in brown overalls and blue RAF caps were busy winching a new Merlin engine into its housing to replace one which had been damaged on a previous raid.

'Excuse me, Chiefie,' said Ad to the flight sergeant in charge, 'I used to be an erk on this station when No. 10 Squadron was here. Do you know if any of the lads are still here?'

'Search me, mate. I didn't even know No. 10 Squadron were ever here. That must have been some time ago. They could have joined the Luftwaffe for all I know. There's a couple of old girls in the NAAFI might know.'

'Tell me one thing, though.'

'I can't stay chatting all morning, mate. I've got to get that engine in place this afternoon.'

'OK, quick question: how long to do an engine change?'

'We can do it in five hours. I must dash.'

'Johnny, that is unbelievable. When I was in the RAF before the war it took us a week to do an engine change. When we had the Wellingtons at Marham it was down to two days and now they've got it down to five hours. That's another thing – when I went to Marham, Wellingtons were the latest and greatest bombers, now they're just used for trainers.'

'I guess that's the marvellous thing about wartime: it takes me from Toronto to England; it takes you from Gloucester to South Africa; and it brings down the time of an engine change down to five hours from a week. Oh, and it also gives you a wife. War is not all bad. What's next?'

They cycled over to a large, very steep, manmade hill. 'This is the bomb dump; let's see what it's like these days'.

They laid the cycles on their side and climbed the hill.

'Crikey! Look at this lot. There is ten times as much here as when I was here before. God, look, there are 1000 pounders, 500 pounders, two 50s and enough incendiaries to blow the Third Reich into very small pieces.'

'Oy! You two!' It was a very officious corporal dressed in a thick leather jerkin over his blue RAF uniform.

'Just having a look.'

'Well, are you an armourer?' The man could see the brevets on their uniforms; it was a totally redundant question.

'No, we're aircrew.' It felt so good to say that, so very good.

'Well, if you're not armourers you can bugger off because this place is out of bounds, CO's orders.'

'Have it your own way.'

'I will, mate, I will.'

Johnny and Ad looked at each other and smiled a knowing look. The prestige of being aircrew meant that a slight from an erk could be safely ignored with impunity. Erks were penguins.

'That's one thing about a war,' said Johnny cheerily as they cycled to the large building on the other side of the bomb dump. 'A war brings people together.' They both laughed.

CHAPTER 7

The large building proved to be a new fusing hut. They watched in impressed silence as a tractor hauled a train of six trollies over from the bomb dump. Inside the fusing hut was such an array of fuses as Ad had never seen before. There were impact fuses, delay fuses and several devices that he had no idea about. It was all so different to two years ago when there were impact fuses and very little else. The new range of delay fuses could postpone an explosion for an hour, or three hours or any other period of time. At the business end the Herrenvolk would have to try to deal with having no idea when it was going to explode.

'Quite a nasty little idea, really,' said Johnny.

'Good,' said Ad and smiled. 'Good!'

Each train of five or six trollies represented a bomb load for a single Halifax bomber. The trolley contained some 14,000 pounds of bombs (6350 kilograms). The armourers were screwing fuses into the nose of each bomb and wiring them up to prevent the fuses becoming active too early and causing an explosion before the bomber had taken off.

An erk saw they were watching and greeted them with a grin. 'You new boys?'

'Yes, just finished at Heavy Conversion Unit. I hope you're making those things safe.'

'Safe as houses this lot,' said the erk. 'Did you hear what happened down at Scampton last week though? One of the big 4000-pound bombs went off when they were bombing up a Lancaster. It destroyed six Lancs, damaged five more, and there was a load of blokes blown to smithereens. Don't know how many got killed but you could imagine.'

They cycled over to the petrol bowsers. A dozen or so Halifaxes stood in line for fuelling.

'How much tonight, Chiefie?'

'Fifteen hundred, mate.' The flight sergeant in charge of fuelling had answered that question several dozen times that day. The tanks of a Halifax could take 1882 imperial gallons, which would take them, with a tail wind, as far as Stettin or even Danzig on the Baltic. So 1500 could take them to Berlin, Frankfurt or Leipzig.

As they cycled on across the airfield, Ad became more excited. 'That's different as well, Johnny; when I was here last time the targets were all Cologne, Hamburg and Bremen, oh, and Essen if they were really unlucky. It was all North Germany. Now it's much further south to Frankfurt and Leipzig…'

'And Berlin if we're really unlucky.' They laughed. Gallows humour is particularly funny, especially when it is your life that you are gambling with. At the next stop the level of the gamble became immediately clear.

Their Odyssey around the airfield had brought them to the hangars where three mighty Halifaxes were being patched up after a raid a couple of nights previously on Kassel.

'What's the operational life of a Halifax?' Johnny asked a corporal.

'Oh, we reckon to get 40 hours out of them on operations.'

That simple fact told Ad and Johnny their life expectancy. From behind them a voice of authority spoke in tones of great irritation.

'Corporal Wilcox!' boomed a very unamused flight sergeant. 'My office now!'

'I suspect he wasn't supposed to tell us that,' said Johnny as they cycled on.

'Do we pass it on to the others, Ad?'

'Would it do any good?'

'Not really, let's just keep it to ourselves. Anyway, some blokes are lucky; the instructors at Honeybourne had completed 30 ops. Maybe we'll be lucky too.'

Ad agreed that they might be lucky, but he knew he had to be very, very loving to Anne because you never knew when…

An average of 40 hours operational time meant that a Halifax bomber could expect to complete some six to eight operations before succumbing to a nightfighter or, less likely, flak. He had known since Operational Training Unit that he was unlikely to complete a tour of 30 operations. Now he knew the extent of the unlikeliness. He would expect to survive six operations or eight if they were lucky.

It would have been very unlikely in that RAF world for the reality of a short life expectancy to put a man off flying on operations. Bert Dowty, who had the honour of being on the first ever Lancaster bomber raid, gave the RAF perspective very well: 'there was a job to

CHAPTER 7

be done'. Whether or not you survived was of meagre importance compared with the imperative of 'doing your bit' and especially, 'not letting the crew down'.

Woe betide the airman who did not understand that principle and understand it well.

CHAPTER 8
AMBROSE'S RAIDS – ST NAZAIRE

2 APRIL 1943

They were airmen now and forged into a team, a unit, a firm and just about to have a crack at Jerry. For the first time they had used the time-honoured expression 'there's a war on'. That meant the station was sealed off. The Flight Office noticeboard showed that Johnny's crew were rostered on. It was a breathlessly exciting day. Each man worried: 'what will I do if things go wrong? I will die before I let the crew down.' They all meant this literally.

Following another time-honoured tradition each man piddled on the rear wheel of the aircraft. They would not be able to 'go' again for some eight hours. Technically they could use the Elsan chemical toilet in the aeroplane but any crew member away from this position for the length of the average piddle (plus the difficulty of navigating the flying suit) would put the whole aeroplane in danger. In any case, it was common practice for the flight engineer to give a crew member the option to throw the Elsan toilet out of the aircraft and onto Hitler's Reich before he closed the bomb doors during a raid.

Ad pulled into his seat in the cockpit on Johnny's right. They began the litany of pre-flight checks. After the intensive training at the Operational Training Unit and Heavy Conversion Unit they could do the flight checks without looking at the checklist which an efficient Royal Air Force had provided for them. Johnny turned on all

CHAPTER 8

the switches for which he was responsible, and Ad turned on all the switches for which he was responsible.

'Ground/flight switch?' asked Johnny.

'On Ground,' responded Ad.

'Fuel cocks?'

'Fuel cocks on, skipper.'

'Altimeter?' asks Johnny.

'Set to FE,' responded Ad.

'Radius shutters?'

'Open.'

The erk with the starter trolley stood awaiting the signal to turn the portable starter motor on to charge up the engines. This was a vital measure to preserve the aeroplane's battery power.

'Confirm trolley connected' was Johnny's much used line. Ad looked out of his window pointedly at the erk. The erk gave a 'thumbs up'.

'Trolley connected, skipper.'

Ad loved this. The whole procedure of pre-flight checks, of test flights, of working with the flight sergeant in charge of the erks, of acting as Johnny's indispensable right-hand man – it was exhilarating. There were no more boring jobs of making bloody barrels. There was no more servicing aircraft in the open air in freezing rain. Now he was to drop bombs on Germany (or at least on German installations in occupied France) and six other men depended on him for their life. This exhilaration was something he had never before known.

Johnny pressed the button to start up the first engine. 'Starting port outer – NOW.' He did this for the port inner, starboard inner and starboard outer.

He then pressed forward a lever with the words 'checking port outer for mag drops NOW' and did this for each of the other engines. Ad checked the gauges, dials and indicator lights to ensure that each was doing what was expected.

Immediately afterwards, Ad checked that the erk with the starter trolley had pulled clear of the rapidly spinning propellers. The erk stood clear so that Ad could see him, and each gave a wave of acknowledgement.

'Ground switch to flight.'
'Ground switch to flight, skipper.'
'Instruments vacuum?'
'Four and a half inches.'
'Pressures and temperatures.'
'One sec, skipper, erm, yes, all OK.'
'Bomb doors?'
'Closed.'
'Hydraulic brake pressure? Is that OK, Ad? It was looking a bit underdone on that last flight test.'
'I got Chiefie onto it, skipper. He found a faulty component and swapped it over. It's showing 300 pounds per square inch.'
'You happy with that, Ad?'
'It's the right pressure but I'll keep an eye on it just to be sure.'

It was a sobering thought. Ambrose Adlam was easily capable of performing such a job of high technology, of the intellectual rigour of diagnosis and solution and of coping with the psychological pressures of a bomber crew member. Why on earth had he just made barrels for a living before the war? There was no time to ponder.

'Auto pilot?'
'Control out.'
'Compass?'
'Set to magnetic.'
'Trim?'
'Set for takeoff.'
'Propellers?'
'Full fine.'
'Fuel?'
'One and two tanks selected, booster pumps on.'
'Flaps?'
'Set for takeoff.'

Johnny looked out of his window to see the corporal give a thumbs-up sign.

'Skipper to crew, are all checks completed?'

In turn they all confirmed that their checks were complete.

CHAPTER 8

Johnny gave the thumbs-up to the corporal on the ground. The corporal gave hand signals to unseen ground crew members beneath the Halifax's mighty airframe.

'Here we go, then, chaps.' He nodded to Ad.

Ad pushed the throttles forward as the erks removed the chocks from in front of the massive tyres. The engines screamed. Ad checked the gauge, which showed propeller revolutions per minute.

'Three thousand revs per minute and manifold pressure 14 pounds per square inch, skipper.' Johnny nodded and pushed the throttle lever gently away from him.

The massive aircraft shuddered forward.

Johnny guided it into the line of Halifaxes now proceeding from their dispersals and onto the live runway. One took off, another took off... now it was Johnny's turn to pull the aeroplane onto the runway. At the far end he could see a red Aldiss light telling him that the last aircraft had not cleared yet. The red light changed to green.

'That's it, skipper, you've got green.' At the far end of the Leeming runway the Aldiss light flashed once, twice, three times.

'Roger, flight engineer.'

Lennox increased the revolutions until the mighty Merlin engines screamed. The aeroplane vibrated like a highly strung horse desperate to start a big race. It moved slowly, like a duckling uncertain of its first steps. Johnny guided the aircraft slowly onto the runway, then more quickly as he straightened it up. Oh, don't let the kite swerve off the runway, if it gets onto that grass it will bog down and it will block the runway for hours! The wingco will go ballistic. Johnny's task now was solely to guide the aeroplane forward and to point it in the right direction. It was Ad's task to hold the throttles forward until they are jammed against the stops. It was Ad's job to count off the ground speed of the aircraft.

Ad looked down, as he had been told, to see a small farewell party at the end of the runway. He could see Wing Commander Clayton's Austin 7 and there was the wing commander giving a salute as they took off. Several of the WAAFs stood beside him and waved scarves and other things he couldn't identify. Beside them stood several of the erks. The more military among them saluted and the more friendly waved.

'Ninety-five knots, skipper, 100, 105, 110 up to 130.' At 130, Johnny adjusts the trim and pulls the relevant levers. The mighty aeroplane shudders. Ad feels slightly weightless. They are airborne.

Johnny's task was to follow the preceding aircraft to the forming-up point at which the entire force from several squadrons and several stations would form into a single massive unit to maximise their force onto Hitler's domain at St Nazaire. The significance of hitting St Nazaire was of the highest importance: it was the only port with dry dock facilities big enough to service the battleship *Tirpitz*, which threatened British shipping in the North Atlantic.

'Good luck, Johnny. Let's hope it goes well.'

'What's luck got to do with it?' Johnny laughed.

'OK, engineer, take up flaps.'

'Flaps up, skipper.'

'Undercarriage up, engineer.'

'Undercarriage up, skipper.'

'Roger, engineer. Navigator, give me a course please.'

'Navigator to skipper, can you see the A1 road?'

'A1 road dead ahead, navigator, we'll pass over it in one minute.'

'Take a bearing of two one zero when you cross the road. Ascend to angels 8 (8,000 feet). Maintain air speed 150 miles an hour and head for forming up place at Ripon. I'll tell you when we're five minutes away.'

After takeoff, Ad left the seat beside Johnny and went to his permanent seat for the flight. This is behind Johnny and slightly to the left.

They had been through the routine over and over and over again. Ad did not even think. He instinctively looked at his dials:

- Electrical charge
- Engine coolant temp
- Oil pressure and temp
- Fuel levels

CHAPTER 8

- Fuel tank selection
- Fuel booster pumps
- Oil dilution.

'Skipper to engineer, how's that port inner engine looking? You said it had overheated when Crockatt had this kite out last week.'

'I've been over it with the erks, skipper, they made a small adjustment and it performed all right in flight tests. It's looking all right now but I'll keep a special eye on it.'

The port inner engine was of particular importance. Apart from holding the aircraft up, it provided power to the rear turret. If that engine was lost, the rear gun turret would not operate and the aeroplane would be vulnerable to nightfighter attack.

At Ripon they found other aircraft arriving for the raid on St Nazaire.

'Engineer to skipper, what a bloody rag bag this is. There must be two of everything the RAF has got flying. I can see Lancasters, Stirlings, Mosquitoes, Wellingtons and Whitleys. I'm surprised there aren't a couple of Sopwith Camels.'

In all there were 55 aircraft on the raid. This was a small raid. They circled in the prescribed manner, formed up into formation for a raid. The Pathfinder aeroplanes went first with the others following.

'Navigator to skipper, ascend to angels 12 now.'

'Roger, navigator. Engineer, turn on oxygen please.'

'Wilco, skipper.' A short gap. 'Oxygen turned on, skipper.'

'Skipper to crew, all crew members put on oxygen masks. If problems let me know soonest.'

'Skipper to navigator, force are all ascending to angels 12. Am going up with them.'

Ad heard the engines surge. The red-hot exhausts were visible in the reflection of the Perspex canopy. He was getting closer to Hitler-occupied France now. This is what he had joined up for. Were there any regrets? None. Below them was the dark mass of southern England. Not a single light was to be seen but roads, the shining metal of the railways and rivers were all clearly visible in pallid moonlight. Now they were over the English Channel.

BOMBS AND BARBED WIRE

After a half-hour's flying time Ad heard the phrase, which told them all to be on their guard.

'Bomb aimer to skipper, enemy coast ahead.'

'Roger, bomb aimer. Skipper to all crew. We have a lot of two-engined kites with us tonight. I want the gunners, especially, to make sure that if you see a two-engined kite that it is one of ours and not a bloody Junkers or Messerschmitt insinuating itself into our bomber stream.'

'Rear gunner to skipper, wilco.'

'Mid-upper to skipper, wilco.'

In the darkness and if visibility was poor it was all too easy for an apparent Whitley to turn out to be a Messerschmitt 110, which would then creep up behind an unsuspecting RAF crew and blow them out of the air. Visibility, however, remained very clear and much as the station intelligence officer had predicted in the briefing.

'Engineer to skipper, you know when the intelligence officer said that all civvies (civilians) had been taken out of St Nazaire? How would they know?'

'Yes, that worried me as well. I don't think they'd make it up, though; what would be the point?'

'Make us feel better about dropping bombs if we weren't going to hit civvies?'

'They didn't say anything like that on the Berlin raids. They seemed to be perfectly happy for us to drop as many bombs as we wanted onto civvies.'

Johnny had undertaken two flights as 'second dicky' (supernumerary) on raids over Berlin. In the Dog and Gun afterwards he had held the crew spellbound with stories of the experience. The flak; the nightfighters; the searchlights; the Christmas tree effect of the markers; the flash of the bombs. He had, of course, forgotten to mention the terror of being there. The crew had understood this but were too diplomatic to ask. They also knew that they would feel the terror, too, when the time came. They could not let their skipper down.

By now, as Ad and Johnny knew from training, Luftwaffe long range 'Freya' radar would have picked up their presence. It would be a short leap of logic to guess that this smallish raiding party was after

CHAPTER 8

U-boat bases. What the Luftwaffe did not know was precisely where the force was going. Would it be Lorient? Would it be Bordeaux or Brest? Would it be St Nazaire? It was not given to the men who flew to know who had planned these raids.

Someone, somewhere, had punctiliously mapped out the flight path to feint first towards one direction and then to another. The landfall was in the area of Lannion, which would threaten Brest, St Nazaire and Lorient. Most importantly of all, the route would be devised to give as wide a berth as possible to Rennes. Squadron 4 of Luftwaffe Nightfighter Wing 5 was based there, and they were deadly. Their wing commander, Heinrich Prinz zu Sayn-Wittgenstein, was as dangerous a combatant as the RAF crews ever encountered.

'Overhead Lannion, skipper, course is now 200 degrees until we pass over Quimper and go out to sea again.'

'Roger, navigator, yes, the force is swinging in that direction. Skipper to gunners, any sign of intruders out there? It's a bit bloody quiet for such a moonlit night.'

'Rear gunner to skipper, not a sausage, skip.'

'Mid-upper to skipper, no sausages here either.'

'Engineer to skipper, I bet it wasn't like this over Berlin, Johnny.'

'Christ, over Berlin there were hundreds of the buggers and then over the target the flak was so thick you could walk over it.'

'Skipper to gunners, this is too bloody quiet. Keep your eyes peeled. Flight engineer, could you stick your head up into the Astrodome please? If you can see anything let me know as soon as possible.'

'Wilco, skipper.'

The Astrodome was mainly intended for the navigator. If an aircraft was lost the navigator could find a position from the stars. Now that aeroplanes were being equipped with electronic navigational equipment it was redundant but served very usefully as an extra observation point to look out for nightfighters.

The force flew over Quimper and the charming fishing port of Concarneau. Not a light was to be seen. The Germans now would not only have radar contact; they would be able to hear them. Still there was no nightfighter activity.

'Just leaving the coast, skipper. Ascend to angels 15 for bombing run.'

'Skipper to navigator, ascending to angels 15 for bombing run.'

The force passed over the small island of Belle Ile and banked due east for St Nazaire.

'Skipper to crew, this is it, chaps, good luck everyone. Gunners, any sign of action?'

'Rear gunner to skipper, none.'

'Mid-upper to skipper, none.'

'Skipper to gunners, roger and out. Bomb aimer take up your position please and advise that all equipment is working properly.' Bomb aimers rode in the front gun turret until approaching the target and would move into their combat position some minutes before the final run-in.

The first of the Pathfinders had arrived at the target and were now starting their runs. The lurid green markers could be seen dropping like neon-lit Christmas trees slowly and dangerously onto the target. The red and orange snakes of tracer bullets were coming up towards them now. The first red puffs of exploding shells could be seen a couple of thousand feet below them.

'We're going in, chaps. Skipper to bomb aimer, take over now.'

'Wilco, skipper. Keep her steady on those green markers, right a bit, right a bit. That's it.'

They all heard the 'plink, plink, plink' of exploding flak shells against the fuselage of the plane.

'Skipper to all crew, any problems with that flak?'

'None, skipper, over and out.'

'Keep her right a bit, skipper… and steady… The greens have gone out but the red markers are exactly in the same spot. Nice marking. Oh bugger! The Germans have started a smoke screen.'

'Can you see what you are doing, bomb aimer?'

CHAPTER 8

'They've started it too late, skipper, yes, I can see the reds perfectly and now we're coming onto them.'

Plink... plink... plink.

Ad kept his eyes on his gauges and all the other various indicators.

'Everything OK, engineer?'

'Everything's fine, skipper.'

'Rear gunner to skipper, there's a kite going down behind us. He's in a bloody mess. One parachute...'

'Can't worry about that, rear gunner. Bomb aimer what are your instructions?'

'Left a bit, that's it, skipper... The reds are coming right into my...'

The massive Halifax bomber suddenly lurched upwards.

'Bombs gone, skipper.'

Now came the worst, and perhaps strangest, part of the raid. The high explosive and incendiary bombs were hurtling downwards but, for a whole minute, Johnny's task was to hold the aircraft straight and level. The reason was that together with the bombs was a photo-flash illuminator. As it descended, this exploded and the explosion in turn caused a camera on the bottom of the aeroplane to photograph it. The photo was of the flash, not the target. Upon return the intelligence staff would confirm that the photo-flash photo was correct, and the raid could be counted towards the completion of the crew's tour of duty. Without the photo the raid would not be counted towards completion of the tour of duty. This minute, crews reported, felt like several lifetimes as flak burst all around them.

Snakes of red tracer moved slowly towards them then accelerated to whizz over the aeroplane at supernatural speed. Those tracer bullets were 20-millimetre cannon shells. If one of those hit the petrol stored in the wings, death would follow shortly afterwards.

'That's it, boys, the photo-flash has gone off, let's get the hell out of here.'

A minute or so later they had banked out to sea and were away from the flak.

'Skipper to navigator, bearing for home please.'

Sergeant Cooke, who was the pilot on another 405 Squadron aircraft that night, also notes that the target was obscured by a German smoke screen, which is why the results of bombing were not observed. Sergeant Cooke also describes this as an 'uneventful trip'.

As they ran up the English midlands, Johnny gave his final orders for the night.

'Skipper to gunners, keep your eyes peeled, boys, we'll be landing in about ten minutes and Jerry has been a bit keen in using intruders of late. I would rather not cop a nightfighter when we're only 20 minutes from bacon and eggs.'

'Wilco, skipper.'

The aeroplane came to a halt at the dispersal. Johnny and Ad shook hands.

'Well, Ad, we've done it, we've bloody done it.'

The crew jumped, fell or sprang out of the small doorway and down onto the ground. Everyone shook hands all around. 'We did it, we bloody did it!' Several of the erks had stayed up to see them home. Everyone shook hands and offered cigarettes all around. God! It was good to draw on a fag!

'How was that port inner, Ad? Did it stand up OK?'

'Yes, Chiefie, no trouble at all, I was watching it all the way through the raid. Not a worry.'

A 3-tonne truck appeared driven by a WAAF.

'Well done, boys, jump in.'

They were immediately taken to the briefing room where Wing Commander Clayton was waiting. They all saluted, then he shook each hand.

'Well done, you guys.'

They were seated in front of an intelligence officer who asked about every aspect of the flight and a WAAF who took notes.

Johnny Lennox's report on the St Nazaire raid reads:

Up 1945   Down 0212

B' (F/O Lennox JW) Reached primary in good visibility at 2226 hours and bombs released from 15,000'. LOIRE ESTUARY identified

CHAPTER 8

visually. Red T.I. markers in bombsight at moment of release. Green markers seen but had gone out. Red markers co-incided well with the green ones. Results of own bombing not observed. One good fire seen close to aiming points and another in N.W. of town. A third fire was seen to the East of the docks. Other bombs were seen bursting and glow of fires still visible 75 miles away on return journey.

Having made the report, the crew had their heavy flying suits taken from them and were ushered into the NAAFI, the airmens' canteen, for bacon and eggs.

There were some things about the raid which were very relevant, but which were not known to the crew.

The reason that they had not seen any nightfighters was that the much-feared German squadron IV/NJG5 had been transferred some weeks before to the Russian front. The night skies to the St Nazaire dry dock were open. This, unfortunately, was of little strategic advantage to the war effort. No evidence exists that this raid hindered the German war effort at all.

A crucial member of Winston Churchill's high-ranking air commanders, Sir Arthur Harris, was not surprised at this. Harris was the head of Bomber Command. He was, and still is, a controversial figure whose committed strategy was to bomb German cities to the point where the country could no longer function and the Allies would win the war. His hand had been forced by the Admiralty into bombing naval bases; although, he himself believed it was pointless. This raid on St Nazaire was destined to be the final raid on the naval bases for the time being.

It was fortunate for Sir Arthur Harris that his country home was within walking distance in the Buckinghamshire countryside from Chequers, the Prime Minister's country retreat. This resulted in many dinner invitations to Harris, which were 'one on one' with Winston Churchill. In the world of politics this was an opportunity of the purest gold. Harris used this frequent and informal access to persuade Winston Churchill that the only way to win this awful bloody war was by massive bombing efforts on the German mainland. As head of Bomber Command, Harris was Ambrose Adlam's ultimate boss and Ambrose Adlam was very much included in Harris's forward plans.

CHAPTER 9
THE RAID ON KIEL

4 APRIL 1943

They were 'blooded' now! They could swagger around Leeming with that glow of combat behind them. They were the equals of other crews; well, except the lucky ones who had survived tens or even twenties of operations. They were learning the ropes and the significance of that telephone box. The first thing on waking up was to look out of the Nissen hut window and look at it: it told the story they all wanted to know.

'Wake up, you lot!' said Ad. 'The telephone box is padlocked. There's a war on!'

Before breakfast they sauntered to the Flight Office. Heck! There were ten aircraft scheduled for the raid. Lennox's crew was scheduled onto aeroplane LQ-J for Johnny.

'You lot go off to breakfast,' said Ad, 'and I'll have a chat with the erks.'

It was great that he could say that. He wasn't an erk anymore. It was useful to Johnny that with Ad's earlier experience as an erk he knew just what questions to ask.

The casualty list on St Nazaire had not been too bad: only one aeroplane had been lost with, probably, three men dead. The experience, though, had bolted home what they had been telling him in training: every man depends on every other man for their lives. For Ad, the job and the vital dependency began long before the aeroplane ever took off.

He bumped into Sergeant Damms from Foley's crew.

CHAPTER 9

'Hi, Dammy, where do you reckon we're off to tonight?'

'Hi, Ad, I've just been over to the petrol pumps. We've got 1700 gallons on.'

'So that's about six and a half hours flying time. We had 1650 on two nights ago for St Nazaire so it's a bit further than that. It's a bit too little for Big City and a bit much for Happy Valley.'

'Big City' (Berlin) and 'Happy Valley' (Essen and the mighty Krupp works) were the two most feared destinations for bomber crews target.

'What do you reckon then, Ad? Rostock? Kiel?'

'Could be, or how about somewhere like Kassel or Nuremberg?'

'Tell you what, Ad, two bob says it's Kassel.'

'You're on!'

Ad went over to the dispersal to find LQ-J.

'Hi, Chiefie, we're on J for Johnny tonight. How's she looking?'

The bond between the members of aircrew was obvious. A less obvious but equally important bond was that between the aircrews – and especially the flight engineer – and the flight sergeant who was in charge of the ground crew. The ground crews were assigned to specific aircraft and took a fierce partisan pride in keeping them in perfect order.

'Hi, Ad! We've had to do a bit of work on her. She was out over Stuttgart with Jago a couple of weeks ago. She took a lot of flak on the port side and we've had to replace some of the electrical wiring and hydraulics but she's been out on flight tests. I would say she's as good as new. She was bloody lucky; that was the operation when Logan and Jennings…', he trailed off. He remembered the unwritten rule: you do not talk about crews who have not come back. It was bad form. It was just not done. Everyone wished Logan and Jennings well, but the likelihood was that they were dead or, at best, in a prisoner of war camp.

There was an unfortunate truth about Halifax bombers, and Lancasters as well, for that matter. Their wing span was too wide to accommodate them in the standard RAF hangers, which had been designed for an earlier dynasty of bomber: the Whitleys and Wellingtons. That, in turn, meant that the erks – the fitters, electricians, specialists of one sort or another – had to work in the open air with minimal cover in all weathers. Work did not stop for bad weather: it carried on until the job was done. There was a war on!

'Pass on to the lads that we're very grateful for their efforts, eh?'

'They know, Ad, don't worry.'

'Do you and your lads want to join us for a pint in the White Rose tomorrow night?'

'That's very kind, we'd love to. See you there at eight!'

Ad hoped they would still be alive to buy those pints. Would he still be alive? Of course he would. He sauntered back to join the others at breakfast. They had done one raid. They had survived. They were carefree.

'Well done, lads!' came from every corner as the established crews welcomed them into the inner circle of 'the men who flew'. The immediate problem was how to spend the day. When an op was due, the Leeming station, like all others, was locked down. RAF police closed the gates. No-one was allowed out. No-one was allowed in.

The day might be spent at the camp cinema, or reading, or playing cards or washing uniforms. The latter was by far the best way to kill time as it carried the vital psychological implication that they would return. Return? Of course they would. The gunners had some additional tasks to do, such as polishing the Perspex of their turrets so that not a single smudge remained. In a few hours' time over a target, an apparent smudge could be a nightfighter. A late call to the pilot could mean death for all of them.

At 2055 the green Aldiss Lamp flashed again.

'Engineer to skipper, you've got green.'

'Thanks, engineer. Skipper to crew, best of luck, lads. Let's hope it's a piece of cake like two days ago.' Up they went.

The ten aircraft from Leeming were to fly to the east coast and meet up with the rest of the force over Spurn Head on the North Sea

CHAPTER 9

in Yorkshire. They circled as ordered until all of the other squadrons had arrived.

'Crikey, Johnny, it's a fair-sized force. I make it about 250, how about you?'

'Yes, I was thinking that'

They were headed for Kiel. This meant flying more or less due east for some three hours. They would only be over Germany for some 30 miles, making landfall near the Danish border in Schleswig Holstein. The great problem was that they would fly parallel to the Dutch and German coasts for some 150 miles (240 kilometres); there were many nightfighter squadrons based there. Their nightfighters – the Junkers 88s and Messerschmitt 110s – were formidable opponents and the pilots were very, very good at their job. The Germans also had an excellent radar defensive line known as the Kammhuber Line after the German Luftwaffe General who had brilliantly masterminded it. There was no possibility of surprising the German defences. The whole trick was to overwhelm them with numbers.

Ad was now beginning to understand another subtlety of operational flying. If they were to be attacked by German nightfighters there was little chance of winning the battle. The nightfighters' 20-millimetre and 30-millimetre cannon shells could down a heavy four-engined bomber in seconds. The gunners only had .303 machine guns with a range one quarter of that of their adversary. The main role of the gunners, therefore, was not primarily to fire guns but to act as lookouts. They had been trained that if they saw a nightfighter the gunner would shout 'corkscrew right' or 'left' as the case might be. Johnny Lennox would take his Halifax bomber into the tightest downward spiral possible with engines screaming, the crew hanging on for grim death and the nightfighter (with a bit of luck) overshooting and losing them because his greater speed would carry him past their position.

'Are you gunners watching in among this cloud?'

'Rear gunner to skipper, can't see a thing.'

'Mid-upper to skipper, same here, skipper, no sign of our Teutonic friends.'

So, it was all the way to Kiel. There was not a single sighting of any enemy aircraft.

Over the island of Nando the Pathfinders dropped yellow flares, which were a marker for the force to turn to starboard to prepare for the final run in on Kiel. The dropping of the flares precipitated sudden and heavy anti-aircraft fire. The clouds largely protected the force, but the heavy explosions from the powerful 88-millimetre shells caused the aircraft to buck and gyrate in the air. They could hear the 'plink, plink' of shrapnel on the fuselage.

'Skipper to all crew members, any problems from that flak?'

The aircraft was unharmed. How long could it remain so?

The operation on Kiel was simpler than the one on St Nazaire: drop as many bombs on the U-boat yards as humanly possible. To hit the 'Konrad' or 'Kilian' submarine bunkers was the holy grail. To hit a partly built submarine on the slipway was highly acceptable. However, to hit machinery to prevent a submarine being built was almost as good. Then, in the hierarchy of acceptable outcomes, came hitting dock gates to render the dock out of action and hitting railway installations and roads to prevent the delivery of vital supplies. Then came hitting workers' houses to make it difficult for them to work and function. From the crew's point of view this was also a good raid in that there was little chance of hitting civilians: anyone killed by a bomb was likely to be someone actively working against the British war effort. The unfortunate casualty, even a 'civvie' was looked on as fair game.

Flak snaked up at them from unseen gun positions somewhere below the cloud on terra firma.

Suddenly the flak stopped.

'Skipper to crew, everyone be alert!' said Johnny.

'What's the problem, skipper?'

'This is what happened on Berlin. The flak stops and then the nightfighters come in.'

The tension in the aeroplane rose accordingly. One minute ago, the risk to their lives had been high enough. Now it was acute.

The sky lit up with a bright orange light that lasted for two seconds.

CHAPTER 9

'Christ almighty!' shouted a voice into the intercom.

'Skipper to crew, it's just a scarecrow. The Germans let them off to scare us into thinking they are planes going down.'

'Mid-upper to skipper, there is definitely a kite going down at 20 degrees. Can't see any parachutes.'

'Skipper to crew, keep calm, boys, and remember we are here to do a job. I want to ask you all to do the job that you are trained to do. Skipper to bomb aimer: take up your position.' 'Wilco, skipper,' echoed around the aircraft.

Two minutes later the lurid 'Christmas tree' of the red markers was dead ahead.

Again, the sky was lit up with a second massive yellow explosion of a 'scarecrow'.

'Never mind that, just see to your tasks. Skipper to bomb aimer, take over please.'

'Wilco, skipper. Can clearly see the red markers.'

On this raid, the 'reds' were the first set of target indicators dropped by the Pathfinders. After the reds came the greens. Tonight's order was 'bomb on greens'.

'Greens quite clear, skipper, stay on this course. Left a bit, left a bit. The greens are going through the cloud, but I can still see the glow quite clearly. Right a bit and right a bit and…'

The aeroplane lurched upwards.

'Bombs gone, skipper.'

'Skipper to bomb aimer, let's hope we hit something.'

'We're right on the greens skipper but God only knows what's down there.'

The photo-flash went off.

'Right, that's it, let's go home.'

Johnny Lennox's report from that night read:

'J' Up 2055 Down 0324.

Primary (target) was reached in 10/10 cloud. Load was released from 16,500 feet at 2334 hours on green T.I. markers. Glow of green marker on cloud was in bombsight at moment of release.

Three big glows were observed through the cloud. A/C returned to base undamaged.

The other pilots' reports read similarly to this. The pilots, almost to a man, gave an opinion that although they could not see the damage through the clouds, the amount of smoke and glare of fires led to a conclusion of success. As long as there were large fires burning over Nazi territory it was all bringing tears to Adolf Hitler's eyes. That was a good thing.

If the time over the target area had been difficult, it was nothing compared to the return journey. The Luftwaffe scrambled nightfighters from Flensburg, Schleswig, Nordholz, Ardorf-Wittmundhafen and Vechte. That night there were to be 69 interceptions of which 8 turned into positive attacks.

'Rear gunner to skipper, kite going down at 150 degrees.'

Johnny looked out of his port side window.

'Christ, they've taken a real pasting.'

At that distance whether the four-engined bomber was a Lancaster or Halifax was difficult to see.

'Rear gunner, can you see any parachutes?'

'I can see two, skipper, no, three. Oh god, she's spiralling now.'

'Poor buggers.'

Once a stricken aircraft had started to spiral down, the centrifugal force made it impossible for a crew member to move to the escape hatch. Their burning aeroplane was a trap from which there was no possible escape. On the other hand, that same force would cause them to pass out in ten seconds so that their last agonising moments would be unknown to them.

'Engineer to skipper, there's another one going down on the starboard side. I can see four parachutes... no, she's spiralling now.'

'Skipper to gunners, keep those eyes peeled, boys. All I need to hear is "spiral left or spiral right" and I will obey your command in less than half a second. I really don't need a commentary on kites going down. OK, guys?'

'Mid-upper to skipper, not seeing any nightfighter coming after us, skip.'

CHAPTER 9

'Rear gunner to skipper, no, they don't seem to be interested in us at all.'

They all knew that 20 seconds from now they could be in a burning wreck hurtling to the ground and that, on average four of them might survive. That was an advantage in being in a Halifax rather than a Lancaster. In a Lancaster only three survived on average if the aircraft was hit. In a Halifax with a slightly greater escape hatch the figure was, on average, four.

Every man felt terror. The training gave them procedures to carry out. They did not have to think. They were perfectly at liberty to feel extreme terror. They were still expected to do what they had been trained to do without flinching. This was where the bond of one crewman to another kicked in very strongly.

'God! The buggers might have let us in but they're not letting us out!'

The nightfighters pursued them 50 miles out to sea. Johnny's crew had been lucky. No nightfighter had been on their tail.

In the Flight Office they noticed that the Halifax with the letters, LQ-N, Foley's crew had not yet returned. This was not necessarily a cause for panic. There were a variety of reasons why aircraft might not return. They may have had engine trouble on the way out and landed at the closest RAF station. On the way back, they may have been shot up and landed at the nearest RAF station.

The clatter of boots at some time between 0400 and 0500 told anyone awake that the Committee of Adjustments men had been in.

A visit to Foley's Nissen hut in the morning would show that all trace of Foley and his crew had been surgically removed. Over breakfast someone would say 'Foley went for a Burton'. This also meant that Ad would now not collect his two-bob bet with Damms. Was Damms dead? Was he injured? Was he a prisoner of war? 'Poor buggers,' someone would have said. Later that day a new crew would have taken residence in that hut. A new Halifax LQ-J would appear. It would be as if Foley and his crew had never existed.

With two raids behind them, Johnny's crew had still not had a nightfighter after them. They knew that this could last for much longer.

BOMBS AND BARBED WIRE

The following piece from the *Adelaide Advertiser* in Australia shows how the Kiel raid was reported to the British at home and across the empire. It is also interesting in that it places Ad's contribution within the context of the vast amount of operations being undertaken against Nazi Germany at this time as World War II was ramping up to its peak of activity.

R.A.F. BLOWS REACH NEW PEAK

Kiel Raid Marks 60 Hours of Non-Stop Attacks

Australia Associated Press LONDON, April 5.

The round-the-clock bombing of Germany reached a new record of intensity last night, when aircraft of Bomber Command in great strength attacked the naval base and shipbuilding yards at Kiel. This completed 60 hours of nonstop raids on enemy targets. Earlier in the day a large force of Flying Fortresses of the US Army Air Force made a daylight attack on the Renault motor and armament works at Billancourt, on the outskirts of Paris. The Allied fighters covering the Fortresses formed one of the largest fighter forces in action this year.

The weather was clear for the Renault raid, and the target was heavily and accurately bombed and left on fire. Strong opposition by enemy fighters was encountered on the return trip, and 25 were destroyed by the Fortresses.

Over the French coast RAF, Dominion and Allied fighters covering the withdrawal of the bombers joined in the combat and destroyed another eight enemy planes. Four bombers and seven fighters are missing. A British United Press correspondent at a Flying Fortress base somewhere in England, says that the Germans threw swarms of crack yellow-nose Messerschmidts against the Fortresses, which dropped their loads "practically down the smoke stacks." as one pilot described it. The pilots agreed that the opposition was the stiffest so far put up against them.

CHAPTER 9

Ad and Johnny and the rest of the crew would have seen a similar report in the *Daily Mirror*. The general impression was that the war, which had been going very badly for Britain during Ad's first stint at Leeming, was now starting to go well during his second stint. The change in fortunes had been long in coming and very slow. It did, at least, feel that Britain was on the winning side at last.

There was another version of the truth contained in the top-secret Night Raid report. This was a digest of all pilot reports, all squadron reports. It was for the most senior eyes only in Bomber Command and the Air Ministry.

The number of aircraft on the raid was not the 250 that Ad and Johnny had thought: it was 577; although, given that the raid was organised in waves, this would not readily be observable. The number of aeroplanes shot down was 12. Several others had been severely damaged by flak or nightfighter activity. The next day the super-fast De Havilland Mosquitoes from one of the Photographic Reconnaissance Units would have overflown Kiel to take photographs to assess damage.

The single most important sentence in the Night Raid Report lies in the conclusion from those photographs: 'very little fresh damage can be seen'.

Eighty-four men were dead or imprisoned, some 3000 had been terrified for hours on end. The belief at Leeming and the other stations was that the raid was successful. The top brass knew otherwise.

CHAPTER 10
THE RAID ON STUTTGART

14 APRIL 1943

At RAF Leeming, the activity, news and points of general interest were rolling in like the endless convoys across the Atlantic. The rain continued to lash down. The skies were grey. Life went on.

Three crews had not returned from a raid on Essen. Lago's crew had gone for a Burton as had Murphy's and Luxford's. The latter two were especially great losses; Murphy was gunnery leader to the squadron and Luxford the bombing leader. They had been responsible for giving lectures in technique and had an educational role in bringing 'sprog' (brand new) crews up to scratch. They also gave lectures to crews on the latest techniques and tips on how to kill without, yourself, being killed. After a raid on Duisburg, Stovel's crew were reported missing.

Edwards' crew had been out dropping mines in the approaches to La Rochelle on the West Coast of France. These were to sink, or at least make life difficult for German U-boats based in the port. They had not returned. Sergeant Kirkham, who was on the raid, saw parachutes open. They must have been caught by a flak ship. 'Poor buggers.'

The psychology on Lennox's crew was profound. Twenty-eight men had disappeared within a few days. The probability was that 16 were prisoners and 12 were dead. They were people that they had known, had shared drinks with and had engaged in squadron banter with. It

CHAPTER 10

did not do to become too close to other crews. It also underlined the importance that every crew member depended on every other crew member for their life.

Ad, whether consciously or unconsciously would have made very, very certain that his checks over the aircraft in which they flew were beyond reproach. The slightest degree of error in an adjustment could mean death.

There was something else that happened on that afternoon. A 'Tate and Lyle' walked officiously into their hut.

'Right, you lot, the wingco is not very happy with Lennox's crew and it is my duty to bring this to your attention. You've been out on two raids and you haven't done your last letters yet.'

'We don't have to do them, Mr Graham, we plan not to be shot down.'

'Look, lads, if you could just see your way clear to write one of these letters the wingco will be off my back and I will be off your back.'

Johnny rolled his eyes to the ceiling. 'What goes into these flippin' letters, Mr Graham?'

'Everybody has to do it, lads; just write a short letter home to your wives or girlfriends or parents or anyone you like. It's a letter which we will send if you don't come back.'

'Is it like a will then?'

'If you want it to be. You can ask for some of your things to be given to someone. Don't forget, though, if you don't come back from the raid, you might still be in a POW camp or on the run or ditched in the channel and be swimming home. Don't give everything away or you won't have any possessions if you do make it back.'

This raised a half smile among Lennox's crew.

'The wingco's advice to all crews is to tell your family you love them and tell them you are determined to do your duty to win the war. Even if you don't come back there is still something for them to cling on to and to be proud of.'

Writing the letter was probably the hardest thing that Ad would ever do. Oh God! Just don't let her ever read it. *Don't let her EVER have to read it!*

BOMBS AND BARBED WIRE

626241 SGT A. ADLAM

405 SQUADRON

14.4.43

My Dear Wife.

Ek is lief vir jou my liefling.

Well, my dear, if you ever receive this letter (which I pray you won't) you will already have been told that I did not come back from a raid. No doubt you will be shocked and everything will seem useless, and that is the way I would feel if anything happened to you.

This letter is to be posted to you should I fail to get back to give you hope and courage for you know that no German can ever kill me and I want you to bear up as I shall most likely be a prisoner or else be trying to get back to you. Do not despair as some day I shall return again to you and I know that is true because I feel it inside of me.

We have been happy together now for a year and I would like to thank you for being my wife.

I took you from your own land and brought you to England. Maybe that was a mistake on my part but time will tell. You do not see much to like here and people seem very frigid and stand-offish but you find that they are real underneath. Anyway, they are my people and I reckon they are worth fighting for. Every time I go out I don't know what is ahead of me but I am not afraid of the unknown. As long as there are Nazis to be killed I shall be willing to assist in killing them. I have seen what their bombs have done here in this country and I would like the German cities to be laid into the dust.

The sooner that is done the sooner we shall win the war and I know we shall win.

CHAPTER 10

Well, my sweetheart you have been good to me and given me great happiness and I hope we shall continue to be happy when I return to you. Make no mistake about it – I shall be back. It may be a few months before you hear anything of me but let your mind repeat "He will be back".

I would like you to give Dad my fishing rod so that it will be in the family still and that is about the only thing I have got as we were never very rich in money but we are rich in our love for one another.

Today is the fourteenth and tomorrow is our first anniversary. When that anniversary commences I shall be in the air over enemy territory but my thoughts will be in the little room with you as they always are.

Give my regards to all the family and write to Mrs Boyce often. Her son is far away and it will be a long time before he is free again. Do not despair and every time you feel downhearted have a look at this letter and remember that they can't kill an Adlam and I shall be back soon to tell you that I love you and have always loved you.

I take a photograph of you with me so if I do come down I shall have your face with me always. Good luck and God bless you and take care of you while I am away.

Until we meet tot sien's liefling and remember that I shall come back.

All my love

Your ever-loving husband

Ad

Alles sal reg kom	Everything will be alright
Ik wil te jou kom	I will come to you.

Having written it he handed it without a word to the adjutant. The adjutant, who had taken several hundreds of these letters in his time, took it without a word. He filed it. He had seen an awful lot of these letters sent out.

A bizarre event was to emphasise the theme of 'I may still turn up'. This was emphasised in a dramatic and grimly amusing way. Pilot Officer Stovel had returned from a 'do' on Duisburg without a crew.

'He's done WHAT?' said Johnny.

'Come on, you lot, he's in the NAAFI talking about it.'

They rushed over to the NAAFI where Stovel was surrounded by two dozen blue-grey clad airmen and erks all spellbound by his incredible tale.

'The icing on the kite was bloody terrible. She had flown like a pig all the way across France. We had let the bombs go and then there was the most awful lot of flak came up at us. There was tracer, there were 88 shells; I tell you, it was a shaky bloody do.'

'Was it just you or was it everybody?'

'It seemed to be directed at us, so they must have got a radar bearing. The cloud was 10/10 so they had no idea what they were aiming at. I went into evasive action and put the kite into a downward corkscrew to get away from the bursting flak. One engine cut; then another engine cut; then another engine cut. Whitteron was the flight engineer and he said, "We've had it, skipper, we can't hold her!" She felt like she was spiralling out of control.'

'Christ almighty! There must have been ten tons of ice on the wings!'

'You could have skated on the bloody stuff! I gave the order "crew make ready to abandon aircraft". I heard Coxy in the rear turret shout, "I'm off!" and he dropped out of the back of the plane. She was starting to nosedive. Whitteron was next out. I shouted, "I haven't given the bloody order!" Wagner, the mid-upper gunner, was out. Blisson, who was flying second dickie, was out. I shouted, "I have not given the order!" again. I tried to steady the kite and fire the engine. It turned on. That gave me more control, but we were losing height fast. I tried another engine, it turned on. We were below the cloud now and everything on the ground was shooting at us.'

CHAPTER 10

'Why didn't you jump?'

'Do you know, I have no idea. Anyway, the ground was coming up fast, but I tried the fourth engine. I thought that if that fired we might stand a chance. It fired. We were at 1000 feet and she steadied. The Germans must have been so impressed!'

'Did they stop firing at you?'

'No, but we were so low that they couldn't train their guns on us. Anyway, the kite steadied, came under control. I asked for a bearing and headed to one of the emergency airstrips in Kent. It's taken us two days to get back here. The bomb aimer came up into flight engineer's seat and pulled the right levers when I told him to so we didn't crash land when we got to whatever airstrip it was.'

The audience did not know whether to laugh or cry.

'Buy you a pint in The White Rose tonight?'

'Thanks.'

The news had also come that the squadron was being given a singular honour. They had been selected as a Pathfinder squadron and were to transfer to RAF Gransden Lodge near Cambridge. Preparations for the move began immediately. This meant that Ad would get to wear the coveted gold eagle Pathfinder badge on his tunic. That would go some way to balancing against his brother Bill's Military Medal. Pathfinders did tours of 45 operations, not 30. He had known that he stood little chance of surviving 30 operations. Now he had virtually none. Wing Commander Clayton made it clear to all aircrews that if a man chose not to go into Pathfinders it would not be held against him. He would be transferred forthwith to another operational squadron which was limited to the normal 30 operations. Few took up the offer of opting out. Ad did not. The Red Cross had sent information that some 20 crews from 405 squadron were listed as prisoners of war in Germany. They had all been on the squadron before Ad and Johnny had joined. This was ultimately to prove unfortunate in an unanticipated way.

BOMBS AND BARBED WIRE

The storm clouds of statistics, probabilities regarding survival were gathering. They were not favourable.

Still, it was not good to dwell on such things. Tonight 'there was a war on' and they all had to think about the complexities of checks and formalities and procedures. It seemed hardly any time before the blood wagon had taken them out to the dispersal where the aircraft sat; they had piddled on the rear wheel and waited for the signal.

'You've got green, skipper.'

'Roger, engineer, good luck, everyone, here we go again!' Tonight, the target was Stuttgart. This was by far the longest trip that they had taken part in. Four hundred and sixty-two aircraft took off from twenty RAF stations across eastern England. As ever, Lennox's crew were only aware of the part of the bomber stream within their own vision. The other thing that they did not know was the rate of casualties. On the way out, the bomber stream had passed through the lurking dangers of the radar, flak and nightfighters in the Kammhuber Line. The German nightfighters had been slow off the mark. As Johnny and Ad had taken off at 2124, they would have passed through the danger area without seeing a casualty. Once the nightfighters were up and active they knocked out three RAF aircraft in three minutes.

The raids were becoming more scientific now. The Pathfinders were dropping target indicators more accurately, guided by instruments and radar. Yellow markers showed the main force where to turn in its Odyssey across Germany. Once the Kammhuber Line was passed there was no further harassment from nightfighters. As the bombing stream approached Stuttgart the flak began. The heavy flak was not remotely as terrifying as the ordeal over Kiel. The light flak hardly worried them.

'Not as bad as Berlin, eh Johnny?'

'So far this is a piece of cake and as long as that flak is coming up we shouldn't have any trouble with nightfighters. Skipper to gunners, keep an eye out, you characters. We've had an easy ride so far, but it won't stay that way.'

'Engineer to skipper, red markers going down now.'

CHAPTER 10

'Skipper to bomb aimer, take over, please.'

'Bomb aimer to skipper, wilco. Keep on this bearing. That's it… that's it. Greens going down now, skipper, I am aiming directly on green markers.'

Still the flak was desultory. No-one had heard a single instance of that 'plink' of flak on the fuselage.

'Green in bombsight now, skipper, right a bit, right a bit…'

The aircraft lurched upwards.

'Bombs gone, skipper.'

It was a clear night over Stuttgart. They could clearly see the valleys and hills below them. There were a lot of fires and several large explosions.

'Rear gunner to skipper, there's a hell of a lot of fire and smoke down there.'

'Well, that should shake up the Herrenvolk. OK, there's the photo-flash, let's get out of here. Gunners, keep those eyes open!

On the return journey the Luftwaffe were waiting in numbers in the area of Mannheim but were not in luck. Only one nightfighter pilot got a kill – in fact, two within 20 minutes.

A second cordon of Luftwaffe nightfighters were waiting in line stretching from Brussels south-westward. This was very much more serious. The squadrons of Nachtjägergruppe (nightfightergroup) 4 bagged 14 of the returning bombers.

It had been a good night for the Luftwaffe. Their pilots Materne, Holler and Altendorf all got two in a single night.

At the debrief, back at Leeming, Lennox was to report:

There was no cloud, and visibility was quite good, except for slight haze. Load was released at 0120 hours from 16,000' on green T.I.s, which were in bombsight at time of release. Bombs were seen to explode in centre of large fire in target area. Three large oil tanks were ablaze in centre of large fire, which was giving off thick black smoke. Fires appeares (sic) sort of scattered but seemed to be spreading. Fires could be seen for 70 miles after leaving target area. Crew believe this operation to have been successful. Landed back to base.

BOMBS AND BARBED WIRE

All returning crews reported seeing a lot of bomb blasts, a lot of fires and scattered fires which linked up. Back at the Flight Office they discovered that Sattler's kite had not made it back. Wing Commander Clayton came to congratulate each crew on a good night's effort. 'Don't worry about Sattler, he's had to put down in West Malling with bloody engine trouble or some such thing. He'll be back in the morning.' That was good for morale.

Ad and Johnny and the rest of the crew swilled back their hot tea and swaggered back to their Nissen hut. Ad could have jumped for joy. He had his aircrew brevet, he had taken everything that they had thrown at him in training and now he had actually been on raids into the heart of the darkness that was the Third Reich.

'You're looking very pleased with yourself,' said Johnny as they peeled off their heavy fleece-lined flying jackets. 'Is this because you're an official RAF Brylcreem Boy now?'

'No, Mr Clever Clogs, it's because it is now after midnight.'

'And?'

'That means it is the 15th of April and that is my first wedding anniversary.' He had already composed a very special letter to Anne. He had got to his first wedding anniversary in one piece. He did not dare think about where he might be for his second anniversary: if anywhere.

'BOYS!' shouted Johnny. 'Did you hear that? It's Ad's first wedding anniversary; he's buying drinks all round in The White Rose tomorrow night.'

Next day, the Photo Reconnaissance Unit sent over two Mosquitoes to take photos.

The report read:

Very heavy destruction was revealed in the North of Stuttgart, where the industries of the town are mainly concentrated and in the outlying districts. Some 40 industrial and commercial concerns were affected, including manufacturers of ball bearings, precision instruments, machinery, ventilators, veneer presses, steel windows, sugar, flour, bricks and coal gas. At Unterturkheim Goods Station, 8 acres of buildings were demolished, while two direct hits were

CHAPTER 10

scored on the tracks at the Main Station. The generator house of the Power Station at Bad Cannstatt was destroyed by fire.

Most of the residential damage occurred in the urban districts of Munster and Bad Cannstatt and in the two villages of Mulhausen and Hofen further north. Altogether, over 300 houses were rendered uninhabitable. One area in Bad Cannstatt covers 36 acres.

Barracks and public buildings sustained a number of hits including Wilhelm Castle, which burned to the ground.

The iconic Stuttgart Gedächtnis church was destroyed. One bomb tragically had a direct hit on an air raid shelter packed with French and Russian prisoners of war: 257 Frenchman and 143 Russians were killed. The death toll for the raid was 619. A further 703 were severely wounded. This represented a new record for a death toll in RAF raids to Germany. The record would not stand for long.

Number 405 Squadron crews felt fairly good about the raid on Stuttgart. They had lost no aircraft and had made a mess of a German industrial centre. There was, oddly enough, a strange aftermath.

A Wellington bomber from another squadron had apparently been hit over the target and had made for the Swiss border. Once over the border the crew bailed out and landed in neutral Swiss territory. The rule was that they would be interned, on parole, by the Swiss authorities until hostilities had ceased.

'Christ! A holiday in Switzerland? That's not bad is it?'

'You don't suppose they could have…?'

'Done it on purpose?'

'No, surely not.'

'No, I'm sure they wouldn't do that!'

Within the mental landscape of an RAF operational squadron the notion of deserting was not present, admissible or even thinkable.

BOMBS AND BARBED WIRE

RAF Bomber Command had a hierarchy of good things and bad things. At the top of the hierarchy was the Victoria Cross, although very few of those were given out. Then came other various medals and promotions. At the bottom of the hierarchy were the three dreaded letters 'LMF'. This meant that your file had been marked 'Lacks Moral Fibre'. This was the most devastating, the most psychologically shattering phenomenon that could happen.

'Christ, have you heard about Harris's crew on Kiel? His bomb aimer has been kicked out, LMF.'

'What, that bloke from Sunderland… wasn't his name Ken something? God! He's done about 20-odd operations.'

'Well, the buzz is that he was over the target, he let the bombs go and then started shouting, "Get out of here, just bloody get out!" Harris was very calm and said, "It's all right, Ken, it's all right." Anyway, he was duty bound to report it to the wingco and so his bomb aimer was off the station within a half hour.'

Some men could carry on a full 30 operations and not panic over a target. Others would panic on their first operation. Everyone knew that they might have a psychological limit and that on the next operation it might be them who lost their nerve. If you were really unlucky you could be steadfast for 29 operations and then crack on the last one.

Some wing commanders took a humane view and transferred the man to somewhere remote. Jack Walshaw of 44 Squadron at Waddington near Lincoln found a man at Lossiemouth in the North of Scotland who had been classified as 'LMF'. The man recognised Jack and avoided any eye contact. Other wing commanders took an authoritarian view and publicly stripped the wings off a man's tunic in full view of the entire squadron. Whichever view they took, wing commanders were more afraid of an epidemic of 'LMF' working its way through the squadron than any other single threat.

Don Charlwood of 103 Squadron said, 'LMF was worse than Happy Valley.' Most airmen would rather keep on flying and risk a grisly death than have those three terrible letters ascribed to them. To have 'LMF' on your personal file was like a red-hot brand that you had

CHAPTER 10

let yourself down, you had let your country down and, worst of all, you had let your crew down.

Later that week a new bomb aimer would arrive for Harris' crew and the enclosed world of 405 Squadron carried on.

CHAPTER 11
WELCOME TO GRANSDEN

19 APRIL 1943

After the raid on Stuttgart, the entire squadron was stood down from operations. The tension dropped. There was levity in the air. They could hitchhike into Northallerton or Richmond and spend the day in a pub. There was no worry about the RAF Police turning up in their white-peaked caps and saying, 'All 405 Squadron back to base.'

And so, it came to pass that Air Officer Commander in Chief Sir Arthur Harris, in his top-secret headquarters at 'The Hole' somewhere below High Wycombe in leafy Buckinghamshire, had detached 405 Squadron from the Royal Canadian Air Force from 6 Group. He reattached it to Pathfinders Force (PFF) in 8 Group. The new station was Gransden Lodge, just outside Cambridge. The local landmark, as they would find out, was to be the windmill. This was to be their vital navigation point returning from an air test or an op.

The move itself proved to be a miserable business. The advance party had paraded at 0730 on the morning of 19 April, then proceeded by rail from Leeming Bar station near Northallerton in Yorkshire to Gamlingay station outside Cambridge. This required five changes and took nearly 12 hours. Such was the pressure on the railways that freight trains with war-priority were given all priority. Non-priority trains could be shunted into a siding for hours until the line was clear of higher-ranking trains. It was also a feature of wartime railways that

CHAPTER 11

all buffet cars and restaurant cars were discontinued: passengers had to carry all their own food and drink and lots of it to cope with the incessant and endless delays.

As it happened, none of this bothered Johnny Lennox's crew. They were part of the air party and flew 18 Halifaxes from Leeming to Gransden Lodge in rather under the hour. The uniquely plentiful supplies of bacon and eggs were not the only perks of being in aircrew! On arrival, the new commanding officer, Wing Commander Fauquier, addressed all ranks to prepare them for the new life of a Pathfinder squadron. There was to be a training course which would last some three weeks. During this time 405 Squadron planes would still be called upon for operations as a conventional bombing squadron until they had mastered the arts of advanced navigation using 'Gee', 'H2S' and 'Oboe' electronic navigation devices. These would help navigators to identify targets and in dropping their target indicators. They were to be inducted into the mysteries of new navigational technologies known as 'Parramatta', 'Newhaven', and 'Wanganui' and, at the peak of technological development, 'Musical Parramatta'.

None of this wizardry would impact Ad directly, it was all for the navigator to master. Nevertheless, all of this high technology had the significance of being yet more nails in Adolf Hitler's much desired coffin.

It would not be lost on Johnny Lennox's crew that they were moving into an elite unit. This was not just because of the electrical wizardry. They were under the leadership of the outstanding Wing Commander Jacques Fauquier.

The *History of Canada's Air Force* says of him:

'There is no doubt that Fauquier was one of the toughest of commanders. He saw his job as getting every available aircraft on the target on every night of operations and had no patience with any incompetence or inefficiency that might compromise that goal. The ground crews thought the world of him because he thought the world of them and never took them for granted, always remembering to take them bottles of beer or other treats if they had worked particularly hard. Many considered him Canada's greatest bomber pilot.

BOMBS AND BARBED WIRE

New Pathfinders also needed training in how to operate with the new role of master bomber. No-one was to be allowed on a Pathfinder operation until he had passed the course and been presented with his certificate and Pathfinder badge. There was one small but important standing order. The Pathfinder badge was on no account to be worn on operations. If an airman fell into the hands of the Luftwaffe he was to give name, rank and number and nothing else. The Germans would have noticed how leading bombers now dropped flares instead of bombs and that this was leading to vastly improved devastation in RAF bombing raids. They would be very keen to identify the men involved and to make them talk about these new and deadly developments.

On the day of arrival, the Pathfinder Navigational Training Unit began its operations at Gransden. On 20 April, Wing Commander Fauquier took over formally as wing commander and outlined the training program. On 21 April the training began in the classroom. On 22 April the training began in the air. Events were moving quickly.

On 25 April, there was a very interesting diversion and one which potentially had a great influence on Ad. Wing Commander Fauquier summoned all ranks to the sergeants' mess.

'What the hell is it?' Ad asked Johnny.

'Search me,' said Johnny, 'I do hope we've been posted to somewhere like the Bahamas, though; we deserve it after all that rain at Leeming.'

'Put money on it?'

'No, not really.'

The chairs scraped back as they stood for the wing commander as he entered the mess together with the squadron leaders.

'Thank you, chaps, be seated if you would. I have a rather nice surprise for you this morning.'

Anticipation ran through the room.

'Bahamas,' whispered Johnny to Ad.

CHAPTER 11

'Now those of you who were here some ten weeks ago will remember that we were on Stuttgart and lost four planes. Well, it is my extremely pleasant duty to tell you that Squadron Leader Logan and Sergeant Jennings not only survived but have got back to Britain…'

There was a huge roar; spontaneous clapping and whistling broke out.

'Pipe down, children, thank you…'

The room was silent. For a moment the only movement was the blue-grey cigarette smoke which lazily ambled its way to the ceiling.

'And they are with us today. Come in, Squadron Leader Logan and Sergeant Jennings.'

The room broke into a frenzy of cheering, stamping and, as Logan and Jennings walked up to the podium, the inevitable chorus broke out:

'Why were they born so beautiful?
Why were they born at all?
They're no bloody use to anyone.
They're no bloody use at all.'

Logan and Jennings laughed the laugh of men who were winners, were first among equals, and were heroes. They conducted the singing in the traditional manner.

'Right, thank you, gentlemen, now the reason that you are here is partly to welcome these reprobates back but also to learn how they escaped and got back to Blighty. Squadron Leader Logan, if you please. Now for the rest of you, I strongly suggest that you hear what these chaps have to say because it may be useful to you one fine day.'

'… Or one fine night!' shouted a wag.

'Indeed, that may be the case, now could I just get you all to let Squadron Leader Logan tell his story?'

'Well, thank you, Wing Commander. We were on our way to Stuttgart. I was flying second dickie. Without any warning there were cannon shells shooting in front of us. The skipper was Bob Dennison; he had no chance whatsoever. The kite just flew into the stream of cannon shells.'

'That man there!' A member of the audience had put his hand up.

'Sir, can we ask questions?'

BOMBS AND BARBED WIRE

Fauquier looked at Logan with raised eyebrows.

'Er, yes, sir, up to a point. When we got back we had a briefing from a couple of Air Ministry types, who told us what we can say and what we can't.'

'Can you tell us where you were shot down?'

'It was somewhere between Amiens and Arras; the Air Ministry chaps have asked not to be too specific because they want to keep it dark where resistance cells are operating.'

'"Air Ministry" bollocks!' Johnny whispered to Ad. 'Those are some sort of secret service wallahs.'

'You reckon?'

'I reckon.'

He was right. From time to time they had seen these rather mysterious men. What drew attention to them had been the way they were dressed in 'civvies' but had a definite military bearing. They only ever spoke with the group captain who was station commander or, rarely, wing commanders. When they had asked the WAAFs who the mysterious visitors had been they were inevitably met with blank stares and 'don't know what you're talking about'. They had been worded up: don't talk about these men.

It was Ad's first unwitting brush with MI9, a shadowy, top-secret organisation, which dealt in evasion and escape from Germany and occupied countries. It was not destined to be the last.

'Well...' Logan proceeded, 'Dennison shouted "everybody out". We had about ten seconds to jump for it. You would think we were scared. We hadn't time to be scared; we just headed for the escape hatch, dropped out and hoped that the chute would work.'

'And did it?' asked a wag to a chorus of raucous laughter.

'Anyway, most of us got down OK. I counted six chutes. Five of us got together very quickly before the Germans could come after us. I have to tell you that Sergeant Lacina and Sergeant McDonald

CHAPTER 11

were not able to get out of the kite and went down with it. Sergeant Kennett did get out, but we couldn't find him. As far as I know he didn't make it back, so I guess he must be a prisoner.'

'Did the Germans come looking for you?'

'Oh, my word, yes. There were patrols going all night. We could hear their trucks roaring around the roads and we could see them shining lights around the local farmhouses. Anyway, the five of us had a quick confab. The first thing to find out was where we were. We knew we had passed away from the German border but didn't know how far over France we were.

'We buried our chutes and got rid of our flying suits and the tops of our flying boots. We decided we just had to chance it. One of the chaps spoke a bit of schoolboy French so we knocked on a farmhouse in the middle of the night; there was an old chap, his wife and daughter. They took us in. As far as we know, no-one even saw us.'

'How did you know they wouldn't give you away to the Jerries?'

'We didn't. But we didn't want to give ourselves up and it was too far to roughneck it across country to the coast. We decided that all we could do was to throw ourselves on their mercy.'

This rang a bell with Ad. Arras, Amiens… His brother Bill had been there during the time of the great disaster before Dunkirk. He agreed: it was too far to 'roughneck' it.

'The family were absolutely bloody terrified. If the Jerries had caught them they would have been put in front of a wall and shot. They gave us a hot drink and a sandwich and told us to hide in the farm buildings and not to come out. We heard the Jerry patrols outside scouring the country lanes for any sign of us. We asked if we should leave so as not to get them into trouble. They told us to wait.'

'Did they speak English, these types?'

'No, they're French farmers; how many farmers out in Cambridgeshire would speak French? We had one guy's schoolboy French and that was all we had. You don't need a degree in the language: wait – go – sleep – eat – hide – the Boches are coming; you don't need much more. We hid in a barn for a couple of days then three blokes came and took us. Oh, if you get shot down, chaps, you don't want to know the name of the family who help you; then the Gestapo can't get it out of you.'

'Squadron Leader Logan, please…'

'Yes, that man?'

'So, is it the case that we can trust the populations in the occupied areas?'

'Hell no! Not at all! There are plenty of French fascists around, supporters of Petain and Laval. Oh, and in France, there is a paramilitary organisation called the Milice and you really want to avoid them; they are very, very nasty. Our family thought they were scum. The family might, actually, have been communists. If you can make contact with communists then that is a good thing. Anyway, on the second day some French civvy clothes arrived for us. They weren't Savile Row but they made us look almost French. They hadn't been to the cleaners too often or even at all, but they made sure that we didn't stand out. Oh yes, if you have to bail out, if a chap is too tall he will stand out. In France, they're mainly fairly short. I'm sorry but it is better if a tall chap volunteers to go off on his own or he will give everyone away.

'The family took away our English underwear; all our English cigarettes and lighters and so forth. They burned our uniforms and just got on with their lives until these guys turned up. They turned up at about 3 a.m. and moved us somewhere else. They put us in the back of a lorry with some tarpaulins and bales of hay to cover us.

'Our navigator says we were moving south-west. There were checks all the time. You could hear the German soldiers: "*Papiere bitte and alle Ausweise.*" They were only a few feet away from us under the tarpaulins. You don't know what "scared" means until you have done that. It was jolly worse than bailing out of a burning plane, I can tell you that.'

The room was silent.

Logan continued. 'We moved in the back of trucks, sometimes under tarpaulins, sometimes we were in farmers' lorries with the sheep and the chickens. The navigator realised we were heading into Central France. No-one would tell us where we were going; I suppose in case

CHAPTER 11

we fell into the hands of the Germans. We avoided towns and moved at night and after a few weeks we realised that the mountains in front of us were the Pyrenees. God, it was cold up there!

'But the mountains are very isolated and, once we got moving, our guides were able to take us away from where the Germans were to the remote mountain paths. We didn't have much to eat but we kept on sleeping by day and moving by night. Eventually we realised that the latest lot of guides…'

'How many guides were there?'

'Oh, let me think… about 15.'

The room let out a gasp of surprise.

'The whole thing is well worked out and these are really brave people who know what to expect if caught. Eventually we dropped down into Spain and the network got us across country to Madrid. Once again we had to watch out for local fascists: General Franco is not short of supporters in Spain.'

'If you had been caught in Spain, would they have given you back to the Germans?'

'Don't think so, but we could have been kept in Spain for the duration. Anyway, we made it to the British Embassy in Spain, and we had to be bloody careful about how we went in. The Spanish have a police force called the Guardia Civil who dress up in Gilbert and Sullivan uniforms but are reputedly quite vicious.

'We knew the place would be watched by Franco's men, so we arrived early in the morning. In our French peasants' gear we looked quite the part, so we just posed as workmen, forced our way in the front door, pushed past a sort of commissionaire wallah and said, "We're RAF and would rather like to go home." Then we got interrogated again to make sure we weren't German plants. Then there was a flight to Gib. Then the navy sent us back on a destroyer. And here we are.'

The whole room stood to give them a standing ovation. 'For they are jolly good fellows' rang around the sergeants' mess.

'Well, chaps,' said Wing Commander Fauquier, 'Squadron Leader Logan and Sergeant Jennings will be around for the rest of the day but have to go back to London on the late train. So, if you want to buy them a pint, they'll be in The Chequers this evening. I'm having a chat with Air Vice Marshal Bennet to get them reassigned to the squadron. I trust that will meet with your approval?'

It did!

CHAPTER 12

THE RAID ON DUISBURG

26 APRIL 1943

Once again, 'there was a war on'. This time it was to the great German nerve centre of Duisburg-Ruhrort. This is a major transport hub where main railway lines and canals come together to meet the River Rhein. It is major point of import of raw materials and components into the Ruhr Valley and a major point of export from the valley of finished goods, arms, munitions, aircraft and U-boat parts being passed on elsewhere in Hitler's war machine.

'You've got green, skipper.'

'Roger, engineer. OK everyone, off we jolly well go.'

Johnny pulled back the levers; the newly-installed Hercules engines screamed like a primaeval animal in pain. The airframe shook and shuddered like a bull caught up in anchor chains. Johnny nodded to Ad. Ad nodded back to Johnny. The skipper gently took the brake off and the aircraft stuttered forward toward the intense pinprick of green light from the Aldiss lamp at the end of the runway.

They were getting quite used to the drill now. This was their fourth trip and the first from the new station at Gransden. Unusually, their takeoff time was after midnight. McSorley had been first up at 0015; Johnny's aeroplane was sixth of eleven, leaving the ground at 0023. The target for tonight was Duisburg. Wing Commander Fauquier had spelled it out in the briefing: this was the next-most difficult target after Essen and Berlin. It was by far the most dangerous raid for Johnny's crew so far.

The docks at Ruhrort formed the world's largest inland port. The railway junctions were sprawling, sinuous and massive. The canal junctions met the Rhein in a complex series of locks. They could expect nightfighters to pick them up as soon as they made landfall in Holland near Egmond-aan-Zee near Alkmaar. They could expect to be harried all the way and, on arrival, they could expect 30–40 kilometres of flak concentrations as they passed over the industrialised Ruhr area.

As with all raids, Wing Commander Fauquier's pre-raid briefing had shown them the central aiming point. Their task was to drop bombs on a concentration of green target indicators in the docks area. The wing commander did not have to say, but they all knew the truth. Even if you missed the target, literally by a mile, the industrial complex at Duisburg was so huge that a random bomb load was always going to hit something of value within the dark heart of Hitler's war effort. The other attractive aspect of this target was that, like Kiel, there was a minimal chance of hitting civvies. At St Nazaire there had been the uncomfortable but suppressed doubt that you would be dropping bombs on French civilians. At Stuttgart there had been the feeling that perhaps not all Germans liked Hitler but you were still dropping bombs on them. Targets such as Kiel and Duisburg had the ultimate moral luxury for a bomber crew: hit whatever you like, it doesn't matter!

To make matters even better the docks were at the confluence of the Rhein and Ruhr and, even in a blackout, the two shining rivers would give them a target nearly as good as the target indicators themselves. The weather officer had given a forecast of clear skies with only a little ground haze. As they flew on to the Wash and the forming-up place with the rest of the squadrons, Johnny's crew could rest assured that Hitler's boys were going to cop it tonight.

As Ad finished his flight engineer's duties and checked the gauges for the electrics, hydraulics and the other paraphernalia of a large and complex aircraft, he had time to think.

CHAPTER 12

The last two weeks since the Stuttgart raid had been very mixed. The move to Gransden had been easy enough for him but, once arrived, the Pathfinder training had started in earnest. It was like playing in a different league. Within 6 Group there was no question that crews were determined, brave and focused. In Pathfinders it was the next level up. The main force which followed them depended on them totally for accuracy and punch. There were few short cuts before: now there were none. They practised and attended lectures and did test flights and drills and more drills and now there were new forms of training. There was training with only three engines. There was training at nil visibility. There was training with half the crew injured.

It was only with difficulty that he could find the time to write the daily letter to Miranda, his own 'Anne'. The training had commenced with easy stuff: lectures and talks on the role of Pathfinders; different types of target indicator; different techniques of deploying target indicators and the new electronic methods for blind bombing: Gee; Oboe and H2S. Then it became more intense and more intense still. The fast evolution of the bomber force from a willing artisan body of men to calculating professionals was very evident. One thing stood out clearly in Ad's mind: he wanted that prestigious golden Pathfinder eagle on his uniform and wanted it very much. Even so, there was so much to take in that he thought his head would burst.

One aspect did command a certain gallows humour.

The RAF was developing a technique whereby a dummy Pathfinder run would drop (say) green target indicators (TIs) on the northern part of a town to get the fire engines, ambulances and rescue teams dashing in that direction. Fifteen minutes later the real Pathfinders would drop (say) yellow TIs on the southern part of the town, which would then be hit by the main force and without any emergency services where the action was. Well, if old Hitler didn't want his towns made a mess of, he shouldn't have started the bloody war in the first place!

BOMBS AND BARBED WIRE

After the lectures came the cross-country flights, the dummy marking runs and the first attempts at navigating with the new high-technology methods. This was getting better and the new navigational aids were sensational. When they had mastered them, the crew would be able to fly to a target with nil visibility at all and still drop their TIs on a sixpence (perhaps that should be a Reichsmark) for the main force to come and do its stuff. As if this were not enough, there was a new method now of sky-markers. Pathfinders were dropping markers attached to parachutes. The main force did not even need to see the ground: their bomb aimer could just aim at the coloured Christmas tree as it floated gently down and into the target area. In turn, this all meant that German attempts to 'sell a dummy' by starting fires outside of towns were rendered useless.

On 22 April the crew had undergone one of the most soul-destroying experiences that any crew could endure: a scrubbed raid. The Flight Office had shown that Johnny's crew and six others were rostered on for a raid. Ad had checked the petrol in the tanks and all moving parts and gauges; the gunners had checked the gunnery blisters, the ammunition belts and the guns. They were keyed up, mentally prepared and emotionally wound up. At five in the evening Johnny had come by. 'Just seen Crockatt, the show's off.'

'There's not a war on?'

'There's not a war on!'

The normal response to a raid being scrubbed out was a long list of invective followed by the words 'the main gate will be open by now; anyone fancy a pint?' And a pint it was, but the chance to knock off one more of those 45 raids was lost. Duisburg would set the record straight again, however.

'Enemy coast ahead, skipper.'

'Thanks, bomb aimer. Skipper to crew, watch out for nightfighters, they are going to be after us.'

CHAPTER 12

Yet again, this was an immense bomber stream. Some 557 aircraft were travelling south-eastwards with malice aforethought. Looking out of the right-hand side of the cockpit it seemed to Ad that the bomber stream went as far to the left and as far to the right as the eye could make out in the gloom of night – albeit on a reasonably moonlit night.

'Rear gunner to skipper, kite going down at 210 degrees.

'Skipper to rear gunner, one of our squadron?'

'Don't think so, skipper, too far away I would say. Say, skip…?'

'Yes, rear gunner?'

'I don't know if it's my imagination, but we seem to be getting less trouble from the Herrnvolk than we would have expected at this point.'

'Know what you mean but keep your eyes peeled, you never know what the Teutonic buggers are up to.'

The truth, had they known it would have astounded them. The truth was known to the Bomber Command high-ups in 'the hole' at High Wycombe, but in those days information was reserved only for those who needed to know, not to Group Headquarters and definitely not to the men who flew the planes in the squadrons.

This Duisburg Raid in which they were taking part was the first in which the Royal Air Force had employed a new weapon, one not even communicated to its fighting squadrons. The technique rejoiced in the name of 'Grocer' and was a system for jamming the frequency of Luftwaffe radios. This meant that when the German radar picked up a target, they could not employ their 'Himmelbett' system to guide a nightfighter onto the rich pickings of a large force. Every radio which was jammed left a Bf110 or Ju88 relying on line-of-sight to find his victim. This meant that the Luftwaffe, while not entirely rendered blind, was certainly reduced to looking for needles in haystacks in the sky.

The force of 557 planes pressed inexorably on towards Duisburg. Ad was frozen, even in his uniform and flying suit. Outside the cabin, the frost glistened on the Halifax's wings, bringing a hint of Christmas to the deadly proceedings. Visibility remained good. He could see the Dutch rivers, the Waal, the Lek and the Maas below; they were a wonderful direction finder pointing with glistening certainty to the heart of the Third Reich. Ad checked his dials.

'Engineer to skipper, everything is looking OK.'

'Skipper to engineer, roger and thanks. Skipper to gunners, any of our little friends out there?'

'Not that I can see, skipper.'

'Me neither, it's very strange.'

'Rear gunner to skipper, kite going down dead astern; it's a long way back, not one of ours.'

Even so, the nightfighter activity remained less than expected.

Ad was well into operations now and was, perhaps, finding himself as he had never found himself before. His 23 years had had their tribulations. His family had not merely been of modest means; they had been poor. This had led to the flirtations with delinquency, 'dodgy dealings' and, conversely, flirtations with the Salvation Army as a place where you could get a meal. Now he had purpose. For this aeroplane to fly depended on his skill, intelligence and dedication. He knew that he would die rather than let them down. He also knew that each other member of the crew would die rather than let him down.

The massive armada droned on.

At that moment he felt the edgy thrill of terror as the armada barged its way over enemy territory. Tomorrow they would be in the pub and reflecting on another job well done… assuming they got back from this one.

He looked down over Holland. It was dark; there was a little flak but still very little nightfighter activity.

The massive armada droned on.

He had to laugh. Here he was, taking responsibility for his part in a deadly serious military operation, six other men's lives and a rather expensive aircraft. Only a couple of nights previously he had taken a drunken dive across a pub floor between two lines of equally drunken airmen who were brandishing flaming newspapers in a game of 'flare path'. Woe betide the publican who would complain about this manly delight, which always had an attendant threat of his pub burning

CHAPTER 12

down. He was likely to be 'debagged' and have the contents of the beer-slop bucket thrown over his bare bottom. Wing commanders also turned a blind eye. There was a war on.

'Navigator to skipper, just passing the German border and about to pass over Kleve. Right on course and right on time. You should see yellow markers in about one minute telling you to make a right turn and then stand by for the bombing run.'

Johnny did not ask Ad if he was ready to open bomb doors on command. He looked towards him. Ad, swaddled in his massive flying jacket and leather flying helmet, nodded. He did not have to confirm that he was standing by for orders. It was understood. They were becoming battle hardened.

As predicted, up ahead the yellow target indicator markers descended slowly to earth like massive Christmas tree lights dropped from Mosquitoes at exceptionally high altitude. As briefed, the entire vast force, which had feinted towards the top of the Ruhr Valley, now swung towards Duisburg. Whatever else they achieved, they had made sure that the entire population of the Ruhr Valley had yet another pitiless night without sleep as they shivered in their air raid shelters dreading the high explosive ordnance that would shortly and inevitably be targeting them.

'Navigator to skipper, arriving at target in five minutes, stand by.'

'Skipper to navigator, roger and out.'

Ad could now see the vast shining ribbon of the River Rhein as it glinted in the moonlight. God! What a river! It was huge! It was too dark to see any detail, but he knew that below them was concentrated the industrial complex, which was the manufacturing heartland of Hitler's Third Reich. Their pleasant task was to drop bombs on it. Tonight, they carried several tons of high explosive bombs, each of 500 or 1000 pounds, and some 100 incendiaries. That lot should bring tears to the eyes of someone or other and quite right, too.

'Skipper to flight engineer, open bomb doors.'

They felt rather than heard the rasping sensation throughout the aeroplane as Ad pulled the lever for the bomb doors to open.

BOMBS AND BARBED WIRE

The aircraft bucked a little as the drag of the bomb doors acted momentarily as a break.

Now the flak was starting. The red, yellow and green tracers of the light flak ambled amiably towards them and then zipped past their wing tip at incredible speed as they searched for a kill. They could see the dull red puffs as the heavy flak exploded all around them. Tinkles of shrapnel began to ring against the fuselage.

'Skipper to navigator, the flak's just kicking off. Where does that put us?'

'Navigator to skipper, oh, that's good. That means we're just over Geldern, which is dead on time. It's jolly decent of our German cousins to confirm that we're right where we should be.'

'Skipper to crew, everyone keep about their job. Never mind the flak; they're not very good tonight.'

'Engineer to skipper, is that a violet-coloured searchlight up ahead or was I drinking too much wallop last night?'

'Skipper to engineer, no, it's violet all right.'

All conversations stopped. All crew members were silent. They had heard of these and knew what this meant: radar guided searchlights. They watched in horror as the pretty violet light caught the wing of a Lancaster perhaps 2000 yards ahead. Within a second some 30 searchlights turned on and 'coned' the hapless aircraft.'

'Dive, you bastards, dive!' shouted Ad into the void as a man might shout unheard from a huge crowd at a football match.

The hapless Lancaster was completely illuminated in a vast bank of light. The pilot dived as fast as his airframe would allow him without pulling the wings off the aircraft.

'Go on! Dive! Dive!'

The dull red reports from the flak concentrated all around the plane. Now, flames could be seen from the burning fuel tanks. The aircraft was starting to corkscrew.

'Two parachutes, skipper, that's all I can see.'

The Lancaster plummeted burning into the depths of the early morning sky. The aeroplane took with it five men. Ten seconds after the aircraft started to corkscrew, gravitational forces would render

CHAPTER 12

them unconscious. Twenty seconds later they would be blackened, unrecognisable slabs of meat. There was no time for such thoughts.

'Navigator to skipper, five minutes to target.'

'Thank you, navigator. Skipper to bomb aimer, take over, if you would.'

'Bomb aimer to skipper, wilco. Stay on this course for the moment. Ah! There are the red markers going down. The greens will be on them in a moment.'

The flak intensified. It thudded, tinkled and crashed against the fuselage.

'Skipper to crew, is any of that flak causing problems?'

'Not yet, skipper, it's tiresome rather than dangerous.'

'How are we going, bomb aimer?'

'Greens going down now, skipper, head into the middle of them.'

The lurid red markers had been the initial marking place. Now the greens were dropping on top of them making a huge, brilliant firework display on which to drop their bomb load.

Ad checked his gauges. The showers of flak had not interfered with any of the working parts of the aeroplane, at least not yet.

'Right a bit, skipper... That's it... Steady...'

The lurid green markers were now lighting up the centre of the docks area. Ad could see the black shapes of ships and large barges in the many basins in the dock area. Still the illuminations of the flak coursed towards them.

'Markers in bombsight, skipper, steady...'

Ad wanted to scream 'let's get out of here' but knew that that would be the end of his operational career. He also knew that everyone else felt the same way but dare not overstep that fatal line.

The aircraft lurched suddenly upward. Ad felt the giddy thrill of the negative G force once again; for a second it took his mind off the fact that he was in deadly peril.

'Bombs gone, skipper.'

Ad looked down at the Duisburg docks and railway installations. In the last minute they had burst into livid orange and red flames from one end to the other. Over to the right something blew up. Whatever it was, that was good. Two or three fires had very quickly flared up and were about to join each other.

He saw that sudden flash of the photo-flash bomb.

'Engineer to skipper, photo flash gone, we've done our bit. No hang-ups, skipper, all bombs have gone. Bomb doors closed, skipper.'

'Skipper to engineer, roger.'

They had, indeed, done their bit for the night but the job was only halfway through. Now they had to get home and the Luftwaffe would be waiting over northern Germany and Holland. In the normal manner, Johnny took the aircraft to the highest possible altitude, ordered the navigator to set a course for home and then, using gravity, flew the Halifax in a shallow dive to speed it as quickly over Holland as it would feasibly fly.

The official report presented the score card the next morning to Butch Harris at High Wycombe.

No of aircraft missing		17
Damaged	(a) flak	66
	(b) fighter	4
	(c) not enemy action	5
Total		**75**

The official report gives the external view as to the results of the raid. The report was not available to anyone at 405 Squadron but the crews who were there saw those planes go down in flames, saw the few parachutes that got out and saw the damage to the planes that came back.

From 405 Squadron, Crockatt's crew had not come back. Only a couple of days previously Crockatt had commiserated with them that a raid was scrubbed. Now he was dead or, at best, a prisoner of war.

'Poor buggers.'

A psychological change passed imperceptibly over Johnny Lennox's crew. They had learned to engage less and less with other crews. Other crews too often did not return. Lennox's crew engaged more and more with each other and formed almost a psychological rampart against outsiders. They trusted each other.

CHAPTER 12

Before their first raid on St Nazaire they had chatted eagerly and excitedly among themselves and other crews. Now, before a raid, no-one spoke. They spent too much time hoping they would be alive this time tomorrow. They smiled as new boys, 'sprog crews', would excitedly chatter before a raid. The same crew did not do so before their second raid, if indeed there was a second raid.

Training for their new Pathfinder duties carried on. At this rate they would be fully-fledged Pathfinders by the middle of May and could wear that very prestigious golden badge.

CHAPTER 13
TARGET FOR TONIGHT: DORTMUND

4 MAY 1943

'How much do we owe you, love?'

'Seven teas, five wads and two cakes; that'll be five bob, thanks. Oh, you're aircrew aren't you? Oh, no, then, nothing to pay. Lads, don't worry about it.'

Lennox and the crew were in a tea shop in central Cambridge. Life was looking up. Cambridge, with its colleges, picturesque buildings and charming River Cam, was an attractive place to be stationed. It was rather better than the grim dampness of Leeming with its limited attractions. When they were not on ops, the life for an aircrew was not too bad. They were largely left to their own devices. They could go to the pictures, go for a walk around town, take out a punt on the river, play cards, enjoy a pint of wallop and flirt with local girls. It was certainly better than the privations of his brother Bill's army with their tented camps and never-ending cold and mud. It was by no means uncommon for shopkeepers, publicans, bus conductors, doctors or tearoom proprietors to refuse payment from aircrews.

'My brother's a wireless op,' she added.

'RAF?' asked Lennox.

'Oh no, nothing like that, he's in 5 Group.'

They all laughed uproariously.

CHAPTER 13

Number 5 Group, at least according to legend, was the bomber group most favoured by Sir Arthur Harris. Harris had been its air officer commanding and they would always be 'his boys'. Five Group noticeably had the best RAF stations, such as the large new one at Waddington. They were given the best crews from Operational Training Units and were generally reputed to be Harris's pet group. What Lennox and his crew knew was that 5 Group also got the toughest jobs and that very few of their crews ever completed a tour of 30 operations.

'What squadron is he with?'

'He's in 106.'

'At Syerston? Oh, they're tough characters those lot, indestructible most of 'em.'

'Oh, my brother's pretty indestructible.'

They laughed. The crew could see that she was trying to be brave. They laughed with her. She knew clearly that her brother had little chance of survival or would become a prisoner of war. There was a special comradeship between aircrews' families and those in aircrews. That is what made her offer the teas free of charge. In all probability, it also led to two of the crew surreptitiously leaving five shillings on the table for her to find when they had left.

The laughter stopped.

In the doorway stood two RAF policemen: the 'whitecaps'. 'Are you 109, 156 or 405 Squadron?' asked the sergeant.

'That's us, we're 405,' said Lennox, the skipper. The pilot always spoke as 'first among equals'.

'Back to base, lads, there's two trucks on the Meadows. They're going in 20 minutes. You've got to be on them.'

'Right, Sergeant, thanks. Is there a war on tonight?'

'No idea, mate, and I wouldn't tell you if I did. Twenty minutes, OK? Have you seen other 405 blokes down here?'

'Good luck, boys!' the waitress said. 'Good luck to all of you. Come in tomorrow and tell me you're all OK.'

The crew walked past the medieval colleges and quaint shops to the Meadows, each man with his own thoughts. 'Maybe the CO just has some special announcements.' It was possible. 'Maybe there is just some special training this afternoon arranged at short notice.' It was possible. Over at 44 Squadron all crews had been called back to base and King George VI had walked in to review them. Such visits were never pre-announced to preserve security from possible enemy eyes.

In the truck, they talked.

'Well, the weather's not looking bad, so it might be an op.'

'Actually, it's more likely just to be a bit of an air test to make sure the squadron is up to scratch.'

'Oh yeah? And what are you basing that on?'

As the truck, full of tense airmen, bumped and ground its way to Gransden Lodge it was better to talk of other things. They were surprised that Darwin in far-off Australia was being bombed by the Japanese. They were all heartened by the events in North Africa where the Germans were being pushed farther and farther back.

They all hung on as the truck made the tight turn, slewed around the corner and into the Gransden Lodge air base. They looked at the guard on the gate. There were extra RAF police on duty with rifles at the ready. It looked as if a raid was on. They looked at the telephone box. It was secured with a chain and padlock. That meant there were no communications in or out.

'There's a war on, gentlemen,' said Johnny.

'I do hope it's somewhere like Italy where we can just bail out and spend the rest of the war sunning ourselves by the Med.' Raids on Italy were also popular because the Italian gunners sought out the refuge of the air raid shelters as the bombs hurtled down. The views over the Alps were reputedly sensational. You could but hope.

Each man was now silent. The burning question now was whether they had been selected for operations.

When a raid was on, all squadron members had to be within the base and sealed off from the general public. Security requirements

CHAPTER 13

meant that no-one had the chance to tip off a member of the public, journalist or possible German spy that a raid was imminent. There was always the possibility that they had just been called back as a routine security measure. Just as long as it was not going to be a scrubbed raid. That was the absolute worst.

Johnny Lennox went straight to the Flight Office.

'It's us, lads! There's a show on and we're flying tonight. There's just three of us going. The detailed briefings start after 1430 and the main briefing is at 1700 hours. Without a word the crew walked swiftly over to the petrol pumps. There she was: Halifax number JB904 with the squadron markings of LQ-E for Easy.

Lennox asked the chief erk 'how many?' He did not need to add 'gallons'.

'Fifteen hundred, Johnny. Where d'ye reckon?'

The total fuel capacity of a Mark II Halifax was 1882 imperial gallons (8556 litres). This meant that the aircraft was not going to be targeting to the limit of its range. 'Big City', or Berlin, was out: a Halifax could not fly there on 1500 gallons. Fifteen hundred gallons would take them perfectly to 'Happy Valley' or Essen.

Equally, though, it could be Bremen, Hannover or Hamburg. Cologne was also a possibility but from what he had heard from other crews there was nothing left to bomb there: it was just a blackened ruin apart from the cathedral. The vital railway yards at Hamm were always a popular target and 405 hadn't hit them for a while.

There was one kind of operational luxury, which, curiously, was denied to 405 Squadron. Other squadrons often had 'soft' operations: 'nickelling' to drop leaflets on the German population or 'gardening' to drop mines in the North Sea, Baltic Sea or between Denmark, Sweden and Norway. These offered considerably less danger. They were often reserved for 'sprog' crews or crews just finishing a tour. For whatever reason 405 Squadron, possibly uniquely, was never called upon for one of these 'soft' raids in the whole of the war.

Ad's job was to find the chief erk to go over all the technical aspects of the aircraft and confirm to Johnny that it was OK to accept responsibility for the plane.

BOMBS AND BARBED WIRE

So, they wended their way back onto base to kill time until the briefing. It was back to the familiar pre-op routine of table tennis, washing or letters home. There was one thought that they did not want in their mind. 'Tomorrow I might be dead.' There was an even worse thought: 'I can walk out if I want to.' And they could! If a man did not want to fly operations he only needed to approach the wing commander and say, 'I can't take this anymore' and he would be off the station within 15 minutes. He would be out of aircrew immediately. He could go home to his wife and children (if any). He would most certainly survive the war, having let his crew down. Oh no! Flirtation with death was highly preferable to that.

At 1420 the Tannoy announced that the pilots' and navigators' briefing would take place in the smaller briefing room in ten minutes. Lennox and Knight would have worked their way there with other pilots and navigators.

At 1500, Graham would have attended a briefing telling bomb aimers of the main aiming point, usually a prominent feature in the centre of town.

Roberts would have received a briefing by the signals officer who would detail the radio frequencies to be used that night. These were printed on rice paper so that they could be eaten if the aeroplane was shot down. They are also advised of 'colours of the day': the colours of flares which are to be used to identify an aircraft as friendly if putting down at another station or to communicate to British flak batteries to stop firing at them. The Royal Navy, in particular, had a policy of 'shoot first and ask questions later'.

At 1700, all three aircrews who were to fly that night gathered outside of Gransden's large main briefing room. The doors to the briefing room were closed and guarded by RAF police. At the appointed hour the police opened the doors and the aircrews filed in. They would take their places on long wooden benches. In front of them was a large map of Europe covered by a curtain. On the stage waiting for them were the station intelligence officer, metrological officer, engineering officer and flying control officer.

First there was roll call. The roll call tonight was short.

CHAPTER 13

Then the platform party entered and everyone stood smartly to attention. The platform party consisted of the group captain in charge of the station, wing commanders and squadron leaders. The RAF police closed the door and stood guard outside to maintain security. Any non-involved air force or civilian personnel approaching a briefing would be arrested immediately.

The station intelligence officer opened proceedings by drawing back the curtain. This is the moment which everyone has been waiting for. Red tapes on the map showed a route from Gransden to a landfall near Haarlem in Holland to… where? It's not actually Essen (sighs of relief all around) but it is close. Where the heck is it?

'Tonight's raid, gentlemen, is on Dortmund. Some 600 planes will take part. Can we have the blinds drawn and lights out please?'

This was the first main force raid on Dortmund. A ripple of excitement, surprise and tension would have passed through the room. The meteorological officer would speak next.

'Right, everyone, here is the situation on the weather. There is a cold front moving across here [he indicated] to be at Kiel by midnight. You can expect to find small amounts of cloud here [he indicated] and much cloud at all levels here [he indicated again]. You will find cirrus over the target area but nothing much below 23,000 feet. On return there will be some fog patches later into the night. On return you will encounter some low stratus over the coast and East Anglia. Visibility is unlikely to be less than 2000 yards. However, tonight's main force is from 4 Group in Yorkshire, 6 Group (which is your home group, anyway) and 1 Group from Lincolnshire. We expect that all squadrons should be able to take off and to land in good order.

'If there are any unexpected weather problems on return the aerodromes at Acklington, Scorten and coastal aerodromes in East Anglia will all be quite free of fog. Navigators, you all know how to find these do you not?'

'Yes, sir.' They had landed at them in flight tests and were quite familiar with the conditions there.

Wing Commander Fauquier would then take over.

'Thank you, gentlemen.'

A projector at the back of the room shone an aerial photograph of Dortmund onto the wall.

'As you all know we have not previously carried out a main force attack on Dortmund. The red spot on the photograph shows the aiming point, of which navigators already have details. Essentially it is the town centre but there are many industrial factories in that area. As some of you will know from earlier in the war, Dortmund is a place where U-boat engines are made and are transported up the Dortmund-Ems canal to the shipyards in Hamburg, Wilhelmshafen and so forth.'

Fauquier looked around to ensure that his points were being understood.

'Dortmund also has a large steelworks called the Hoesch Werke. We would like to put that out of action as well.'

The crews nodded in enthusiastic assent. The Dortmund-Ems canal had been a much-hit target in daylight raids earlier in the war. Dozens of planes and crews had been sacrificed. Despite tales of heroism and sacrifice plus a couple of Victoria Crosses, little had been achieved. The canal had kept open and this had kept the production of U-boats in full swing.

'You might also like to know that Dortmund is a major brewing centre. If we can put the breweries out of action, we will be doing our bit to ruin the Jerry morale.'

The wing commander waited until the laughter had died away. The slightly too keen laughter betrayed the nervousness in the room. He would not have expected anything else.

'We are to meet up at this point here [he pointed to the map] with a Pathfinder force of Mosquitoes. These are fitted with Oboe and will show us the way.'

Oboe was a relatively new direction-finding technology which allowed bomber squadrons to find their targets. Before the advent of new technologies, crews navigated by dead reckoning or even the stars. This had led to a situation where less than one bomb in three was within 8 miles (12 kilometres) of the target. The Germans had shown the way with direction-finding equipment, notably on the Coventry

CHAPTER 13

raid. The RAF was now, essentially, copying the German lead, albeit with different technology.

'The Oboe Mosquitoes will be backed up by 22 Lancasters that will be marking the target from 156 squadron at Warboys. I understand from Group that marking is getting better. We don't want another Saarlouis!'

This would have raised some wry smiles, but the point was well made. Some weeks earlier a Pathfinder squadron had brilliantly lit up the town of Saarlouis, which was impressively and effectively taken off the map by the main force. The problem was the target for that night was nearby Saarbrücken, which remained totally unscathed. Sir Arthur Harris had not been amused at this. His wrath had found its way forcibly and unequivocally down the chain of command.

'The takeoff time is 2143 for Weiser's crew, in LQ-T for Tango. Harty, you are in LQ-A for Able and will take off at 2149. Lennox, you are in LQ-E for Easy and will take off at 2150. You'll see the Warboys kites probably before you take off, they'll be waiting for you over St Neots to form up with them. You'll then form up and proceed to 52° 24' north, 0° 33' east making landfall at Bloemendaal aan Zee before following this course to Dortmund, which is at 50° 10' north, 1° 37' east. As usual, Group have included a couple of dog legs on the route to confuse the Hun.

'The Mosquitoes will lead the way and will drop the first yellow long burning target indicators from 50° 52' north, 1° 26' east. This will keep Jerry guessing as to whether we are heading for Essen, Hannover, Hamburg or, indeed, Dortmund. These Mosquitoes will drop a salvo of green target indicators over the target area between 0057 and 0137 hours.

'If green target indicators are not visible for any reason, pilots will order navigators to calculate the central aiming point and overshoot it by one second between 0102 and 0141.

'The main force of Lancasters will commence their bombing run at 0102 and will aim red on green markers. Any questions?'

'Is there any intelligence on nightfighter activity in Holland, sir?'

'Nothing special but we all know where they lurk.' He pointed out the Kammhuber Line. You will certainly find a lot of searchlight activity as you pass through here and you will certainly be targeted by nightfighters. However, with a main force of 600 and the speed at which they will be travelling it is unlikely that Jerry will pick many off. If there is the slightest doubt of enemy activity in the form of a nightfighter do not engage, corkscrew and get the hell out of it. You're not bloody Roy Rogers!'

A current of nervous laughter doubtlessly ran around the room.

'Well, you're all experienced chaps so there's no need to tell you that Jerry is using a lot of "scarecrow" shells at the moment. You will probably see some tonight. Don't let them worry you unduly; it's just a load of Teutonic pyrotechnics trying to put you off your job.'

The crews smiled knowledgeably and gave each other knowing looks.

'There is something else that you need to know about as well. There are some kites going over to Rheine at a similar time. Make sure you stay with your own operation or the group captain will be on to us like a ton of bricks. Oh, and I take it that you have all written your letter to your next of kin and given it to the squadron adjutant?' He looked searchingly at them.

'Yes, sir.'

The wing commander would then proceed to give estimated times of arrival at each control point on the route out and the height for bombing.

The flying control officer is the next to speak.

'Tonight's duty runway is runway A. Start-up times are at 2100 hours and we want you marshalled and ready for takeoff at 2130. Synchronise your watches; the time is now 1727.'

The station commander would close the proceedings.

'And I would like to wish you all a successful trip and a safe return. Now if you all file past the intelligence officer's table he will give you your escape kits.'

They picked up escape kits and survival packs in case of being shot down. Escape kits included packets of foreign money as well as maps of Europe printed on silk and showing the best escape routes. Each airman also carried photographs to be used in false documentation if they could contact the local resistance. A group of WAAFs then

CHAPTER 13

enter the room with bags for personal items. Every item in the aircrew member's pocket had to be put into one of these bags. This included Ad's photo of Miranda. Even a ticket stub from the local cinema could tell a Luftwaffe intelligence man 'Cambridge: 1 Group or 8 Group.'

Lennox would have proceeded to the map store for the night's map and to mark out their route. The navigator, Knight, went off to another room and drew tracks to Dortmund on Mercator maps, checking and double-checking calculations with slide rules and protractors. Then the crews would return to the mess for the pre-operation meal. Dennis Over of 206 squadron recalls:

We would be given the time for our 'aircrew meal' serving the one luxury that we all looked forward to, eggs, bacon, sausage, baked beans, unlimited cheese that we independently cut from a large cheese on each table, an urn of fresh milk, fresh fruit and of course the large bowl of 'wakey wakies' on each table, which we used to take by the handful. God alone knows why we did not all become junkies. In retrospect, to think that we used to then jam ourselves into our turrets for up to 12 hours, we must have had cast iron digestive systems. We were each issued with refreshments for the trip, typically a bar of Cadbury's Bourneville chocolate, fresh fruit, Horlicks tablets and anything else that we could purloin such as cheese, unused cold bacon, sausages, any other leftovers from the aircrew meals and two flasks of tea in RAF issue thermos flasks.

Some would be quiet. Some would eat heartily. Some would not eat at all, although it was better to eat to summon up energy to meet whatever challenges lay ahead. It was easy to pick out the raw crews on their first trip. They were eager and asked questions. The old hands were mainly quiet. There was an unwritten rule that any conversation had to be cheerful. But each was locked up with his own thoughts and they must have wondered who was to have the last supper tonight. At this point it is highly likely that there was near silence. Perhaps there were some weak jokes that everyone laughed at in too hearty a fashion. Or perhaps not at all.

The crew would cycle to the stores to pick up fresh parachutes and Mae Wests. They then proceeded to the locker rooms. This was where they 'suited up' and pulled the Sidcot flying suit over their uniforms. The rear gunner had a different kind of suit, appropriate to his freezing position in the tail of the plane. This was a massive suit with internal heating to prevent him from dying from hypothermia in the below freezing temperatures in the rear turret. Finally, they pulled on the heavy flying boots lined with lamb's wool. These were cunningly designed with a pocket for escape documents and detachable sides so that in the case of being shot down they could be removed and the remainder would resemble normal shoes.

WAAFs handed out sandwiches and flasks of tea together with chocolate and barley sugar. There was one more piece of equipment which was actually rather intriguing. It was as vital as it was non-standard-issue: an empty 1-gallon Tate and Lyle syrup tin. This was specifically one with a closely fitting lid. Gunners had to be at their post for the whole of an operation and had to make alternative arrangements. A mid-upper gunner such as Prieur could not desert his post for a toilet break for five minutes without endangering the entire aircraft and crew. Hence the syrup tin and especially that closely fitting lid!

Some crews whose families had suffered bomb damage also took rubble from home to throw through the open bomb door with a dedication such as, 'You did this, you can bloody well have it back!' Empty beer bottles were also popular items to be thrown out as they sounded like a falling bomb as they fell. Some wags with a particularly macabre sense of humour would paint cheery slogans on bombs such as 'From all in Coventry!'

Perhaps the most harrowing part of the process was the point where each crew member surrendered his locker key to the NCO i/c locker room. This was a precaution, just in case they didn't make it back. Outside of the locker rooms the crews would wait for the vehicle, jovially called the 'blood wagon', to take them to their dispersal.

One airman wrote:

I for my part hated the feeling of standing around in the crew rooms waiting to get into the vans that will take you out to the aircraft. It's a horrible business. Your stomach feels as though it wants to

CHAPTER 13

hit your backbone. You can't stand still. You laugh at small jokes, loudly and stupidly. You smoke far too many cigarettes, usually only halfway through and then throw them away. Sometimes you feel sick and want to go to the lavatory. The smallest incidents annoy you, and you flare up on the slightest provocation. When someone forgets his parachute, you call him names you would never use in the ordinary way. All this because you're frightened, scared stiff. I know because I've done all those things. I have always felt bad until the door of the aircraft clangs shut: until the wireless operator says 'Intercom OK' and the engines burst into life. Then it's all right... Just another job.'

The airman was Guy Gibson VC, DSO and bar, DFC and bar.

A corporal would stand by the bus telling the crews when to get in.

'Right, you lot, the blood wagon is ready. P-Peter, are you ready? 'E-Easy, you're next; can we be having you please?'

By this time the ground crew will have bombed up the planes. The belts of .303 ammunition would be loaded into the aeroplane ready to be fired. Lennox would do a check of wing flaps, tyres, elevators and undercarriage gear and check that all other crew members are happy with their equipment. Ad, as flight engineer, was a key participant. He had to confirm that all of the instruments, equipment and gadgets for which he was responsible were in working order. It was Ad's job to confirm to Lennox that he could sign the form 700, which he gives to the ground crew corporal to formalise acceptance of the plane.

The crew then sit on the grass and smoke and talk to pass the time until the control tower fires a flare from a Verey pistol to tell the squadron to get into their planes. The conversation could be about football, a beery night in a pub or anything. Well, anything except the upcoming operation.

There is just one thing to do before getting into the plane: the obligatory last piddle on the rear wheel of the plane.

After the war the discovery was to be made that the Germans had no 'scarecrow' shells. There were only bombers, which were exploding with their full bomb load in mid-air. RAF crews did not know this.

CHAPTER 14

ENEMY COAST AHEAD!

4 MAY 1943

'Engineer to pilot. Rear hatch closed and secure. OK to taxi.'

Both he and Lennox sat high in the cockpit looking forwards.

'Wireless op to pilot, intercom OK.'

'Skipper to crew, all OK to taxi?'

'OK, skip!'

'We've got green, skipper.'

Ad's observation was redundant. Both could see the piercing green flash of the Aldiss Lamp at the end of the runway. Sometimes you just had to say something to break the tension.

'Off we jolly well go, then, chaps. Chocks away, Ad.'

The unbearable nagging tension dissipated. Each man had a job to do and all focus had to be on that. Fear of the unknown was forgotten, at least for the moment. As they all knew, fear of the known would later replace it.

Lennox looked down on the port-side erk who held the rope attached to the chock. Ad looked down on the starboard-side erk. They both gave the thumbs-up sign together; the chocks were removed. The erks ran to escape the vicinity of the huge aircraft. Lennox kept the brakes on as he revved the massive engines, and released the brake. The Lancaster LQ-E shuddered forward, still under a controlled speed as Lennox took it off the dispersal and onto the runway.

CHAPTER 14

It was now Ad's job to operate the various mechanical, hydraulic, electrical and fuel systems.

As the aircraft gathered speed he and Lennox waved at the sending-off party. Towards the end of the runway were the wing commander, group captain, several other crews who were not flying to night, several WAAFs and perhaps a dozen erks. Most wave; the wing commander and group captain salute.

Johnny and Ad now go through the familiar litany of procedures, checks and confirmations. They were not yet at the point where they could do it unconsciously, but after countless air tests and five operations they were well on the way to achieving that.

With a bump the aeroplane leaves the ground.

'Course two five zero, skipper,' says Knight, the navigator, from his cubby hole covered in curtains. 'Go up to angels ten, we should pick up 156 there.'

'Undercarriage, engineer.'

Ad pulls the lever to retract the undercarriage. The aeroplane shudders as it clicks into its housing beneath the fuselage.

'Undercarriage up, skip.'

'Ad, can you see any of our mates up there?'

'Yes, at three o'clock, you can just see the glow of the exhausts.'

'Ah yes, and right on time; let's join the party.'

The force headed due east and climbed to 17,000 feet. Ahead, Ad could see some 30 aircraft, their dark, deadly bodies glinting in the moonlight as they played hide and seek among the scattered clouds.

In a few minutes he could see the shining expanse of the North Sea.

'Right, chaps,' said Lennox into the intercom. 'Jerry will know we're on our way by now. Mid-upper, just check that your guns are working, would you?'

A rattle which could be heard from above the din of the four engines shook the aeroplane.

'Yep, OK, mid-upper. Rear gunner, could you give us a burst, please?'

A second rattle shuddered through the aircraft before it settled into a now-familiar routine.

BOMBS AND BARBED WIRE

An hour after leaving Gransden, the intercom crackled with Prieur's voice. 'There's some flak up ahead, skipper, at ten o'clock.'

'Thanks, mid-upper. Doesn't look too terrible for the moment. Bloody hell, though, I do hope it's not the Royal Navy trying to shoot us down again!'

Ad saw green and red signal flares burst in the black night sky. They had been fired from the lead Mosquito to identify the aeroplanes as British to whatever ships were passing beneath. They waited for the flak to stop. It did not do so.

'Bugger! They're Jerries.'

'Skipper, permission to fire in the direction of the flak?'

'Permission denied, rear gunner, and permission denied mid-upper as well. We can hardly see the buggers and there's too little chance of hitting anything.'

'Order received, skip, wilco.'

The convoy escort vessels which the German navy used were normally converted fishing boats. Nevertheless, some were equipped with single high-powered 88-millimetre artillery and most had 20-millimetre or 30-millimetre cannon. Their firepower was not vast but quite capable of bringing tears to the eyes of an unlucky crew.

An aeroplane burst into flame and began to lose height rapidly.

'Bernie, is that a Halifax or a Lanc?'

'Looks like a Lanc, skip, not sure, though.'

The aeroplane plummeted towards the sea; a parachute could be seen. Then the aircraft lost control and began to spiral down.

'Poor buggers.'

An aircraft burst into flame on their port quarter.

'Rear gunner, mid-upper, can you see who that is? It looks like one of our Halifaxes.'

Lines of red and orange tracer were now wheeling towards Lennox's crew with menace. The line of the shells would seem to come their way so slowly and then whiz past before the crew could duck or wince.

'There's LQ-A on the side, skipper, it's Harty.'

'Is he going down?'

CHAPTER 14

'Don't think so, skip, the fire's diminishing so he must be using his extinguishers. He's losing height, but I don't think he's out of control, he's going back to Gransden.'

The crew would have breathed a sigh of relief for Harty.

'Oh well, with a few holes and burn marks the wingco shouldn't chew him off too badly.'

Pilots who turned back, or 'boomeranged', were routinely grilled by wing commanders. A pilot who could not summon up a convincing reason might be posted to the Orkney Islands or (if possible) worse. A lesser case might be 'sent to Sheffield' to the centre for restoring those with faltering motivations back to a suitable level of homicidal enthusiasm.

The last of the flak came up to meet them and died away beyond their slipstream.

'Enemy coast ahead, skipper.'

'Thanks, bomb aimer.'

Below them they could see through the patchy cloud to where the shimmering sea stopped and the blackness of the land began. Under its German masters, Holland had to keep a blackout after dark every bit as complete as that in England.

'Hey, Johnny, look over there!'

In the darkness from the ground a flashlight gave three short flashes and a long one. Then again; three short flashes and a long one. Dit dit dit dah. It was Morse code for 'V' (for Victory). These sightings were common for bomber crews flying over German-occupied territory. They were a wonderful morale booster for crews. At least the people on the ground were telling them that it was worth it.

'Thanks a lot, you crazy Dutchman, but I hope the Gestapo don't get you.' Ad laughed at Johnny's fervent prayer.

'Rear gunner to skipper, there's two kites down behind us. They look like Lancs, oh and there's a Halifax going down as well.' The bastard nightfighters had been waiting for them. A feeling of terror chilled the crew to their boots. They also noticed that there was no flak coming up at them. Lennox and Adlam and the rest of the crew knew what that meant. Up ahead there were more nightfighters waiting for them.

'We'll be into the danger zone in a minute or two, chaps. Keep your eyes peeled and if there's even a doubt shout "corkscrew!"'

'Got it, skipper,' chorused the gunners.

'Navigator, there's yellow markers going down ahead from the Mosquitoes. Does that fit in with your readings on the Goon Box?'

The 'Goon Box' was a navigational system currently being rolled out to all bombers. It was intended as a means of bombing accurately without the need for a bomb sight. As the technological cat and mouse game between the RAF and Luftwaffe progressed the Germans became adept at jamming the signals, but it remained a very useful tool for navigation.

'Looks spot on to me, skipper, Dortmund here we come.'

'Rear gunner to skipper, I can see two kites going down behind us. They're a bit far off. They've got short wing spans. I think they're Stirlings. CHRIST ALMIGHTY!'

A livid yellow flash lit up the sky. In the glow for three seconds Ad could see the size of the force behind him. God! It was huge! There were rows upon rows of Lancasters, Halifaxes, Stirlings and even some old two-engined Wellingtons, which, being four years old, were now obsolete technology.

The flash died away. Burning debris trailed away down to earth.

'Skipper to all crew positions, not to worry, chaps, just one of those Jerry scarecrow shells.'

Ad heard knowing chortles over the intercom.

'Navigator to skipper, we're passing beyond the main German air defence. We are on course and spot on time for Dortmund.'

'I don't care if we are past the main defences, keep your eyes peeled, all of you.'

'Rear gunner, skip, I can see more kites going down behind us. Two Lancs, I think. Christ! Jerry is having a field day out there.'

After a couple of minutes, they could see no further aircraft go down. The aeroplane rumbled on towards its destination. It was up to Lennox to calm the crew down and keep them focused on the job at hand.

'Skipper to engineer, have you heard from your brother at all, the one in Commandos?'

CHAPTER 14

'Not for a while, skipper. Last I heard he was on some top-secret training thing up in Scotland. He would love that. I saw him at Christmas and told him to keep on enjoying himself while we fought the real war.'

Lennox laughed. Ad could hear laughter from other members of the crew.

'Skipper to engineer, he was on that show at Dieppe wasn't he? Brilliant piece of work that, really showed Jerry what was what.' It was very much part of a skipper's job to keep the atmosphere as relaxed as possible. Chat was not merely social contact; it was a way of keeping the terror at bay.

Ad was uncertain. It was clear that Bill had been told not to talk about the Dieppe Raid, which the powers that be were presenting to the public as a great triumph. Ad had been taken aback at Bill's reticence to talk about it. Still, there was a war on and, as the official posters proclaimed, you had to 'Be Like Dad: Keep Mum!'

'Searchlights, skipper! You'd better start ducking and weaving.'

'Skipper to navigator, where the hell are we?'

'Just over the border of Germany, skipper. It is now 0055; we are due over the target at 0115 and are where we should be. No need to speed up or slow down.'

'So, there it is, boys. That's the lair of the beast down there. Twenty minutes from now…'

'Rear gunner to skipper, I think there's something out there, Johnny.'

'What is it, Bernie, do we corkscrew?' He hoped the answer was no. If he corkscrewed it could make him late over the target. That could lead to raised eyebrows by the wingco when he got back.

'Not sure, skip; hang on, bugger it, whatever it was has gone into that bank of cloud.'

'How many engines, Bernie?'

'Two, skipper, could be a Wellington, I'm just not sure.'

'Mid-upper, what can you see?'

'Can't see a thing from up here, skip. There's loads of kites but they're all four-engined jobs and they're all ours.'

'Bernie, keep your eyes peeled whatever else you do. If you think it's a Jerry kite just shout "corkscrew!"' Get it?'
'Got it!'
'Good!'

CHAPTER 15
HAUPTMANN THIMMIG BOOSTS HIS TALLY

4 MAY 1943

For Wolfgang Thimmig, 31, life was really not too bad. He was lucky and he knew it.

A Saxon from Dresden, he had joined the Luftwaffe and had enjoyed a commendable record of promotion. He had missed the bloodbath of the Battle of Britain. His communication skills led to him being more valuable as a trainer of fighter pilots. Just after the Battle of Britain he had been promoted to Oberleutnant (Flying Officer) with his training squadron V./LG 1 and had been appointed the squadron's adjutant.

In October of 1940 he was sent to the front line against the RAF bombers in a squadron based at Mönchengladbach. The people in the Ruhr area spoke rough farmers' Plattdeutsch, which was an affront to his refined Saxon sensibilities. The industrial 'Gladbach' was so much less civilised than the airy boulevards and Rokoko spires of Dresden. It was still better than being stuck on some wind-swept back-of-beyond on the North Sea. Not only was he transferred but was immediately made Staffelkapitän. The 'Staka' was senior officer in the squadron. He was now one of the standard bearers for the Red Baron; a hero of an earlier war. This stamped him, in Luftwaffe parlance, as an 'Expert'. As a call sign he had chosen the name 'Ameise' or 'Ant'.

Nevertheless, something bothered him. He had not yet opened his account by shooting down an enemy plane. You cannot have an 'Expert' who has not actually shot down an enemy plane. You cannot have an ant that does not sting. This was not good for a Staka, who was expected to lead by example.

Fortunately for Thimmig, the kills had come along. By the time of his next promotion in June of 1942 he had already shot down some six RAF bombers: variously Whitleys, Wellingtons, a Hampden and a Halifax. This led to his being presented with the Iron Cross (second class).

For a nightfighter pilot with so few kills his promotion must have raised eyebrows. Despite being four kills short of being an 'Ace' he was promoted to Hauptmann (flight lieutenant). This doubtlessly raised eyebrows in the Spartan meritocracy of the Luftwaffe. Helmut Lent of a neighbouring squadron had got 20 kills in 1941 alone and many others had long since outstripped Thimmig's modest score.

Not only this but Thimmig was attached to the Stabschwarm III/NJG1. This was a considerable honour. The Stabschwarm was formed from leading pilots across several squadrons. The Stabschwarm were in leadership positions. They had enormous prestige and set the whole tone for pilots within the group. Thimmig's joy and his parents' pride did not end there. He was promoted to Acting Kommandanteur of the Stabschwarm; which made him the top pilot within his group. Thus, his substantive rank may have been at flight lieutenant status, but his prestige was equivalent to squadron leader or even wing commander level.

Three months later he had received his Iron Cross (First Class) and had the ten kills to stamp him as an Ace. Shortly after, he received the 'Ehrenpokal': the honour goblet of the Luftwaffe. This was an award presented to pilots who already had an Iron Cross (First Class); who had fought very well but had not qualified yet for a Knights Cross or German Cross.

Wolfgang Thimmig was very much a young man on the way up.

CHAPTER 15

Tonight, 4 May 1943, the weather conditions were suitable for a large attack. The entire Luftwaffe was just waiting for it. The question was when it would come. As Staka he had ordered everyone to be on base and to stay within earshot, 'just in case'. Thimmig flew Messerschmitt Bf110gs: three-seater nightfighters equipped with Lichtenstein radar to find British bombers and 20-millimetre cannon to shoot them down. His first crewman was responsible for navigation, the radio and, if called on, to use the backward-facing machine gun. The second crewman operated the radar whose screen would show the presence of an enemy bomber and his role was to guide the pilot towards the bomber.

As Staka, it was Thimmig's job to assign sectors to each of the nightfighter squadron. Powerful coastal Würzburg radar would see the raiders approach and report strength, bearing and speed. As bombers approached, ground control would scramble the assigned nightfighter to enter the sector and shoot down anything in it. As there was only one nightfighter per sector it followed that any other aircraft in the sector had to be British.

And so they waited. At 2300 hours reports began to come in of a very large force passing over the Dutch coast north of The Hague.

'So, Jungs and where do we think the English gentlemen will strike tonight?'

Thimmig and his fellow pilots would have studied a map. On that course they could be going for Bremen, Hannover, Hamburg, Wilhelmshafen, Berlin or anywhere in the Ruhr. They knew that the British never flew in a straight line anywhere and were likely to make sudden diversions to throw the defences off balance like a footballer changing direction at the last moment.

The report came in that Lent had two kills already, near Enkhuizen, just inside the Dutch coast.

The mood in the Luftwaffe Flight Office was tense. Thimmig was tense. Lent was making him look like an amateur.

At 2320 the shout came over the Tannoy.

'Alarmstart! Alarmstart! Scramble! Scramble! All nightfighter crews to be ready for takeoff in ten minutes. The enemy are on course for the Ruhr area and will be with us in about 20 minutes.

Come on, you two, let's move! We have no time to lose!'

'All ready to go, Herr Hauptmann.'

Within seconds all three-man crews were ensconced in their aircraft; the engines were turned on and they were ready for takeoff.

'Los, Jungs! Los!' It was the voice of the major (wing commander) over the radio.

A minute later the Bf110 was in the air and Thimmig was asking nervously what was showing on radar screen. There was one of the bastards ahead of him. He saw the hot glow of the exhausts; he crept under the aircraft about 500 metres below it. He began to close.

Without warning the aeroplane corkscrewed to port. Scheissdreck! They had seen him. He tried to throttle back but he was going too fast. He overshot the aeroplane and lost it in the blackness of the night and the puffy cloud.

'Don't worry, Jungs, there are so many of them we'll get one or two tonight.'

'Herr Hauptmann, there is a large machine 2 kilometres ahead. Looks like a four-engined bomber. Fly on a course 95 degrees. Yes, you're closing, you're closing.' Thimmig brought his aircraft down to 500 metres below the RAF bomber.

'That's nice, that's nice... Yes, I can see him now.'

He followed the red-hot exhausts.

'Don't think he's seen us. He's getting close to the edge of our sector. I'd better close on him quickly before someone else gets him. The bomber was now a kilometre or so ahead of him. The aeroplane shook as the heavy 20-millimetre cannons spat their shells ahead of the aircraft's port side wing. He saw a burst of flame as the wing flew into his stream of tracer. The wing burst into flame.

'Hang on, lads, hang on to your panties!' The Messerschmitt lurched violently to starboard as Thimmig winged over to port to escape the hail of debris and junk which might be coming at it from the stricken bomber.

'Right, that was a Halifax.'

'What's the time and place, navigator?'

'It's 0050 and we're just over Gronau Herr Hauptmann.'

CHAPTER 15

'Does that look like a kill to you?'

'Yes, he's a goner. Just as well you got him, sir, he's right on the edge of our sector.'

They watched as the Halifax bomber fell to earth in flames in the next sector. Three parachutes dropped out of it. Another aircraft showed on his screen. He gave chase and closed on the radar image. Once again, perhaps a kilometre ahead, he could see the red-hot exhausts. He dropped 500 metres below the aeroplane ready to come up underneath it. From the back of the aircraft he saw a twinkling of machine guns. The rear gunner was firing at him. He was well aware that the effective range of the British .303 machines guns was 500 metres at best. He was also aware that the range of his own 20-millimetre cannon was over a kilometre. Still, this guy was a bit too aggressive. He may as well let him go and find an easier kill.

'Let's get further inside the sector; which way, navigator?'

'Thirty-five degrees, Herr Hauptmann.'

Within minutes a third aircraft came onto his radar screen. Once again, they had not seen him. He lined up the Messerschmitt so that the wings of the British bomber were above his line of fire. He pressed the button and the 20-millimetre cannon gave out their deadly ripping report. The light-coloured tracer from the shells formed a barrier just in front of the aeroplane's wing. The Hailfax flew directly into the stream of shells and debris from the starboard wing and engines splattered into the night.

Thimmig made a sharp turn to port and gained height quickly. Once again, he avoided any debris from the stricken Halifax from hitting his own Messerschmitt.

'Navigator, can you see if he is going down?'

'Ja, Herr Hauptmann! He is spiralling to starboard… there! He has crashed.'

Thimmig gave out a whoop of joy. That bugger Lent might have got two, but he had got two as well.

'Time and place, navigator?'

'It's 0050, sir and we're just north-west of Stüttorf.

Five minutes earlier, Lennox and Adlam had been flying across Holland. They had seen several aircraft go down.

'Gunners, keep your eyes peeled! The Luftwaffe are bloody hot tonight!'

'OK, Johnny, we're watching out. Nobody seems to be worrying about us.'

With the stark inevitability of a Greek tragedy, Lennox and Adlam were now on collision course with Hauptmann Thimmig and his appetite for kills to earn his Knight's Cross.

'OH, BLOODY HELL!'

The wispy light grey trails of cannon shell shot out in front of the starboard wing. They were flying right into it. A nightfighter had them in its sights. Ad and all of the crew felt the terror of immediate death. A sharp burning sensation stabbed into the back of Ad's neck.

'Oh Christ! I'm hit, Johnny, I'm hit.'

'Corkscrew, skipper, corkscrew to port!' Who had said that? It was not the voice of one of the crewmen that he knew. It was the voice of terror. The huge aircraft lurched to the left with violence. Ad felt a wave of nausea well up in his stomach, but instinct told him to hold it in and not be sick.

The cannon shells ripped across the fuselage and into the leading edge of the wing as the aeroplane winged further over to its left. With the power gone from two engines the manoeuvre was futile. One, or possibly two, crew members shouted desperate warnings. The intercom crackled, the sound of their desperation faded into the crackles and then radio silence. Parts of the wing and engines exploded into the cold night air in a shower of sparks. Ad held on waiting for the inevitable.

The petrol stored in the starboard wing burst into flame. Within an instant the livid glare of the blaze lit up the inside of the aeroplane through the portholes. There was no hope. They had never caught sight of their executioner, who by now would be flying as far away from the stricken Halifax as he could manage.

'Everybody out!' It was the code word. It meant that in 20 seconds or so the fire would reach beyond the wing roots and into the fuselage,

CHAPTER 15

frying everyone to death. In roughly that time, also, the Halifax would start to corkscrew downwards out of control and G-forces would render them unconscious. There was no time to lose. Already, Ad was feeling that his body was weighing a ton; he had never felt so heavy in his life. Could it be the effect of the wound in his neck? No, clearly, it was the aeroplane's corkscrewing momentum. He felt heavier, heavier still. He experienced nausea.

His body was now trying desperately to be sick. He had to hold it back. He felt a terror that he had never felt before. The pain in his neck was screaming for relief. His body was also trying to go to sleep of its own accord as the blood drained from his head. He knew that passing out was now close. He knew that if he gave in to it then he would never wake up, never see Miranda again. He had to click open the safety harness which held him in his seat and start to move as fast as he could. He had to move quickly, desperately quickly. His body would not obey his commands. It was similar to being very, very drunk but he knew there would be no waking up with a hangover. There would be no waking up.

What the hell was he going to do? The air force had not trained him in how to exit a stricken plane. There were no rules. It was every man for himself and death was now only seconds away for the slow or the unready.

The bomb aimer was the first from his position in the forward turret to the escape hatch. Ad felt the blast of cold air as the escape hatch was pushed free. He saw the bomb aimer disappear through the hatch. Ad forced himself to move; he ripped out the wireless connection from his flying helmet and eased himself slowly, painfully... Oh God! Was he going to vomit? He was next in line, the shrapnel shard now forgotten. He hooked his legs over the precipice and jumped. He was relieved to be out of the burning aircraft and felt the terror-thrill of falling through the night sky. Three... four... He counted as he had been told. He had not been trained, however. He had never made a parachute jump. Nor did he know what to expect. He only knew that if he launched himself into the cold night air he might survive another 30 seconds. If he did not do so he would certainly only survive for 20 or possibly even less.

He pulled the rip cord and hoped and… He heard a rush of activity immediately behind his back. The chute had opened. He braced himself and – WHAP! – he felt the violent tug as the parachute did its job and the harness jerked on him. Oh God! His neck felt that piece of shrapnel now! Oh Christ, he was in pain.

He still had just enough self-awareness to pull the straps aside and look at the burning Halifax. Its death curl was already starting. In a few more seconds no more would get out. There was one more parachute behind him, that would be Knighty. Then another, that would be Robbie. Then another, that would be either the mid-upper gunner who had escaped through the same hatch as Ad or the rear gunner who had escaped backwards out of his turret. The aeroplane was now spiralling down and clearly losing height very quickly. There were no more parachutes. His terror heightened to screaming proportions as he realised that two, or three or four of his friends were about to die!

The spirals and gyrations of the Halifax were quicker now; the fire had worked its way into the fuselage. After a few seconds the fuselage was a mass of flame as it plummeted then became unstable in flight and gambolled and gyrated like an animal in pain on its way down to crash in a crimson blast of burning petrol and high explosive bombs, far below him.

The night was quiet now. His descent was quite controlled. He had to think about landing. He ran through the training: land with your knees bent and go into a forward roll. Oh, Christ! How could he do a forward roll with this piece of shrapnel sticking into his neck like a supernumerary vertebra?

Below him was a farm. He saw the farmhouse, the fields, the sheds. It was enemy territory and the heart of the Nazi world that he loathed. Ironically, it looked very much like any English farm in the fields around Cambridgeshire as it rushed towards him. There was a pond. He was headed straight for it. How deep was it? He pulled the straps to arrest the fall. He splashed into the pond, which broke his fall and gave him an easy landing. It was shallow. The coldness of the water penetrated his flying suit and uniform. He struck the parachute release mechanism and swooshed his way through the cold, shallow, weedy

CHAPTER 15

water. Free. The water felt uncomfortable, making his heavy flying gear wet and soggy, but he was alive. He was actually alive.

It was the middle of the night. He was in a rural farm complex somewhere in the countryside and not far from the Dutch border. In fact, if he was lucky, he might still be in Holland. Meanwhile, overhead several hundred bombers were still passing over on their way to Dortmund. Their crews would have seen the crash and said 'poor buggers'.

Could he find the other crew members? Who was alive and who was dead? He had not even said 'goodbye' but that was understood. They would not have expected it. The time to say 'goodbye and thanks' was more time than it took for the fire to engulf the entire inside of the plane.

Ambrose Adlam from Gloucester was a British airman, in uniform, very alone. If he was lucky, he was in Holland. If he was unlucky, in Nazi Germany.

CHAPTER 16
IMPRISONMENT – THE FIRST DAYS

5 MAY 1943

The thing that struck him was the silence! The final planes on the raid had now receded in calm, determined procession eastwards to visit fire and mayhem on Dortmund. The throbbing sound of the armada droned and faded and passed away. That was useful! If he went in the opposite direction he would head into Holland and potentially friendly territory. Logan and Jennings had been lucky, and he could be lucky as well.

After the incessant roar of the bomber's engines, which had assailed his ears for the last two hours, he was now engulfed in an endless, black, inky silence. The dark and the silence together were like a living entity, cocooning him within it. He had extricated himself from the duck pond, the weeds and the parachute harness. He lay alone, in his sopping wet flight suit, in a field. Over on the horizon he could perceive a dull livid yellow glow of a burning Halifax bomber. Some crew members, probably Johnny and one other, were in that plane, or the hideously burned remains of them. Then it struck him. He had no emotional response to their death. He had to pull his wits about him. He had to consider that he was probably in Nazi Germany in RAF uniform and in some peril of his life. There was no response to that either. This was very odd. It might be years before he saw Miranda, his Anne, again. He might

CHAPTER 16

not see Miranda ever again. Miranda might be destined to become a widow. No! There was no emotional response.

Then something else struck him. His senses seemed to awaken. It was the farmland smells that came first: the damp grass in the small hours, the smell of manure, the powerful scent of the wildflowers. As he looked up he could see a few stars through the broken cloud, but the brilliance of those stars was something that he had never seen before.

Why was the scent of the wildflowers so overwhelming when he could not even grieve for Johnny? There was no time to worry about this. He had to get home.

He really did have to think very hard, was he in Nazi Germany at all? The aeroplane had flown agonisingly slowly but from the last navigator's report, he knew they had been close to the Dutch border. He had seen those 'victory-V' signs from Dutch farmers. Perhaps he could find one of those friendly farmers and go through them to the Dutch resistance. He had to get the flying suit off; it would be far too conspicuous when daylight came. He peeled off its clinging wetness. Oh! The stench of stagnant water was as overpoweringly awful as the scent of the wildflowers was wonderful.

Something else occurred to him. He was not frightened. Why on earth was he not frightened? He should be scared stiff. This felt wrong. It was all wrong, but he had no time to contemplate what was happening to him. The shock, the emotional overload and the vast burst of adrenaline had rendered him calm and untroubled.

He hid the parachute, flying suit, flying helmet and various cords and connections deep under a hedgerow. He removed the upper parts of his flying boots so that the remaining part around his foot resembled normal shoes. He undid the fly of his trouser and ripped off the top button. In the dim half-light he could just see well enough to undo the cover to reveal a small compass. West was – that way over there – so he set out walking. Just as he had thought, it was the opposite direction to that in which the bomber stream had been flying.

The blaze of the aeroplane was still some miles away and he could hear sharp reports as the last of the ammunition exploded. He also heard the bells of a fire engine sent out to douse the blaze.

BOMBS AND BARBED WIRE

He began to collect his thoughts. The first thing was to find out whether he was in Germany or Holland. He skirted around a couple of farmhouses and disturbed dogs but no-one responded to the alarm. He worked his way across a field and, on passing through the hedgerow, found himself on a road which led – he checked the compass again – due west. This was brilliant. There was no traffic and he could just follow it. A signpost gave directions to Isterberg, Schüttorf and Bad Bentheim.

That did not tell him which country he was in, but he did notice that 'ü'. Bollocks! It meant that he was, in all probability, in Germany.

Behind him the headlights of a vehicle swept the landscape. He dived into the hedgerow and knelt down to make himself as small as possible. It was a large truck. It was full of service personnel. As it passed by him he could see that they were armed with rifles. They were after him. Sod it! At least they had not seen him. It passed by slowly then disappeared.

He carried on along the road still walking westwards. The Dutch border had to be some way in this direction. The adrenaline rush passed away from him. The first sharp pangs of fear began to gnaw inside him. He could hear how his breathing now was laboured as he walked. He saw headlights again; that truck was coming back. They were looking for him and any other crew survivors. He crouched down in the hedgerow so that the whiteness of his face would not be seen. Maybe it would be easiest just to attract their attention and turn himself in?

He imagined himself after the war having a pint with his brother Bill in Gloucester (not that Bill actually drank alcohol) and saying, 'I gave myself up.' To be precise, he would have to say, 'I gave myself up' to a guy with a Military Medal and who had taken part in Commando raids on some island in Norway and shot up Germans by the score during the Dieppe Raid. What would be the look in Bill's eyes when he made that announcement? No, he was better off being shot!

It was getting lighter now. He opened his soggy, heavy uniform tunic and ripped open the lining. Inside was a map printed on rice paper. He was lucky. The water had not penetrated that far. It was

CHAPTER 16

still legible. If he positioned himself correctly with the moonlight falling on the thin paper, he could just make out some towns in northern Germany. There was Dortmund, but he had never got that far. They had flown just over the German border on a south of east course so he needed to go back on a course north of west and he was near the German border. Which side of the border was he on, though? He seemed to be heading for Arnhem or possibly Enschede. There was not enough detail. He replaced the map in its hiding place. The important thing was to be sure that he was over the Dutch border.

The fear was overtaking him like a tidal wave now. His heart was pounding. What would happen if they caught him? Would they shoot him out of hand? The Geneva Convention was all very well in Geneva but he was somewhere near a place called Bad Bentheim; had they heard of the Geneva Convention? Had they heard of Geneva? If an angry farmer with a pitchfork caught him, would such a man feel bound by the Geneva Convention? Some farmers in Kent had definitely not felt encumbered by the Geneva Convention during the Battle of Britain. They had meted out rough justice with no comebacks or raised eyebrows of any kind.

He would follow the road until daylight made it dangerous and then he would try to move parallel with the road in the fields. To his surprise the countryside within the lair of the Nazi beast resembled closely the rolling farmland of Gloucestershire, although the farmhouses which were semi-visible in the growing light of dawn showed a style of architecture that emphasised that he was not in England.

The military truck appeared on the horizon again, which made him duck for cover into the hedgerows. Or was it another truck? There were at least five of the crew at large and it could well be that there was more than one.

'He! Du da!'

From the top of a field a farmer was shouting at him. He had been seen; he had to move quickly and melt into the hedgerows. His heart was pounding. His mouth was dry. He was aware of the sound of his own breathing: short and in rapid gasps. In his stomach he felt fear. In the back of his neck the pain was getting worse. There was no question now. He was in the heartland of the Nazi beast and Nazis murdered people.

Ten minutes later a truck ambled slowly along the road with men hanging on the side flashing powerful torches and looking for him. He crouched down. The truck passed. If he could make it across the field, he could disappear into a hedgerow up the hill and away from the road and make it difficult for his pursuers. He remembered from a briefing 'if on the run, sleep during the day and travel by night', but things were not going his way.

The truck had passed, and he ran under the shadow of a hedgerow. Behind him he heard a guttural shout.

'Da ist er! Dort oben, links!'

Now all he could do was run. They would be after him on foot now. He hoped they had not got dogs. In his heavy uniform, which was still wet, it was difficult to run.

'Halt oder wir schießen!'

'Christ knows what that means,' he thought and sprinted as fast as the heavy thick wet material would allow him.

Two bullets went over his head with a 'thwack'. One hit a tree and bark splattered in a fine shower of material. These people were not joking.

'Halt oder wir schießen du dummer Affe!'

He kept on running. Two more bullets flew over his head. Then came a blow in the back of his arm. It was just like when he had hit his hand with a hammer but now came the burning sensation. The bullet was as hot as the oven when Miranda used to make rice pudding on Sundays. He screamed involuntarily and stopped. He felt another hammer blow in the back of his leg and again the burning sensation. Now he fell. The burning sensation made him scream with no concerns about the indignity of it all. He looked up and saw the sky. It was early morning now and through the screaming the sky was very blue and with puffy white clouds.

He heard footsteps running up the hill behind him. A face looked down at him.

CHAPTER 16

The man was about his own age, carrying a rifle. The blue uniform proclaimed that he was from the Luftwaffe. The rank badges suggested that he was of officer rank. He barked out an order.

'Sichere, daß er keine Waffe trägt.'

Was it an order to shoot him as he lay there? Would he see Miranda again? Hands passed themselves over his body. As the hands went over his wounded arm and wounded leg he screamed in agony.

'Keine Waffe, Herr Oberfeldwebel.'

'Du, Messner, hole mal die Sanitäter und zwar so bald wie möglich. Das Bein ist ihm schwer verletzt.'

So that was it then, the orders had been given to shoot him and probably bury him in the field.

'Gefreiter Mohren, komm mal her and ihm erklären was geschieht.'

'Hello, you speak English, yes?' Ad nodded.

'I am Corporal Mohren. You are captured by the German Luftwaffe. We await medical orderlies in order to dress your wound.' The others of the platoon sat around on the grass smoking and talking. They did not take any special interest in Ad; they did 'pickups' such as this three or four times a week.

By now, the pain from the leg and arm were all consuming. The throb and the agony took over his entire being. There was nothing else that he could think about.

'The medical orderlies will take about a half hour to arrive. Just rest.'

Someone ripped open the leg and arm of his uniform to gain access to the wounds. He felt a sharp pricking sensation. The pain faded like the morning dew. The officer produced two pads, dusted them with antiseptic dust and fastened them to the wounds with a bandage.

The officer offered him a cigarette. Compared to decent civilised cigarettes like Players' Navy Cut or Wills' Woodbines it tasted dreadful. At least if they were offering him cigarettes they weren't shooting him. The officer spoke to Ad via Mohren.

'You are a lucky man. For you the war is over. You still live. You walked for the Dutch border?'

'Yes.'

'It is about 10 kilometres but the SS watch the border. If they catch you, you are dead immediately, and no bandage and no bloody cigarette. Why did you run?'

'Well, I would rather like to get back to England.'

Mohren translated and the officer laughed.

The officer pointed to his heart: 'Hier gut.' He pointed to his head: 'Hier nicht gut.'

They all laughed. Mohren translated. 'The Oberfeldwebel says you are strong in the heart but weak in the head.' He smiled through the pain. It was incredible. He was sharing a joke with Nazi thugs. In reality the officer appeared civilised and pleasant. The excellent cut of his uniform gave him an air of professionalism. The man was clearly educated and no thug. Like himself, the officer had the air of a civvy-in-uniform rather than a hardliner military professional, as was his brother Bill.

It occurred to Ad that there was something out of place that he could not put his finger on. It came to him in a flash. The Luftwaffe personnel saluted in the same manner as the Royal Air Force. They did not do the 'Heil Hitler' salute. Well, that was a surprise.

As he collected his thoughts he asked about the rest of the crew.

'That aeroplane over there?' asked Mohren. 'The pilot and one other are still in the plane. The others got out, but I do not know if we have picked them up. We got dozens from last night.'

'What happens to the remains?' That was Johnny and, most probably, Bernie in there.

'The Luftwaffe buries all of your dead with full military honours as the RAF does with ours, you need not worry about that.'

'Can civilians get into the aeroplane to take souvenirs?'

'No, there is a death penalty for any unauthorised person to enter a shot-down aircraft. The German government considers them as war graves and not for silly people to enter for amusement.'

That was a great relief; the thought of senseless civvies pawing over Johnny's remains was sick-making. He did have to give pause for reflection. This was not quite the fire-breathing Nazi state which the *Daily Mirror* had been promoting for the last six years.

CHAPTER 16

There was something else to think about as well. Miranda would be worried sick about him. He had written the letter as Warrant Officer Graham had suggested and now it was really useful. She would be receiving that today or, at least, in the next couple of days. Then would come the telegram telling her that he had not returned. That would be the worst bit. She would not know if he were alive or dead. Oh God! He hoped the family would rally around. Surely they would? He had seen other families of men gone missing. Everyone piled in to help.

Then there would be the second official telegram saying that the Red Cross had him on a list as a POW in Germany and some means of contacting him. At least she would know he was alive, but how long would it be before he was able to contact her? He could not spend too much time thinking about it.

Local farmers, used to an early start, had their curiosity aroused by the gathering. They asked questions of the Luftwaffe men. In contrast with the professionalism of the German airmen, the locals were not so detached about matters. Ad did not understand what they were saying but he did get the gist that it was not good. They looked at him with an undisguised and visceral hatred. The officer spoke to them severely.

'Haut mal ab! Der Kerl wird verhaftet und ist unter unserer Verteidigung! Na! Noch wieder! Haut mal ab oder die Polizei kommt.

The men slouched off grumbling and looking at Ad in a very hostile manner.

'They want us to hang you,' said Mohren brightly.

The medical orderlies duly arrived. They ripped away the uniform. They cleaned the wound tracks as best they could. Ad winced as they dabbed some form of antiseptic liquid onto the wound.

'The medical orderlies advise that the wound in the leg may get infected. Probably the bullet carried pieces of uniform into it. We will take you to the air base at Rheine and have a doctor look at you. There are good facilities there.'

Rheine? Wing Commander Fauquier had said that there was a raid on Rheine that night and that the three 405 Squadron aircraft should not stray into their bomber stream. He would see what a German town looked like after an attack.

BOMBS AND BARBED WIRE

The medical orderlies stretchered him onto the truck; it was probably the same one which had been searching for him in the early hours. The small industrial town of Rheine was, indeed, showing signs of the attack from the previous night. The smell of burning hung in the air. Firemen, police and soldiers were in the streets, weary and exhausted. Houses and factories were still burning. The streets were strewn with rubble and untidy seas of exploded flak littered the streets. In the street Ad saw Hitlerjugend boys with their distinctive yellow-shirted uniforms. They took part in air defence work. Now he saw 'Heil Hitler' salutes.

They took Ad by truck to the nearest operational air base, in this case at Hopsten just outside of Rheine. His first impression would have been fascinating for an RAF man. The base served the daytime and bomber needs of the Luftwaffe in that area. He would have seen Messerschmitt Bf109s; Focke Wulf 190s; Heinkel 111s and the bizarre insect-like Heinkel 219s. 'If only I could describe this lot to the RAF,' he must have thought but, as Mohren had said, 'for him the war was over'. The German pilots in their exquisitely cut leather jackets made quite a dashing figure, especially the ones with the red ribbons of the Knights' Cross around their necks.

The second impression would have been a discovery of the strange relationship which existed between the Luftwaffe and Royal Air Force. In the air they tried to kill each other in as many vicious and imaginative ways as possible. On the ground there was a mutual respect as may be found between two elite sports teams who are happy to have a beer on the ground and a gentlemanly handshake before the slaughter at 15,000 feet recommences.

A doctor cleansed Ad's wounds thoroughly. The bullets and the shrapnel from his neck made a harsh metallic sound as the doctor dropped them into a metal bowl. He put in stitches to help recovery.

Ad waited for interrogations – and possibly rough stuff – to start.

None did. The Luftwaffe did indeed want information but knew that there were better methods to obtain it.

The next morning an escort was arranged to take him to his next port of call.

CHAPTER 16

The officer visited him with Mohren to explain. 'Tomorrow we bring you by train to Auswertestelle West, which is a clearing house for prisoners of war. Then you will be assigned to a permanent camp.'

'Oh, is Dulag Luft closed down, then?'

The officer laughed. 'You are very well informed. Sergeant Adlam. The Dulag Luft camp was renamed some weeks ago. The name is still used but only for the small transit camp in the centre of town.'

'Which town is that, sir?'

'Oberursel, just outside Frankfurt am Main.'

Ad had to ask if he could trust his senses. Was this all really happening? He had joined up with the specific intention to drop bombs on Nazis. Nazis were vile creatures who wanted to take over the world or, at least, Europe. They were people who, at worst, had murdered their own and for some unfathomable reason had a psychotic hatred of Jews. On a more banal level they or their British admirers thought it was a good idea to write the word 'Jew' on Montague Burton's outfitters shop in high streets in England. Yet here he was having a rational discourse with a perfectly civilised air force officer who looked like an RAF officer except that his uniform was rather better cut. The 'degenerate Nazis' had protected him from a mob, had dressed his wound and, on the whole, seemed strangely civilised. He did not know how to process this. He knew he would have plenty of time in which to do so.

The journey proved fascinating. Because of the severe leg wound he was carried by stretcher to the first train and then by various other trains through Münster, which was Johnny's next navigation point on the way to Dortmund had they ever got there. Then they passed through Dortmund itself, which gave him the chance to see the damage the raid had done. The last of the fires were being put out now, but it was clear that the main force of 596 bombers had done a gratifying amount of damage. That felt good. That is what it was all about. The place was, however, still open for business. Passing through

BOMBS AND BARBED WIRE

Essen, he would have been even more gratified at the vast amount of devastation which Sir Arthur Harris had caused with his endless bombings of the Krupp munitions factories there.

On the stations, passengers would see that his uniform was of the Royal Air Force and not of the Luftwaffe. Many of those passengers had lost houses, jobs, family members, possessions and friends. They had been subjected to night after night of heavy bombing raids and knew the feeling of bombing terror. One aspect was not lost on Ad. That hatred of bomber crews was the feeling which the German Luftwaffe had brought into the world when they had undertaken the first ever bombing raid on the Spanish town of Guernica only seven years previously. They shook their fists. They mouthed obscenities. They appealed to the guards to hand him over to them for immediate and summary justice. The guards ignored their would-be barbarity and arranged for Ad to be given a drink by the smartly dressed women and girls of the Nationalsozialistische Frauenschaft (Nazi women's organisation) or Bund Deutscher Mädel (League of German Girls).

Perhaps the Luftwaffe people were just very professional and not particularly of a Nazi persuasion at all. Now Ad was coming up against some undoubted Nazis. The members of these organisations undertook many auxiliary jobs throughout the Reich but were extremely loyal to Hitler personally. As he noticed, they used the 'Heil Hitler' salute. A pretty blonde girl passed him a cup of the barely drinkable brown sludge that had replaced coffee in Germany. She gave him a snappy 'Heil Hitler' greeting with a look halfway between hero worship for a war hero and disdain for a vanquished foe.

'*Schmeckt's gut?*' asked a guard. This obviously meant 'does it taste nice?' In fact, it did not. He was to discover that it was a coffee substitute made from acorns and called Muckefuck. It tasted as though the pretty blonde BDM girls had piddled into it. Indeed, they may well have done. Nevertheless, this was not a time to upset his hosts.

Then his train brought him to Cologne. He would have been rendered speechless. The city was a blackened Pompeii-like ruin from one end to the other. From the railway station he could see that the massive medieval cathedral was the only building in the town centre

CHAPTER 16

which was substantially undamaged. After Cologne the contrast into the wonders of the Rhein gorge was wonderful. It was utterly beautiful with breathtaking views up onto the heights where the robber barons had had their castles. There was no denying it. The dark-hearted lair of the Nazi beast was beautiful beyond belief!

At last a local train grated and wheezed its way from the main station at Frankfurt am Main to the pretty rural backwater of Oberursel. By now other RAF prisoners were coming together, although in a trickle rather than a steady flood. The Dortmund raid had been the only main force raid since Duisburg was hit on 26 April. The airmen chatted together to keep spirits up. They offered cigarettes around. They asked questions about crew members who had not been seen. Even after just a day it was remarkably comforting to hear some British voices again. It was most probably here that he heard the major news from North Africa: the Afrika Korps had been knocked out of Tunisia by Montgomery. The British were winning on one land front at least! In the air they had certainly struck a blow to Hitler's Germany, although Ad's train ride attested to a very inconvenient fact: despite the endless bombing, Germany was still a very highly functioning country.

Ad would soon be at the dreaded Dulag Luft (or Auswertestelle West or whatever they wanted to call it). He had to think what he had been told. You are to give your name, rank and number. There may be rough stuff. They may offer punishments if you refuse to talk. They may offer inducements in the form of extra food, or privileges such as trips out, cinema shows or visits to prostitutes. Some of the possibilities were more enticing than others but, cutting through the complexity, there was one clear imperative from RAF Bomber Command. 'You are to give your name, rank and number only.'

Ad wondered what would happen next.

CHAPTER 17
DULAG LUFT – THE SUBTLE OPPRESSORS

7 MAY 1943

Auswertestelle West was one of those places which had been renamed officially but which, perversely, retained its previous name in common parlance. Its name was Durchgangslager der Luftwaffe (Luftwaffe Transit Camp) or Dulag Luft for short. Dulag Luft had one single mission. It was to extract valuable information from prisoners before assigning them to permanent prison camps.

What information might they want to know? Aircrews would not know RAF grand strategy, but they could comment on civilian morale. They might know of the difficulties of living in wartime London, Manchester or Glasgow. They might know of shortages. They might know of friction between the British and their American allies.

On a more military front, airmen would know of aircraft deliveries, of the impact of losses on operational squadrons or of new technological developments. Top of the list were snippets of information on photographic reconnaissance, radar, new aircraft types, navigational devices or armaments. 'Order of battle' information might also be very attractive to the interrogators.

CHAPTER 17

Every single piece of information was noted down, however trivial it might seem, and catalogued before being included in a daily written report. The report was of such high importance that digests of the information gleaned were rushed each night by a dedicated Fieseler Storch light aircraft to the Abwehr (German Military Intelligence) in Berlin. These were analysed, and intelligence officers wrote daily reports for Oberkommando der Wehrmacht: the German Forces' High Command.

Ad had just flown in 405 Squadron, which was newly transferred to the elite Pathfinder group. The Luftwaffe would already have known about the transfer. Being a Pathfinder, albeit a 'sprog' Pathfinder, would make Ad a 'person of interest'. He might just know about new navigational and target-finding techniques.

He heard the sound of a key in the door to his — what was it? Was it a hospital ward? Was it a cell? Was it a holding pen of some kind?

There was a knocking at the door, tentative but insistent.

'Come in.'

A man in the uniform of a Royal Air Force pilot officer entered. He was balding with a resplendent moustache, which many people in 'Civvy Street' thought all RAF officers sported but in practice few did.

'Hello, old man! I'm from the quartermaster's store down at the main camp. Benson Freeman is my name. I heard you are in need of some new trousers. Well, look, I've got some here. They're in better condition than yours. Give me those ones to get rid of and put these ones on.'

'I'd prefer to have my own trousers back if I could, sir.'

If he lost his trousers he would lose his compass, which might be of vital importance if he had the chance to escape.

'Don't be silly, man! Those were in a disgraceful condition. They are ripped where the medical orderlies tended to your wound and are covered in blood. Back in Blighty you would be court-martialled.' He laughed ingratiatingly.

Ad duly dressed in the foul-smelling uniform, with some help from Freeman.

'Where exactly are we?' he asked.

'Well, the Luftwaffe wallahs will have told you this is Dulag Luft, the transit camp. The main camp is down the hill. This is the Hohemark clinic where they send the types who have been shot up. The medical staff are reputedly quite good.'

After the ordeal of the shooting down and the two days of being in the hands of the Luftwaffe, not to mention the murderous civvies on the railway, it was an enormous relief to see a friendly face. He was glad to chat with Freeman who was personable enough. His visit was the nearest thing to a normal world that Ad had experienced during those few days of terror, pain and trauma.

As Freeman left he said, 'I expect the Luftwaffe people will want to have a natter with you. They're reasonable blokes, so I wouldn't worry too much. Toodle pip!'

Perhaps a half hour later came a second knock on the door. This time it opened without being invited.

'Eberhardt! I am the receptionist.'

A smallish man, blond and bespectacled, entered and clicked his heels. As he had passed through the German procedural machine since Rheine, Ad had been amused to note that Germans actually did this. He had thought it was only something shown on films to make them look stupid. Eberhardt wore the uniform of a Luftwaffe lieutenant. He was brisk and businesslike. His high forehead and rimless spectacles gave him the air of a prim but earnest schoolmaster. This was not inaccurate; Heinrich Eberhardt had been a university lecturer at Giessen, having earlier studied British History at London University.

'You are...' he looked at a note on a clipboard... 'Sergeant Adlam of 405 Squadron?'

'Yes, sir, I'm afraid I can't get up.'

Oh NO! He had just given information away. He had been told 'name, rank and number only' and he had given away that he was a Pathfinder from 405 Squadron. He would not give an outward sign of any personal discomfort at this unmitigated blunder, but he would have to be much, much more careful than this.

'Oh, don't worry about that, we need to get that leg mended as soon as possible. If your condition stabilises we will move you to the main

CHAPTER 17

camp. If not, we will pass you to Camp IXC, which is the hospital for prisoners of war at Bad Sulza.'

Ad nodded.

'Can I ask a question, sir?'

'Certainly.'

'Do you have any information about the rest of my crew? They are Lennox, Knight, Graham, Roberts, Prieur and Moody.' He knew that there was not much hope for Lennox and Moody, but the others might well have survived the crash.

'Not immediately, Sergeant Adlam. In the main camp we have some 200 men and we bagged some 30 planes last night. Men will be coming in for the next three or four days.' He made a note on a paper attached to a clipboard. 'I will make enquiries and see what I can find out.' He did not seem too bad a chap.

'Now,' Eberhardt proceeded, 'you had your wound dressed at the Luftwaffe station where they took you?'

'Yes, sir, and they dug the bullets out, plus the piece of flak in my back.'

'Good, the orderlies have reported to me that the arm and neck wounds look clean and are not infected. The leg wound does look severe. I have arranged for our new medical officer, Dr Ittershagen, to visit later this morning. He is just starting with us but seems to be a good man. Now, I just have to leave this Arrival Report Form with you, which is from the International Red Cross, the protecting power for prisoners of war. It will allow the Red Cross to pass your information back to England. Please fill it in and pass it on to the next officer who will visit you.'

'Right, and thanks for your help.'

'Yes, we help you and we dress your wounds: a man who came to bomb our cities. Who is civilised Sergeant Adlam, Britain or Germany?'

'Well, let there be no doubt about it. I joined up to drop bombs on Nazis. So, I am grateful to you for your help – I really am – but the civilised world needs you to lose.'

Eberhardt did not bite.

BOMBS AND BARBED WIRE

'Just fill in the Red Cross form if you would, Sergeant Adlam. We need to give your details to the Red Cross, who can then pass details on to your family.'

The heels clicked again. The door clicked. Eberhardt's precise steps disappeared down the highly polished corridor floor. Ad was left alone with his thoughts.

The first thought was, 'How the heck did this man know about 405 Squadron?' His second thought was, 'When does the interrogation start?' He must remember 'name, rank and number'. What would it be like when it started?

Ad did not know it, but the Luftwaffe's information collection was already into its third stage.

Like many airmen, Ad was doubtlessly impressed to learn that in Germany shot-down aircraft were treated as war memorials. Admittedly, the death penalty for prying civvies seemed a bit steep. There was more to it. Immediately a shot-down aeroplane was cool enough to enter, trained Luftwaffe Intelligence personnel would ransack the wreck for information. They recorded absolutely everything. The squadron letters LQ-E confirmed that they were from 405 Squadron.

They knew that the aircraft's serial number was JB904. This would confirm that it was a Halifax Mark II. None of this was new to them.

The intelligence personnel would also search the aircraft for any papers, maps or evidence of any kind that might be of interest. Even a bus ticket, cinema ticket or café receipt could alert the Luftwaffe that 405 Squadron had moved from Leeming to Gransden.

In his initial visit, Leutnant Eberhardt had also made note of something else: this man was not wearing a ring. The wearing of a wedding ring gave the Interrogators a valuable trump card: 'your wife will never know what happened to you'. It was crude and it was ungentlemanly but it worked so very often. Ad, however, had made a decision. He never wore his wedding ring on operations. That meant that if ever he failed to return, Miranda would be given his wedding ring together with his other possessions. Eberhardt would have written a report that the man had answered him back, that he was not wearing a wedding ring. Other methods might, in due course, be needed.

CHAPTER 17

Late in the morning, Ad heard the key in the lock again. Dr Ittershagen arrived together with a Polish doctor and the medical orderly who Ad had seen previously. Ittershagen had only come to Hohemark a day or so before Ad and was, himself, very much the new boy. He had the orderly remove the bandage on the arm.

'That wound is clean and quite neat, I do not think you will have much trouble with that. Try not to use your left arm for the next week or so. I will have the orderly dress the wound once a day, but I do not require to see it until you are finally discharged.'

He had Ad lie on his stomach. Ad felt the adhesive bandage rip away around the shrapnel wound in his neck.

'Ganz sauber find ich,' said Ittershagen. Ad really wished they would speak in English.

'Nach meiner Meinung auch,' said the Polish doctor.

'Your neck wound provides no complication as long as we keep it clean. You did very well to jump out of an aircraft with that wound; it must have hurt very much.'

'I can't remember it hurting at all, sir, I was too bloody frightened to worry about pain.'

The two doctors laughed. Surely people who tended his wounds and who could laugh with him could not be the Nazi monsters of British propaganda?

Ittershagen had the orderly remove the bandage from the wound in the back of his thigh.

He heard Ittershagen's voice.

'Das finde ich schlimm. Sauber ist sie schon aber die ganze Wunde ist eine Schweinerei. Meiner Meinung nach sollte das Bein weg.'

The Polish doctor replied.

'Schlimm schon aber schlimm ist relativ. Ich gebe zu, daß es etwas Lebensgefahr gibt aber ich finde, daß so eine Lösung vielleicht übertrieben ist. Hast du Hunger?'

'Schon! Diskutieren wir das während des Mittagessens.'

What on earth were they wittering about?

Ittershagen spoke.

'Sergeant Adlam, the wound in your leg is in a very serious condition. I must inform you that in my opinion we may have to take it off. I will make the necessary arrangements to bring you to hospital in Frankfurt, where they have much better facilities than here.'

They left.

The shock was worse than the bullets which had hit him and which, God knows, had hurt enough. How long was it since he was in Cambridge and happy and married and with his mates and in one piece? It was only three days. In that single minute between the Halifax being shot and him landing in the pond his life had changed so dramatically. Being shot down was bad enough. Being captured was worse. This latest piece of news was beyond awful. He would go through life in Gloucester – if he ever saw it again – as a cripple. In the hours after the shooting down he had been amazed at how little fear, anxiety or pain he could feel. That phase passed. Now he was frightened and desperate, and hope was diminishing by the second.

The medical orderly put his head around the door.

'Essen? Food?'

He shook his head. His appetite had disappeared down that same track, down which his left leg was about to disappear.

Some three quarters of an hour later he heard footsteps echoing down the corridor and coming in his direction. It was the Polish doctor with the orderly.

The orderly took away the bandage. The doctor examined the wound closely, prodded it, which made him wince, and smelled around the centre of the wound.

'Schon gut,' he said, and had the orderly redress the wound.

'Sergeant Adlam, I have discussed your wound over lunch with my colleague. He is worried about gangrene. I think gangrene is possible but not probable. My colleague is an orthopaedic surgeon with a high recommendation, but war wounds are not really his field, or, at least, not yet. I have specialised in war wounds for four years. I will advise him of my opinion and recommend a course of treatment which will bring your leg back to health. I am leaving in a few days' time but will see you before I leave.'

CHAPTER 17

'Oh, thank you, Doctor, I cannot thank you enough.' Ad's face and eyes and demeanour would have shown his gratitude and profound happiness at the news.

'Bitte schön, Sergeant Adlam, and this is probably more than you deserve for being a terror-flier over Germany.'

'I thought you were Polish, Doctor?'

'Polish, yes, but Volksdeutscher. I am ethnically German. I am from Oberschlesien, a part of Poland which is traditionally part of Austria and has now been rightfully reunited with the Reich. We Volksdeutscher have the reputation of being more German than the Germans. You may talk about Britain being civilised, Sergeant Adlam. I just know that when Adolf Hitler took my Silesia out of the idiotic fantasy land of Poland "Heim ins Reich" and back into Germany the standard of living and level of civilisation went sharply up, not down. Heil Hitler!'

He left. He had used the word 'civilised': that was interesting. Eberhardt had used the word also. So, they compared notes, then. The information gatherers were working as a team. That was useful to know.

'The Kübelwagen is ready outside the main entrance, Herr Leutnant.'

Gustav Bauer-Schlichtegroll pulled on his uniform hat and picked up his document folder.

'Very well, Corporal, just take me to the Hohemark if you would and wait for me until I have finished talking to the prisoner.'

He sat in the back and perused the documents. The man was called Sergeant Adlam. He was from 405 Squadron based at Gransden Lodge near Cambridge. The intelligence officers at Rheine had noted the aircraft's markings and reported accordingly. Adlam had been shot down on his way to that big raid on Dortmund.

Eberhardt's initial report stated that Adlam's attitude was anti-German but he seemed intelligent and therefore amenable to reason. He recommended a nice chat to persuade the man as to Germany's righteousness in the war. Occasionally these chats worked and when they did the levels of intelligence which they afforded were pure gold. The man did not appear to be fearful so Eberhardt did not recommend 'higher levels of interrogation' until later in the process.

Adlam carried wounds from 'making a run for it'. Doubtlessly, he and the RAF would see this as heroic. The Luftwaffe saw it as idiotic, but then the entire British war effort appeared idiotic in Germany. As Adlam did not wear a wedding ring Eberhardt recommended that Bauer-Schlichtegroll should establish early whether he was married. This was always the best sensitive point on which to apply pressure. The first and most important point was to get him to fill in the Arrival Report Form.

There was a knocking at the door.

'Come in,' said Ad.

He heard the key in the lock.

An exceptionally tall man with a prominent nose and the air of the upper middle classes entered the room. He did not know Ad but Ad knew him. He was one of the posh people. He was one of those who had ridiculed him at school because his shoes were dilapidated, and which had led to the fights and the expulsion. It was not Bauer himself, of course, who had persecuted him, but Bauer was of that same ilk. His social pretensions, his easy superiority and his smugness hung around him as a two-dimensional aura which said 'twofold enemy': Nazi and class. Had Ad known that he dropped the second part of his surname, Schlichtegroll, because it was too difficult for English tongues it would merely have served as confirmation as what he already knew about this man's status. He was the enemy in every imaginable way.

'Hello, old chap, my name is Lieutenant Bauer, I understand you had some queries that you left with Leutnant Eberhardt?'

'Oh yes, about my crew?'

'That's right. Now,' he said, pulling out a paper from his brief case, 'we have four of the crew at the main camp down the hill. They are

CHAPTER 17

Knight, Graham, Roberts and Prieur. They are all well. They landed without mishap. They did not provoke anyone to shoot at them and they send their best wishes to you.'

'What about Lennox and Moody?'

'We have no details of them.'

'If they had survived the crash would they have been here by now?'

'Possibly. I am sorry to inform you that their absence probably means that they did not survive the crash, but men do sometimes come in a week or so later.'

Ad nodded. 'Well, thank you for advising me, anyway.'

Bauer-Schlichtegroll sat down without being asked.

'You know, there is another way of looking at it.'

'What is that, sir?'

'Well, you have lost two friends and you have my personal sympathy. I have lost many friends in this endless bloody war.'

'Good,' thought Ad.

'Do you mind if I ask you a very leading question?'

'I imagine you are going to anyway.'

'You are with 405 Squadron, you were on your way from Gransden Lodge to Dortmund and your raid killed 600 people.'

'Brilliant!' thought Ad. If there was one thing that he really loved about his job in Bomber Command, it was the thought of killing vast numbers of Nazis.

'I just wondered how you felt about that. You know, as one airman to another.'

Ad was beginning to get this man's measure. As with so many others in the war, he knew a military man when he saw one. He had seen them at Gransden Lodge and met them in pubs in Cambridge. He had seen the Luftwaffe pilots at Rheine. They had the look of military men. This man was yet another civvy in uniform. One airman to another, eh? What was this man after?

'Well, sir, there is a war on. You bombed London, Manchester, Liverpool, Birmingham and especially Coventry. So, we are going to bomb you back. It was you that started it.'

Bauer-Schlichtegroll was impassive.

He smiled the smile of the deeply confident. Ad was beginning to distrust, dislike and even detest him.

'Who started it, Sergeant Adlam?'

'You did.'

'You will recall that your Mr Chamberlain declared war on us on 3 September 1939. In Germany we were utterly shocked. We could see no reason for you to do so and, quite frankly, most people in Germany still do not know why you did so. You may have noticed that people shouted abuse at you on your journey from Rheine?'

Ad nodded assent.

'People are frightened of your war machine, that is clear. There is also frustration. They do not know why you declared war on us. German people are not bad people. They feel that Britain is punishing them, and they do not know why this should be.'

'You took over Austria, you invaded Czechoslovakia and you invaded Poland. That is quite good for a start.' That film *Dawn* went through Ad's mind. Should he say it? 'You bloody shot nurses in the last lot, you cowardly pigs.' He decided to hold his tongue, well, on this occasion anyway.

'The areas that we moved into in 1939 were lands that were stolen from us 20 years previously by the so-called Treaty of Versailles. In the eyes of every German that was theft. We merely reclaimed what was ours.'

'You signed the Treaty of Versailles.'

'Sergeant Adlam, if someone put a gun to Mr Churchill's head and told him to sign away Scotland, would you expect him to honour that signature?'

'Churchill? Not bloody likely, he'd fight tooth and nail to get it back.'

'And when the British Expeditionary Force went to France in September of 1939 how long was it before hostilities started?'

'About eight months.'

'Yes, about eight months, Sergeant Adlam. In 1939 Germany had no army on our Western Front. No-one expected an attack. We only moved armies beyond the Rhineland months after you had threatened

CHAPTER 17

our flank. You and France had half a million men in that area; we had no strategy to cope with it, no men and few tanks or planes. Did you ever wonder why it was eight months before something happened?'

Ad had wondered. He had talked to his brother Bill, who had been with the Fifth Gloucesters in Alsace. He did not say anything. He had nothing to counter Bauer's logic. He was deeply uncomfortable and knew that his demeanour showed it.

Ad chilled. He had fallen into Bauer's trap. If he were to agree with Bauer's logic, then he was accepting that Britain was the aggressor and not the hated Germans. If Britain were the aggressor then as a member of Bomber Command, he was also an aggressor and not the defender that he thought he had been. It also meant that all of the information which he had been fed was cynical propaganda. Ad needed to break the silence and break it quickly. He was not winning this argument.

'Look, we've had our little chat, now was there anything else?'

'Just a couple of things. As you so clearly enjoy dropping bombs on German civilians, do you appreciate what your raid did?'

'Yes, it bloody cut back your war effort.'

'Really, Sergeant Adlam? You came down from Rheine by train. You passed through many industrial towns: Münster, Dortmund, Hagen, Wuppertal, Köln at a guess. You passed through Frankfurt. Köln is certainly a mess and you certainly did see some damage, but does it look as if the German war effort is on its knees? Don't worry, you don't have to answer. Oh, and in the 1933 election do you know what proportion of Germans voted for the Führer? It was about a third. So, of the 600 people you killed, proportionally 400 did not vote for the Führer at all. You have just taken part in the government-sanctioned murder of 400 civilians. Look, old chap, this is not an interrogation, it is just to serve my curiosity.'

'Oh no it isn't,' thought Ad. 'You are softening me up, you bastard.'

'I thought you might like something to read,' Bauer-Schlichtegroll proceeded airily. 'We don't have a lot, I'm afraid. There are a couple of old copies of Dickens. Have you read *Bleak House*? Otherwise there are a few copies of *Der Adler*, which is the Luftwaffe magazine. With all the British airmen we have in captivity we should probably have an English-language edition but Reichsmarschall Göring has not got around to it yet. It's a pity because it's actually quite good; you should find the photographs interesting, anyway. Ach, Dummkopf! I don't seem to have brought them. I will send them up to you.'

That was another thing! The two men that he had talked to so far had a sensationally good command of the English language. Their command of the language was better than most people that he had known in Gloucester. That was surprising. It was significant. What did it mean?

He was also beginning to wonder when he would come across some other British personnel. They had given him a room to himself, which he had thought was generous. Now came the first inkling. 'I am not in a generously provided hospital ward: I am in solitary confinement.'

Inside he chilled. He was part of some machination but what did it all mean and what was going to happen next?

'Oh, have the nuns started reading to you from the Bible yet? I am afraid that Hohemark is actually run by a religious order from the Evangelische Kirche, which is Lutheran. People who are members of your Anglican Church say they feel it is very similar. I am afraid that the Kommandant up here, Hauptmann Offermann, is a strong member of the church and insists that the patients here attend his nightly Bible readings, which are in English. When you are feeling a bit better they will probably invite you. "Invite" is probably the wrong word but you get the general idea.' Bauer-Schlichtergroll laughed conspiratorially.

'We have had men ask if they can be moved from here and put in the charge of the Gestapo people down in the main camp.'

Ad laughed.

'You see, we Germans do have a sense of humour after all.'

'Oh, just one other thing, Sergeant Adlam. Lieutenant Eberhardt asked if I would pick up your Arrival Report Form for the Red Cross.

'Yes, here it is.'

'But you have not filled it in.'

'I am under orders from my wing commander. If captured, the Geneva Convention requires us to give only name, rank and number, as you very well know.'

CHAPTER 17

'I do not think the Red Cross will accept it in this state; in fact, I am sure they will not. They will reject it and your parents and wife will not know what has happened to you.'

'No, I have my orders.'

'I cannot believe that Wing Commander Fauquier would give such an order, it is crazy.'

Fauquier? Ad was quiet. How on earth did this man know about Fauquier? Fauquier had only been on the squadron for a week! Bauer-Schlichtegroll was quiet. Ad had not contradicted this man about having a wife. Now they had a pretty good idea that he had a wife. Now they had a point of vulnerability over him.

'By the way, Lieutenant Eberhardt mentioned a Red Cross parcel. When can I have it please?'

'My dear Sergeant Adlam, you bomb our cities on some crazy notion that Germany started the war; you kill 600 people; we tend to your wound and make you comfortable… and we have, have we not?'

'Yes, you have, and I am very grateful but…'

'You display wilful behaviour by not completing a form for the Red Cross, which is nothing to do with the Luftwaffe, and then you demand a Red Cross parcel. I am sorry, my dear chap, but this is just not done. Every other airman here has completed it correctly and you should do so, also. When we see a little less childishness in your demeanour and a little more, frankly adult behaviour then we will see what we can do about delivering the Red Cross parcel, which is, I can tell you, already allocated to you. There is also one other thing.'

'Yes?'

'When you have completed the Red Cross form, as everyone else does, I will personally see that you get writing materials to write to your wife. I shall leave now. Good day.' So saying, he clicked his heels in a perfectly polite manner.

The stakes were starting to become higher. Bauer had casually dropped into the conversation that the Gestapo had a presence at the camp. Now he began to feel vulnerable. What an utter bastard to pressure him to give vital information away by holding the possibility of a letter to Miranda over him; what an utter, utter bastard. War was a nasty business as he was now finding out; it was nasty every day and in every possible way. Perhaps the worst thing was the way they had got him to reveal that he was married without him even telling them. Now he was vulnerable, and they would play on it.

In his newly realised solitary confinement, he felt more alone than in any part of his life.

626241 Aircraftman 2 Adlam A.A. Ad joins the Royal Air Force before the outbreak of hostilities in 1939 (Adlam Family Collection).

Ad the 'erk' in the boiler suit he wore to service the Wellington and Whitley Bombers (Adlam Family Collection).

'Erks' often had to work in the open air. No complaining! There was a war on (Royal Canadian Air Force History and Heritage).

Miranda in South African Air Force uniform gives a 'love of my life' smile to Ad (Adlam Family Collection).

Ambrose (Ad) and Miranda (Anne) in bliss in South Africa (Adlam Family Collection).

Ad in tropical kit, South Africa 1941 (Adlam Family Collection).

Pilot Officer John Lennox RCAF with his wings.

John Lennox in flying gear, ready to drop bombs on Hitler.

405 Squadron Handley Page Halifax Bomber on a test flight
(Royal Canadian Air Force History and Heritage).

405 Squadron Pilot shows a wicked grin to go with his gallows
humour (Royal Canadian Air Force History and Heritage).

Handley Page Halifax Bombers in silhouette at Dispersal. Their crews could well be already at briefing for tonight's target (Royal Canadian Air Force History and Heritage).

Halifax Bomber with 'erks' making it ready for the next operation over Hitler's Germany (Royal Canadian Air Force History and Heritage).

6262241 SGT. A. ADLAM.
405 SQUADRON.
14 · 4 · 43.

My Dear Wife,
    Ere bed you lay my darling!
Well, my dear, if you ever receive this letter (which
I pray you won't) you will have already been
told that I did not come back from a raid.
No doubt you will be shocked and everything
will seem useless, and that is the way I would
feel if anything happened to you.
    This letter is to be posted to you
should I fail to get back to give you new hope
and courage for you know that no German can
kill me and I want you to bear up as I shall
most likely be a prisoner or else be trying to
get back to you. Do not be afeard as some day
I shall return again to you and I know that
is true because I feel it inside of me.

Ad's 'goodbye letter' to Miranda. When she read this the bottom
would have dropped out of her life (Adlam Family Collection).

2

We have been happy together now for a year and I would like to thank you for being my wife. I took you from your own land and brought you to England. Maybe that was a mistake on my part but time will tell. You do not see much to like here and people seem very frigid and stand-offish but you will find that they are real, underneath. Anyway they are my people and I reckon that they are worth fighting for. Everytime I go out I don't know what is ahead of me but I am not afraid of the unknown. As long as there are Nazi's to be killed I shall be willing to assist in killing them. I have seen what their bombs have done here in this country and I would like the German cities to be laid into the dust. The sooner that is done, the sooner we shall win the war and I know we shall win.

3

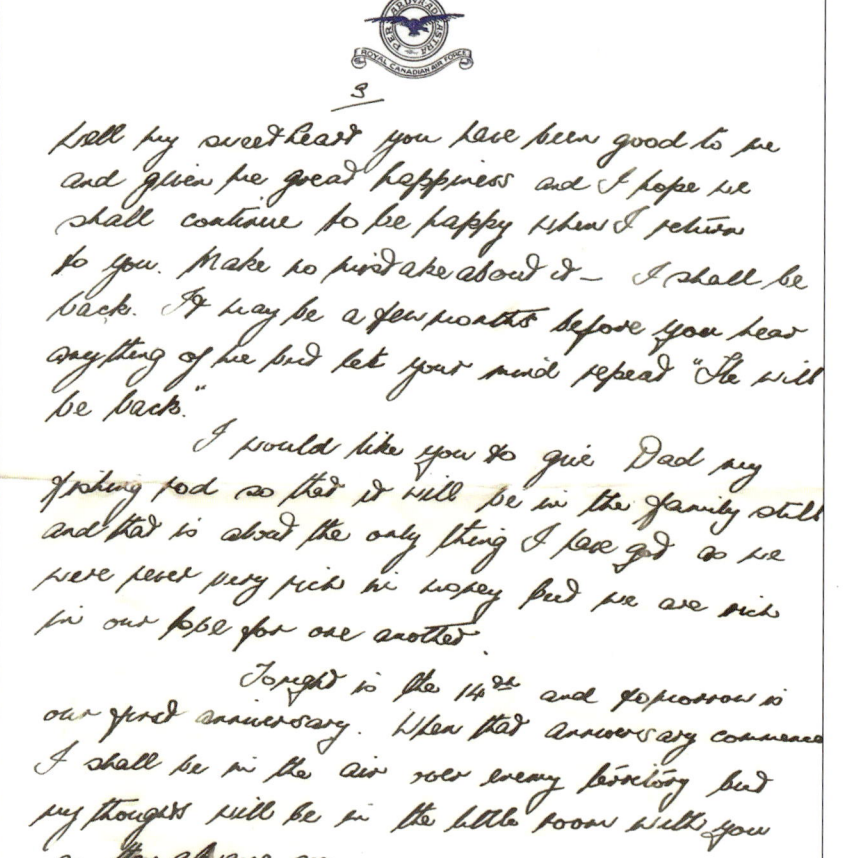

Well my sweetheart you have been good to me and given me great happiness and I hope we shall continue to be happy when I return to you. Make no mistake about it — I shall be back. It may be a few months before you hear anything of me but let your mind repeat "He will be back."

I would like you to give Dad my fishing rod so that it will be in the family still and that is about the only thing I have got as we were never very rich in money but we are rich in our love for one another.

Tonight is the 14th and tomorrow is our first anniversary. When that anniversary commences I shall be in the air over enemy territory but my thoughts will be in the little room with you as they always are.

4

Give my regards to all the family and write to Mrs Boyce often. Her son is far away and it will be a long time before he is free again. Do not despair and everytime you feel downhearted have a look at this letter and remember that they can't kill an Adlam and I shall be back soon to tell you that I love You and have always loved you.

I take a photograph of you with me so if I do come down I shall have your face with me always.

Good Luck Anne, God Bless You and take care of you while I am away.

Until we meet, Kid Seems keep{ing} and remember that I shall come back.

All my Love.
Your ever Loving Husband.
Ad

Alles sal reg kom.
Dit sal te reg kom.

An RAF Briefing Room before an operation.

The 'blood wagons' which took airmen out to their aircraft before an operation.

Map of the route of 405 Squadron on the St Nazaire raid.

St Nazaire after the raid. The raid was not successful despite the large amount of damage.

Pathfinders drop target indicators for bomb aimers to aim their bombloads.

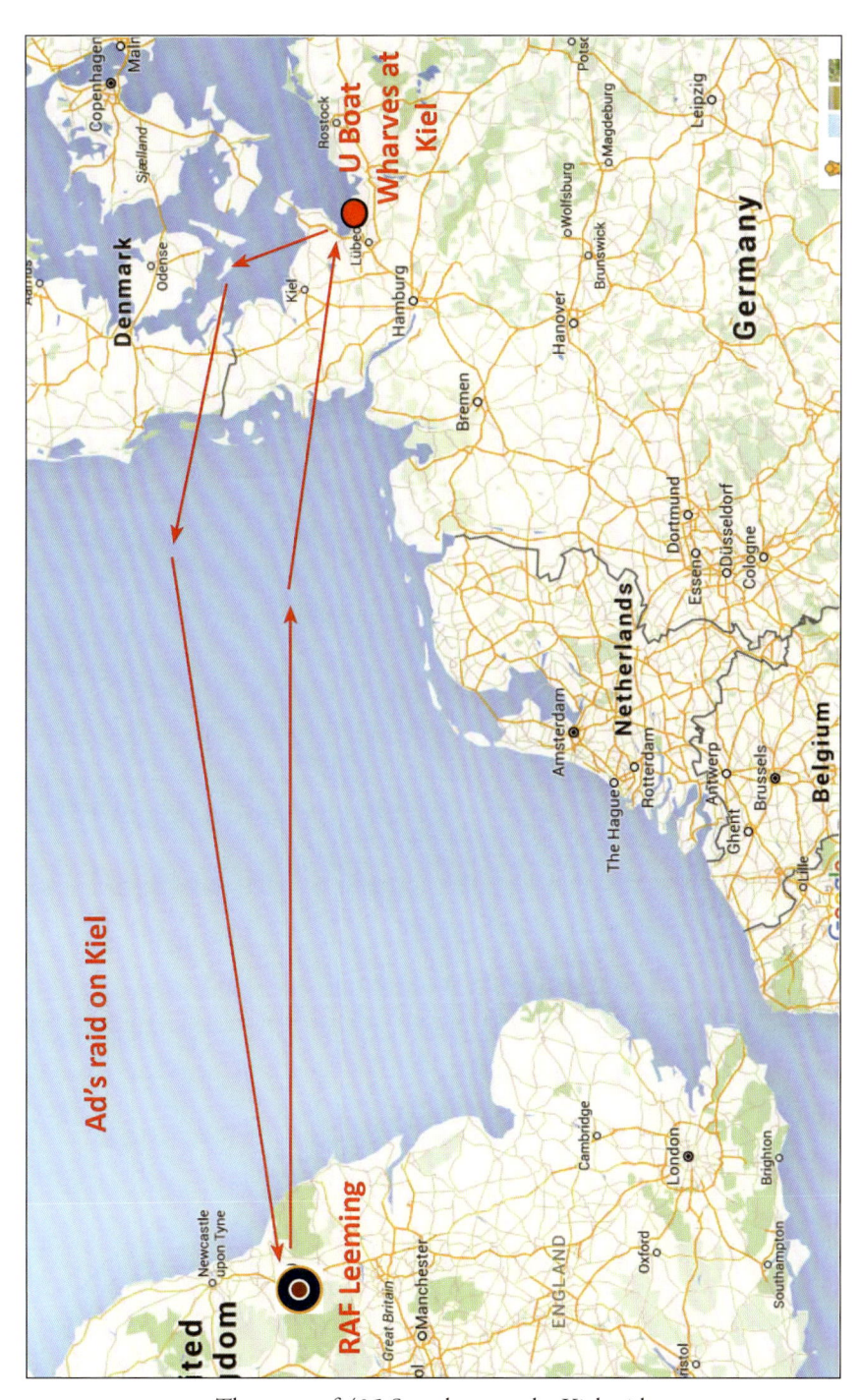

The route of 405 Squadron on the Kiel raid.

The route of 405 Squadron on the Stuttgart raid.

The route of 405 Squadron on the Duisburg raid.

The final raid to Dortmund showing where the aircraft was shot down.

No 405 Squadron
Gransden Lodge
Cambridge
Cambridgeshire

6th May 1943

Dear Mrs Adlam,

I regret to inform you that your husband is at present missing.

The squadron carried out bombing operations yesterday. The aircraft in which your husband was flying has not returned.

No confirmation of events has been received neither has any news come to hand as to any survivors being picked up, although there is always the possibility that such information may be forthcoming.

If any definite news comes through, I will immediately inform you and in the meantime please accept my sincere sympathy and also that of the whole Squadron in your present anxiety.

Yours sincerely

Wing Commander J. Fauquier

Officer Commanding 405 Squadron, RAF

The formal letter from Wing Commander Fauquier to Miranda which tells her the worst (Adlam Family Collection).

GOVERNMENT ABSOLUTE PRIORITY

Charges to pay NEWBROOK

POST OFFICE

OFFICE STAMP

BF/T ADLAM 14 4/5 1943 A A 405 +

37

OOT OOT 237 11.28 BF/T OHMS 47

IMMEDITE PRIORITY MRS M A ADLAM 14 NEWBROOK STEEET GLOUCESTER

= REGRET TO INFORM THAT YOUR HUSBAND SGT A A ADLAM IS MISSING AS A RESULT OF AIR OPERATIONS 4/5 MAY 1943 STOP ANY FURTHER NEWS WILL BE COMMUNICATED TO YOU IMMEDIATELY STOP LETTER FOLLOWS = OC 405 SQUADRON + +

Charges to pay RECEIVED

POST OFFICE TELEGRAM

OFFICE STAMP

TS 36

236 B 3.18 LONDON TELEX 65 =

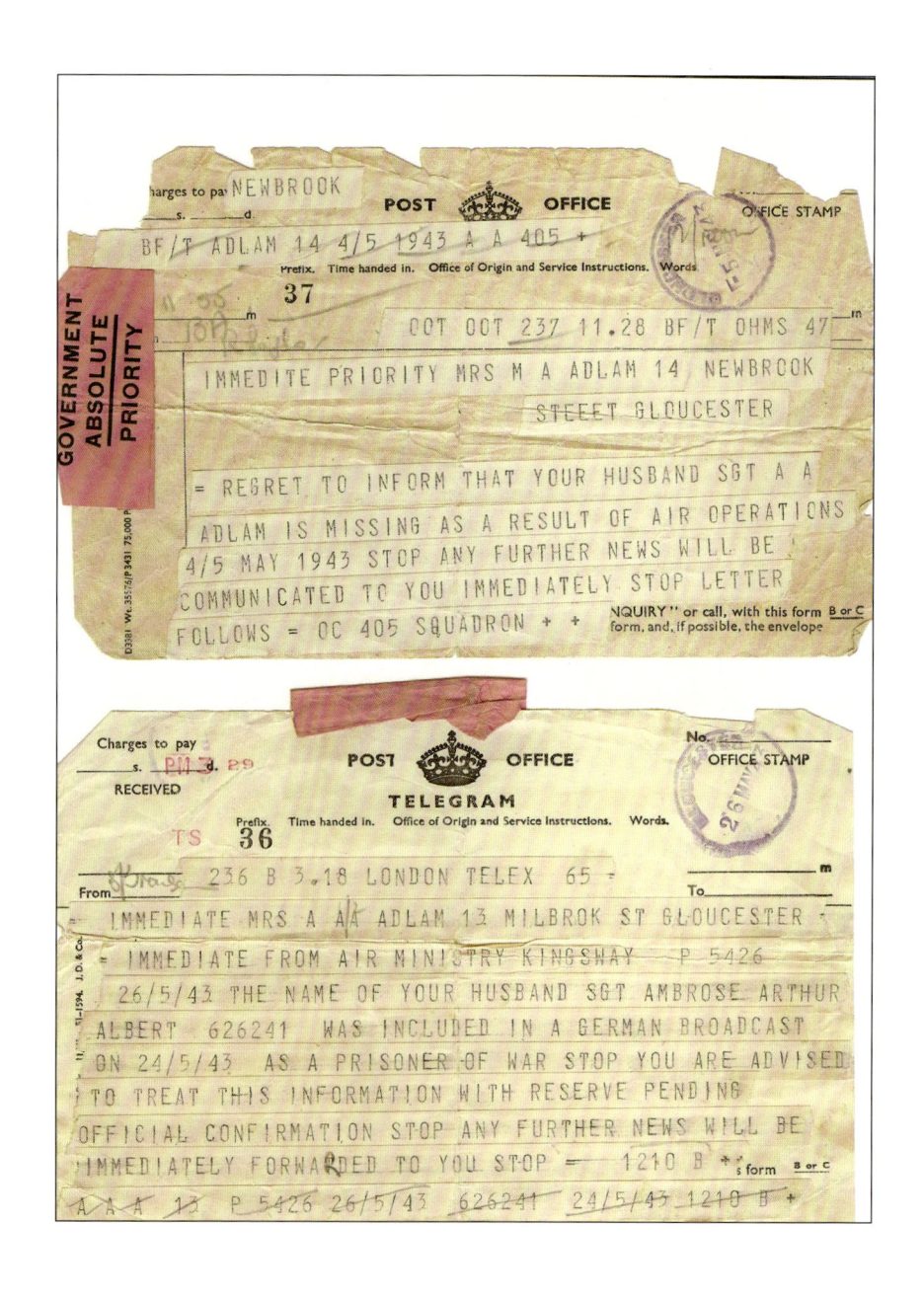

IMMEDIATE MRS A A ADLAM 13 MILBROK ST GLOUCESTER = IMMEDIATE FROM AIR MINISTRY KINGSWAY P 5426 26/5/43 THE NAME OF YOUR HUSBAND SGT AMBROSE ARTHUR ALBERT 626241 WAS INCLUDED IN A GERMAN BROADCAST ON 24/5/43 AS A PRISONER OF WAR STOP YOU ARE ADVISED TO TREAT THIS INFORMATION WITH RESERVE PENDING OFFICIAL CONFIRMATION STOP ANY FURTHER NEWS WILL BE IMMEDIATELY FORWARDED TO YOU STOP = 1210 B +
AAA 13 P 5426 26/5/43 626241 24/5/43 1210 B +

The follow-up telegrams from the Air Ministry. We can only imagine Miranda's emotional response (Adlam Family Collection).

MRS A A A 13 PC 564 ONE 23/6/43 1708 B ONE

RECEIVED PM 7 54

GOVERNMENT ABSOLUTE PRIORITY

m 28

GLOUCESTER 23 JUN 1943

From 328 7.19 LONDON TELEX OHMS PRIORITY 49

IMMEDIATE MRS A A A ADLAM 13 MILLBROOK ST GLOUCESTER = IMMEDIATE FROM AIR MINISTRY KINGSWAY PC 564 23/6/43 INFORMATION RECEIVED THROUGH THE INTERNATIONAL RED CROSS COMMITTEE CONFIRMS THAT YOUR HUSBAND SGT AMBROSE ARTHUR ALBERT ADLAM IS A PRISONER OF WAR UNWOUNDED IN GERMAN HANDS LETTER CONFIRMING THIS TELEGRAM FOLLOWS = 1708 B +

No. 405 Squadron, RCAF,
Gransden Lodge, Beds.,
11th of May 1943.

File: 405S/408/76/P.

Mrs. M.A. Adlam,
13 Millbrook Street,
Gloucester.

Dear Mrs. Adlam:

Before you receive this letter you will have [been noti-]fied that your husband, Sergeant A.A. Adlam, is mis[sing] after an operational flight.

On the night of 4/5th May 1943, your husband, a[nd] his crew and other members of this Squadron, were eng[aged in] action over enemy territory. Unfortunately his aircr[aft did] not return from this operation. It is the sincere w[ish of] all of us here that he is safe.

We lost one of our very best crews when this a[ircraft] did not return. Your husband was an excellent Fligh[t Engineer] and his thorough knowledge of the job he was doing i[n the] air was instrumental in making all the attacks he to[ok part] in, successful ones.

He was very popular in the Sergeants' Mess and is regretted by all.

There is always the possibility that he may be [a prison-]er of war, in which case you will either hear from h[im] or through the Air Ministry, who will receive advice [from] the International Red Cross.

Your husband's effects have been gathered toge[ther and] forwarded to the Royal Air Force Central Depository [where they] will be held until better news is received, or in any [case] for a period of at least six months before being forw[arded] to you.

May I say in closing how very sorry I am to have [to] write this letter to you and how much we are all hoping [that] he is safe. If there is anything further I can do for y[ou] at any time, please do not hesitate to write.

Sincerely yours,

J.E. Fauquier

(J.E. Fauquier) Wing Commander,
Commanding, No. 405 Squadron, R.C.A.F.

The formal letter from Wing Commander Fauquier to Miranda which tells her the worst (Adlam Family Collection).

The rather attractive entry to Dulag Luft where Ad was interrogated by the Luftwaffe; also where they saved his leg.

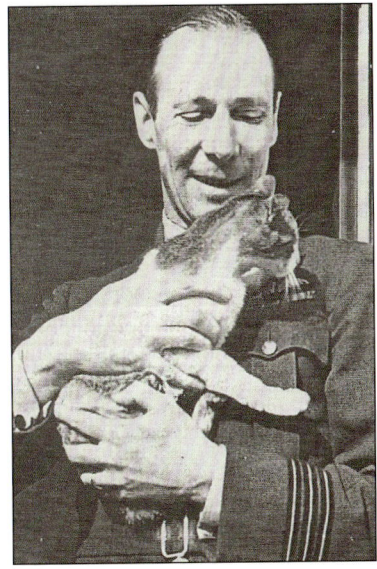

Left: Squadron Leader Roger Bushell who organised the Great Escape. Taken at Stalag Luft III. His physical condition is evident.

Right: Squadron Leader Harry Day, the de facto Senior British Officer in the North Compound where the Great Escape took place. The photo was taken for the Luftwaffe's 'Der Adler' magazine and opened Day to charges of treason when he returned to the UK.

Taken at Stalag Luft 1. On the right is John Casson who later was transferred to Stalag Luft III. In the centre is Lt Commander Jimmy Buckley who attempted to escape in a canoe but was not seen again (Casson Family Collection).

The entrance to tunnel 'Harry'. The mysteriously disappearing Klim cans are quite clearly visible.

The interior of tunnel 'Harry' showing one of the trolleys used to remove subsoil.

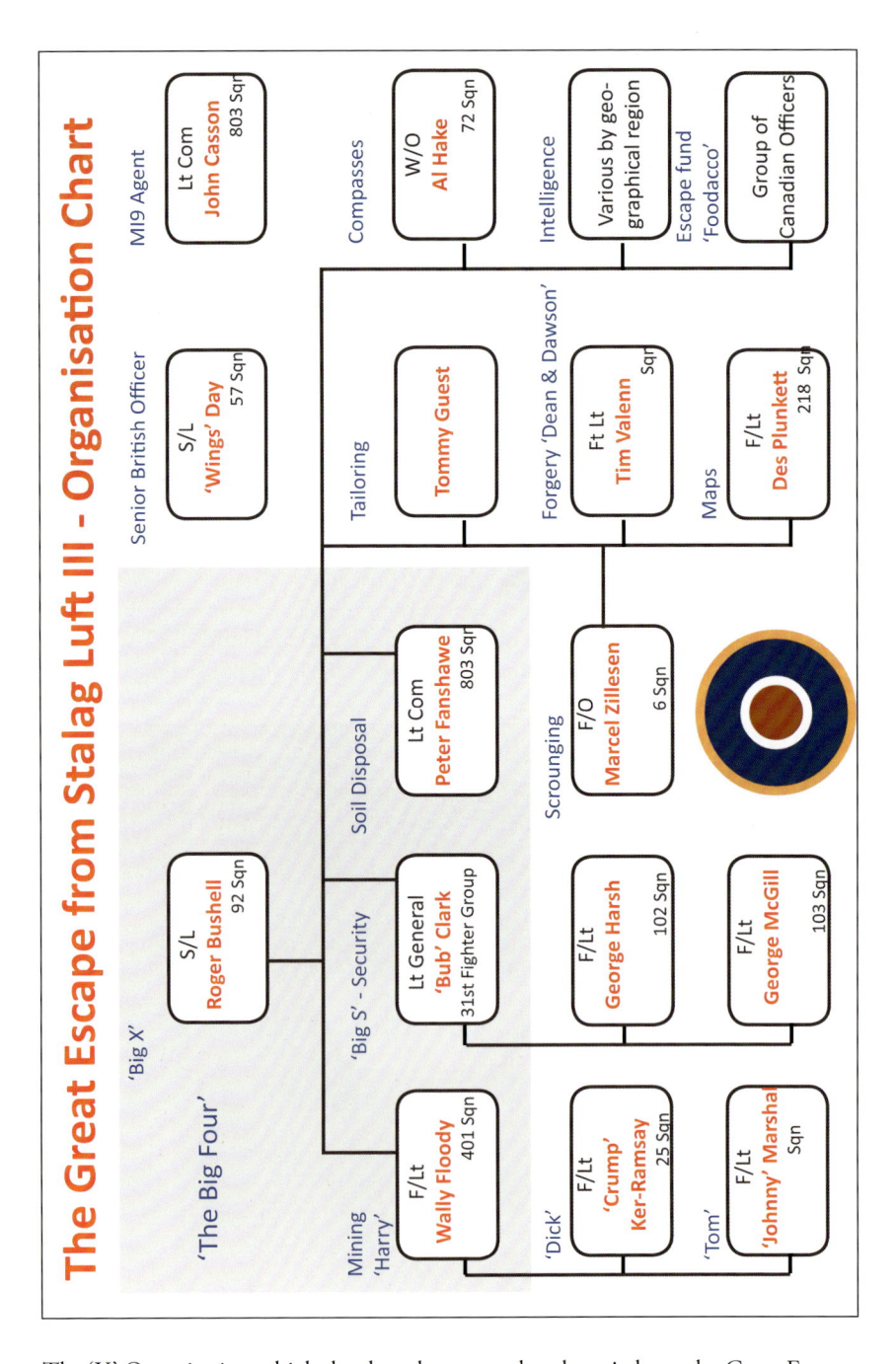

The Great Escape from Stalag Luft III – Organisation Chart

MI9 Agent
Lt Com **John Casson** 803 Sqn

Senior British Officer
S/L **'Wings' Day** 57 Sqn

Compasses
W/O **Al Hake** 72 Sqn

Tailoring
Tommy Guest

Intelligence
Various by geographical region

Forgery 'Dean & Dawson'
F/Lt **Tim Valenn** Sqn

Escape fund 'Foodacco'
Group of Canadian Officers

Maps
F/Lt **Des Plunkett** 218 Sqn

'The Big Four'

'Big X'
S/L **Roger Bushell** 92 Sqn

Soil Disposal
Lt Com **Peter Fanshawe** 803 Sqn

Scrounging
F/O **Marcel Zillesen** 6 Sqn

'Big S' – Security
Lt General **'Bub' Clark** 31st Fighter Group

F/Lt **George Harsh** 102 Sqn

F/Lt **George McGill** 103 Sqn

Mining 'Harry'
F/Lt **Wally Floody** 401 Sqn

'Dick'
F/Lt **'Crump' Ker-Ramsay** 25 Sqn

'Tom'
F/Lt **'Johnny' Marshall** Sqn

The 'X' Organisation which developed, managed and carried out the Great Escape.

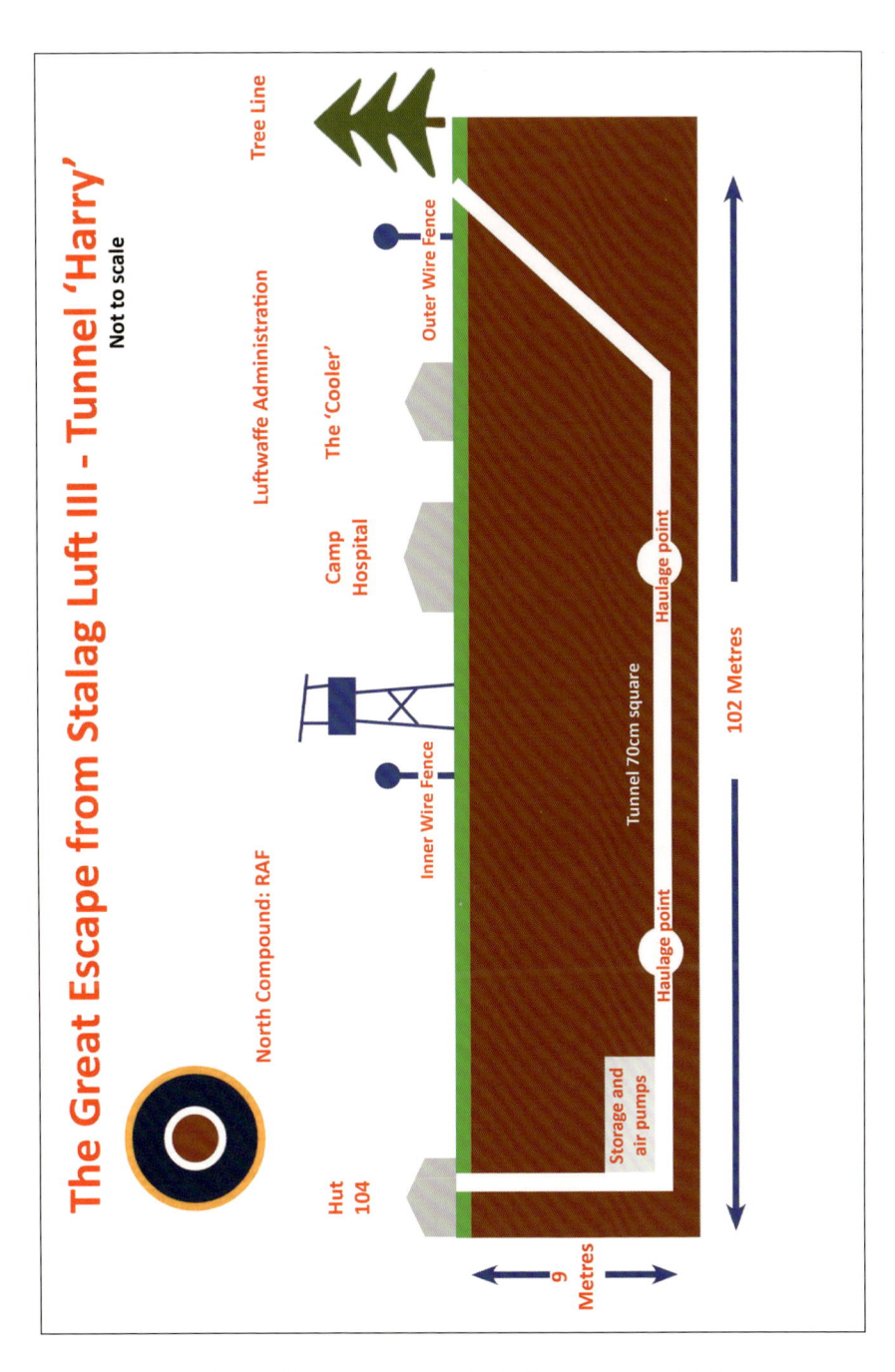

The Great Escape from Stalag Luft III - Tunnel 'Harry'
Not to scale

- Tree Line
- Outer Wire Fence
- Luftwaffe Administration
- The 'Cooler'
- Camp Hospital
- Inner Wire Fence
- North Compound: RAF
- Hut 104
- Haulage point
- Tunnel 70cm square
- Haulage point
- Storage and air pumps
- 102 Metres
- 9 Metres

Schematic of tunnel 'Harry' showing the brilliant concept. Unfortunately the 'free' side was just a few metres the wrong side of the tree line.

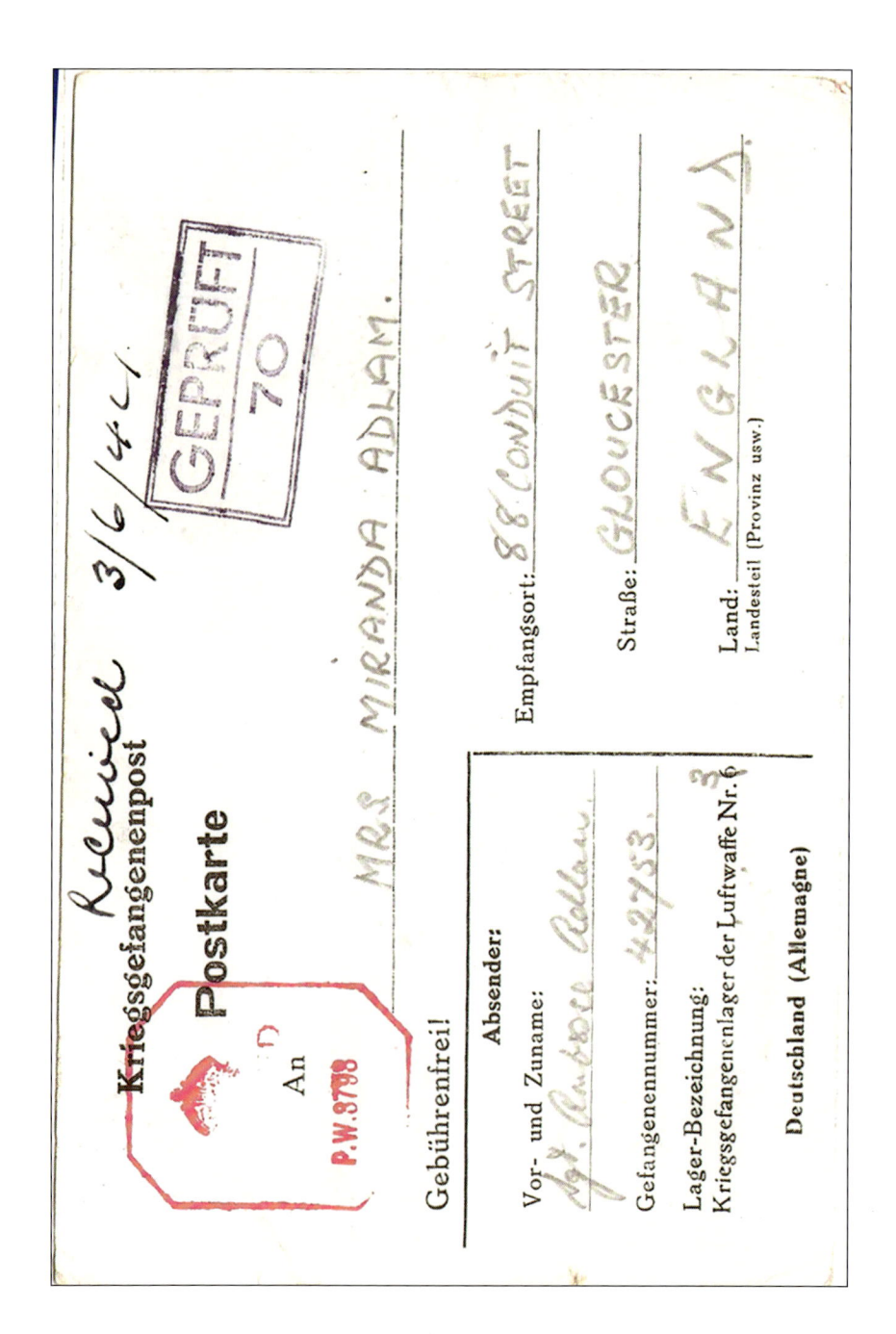

Ad's letter to Miranda, which he wrote on the day that the Great Escape took place and when the Luftwaffe guards had just found the tunnel (Adlam Family Collection).

Kriegsgefangenenlager

Datum 23 - 3 - 44

My Own Dearlife, Received a letter from you today Gladys you are well sweetheart not anytime soon you have moved dear, Hope you like your new lodgings Glad you are cycling around and keeping fit. No photo yet sweetheart Dad forgot to send it I know Extra Keep smiling dear and keep on loving me as I love you dearly ever Thinkof you always Keep on the Aurie dear, soon sweet will be together for always All my love Lid XXX for You, Yr. Ever Loving Husband, Ad

Refugees escaping from the barbarities of the Russian army.

John Lennox's war grave at Reichswald Forest War Cemetery near Kleve (Adlam Family Collection).

J16481 (DPC)

OTTAWA, Canada, March 24th, 1949.

Mr. W.J. Lennox,
300 Wellington St., W.,
Chatham, Ontario.

Dear Mr. Lennox:

It is with regret that I refer to the loss of your son, Pilot Officer John Watt Lennox, who lost his life on air operations against the enemy May 5th, 1943, and who was reported to be buried in the cemetery at Lingen, Germany, but a report has been received from our Missing Research and Enquiry Service that your son has been moved to the permanent British Military Cemetery in the Reichswald Forest British Military Cemetery, Germany. The cemetery is known as the Reichswald Forest British Cemetery, and is located three miles southwest of Cleve, Germany, or twelve miles southeast of Nijmegen, Holland. Your son is resting in Grave No. 14, Row F, Plot No. 15.

Moving the grave of your son to a British Military Cemetery is in accordance with the agreed policy of the Nations of the British Commonwealth that all British aircrew buried in Germany would be moved to British Military Cemeteries located in Germany, where the graves and cemetery will be reverently cared for and maintained in perpetuity by the Imperial War Graves Commission (of which Canada is a member). The cemetery will be beautified by landscaping and the planting of trees, shrubs and flowers, and the Commission will also erect a permanent headstone at your son's resting place and will write to you before the stone is prepared.

It is my earnest hope that you will be comforted with the knowledge that your son's resting place is known, and that it will be permanently maintained, and I would like to take this opportunity of expressing to you and the members of your family my deepest sympathy in the loss of your gallant son.

Yours sincerely,

(W.R. Gunn) Wing Commander,
R.C.A.F. Casualties Officer,
for Chief of the Air Staff.

WRG:LC

The letter to Lennox's family from the RCAF Casualties Officer.

CHAPTER 18
DULAG LUFT – THE UNSUBTLE OPPRESSORS

12 MAY 1943

Emptiness! Blackness! Loneliness! After the initial flurry of visits the follow-up was… nothing.

The orderly came in each day to dress his wounds and to bring him something to eat. The man could not – or would not – speak English. The food portions were diminishing. He was beginning to feel constant hunger.

The first thing was to keep his mind active.

He ran through the events since he had been shot down. What did he think of the Luftwaffe? They were well organised, professional, and he had felt surprisingly at home in the milieu of the Luftwaffe station at Rheine; it had been very similar to Gransden Lodge, except for the uniforms and that the one was a bomber station and other a fighter station.

What had he noticed of Germany? The industrial towns were not unlike Gloucester, but the houses were rather more charming, with steeply pitched roofs reminiscent of Disney cartoon houses. Like England, there were people in military uniforms but of different colours. He also saw people doing the 'Heil Hitler' salute.

BOMBS AND BARBED WIRE

The German countryside was lovely and Rheinland truly wonderful.

Yes, keep your mind active, man, keep it active. Those marks on the wall. He stared at them. He was starting to see patterns on the wall. The patterns turned into faces. Good God! Was that Miranda's face he could see there?

What of Frankfurt station? If the people there could have got their hands on him they would have lynched him, lying on a stretcher or no stretcher. Oberursel was a very pleasant town. Here he had seen many other airmen who had been shot down. Most were still in shock and not saying anything. Where were the other shot-down airmen now? Were they in solitary confinement as he was?

Keep your mind active! Think of Miranda. Think of making barrels in the oil mill, what was the procedure? Think of Miranda.

He thought of his surprise at seeing a garage outside the station. It had a Coca Cola sign. That was a major surprise. Outside the station was a drinking fountain. A local old lady took exception to British airmen drinking out of it and began to hit them with her umbrella, much to the general merriment, until the guards respectfully shooed her away. But again, the guards were not the Nazi stormtroopers that he might have expected, they were firm but polite with her.

His own transport to Hohemark had been by truck because of his wounds, but the others went by tram under a light guard. That was peculiar in the extreme. Somehow being shot down in the lair of the Nazi beast did not raise expectations of a tram ride.

Oh God! If only he could talk to someone. The light was dimmer now. Somewhere else in the Hohemark he could hear a prayer meeting and some hymns. He listened intently to the hymns. They sounded like the same ones that he had sung in school. Did the Jerries sing the same boring old hymns but in German?

Then he thought of the entry to Dulag Luft. There had been the sign above the gate which had made him laugh. Beneath the official military sign was another sign, presumably put up by a former inmate: 'I told you it wasn't a Spitfire'. All the brand-new prisoners of war had seen it and laughed out loud; it had been a wonderful tonic to men about to enter realms of despair.

CHAPTER 18

The main Dulag Luft building was like a large prosperous farmhouse. The outside shutters were painted with red and white diagonal stripes, which made them look very military and rather festive; not at all like a place where nameless tortures would be visited on allied aircrews. The Luftwaffe officers and guards who had met them at the station had the air of slightly bored but efficient school teachers shepherding their charges on an excursion to Cologne – or Gloucester – Cathedral.

Yes! Keep on thinking!

He thought of what his brother Bill had done: he had won a Military Medal on the Maginot Line; he had been through hell at Dunkirk; he had volunteered for Commandos; and had been on a raid in northern Norway. This had been featured on newsreels throughout the UK. He had been on the Dieppe Raid and hinted to the family that it was not the triumph that the newspapers had claimed.

And so his thoughts meandered on. He went through all the streets in Gloucester in his mind and all of the people who he worked with at the Gloucester Oil Mills; he went through one thing after another after another to keep his mind active. Having been through the streets he went through the streets again. He went through his first date with Miranda. He went through his wedding day in South Africa and the journey back to Blighty and then back through the streets of Gloucester.

He thought of the Crown and Cushion pub in Great Gransden where he and his mates had had such spirited evenings. He thought of Johnny. Johnny was dead now. He thought of the cross-country flight tests and how they had navigated back by the one significant landmark in that flat part of the world: the Gransden windmill.

Come on, man! Keep on thinking.

His brother John was in the navy. Yes, what was it like on a naval ship? Cramped, claustrophobic, everything 'shipshape and Bristol fashion'. Whatever did that mean? What was it like on a ship in the middle of a huge gale? How could you do your job if you were seasick?

Despite Ad feeling abandoned and forgotten, this was not so. It was part of the softening-up process. After three days, or perhaps four, he was happy to talk to anyone about anything. He was not only happy to talk, he was dying to talk. He was coming to the point where he would talk to anyone about anything. That was entirely what his captors had in mind. The easy familiarity of Eberhardtand Bauer-Schlichtergroll was about to give way to different methods.

Ambrose Adlam heard the key in the door. It was too early for the orderly's late afternoon round.

'My name is Major Junge. This is Mr Bräder. We wish to ask you some questions.'

The game had changed. These men were not going to have a pleasant chat. Junge was short, very short for an airman, but with the pointed sallow face more of a policeman who was used to dealing with the unpleasant side of life. Bräder had the pinched face of the vocational policeman who positively thrived on the unpleasant side of life. Given more time, Ad might have wondered who this lugubrious civilian was but was not accorded the chance.

Junge stood beside his bed, coming just a little too close to his comfort zone.

'Red Cross form!'

'Here you are.'

'This is unacceptable! UNACCEPTABLE! You were told to fill it in properly.'

'I was told to give name, rank and number by my wing commander.'

'Perhaps Wing Commander Fauquier is a fool, then. This is what is required by the International Red Cross, who are the protecting body for prisoners of war.'

'Well, that is what he told us, and he is my commanding officer.'

Bräder remained impassive.

'You are probably wondering how we know about Fauquier. How do we know about 405 Squadron of the Royal Canadian Air Force and how do we know about Pathfinders? You are wondering how we know about Gransden Lodge and how we know that your crews drink in the Crown and Cushion and that we know all about the windmill. That has been on your mind hasn't it? You won't see the windmill again.'

'Not especially.' But he did find himself wanting to enter a

CHAPTER 18

conversation with these men. After three (four? five?) days of solitary confinement the urge to speak to someone and have them speak to him was so overpowering.

'So how do you know about the Crown and Cushion then?'

'The same way that we know about so many things, Sergeant Adlam. Now, another thing we know is that your Pathfinder squadrons are all re-equipping with Mosquitoes, aren't they? Come on, we know already.'

'I haven't got the foggiest, we just use…'

Ah! The trap was being set.

'Halifax IIs, Sergeant Adlam. Halifax IIs is what you were going to say.'

'Like I said, we were told to just give name, rank and number.'

'Oh, come on, old man, just tell us, we know anyway. All of the Pathfinder squadrons are re-equipping with Mosquitoes, aren't they? When will the re-equipment be complete?'

'Go and ask them in the Crown and Cushion, you know so much about us.'

'Das ist eine Frechheit!' shouted Bräder. That is impertinence! 'You are addressing a Luftwaffe officer and have not once called him "sir"! Is this the professionalism of the Royal Air Force murderers?'

The mood was becoming more threatening.

'When will 8 Group finish their re-equipment? Sergeant Adlam?'

'How the hell do I know?'

'I think you mean "how the hell do I know, sir". But I think that you do know because you go on cross-country flights, don't you?'

'Yes, sir.'

'You go on flight tests, don't you?'

'Yes, sir.'

'And you land at other 8 Group airfields, don't you?'

'Sometimes, sir.'

'And when you land there you see Mosquitoes, don't you?'

'My name is Adlam, Ambrose A, Sergeant, number 626421.'

'Sergeant Adlam, it is better not to play these games with us. Your Red Cross form has not gone forward; no-one knows where you are. You can choose to tell us one or two things which we know already. We can arrange to have your rations increased. We can give you the food parcel, which is determined for you. We can arrange to let you meet other prisoners, possibly even members of your own crew. I think they are still here down in the main camp.'

Bräder slammed a metal disc on the table. It read 'Geheime Staatspolizei': the Gestapo. Ad's blood ran cold.

'Or, Sergeant Adlam, you can choose a different fate: a more difficult one.'

Bräder looked into his eyes. This man was clearly someone who would browbeat, torture, murder, maim or do anything whatsoever to achieve his aims. His demeanour was that he enjoyed his work.

'You can be here for a very long time, Sergeant Adlam. Or, if you wish, we can transfer you to a different camp. The concentration camp at Buchenwald is only an hour or so by rail from here.'

'You can't send me to one of those; I am a British airman in uniform, captured in action.'

'I am afraid that is not necessarily the case,' said Bräder with a slight smile. 'According to your file you were hiding in the woods until a Luftwaffe patrol located you and then you ran and were shot. Does that sound like a Royal Air Force man to you, Major Junge?'

'To me it sounds like a spy. I must congratulate you, though, Sergeant Adlam; your RAF uniform is perfect and threw us right off the scent. You have told us nothing about 8 Group and the re-equipping with Mosquitoes because you do not know. You are a spy and we will make arrangements for you to be transferred to Buchenwald. I am afraid the comforts are somewhat less than you have enjoyed here but then you can reflect that you brought it on yourself.'

'I am a British airman and I was shot down on a raid.'

'Really, raid to where?'

'We never got there; we were shot down before we reached the target.'

'And the target was?'

"My name is Adlam, Ambrose A, Sergeant, number 626241.'

The interrogation proceeded. Junge, the small man, was now like a malignant rat gnawing at a bone. He was dispassionate and merciless.

CHAPTER 18

As Junge would attack him from one direction with questions about Mosquitoes, Bräder started asking questions about lights from the ground to show the way.

'Our nightfighters have seen them, Sergeant Adlam.'

Ad had seen the lights as well: Dutch farmers flashing 'dot dot dot dash': the Morse 'V' for victory. He could not endanger them.

'No, I haven't seen anything like that.'

The policeman in Bräder asserted itself.

'Sergeant Adlam, before I joined the Geheime Staatspolizei, I was in the civil police. We know when people are lying to us and you are lying. You have seen those lights.'

'No, for Christ's sake, how many times?'

Now he began to feel fear. They were not letting him go. What would get them to stop asking these questions and get them out of the room? Could he give them some small amount of information which might satisfy them?

'Come on, Sergeant Adlam, we know that lights from the ground show you the way to your targets in Germany.'

'That is utter bollocks. There are no lights on the ground that show us the way, you are just dead wrong.'

'So, then, why are your raids suddenly so much more accurate? Last year you could barely find a city of half a million people, now you can locate a specific factory, why is that?'

'I don't know, I wasn't flying then; ask someone who was.'

Without warning Junge smashed him across the face with the flat of his hand, making his head ring.

Junge's face now was close to his. 'Do not give smart, clever answers, Sergeant Adlam; you are not in any position to do so. Not in any position at all. What navigational equipment do you use?'

'Don't ask me, ask a bloody navigator.'

Junge moved to slap him again.

'Come on, Sergeant Adlam, what do you use? Gee? Oboe? H2S? What else are you being equipped with now.'

Bräder came back again. 'The lights on the ground, Sergeant Adlam, who organises them? Who is flashing the lights? Is there a coded signal that they send up?'

'There are no bloody messages from the ground.'

'Then you are using new navigational aids.'

'No, I don't know. Look, I'm not a navigator.'

'The new Mosquitoes, Sergeant Adlam, when does 405 Squadron re-equip with Mosquitoes?'

'I've no idea. I'm a sergeant, they're not going to tell me that.'

'But you have been to other airfields and seen Mosquitoes with your own eyes.'

'I'm not telling you anything but my name, rank and number.'

Junge stood up, opened the door and called the orderly.

'Herr Gefreiter, we are going to let this prisoner consider his position. When he knocks on the door, you are to inform me immediately and I will come to visit again, do you understand?'

'*Ja, Herr Leutnant.*'

'Oh, and cut his rations by 50 per cent.'

'You bastard!'

'You brought it on yourself, Sergeant Adlam, by your intransigence. Anyway, do you imagine that it would hurt me to be called a bastard by a man who volunteered to murder women and children? Herr Gefreiter, is everything clear?'

'*Jawohl, Herr Leutnant.*'

'Dismissed.'

'So, Sergeant Adlam, we will leave you with a very simple choice. Just tell us a couple of very simple things and you will find your rations restored; you will receive your food parcel and you can meet some of the other prisoners. There is also the small matter of the letter to your wife, is there not?'

'I'm not telling you anything, so you can just bugger off.'

'We will see, Sergeant Adlam, we will see. Now, Herr Bräder how long would it take to organise this man's transfer to Buchenwald?'

'Two or three days at the most. Personally, I think we should just send him there. He wastes our time with his childish answers. As far as I am concerned he can enjoy his time in different surroundings.'

CHAPTER 18

The door closed. Ad heard the key turn. The final 'click' resounded around the room.

Again, there was silence, black and oppressive, in the room.

Buchenwald? Concentration camps? The bastards had the upper hand: he still had possession of the Red Cross form so all Miranda knew was that he was missing. By now the RAF would have advised that it was unlikely that he would be coming back. The key thing was that she did not know if he was alive or dead. It had been – how long? – a week now?

He wouldn't give them anything. But to be sent to a concentration camp, what did it mean? There had been reports in the press before the war of Dachau and possibly this one – Buchenwald – which they had mentioned. The fear chilled him. Chilled him in the oppressive endless silence that competed with the hunger in his stomach.

He did not think now of the Gloucester Oil Mills or the first date with Miranda. He thought of what it was like to enter one of those places of horror and never be heard of again. Maybe there was some small thing, some small innocuous morsel of information which he could give them and buy them off. Oh, no! These were professionals, especially that Bräder. If he ever once gave them a morsel of information, they would have well-tried techniques to get more out of him. Then again, what did he have that could be of use to them? It could easily be something whose importance he did not know but which, to them, would be the purest gold. It was best to say nothing and ride out the storm if he could.

He was alone in his world. He was totally alone in a pitiless, darkening room with the prospect of never seeing Miranda or Gloucester or his brothers or even the outside world again.

He did not sleep that night.

The days now developed into a carousel of threat, browbeating and humiliation.

In the morning his breakfast had been reduced by half. He tried to think of Gloucester, films he had seen, railway engine names or anything to keep his mind active. It did not work. He could only think of the tunnel of horror which would lead him to Buchenwald.

What did he know of the place? Nothing, in fact. There again, Bräder was in the Gestapo, so whatever was there represented a universe of pain and agony in some form. Mid-morning, the orderly would dress his wound, but when he tried to speak to the man there was still no response.

The worst part was in the afternoon when the shadows lengthened a little and the light mellowed. Then he would hear the key in the lock; he would hear the final 'click' as it opened and Junge and Bräder would be standing there.

'So, Sergeant Adlam, you have had time to see sense. Now, what have you got for us?'

'Just this, matey. You can bugger off!'

'Now, now, that is not suitable language for an English gentleman, is it?'

Then the browbeating would start. He was a murderer of women and children. They would show him photographs of hideously burned bodies. They would remind him that his transfer to Buchenwald was progressing. 'After all, we only have your word that you are an airman. We think you are a spy.'

'Well, I can't be dropping bombs on innocent women and children and be a spy on the ground.'

'You are quite right in that, Sergeant Adlam.' Bräder laughed a confidential laugh. Normally, that tone would be one between friends. Then came the sting: 'But who is going to listen to your cry from the heart? Your cry of righteous justice? Apart from ourselves, no-one knows that you are here or even if you are alive or dead.'

'Just leave me alone.'

'Of course we will leave you alone.'

Then came the demand for information. What Mosquito deployments have you seen? What new navigational methods have you seen? What do the lights on the ground mean? Do you follow them? Who sets them up?

The sessions would go on and on and on.

CHAPTER 18

They would leave abruptly usually with a casual remark about the progress for 'the transfer'.

Sometimes there would be a throw-away remark.

'Laß den Kerl mal weiter kochen.' What did it mean? Then they would disappear. He would have to learn German as quickly as possible.

Then he would try to think of Gloucester again. He could not concentrate. As it got dark he noticed that every night a light aircraft would take off. It was noticeable because it was so regular. It sounded like a British Auster spotter aircraft but obviously could not be.

Sometime later he heard the nightly singing of hymns to a wheezing old harmonium which sounded as if it might be consumptive.

Then came the darkness of the night and the terrifying prospect that he would not see Miranda again and, in a few days, would be in some Nazi concentration camp to face a hideous death.

Then the cycle would start again. The footsteps in the corridor, the turning of the key, the click.

With each succeeding day the threat of that click would bring him out in a cold sweat; an ever-increasing feeling of terrorised nausea settled in his stomach along with an ever-increasing Pavlovian response of helplessness, friendlessness and hopelessness.

CHAPTER 19
AMBROSE IN WONDERLAND

15 MAY 1943

There were footsteps in the corridor: a short, precise, military gait. His heart beat faster. His mouth dried. His stomach felt a deep nauseated sickness. The footsteps were coming his way. 'Go somewhere else! *Go somewhere else!*' The footsteps stopped outside his door. Were they coming to take him to a concentration camp? Was he to be given over to Bräder and his Gestapo thugs? Would he ever see Miranda again? Would he ever see England again? The key turned in the lock. His breath came in short gasps now. The lock gave that final defining 'click' and the door opened.

He suddenly wanted to visit the toilet, but it was too late… the door was opening. Would it be Junge? Would it be Bräder? Would it be Gestapo henchmen coming to take him away? The few seconds turned into hours as the door briskly opened.

To his utter surprise, a man with a short, well-trimmed beard and a shabby, threadbare, dark-blue uniform walked in. To his even greater surprise it appeared to be a British naval uniform, albeit dishevelled and definitely not 'shipshape or Bristol fashion'. He carried a file of papers and a parcel. His features were intelligent and sympathetic. They said 'solid middle-England' rather than 'Teutonic middle-Europe'.

'Hello, old chap, mind if I come in?'

'Who the hell are you?'

CHAPTER 19

'Lieutenant Commander John Casson at your service. I'm adjutant to the SBO: Squadron Leader Elliott.'

'What the hell is the SBO?'

'Senior British officer in Kriegie language.'

'And what the hell is a Kriegie?' Despite the continuing feeling of terror, dread and nausea this conversation was beginning to sound like an apocryphal addition to Alice in Wonderland.

'You're a Kriegie. It's short for Kriegsgefangener, which is the German word for prisoner of war. Now, you are...' he looked at the file, '... Sergeant Adlam, A. A. from 405 Squadron RCAF and shot down last week. I see you have a wound in the back of your neck which is not giving too much concern, and a bullet in the leg, which is rather nasty. Anyway, it is my pleasant task to deliver you your food parcel and also a letter form to allow you to write to your wife.'

The feelings of hunger would have to wait for a moment.

'So, Jerry must have files on the rest of the crew as well? Lennox, Knight, Graham, Roberts, Prieur and Moody?'

The naval officer looked into a file which he carried.

'Knight, Graham, Roberts and Prieur were all here but have all moved on. For whatever reason they seem to have gone to separate camps. There was no Lennox, I'm afraid, and no Moody.'

'Could they have gone to some other centre?'

'No, this is the only one. Look, old chap, I am terribly sorry and all that but I'm afraid you do have to assume the worst. They may have survived and be on the run but, in all honesty, not many do that and even fewer achieve it.'

'Yes, the first interrogator said as much. Thank you for informing me, anyway. Talking of the interrogators, what has happened? Have they lost interest in me?'

'You're rather in luck, as it happens. The Herrenvolk have just shot down their first American planes – B26 Martin Marauders – and they've got all hands to the pump in interrogating those crews. The Yanks sent 11 of them on a power station raid in Holland. Every single one of the buggers went for a Burton. Anyway, there's several dozen Yanks come in overnight and to the interrogators it's the greatest source of delight since sauerkraut was invented. It's all new material for them rather than going over old ground with Lancaster and Halifax crews, where they've heard it all before. Look, don't stand on ceremony, please open your food parcel. I expect they've had you on reduced rations have they?'

Ad wolfed into the easiest and most accessible item: a bar of chocolate. Common sense told him that he had to be wary of this man. The Germans had tried the 'as one airman to another' technique. They had tried to wheedle information out of him. They had tried heavier stuff and threatened to send him to a concentration camp. It was completely within the bounds of possibility that this man was a turncoat and working on their side. He appeared affable, solicitous and dependable but Ad needed more before he trusted him.

Then something occurred which made Ad feel that this man was on his side and could be trusted. He held up a piece of paper. On the paper were written the words 'Careful what you say! MICROPHONE'.

Ad nodded silently.

'How long have you been here, sir?'

'Oh, dash it all, we don't stand on ceremony here. Call me John. I've been here almost three years. I flew off the Ark Royal in a Blackburn Skua. I don't suppose you Brylcreem Boys would have one of those kites?'

'Never heard of them,' replied Ad as he ripped open the packet of biscuits.

'Two-seater, carrier-born but far too bloody slow against the Messerschmitts. Anyway, our operation was to bomb the *Scharnhorst* in Trondheim. There were 109s and 110s all over the place. I think it was a 109 got me. They were about 80 miles per hour faster and armed with rather effective cannon. Down we came. We got out and landed in a Fjord. "We", by the way, means my navigator and myself.'

'Did the navigator survive?'

'Ah, old Fanshawe, I have no idea. I know the Norwegians fished him out of the drink but what happened after that, goodness knows. That's what happens. You come down, you get separated. You lose touch immediately and never see a chap again.'

CHAPTER 19

Ad was silent. He wondered if he would ever see his crew again. He would not, but surprisingly he would meet Fanshawe. World War II provided an endless unfathomable kaleidoscope of strange meetings and separations.

In the time-honoured RAF manner he pulled himself together. 'That's interesting about you crashing into the drink,' said Ad, smiling. 'I landed in a duck pond, when I came down to earth.'

'Well, there you are. But the navy was always more stylish than the air force! Anyway, a couple of the local Norwegian chaps were nearby and thought we looked somewhat bedraggled, so they hauled us out by means of a boathook. They took us home and warmed me up or I would have died of hypothermia. They had to give us up to the Boche, for which I do not blame them. The buggers were shooting Norwegians who hid British aircrews. I know that my navigator survived but don't even know if anyone else from the squadron got back to Blighty.

'Anyway, you have probably seen enough of these four walls. I've got a wheelchair outside; I wonder if you might fancy a spin around the Hohemark?'

'Nothing would please me better.'

'I'm afraid I can't run to a parachute so if we prang you're on your own.'

'I'll take the chance.'

Parallels with Alice in Wonderland grew by the second. Within five minutes, Ad had left the confines of that small room in which he had known a stomach-turning terror. He now found himself wheeled around by a solicitous British naval officer. The Hohemark clinic proved to be rather pleasant. It was a 19th century country mansion which had presumably belonged to the landed gentry. The gardens were enormous and were very well cared for. It reminded Ad of some of the stately mansions around Gloucester which he had passed by but only ever seen through the wrought iron bars of the main gate.

Most strangely, perhaps, British prisoners of war, all with bandages, crutches or slings, mingled freely and chatted with German civilians and women in the medieval garb of a religious order. Who was on whose side? Who was friendly with whom? Where were the boundaries? Were there boundaries at all? It was all becoming curiouser and curiouser.

'*Guten Morgen, Herr Leutnant,*' said a passing nun.

'*Guten Morgen, Schwester Heuer.*'

'She really is a sweetie,' said John Casson.

'You speak German?' Ad asked suspiciously.

'Only Kriegiedeutsch. After three years one does pick a bit up. Although, you'll find that everyone here speaks absolutely excellent English. Frankly, most of them are more fluent in English than people I've met from Glasgow or Newcastle.'

'Yes, I've noticed that.'

'The point is that this place is entirely dedicated to soaking whatever information they can squeeze out of shot-down airmen; no morsel is too small or too trivial. Now, that brings me on to one or two things I need to brief you on. Do you mind if I speak terribly freely?'

'No, you might as well.'

'Most people are very cautious when they come out of interrogation. What I normally do is to assure new boys that I will not ask any questions and they do not have to tell me anything that they feel unsure about.'

'About that microphone…'

'Yes, whatever you do, do not talk about anything sensitive inside the room. Every room in the clinic has a microphone. Now, if you find the microphone, do not disturb it or destroy it. As long as the Germans do not know we know it gives us an advantage.'

'Right, thanks.'

'Secondly, I want to congratulate you for not giving anything away to the interrogators. Dashed good show, if I might say so!'

'How the hell do you know what I gave away or didn't give away? Are you so well in with the Germans that they would tell you things

CHAPTER 19

like that?'

'No, despite the friendly surroundings, I can assure you there is still a war on. They are not going to tell me that. How I know is simple, old chap. You went through the routine of nice interrogator and increasingly nasty interrogator and we know you didn't give anything away because of the timing. If they had marked you as someone from whom they could get information, they would have grilled you for another week or even longer, I can tell you.'

'Do they really send people to concentration camps?'

'Some RAF personnel have disappeared, and we think that the SS got them. They are mainly pilots of Lysanders caught dropping agents off in Holland and that kind of thing. I can't think of any normal bomber crews that were handed over to the SS or the Gestapo.'

'They really are bloody clever the Jerries; they had me terrified out of my wits and this whole process of dragging information out, it's just bloody typical of the Nazis isn't it? I mean there is no sense of decency about them at all, it's just "win at all costs".'

Casson laughed uncontrollably and Ad felt his wheelchair wobble in its tracks.

Ad's decades-old and ingrained mistrust of people with those sorts of accents sparked into life.

'Right, just take me back please, I'm not going to be laughed at like that.'

'Before I take you back, then, can I just ask you one question? Where do you think the Germans got the idea for interrogating airmen like this?'

'Because they're bloody criminal scum and any sort of malpractice – is that what you call it – comes very naturally to them.'

'Well, I have to tell you that everything that happens here is entirely based on the British model.'

'What? You mean we have one of these places?'

'We certainly do! We invented this method of interrogation. It's as British as cod and chips and it operates on exactly the same lines, almost to the last detail.'

'Where is our interrogation centre? I've never heard of such a thing.'

'I've no idea. There's a war on and its location would be classified as most secret but how they found out about it is a dramatic story in its own right.'

Ad was intrigued.

'One of their airmen, Oberleutnant von Werra, was shot down during the Battle of Britain. He went through the centre, wherever it is. Then he was sent to Canada and escaped from a train. He got over the border into America, which was not in the war yet and had himself repatriated to Germany. When he got back, he got a personal interview with Goering. Being a baron, he got easy access to the highest places. Anyway, he told Goering about the British interrogation methods. As a result, this place was set up. Von Werra's a very nice chap actually.'

'You met him?'

'Yes, he came here several times and I had lunch with him, the SBO and the previous Kommandant, Major Rumpel.'

'Hang on, you had lunch with Luftwaffe blokes? Just whose side are you on?'

'I'm on the side of his Britannic Majesty. Well, I did rather risk my life for him. It's a damned ticklish business here. If we carry on like the Battle of Rourke's Drift, we are not going to win. There are more Germans here than there were Zulus there and we don't have any guns.

'As you settle in to Kriegie life you'll find how the relationship works with the Boche. At a personal level RAF chaps and Luftwaffe chaps get on more or less very well. They have a respect for us and we have a professional respect for them. It's rather like two rugger teams who biff the hell out of each other on the field and have a drink in the bar afterwards. There is something else as well. You will also find that getting on with the guards is a good thing because they can be bribed and that is very useful. However, we don't tell them anything that they shouldn't know.

'What's more, when you get on good terms with the guards, as you doubtlessly will, remember that line from *The Merchant of Venice*: 'and if you wrong us shall we not revenge?'. The Germans started this bloody war and I understand some British cities are looking unhealthy

CHAPTER 19

as a result.'

'London, Plymouth and Liverpool, and especially Coventry are looking bad but not as bad as Holland or Poland,' Ad replied.

'And shall we not revenge? Just remember that always.'

Ad nodded silently. One thing about this war, it brought him into contact with people who could casually quote Shakespeare. That did not happen in the barrel factory in Gloucester.

They turned the corner into a leafy garden, splendid with summer flowers.

'Let me tell you how far the relationship can go,' Casson continued breezily. 'Some months ago, when Major Rumpel was still here, he used to have some of us up to his house for dinner. We would have a chat with Rumpel and his wife. She's from the Dutch East Indies and is absolutely charming. Anyway, one time we were up there and he got so sloshed that he passed out. His wife had long since gone to bed and we were prisoners of war in the Kommandant's house with him unconscious. That put us in a difficult position.'

'You could have made a run for it!'

'In the middle of the night and in British uniforms? That does not sound like a dead cert winner to me. Anyway, we were on parole.'

'Bloody posh people and their stupid ideas,' thought Ad.

There was, however, something that John Casson did not share with Ad. It was a secret 'as deep as e'er plummet sounded' as he might have said himself. The truth about John Casson would not come out until some decades after the war was finished but Ad would find out later.

'Our task was to get back into the main camp without being found by a Luftwaffe patrol, who would certainly have thought we were escaping. Even worse, the SS run patrols from time to time and they would just have shot us.'

'So what did you do?'

'Well, we were fairly the worse for drink as well, so we just walked – and it was rather unsteadily, I would have to say – down the middle of the road where we were in full view. We passed a couple of Germans of other ranks in uniform; they saluted and we returned the salute. It was pretty bloody dark, and they didn't give us a second glance so we breezed up to the main gates.'

'What happened then?'

'There is a vital thing to understand about the Germans. They live in a world where order and authority and correctness are as beautiful as the *Mona Lisa*. If everything looks in *Ordnung* (you will need to learn that expression) then all is well in their Teutonic world.

'One of our fellows, who speaks German rather more convincingly than I do, walked up with full military authority and said, *"Gefangener auf Bewährung."* The guard opened the gate and let us in with a splendid military salute.'

'What does that mean?'

'Prisoners on parole.'

'What about escapes, John, has anyone tried it?'

'I have one or two other chaps to see, so I will tell you about that the next time I come. Now, old chap, must take you back as fast as possible, or I shall be in for a wigging.'

The orderly who had brought his food chanced to pass by at that moment.

'I say, Gefreiter Kohns, could you take Sergeant Adlam back to his hotel suite? Oberstleutnant Killinger wants to see me down at the main camp on some damn silly administrative thing.'

'Certainly, Herr Leutnant Kommandeur. I understand the interrogators have finished with him now.' Kohns took him back to the room.

'Bye, old chap, I'll come back and see how you are getting on. Doctor Ittershagen will pass you fit at some point and you will pass further into the Kriegie sausage machine. It's my job to make sure that if he passes you as fit then you really are fit. They were a bit keen to pass people on with open wounds in the early days, but we seem to have got them more under control these days.'

'Oh, you speak English then?' said Ad to Kohns.

'Now that you have finished interrogation I can speak it rather well. I taught in a school in Nottingham before the war. Incidentally, do you realise who the Leutnant Kommandeur is?'

'No, not at all. I didn't know many naval blokes in Blighty.

CHAPTER 19

'You've heard of Dame Sybil Thorndike?'

'Of course.'

'She is his mother.'

'What? Crikey! I've seen her in so many films. She was fabulous in *Hindle Wakes*. I saw her in *Major Barbara*, just a year or so ago.'

'Yes, I'm afraid we don't get to see that one in Germany.'

'I suppose you saw *Dawn* about Nurse Edith Cavell? It didn't make your countrymen look very good, did it? Killing nurses is not what I would call civilised behaviour, but perhaps you do.'

Silence.

Ad did note with amusement that Casson's fluency with Shakespearian quotes was now clear. Back in his room or ward or cell there was much to think about.

In the next days, Ad was to learn more about this strange institution. The first was a painful encounter with Casson.

He entered in his normal businesslike manner but was noticeably curt in his address.

'Are you OK, old chap?'

'Yes, I think so, as well as can be expected.'

'Wizard.'

He looked at Ad pointedly. 'Let me take you for a spin in your wheelchair, the garden is looking lovely!'

There was some other agenda going on, Casson was clearly removing him from the ambit of the hidden microphone.

'I understand you have been implying that the Germans are not civilised or some such thing? Well, I have to tell you, old man, that this sort of thing is simply not done.'

'What? It was your mother in the *Dawn* film wasn't it? They weren't bloody civilised with Edith Cavell.'

'That is neither here nor there and is of no possible significance here. Let me spell the situation out for you. Here, we are in the hands of the Luftwaffe and we have the International Red Cross as protecting power. Now, have you heard of a man called Heinrich Himmler?'

'Isn't he that creepy crawly SS bloke?'

'That is correct. Well, behind the scenes he is trying to get the prisoners of war into his sticky fingers. Do you have any idea what that means?' He was silent and looked searchingly at Ad. This was clearly not a casual question.

'Er, no, not really.'

'Well, what it means is that if the SS take us over they are capable of shooting us or starving us to death or using us as slave labour. They've starved about two million Russians to death. They won't be nice guys just because we're British.'

'Well, what has that got to do with me?'

'We don't want to insult the Jerries unnecessarily. As it happens, Kohns is an Anglophile and knows the score; that is why he came to me. He is worried that if you shoot your mouth off you are taking every British prisoner one step closer to the SS. It might just be one step, I grant you that, but it is one step too many. Remember what I told you about not fighting the Battle of Rourke's Drift?'

'OK, sorry if I spoke out of turn. This is just such a new world to me.'

'It is to all of us. We just have to be very careful. The last senior British officer, Wing Commander Day, got himself into terrible trouble through something totally innocent. The German Kommandant, Major Rumpel, gave him a cat. His photo with the cat got into the *Adler* magazine, which is the Luftwaffe newspaper. If and when he ever gets back to England, he is likely to be court-martialled for collaboration or even treason. We all have to be so bloody careful in everything we do and say. Don't worry, old man, you're not the first to put your foot in it and there have been worse cases but for God's sake be careful.'

Casson – in the privacy of the garden and away from the microphones – told him about escape attempts of which there had been several. One RAF officer had breached his parole when given a pass into the town. He had tried to escape but had been recaptured very quickly. The breach of parole was thought to be 'bad form' as much by the British as by the Luftwaffe personnel.

Sometime later, Flying Officer Foster had cut through the barbed wire at the Hohemark and got out. He had been caught immediately by the local police. Sometime later again, four officers had escaped, again from the Hohemark, all to be recaptured within hours. These piecemeal

CHAPTER 19

efforts clearly showed little merit and were hardly worth the effort.

An even worse attempt had been made by Bob Kee, a Hampden bomber pilot. He had secreted himself in the roof of the goat shed with the intention of slipping over the wire in the middle of the night. Casson had warned him that the Germans were perfectly aware of this ruse. Kee had insisted. He was instantly apprehended.

Also, at the main camp, a rather more determined attempt had been made. A Kriegie called Alex Gould, who had studied geology, had designed a tunnel. This had been taken up as a project by Roger Bushell, a South African barrister who was completely larger than life. The plot was elaborately worked out in detail with the provision of civilian clothes with Reichsmarks bribed from the guards. They were carefully husbanded together with forged German *Ausweise* or passes. 'London had supplied maps on rice paper,' Casson informed Ad.

'How on earth did London supply maps?' Don't ask! Ad was starting to learn the game.

He remembered that Logan and Jennings had spoken about having dealings with some shadowy organisation to do with their escape after being shot down. There were clearly things going on behind the scenes. This was more *Alice in Wonderland*. Ambrose Adlam may have felt profoundly uncomfortable in captivity, but he had to admit it was a world with a certain macabre fascination.

Eighteen men were to get out down the tunnel. Bushell was to hide in the goat shed and slip out after the alarm had gone off for the main escape. Almost all were captured within 20 miles of Dulag Luft but three, including Bushell, were to make it to the border with Switzerland before being recaptured. It was, however, not lost on the escapers that the local army, police and Luftwaffe had deployed 3000 men in a manhunt to apprehend the escapers. Ad was destined to meet Bushell some months later.

'There are some other things that I have to tell you about as well,' Casson had told Ad in one of the later visits to check on his progress. 'We have two men in this camp who you will trust at your peril. The first is called Michael Joyce. He is Irish, very much an IRA sympathiser and extremely anti-English.'

'Joyce? Is he any relation to William Joyce, Lord Haw-Haw?'

Lord Haw-Haw was a Nazi sympathiser who made daily broadcasts from Hamburg to the British public on behalf of Adolf Hitler. The level of loathing for Joyce outstripped that of Goering, Goebbels or Hitler himself.

'He's not a relative of that bugger as far as I know but it would have to be possible. Anyway, the other traitor to worry about is Benson Railton Metcalf Freeman. He is a devoted supporter of Sir Oswald Mosley and a former member of the British Union of Fascists.'

'Freeman? What? The bloke from the clothing store?'

'That's him, have you met him?'

'Yes, my trousers were in tatters after the excitement of getting shot down and he brought me some revolting, smelly Polish uniform trousers.'

Casson looked at him intently.

'Sergeant Adlam, would you tell me please how the conversation with him went?'

'Well, he seemed like quite a nice chap. He apologised because the trousers were not very clean but said I could clean them myself when I was mobile.'

'Anything about the Royal Air Force?'

'Oh bugger! I told him I was from 405 Squadron at Gransden Lodge and that we were a Pathfinder outfit. I also told him we were heading for Dortmund when we were shot down. Oh bugger! It never occurred to me that an RAF bloke would be working for the Jerries. Christ almighty, have I given away too much?'

'Don't worry, old man, the Germans knew all of that before you even got here. What else did he ask you about?'

'Well, he said that he was shot down after Dunkirk I think it was. I think he said he was in Wellingtons and that they didn't have any of our navigational aids. He tried to talk to me about the Goon Boxes, you know, Gee, Oboe and H2S and that sort of thing.'

'What did you say?'

'I said I'm a flight engineer and didn't know much about that sort of

CHAPTER 19

thing. I said there are lots of navigators who used those things every day.'

'I'm sure that's not lost on him. The Jerries are mad keen to know about those things. What else?'

'Well, he started talking about how nice England was and what a threat the communists had been. He talked about the General Strike and the threat that the communists posed to the country.'

'Now look, old chap, this next bit is really important: what did you say back to him?'

'I just said that I didn't know much about communists but we used to see Moseley's fascist scum giving out leaflets outside Woolworths in Gloucester. I said that I don't remember anybody accepting one of their leaflets, but I do remember that a lot of people told them where they could stick them.'

'Right, well, Freeman is one of the fascist chappies in no uncertain terms. His tack is to see if someone shares his ideas. Then he tells the Luftwaffe people and they work to turn him over to their side. You gave good answers; they would not have had much hope of turning you after that pithy but clear exposition of your views.'

'Bloody hell, though, if a bloke is a British fascist what is he doing dropping bombs on his Nazi mates?'

'I don't think Freeman actually dropped bombs on them. From memory he was caught on the ground when the Germans overran the British. One thing we do know, though, is that the bugger wrote to William Joyce in Germany…'

'What? Bloody Lord Haw Haw?'

'The very same. Freeman offered his services to Haw-Haw in the fight against Bolshevism. It is interesting how information gets around. He was talking to the old Kommandant, Rumpel, and the Kommandant let it slip when he had had a few too many. I actually don't think Rumpel likes traitors any more than our people do. We had also noticed that Freeman was getting rather a lot of privileges from the Germans, extra rations and that sort of thing.'

'Hang on, you went drinking with the Kommandant, you said. So how were his privileges different from yours?'

'There is friendliness and friendliness and you need to find out very quickly, old chap, where the line is. You need to decide which side of that line you are on. I might also mention that Squadron Leader Elliott had Freeman's room searched and found a Luftwaffe communication which commended Freeman for his anti-Bolshevik attitudes and friendliness towards Germany. Anyway, as adjutant it is my duty to ensure that all of our chaps know about this bloody bad egg.'

'Christ! If I ever met him I would want to punch the bastard's lights out.'

'No, you won't, Adlam, and that is an order. It is a formal order, do you understand? As long as Freeman does not know that the airmen passing through here are on to him we have a means to neutralise his poison. If you or anyone else tip him off it will help the other side. Do you understand this order?'

'I understand, sir… John.'

'I have another reason for the visit today. The Kommandant has made arrangements for you to be transferred to the POW hospital at Bad Sulza. There is a waiting list to get in there and quite honestly, I would not be in a hurry. We don't have a date for your transfer yet, but forewarned is forearmed. It is not likely to be as nice as the Hohemark.'

John Casson withdrew and Ad was left alone with his food parcel, bars of Cadbury's chocolate and, wonderfully, a form to let him send a letter to Miranda together with a pencil.

The first letter from Ad to Miranda is dated 12 May 1943.

Kriegsgefangenenlager   Date 12. 5. 43

From 626241 Sgt Adlam
To Mrs M. A. Adlam
Gloucester
13 Millbrook St
England

My own dear wife. I hope you receive this OK, dear, and that you are well. I am fine and am hobbling around. I shall be perfectly well

CHAPTER 19

within weeks. Can't give you an address but chin up! It won't be for long. I am well looked after and the odd scratches are all healed. I love you and wait for me. Regards from your loving husband Ad.

As Ad gradually became stronger he was able to move around the Hohemark on crutches and make contact with other prisoners. He noticed their reticence to talk freely on any operational matter. It was clear that they had been through the same ordeal as himself.

They talked of life in Blighty, how they missed the pubs, their girlfriends and the excitement of life on an RAF operational station. There were always rumours. There were benign rumours of repatriation. There were disquieting rumours that the SS wanted to take over all of the prisoner of war camps. There were rumours that the quietness on the Eastern Front meant that the Germans and the Russians were discussing an armistice. There were rumours that the RAF and Americans were bombing the hell out of Germany. There were rumours that the Germans had organised for the detestable Benson Freeman to have female company brought in as a special privilege. That was the rumour that raised the most bile, unsubstantiated though it might be.

About the raids, they had all heard many, many bomber fleets rumbling overhead on their way to bomb Frankfurt, Munich, Stuttgart and Nuremberg. Indeed, the Kommandant had had the words 'POW' spelt out in large letters on the roof of one of the buildings.

'Always useful to keep the RAF away during a night raid,' one wag had ventured.

Ad was beginning to make sense of the Alice in Wonderland world. He had learned that there was an overt layer of reality where the Kriegies worked together with the Germans: tending gardens, distributing uniforms or bribing for the odd favour. Then there was a covert layer of reality which concerned information that was related to hostilities: the secret source of BBC broadcasts; how you learned to trust – or mistrust – a fellow prisoner; and, especially, the cat and mouse game with the established traitors, Freeman and Joyce.

There were other rumours. There were stories of blazing rows between Casson and Freeman. No-one knew what the rows were about, but the rumours told of extreme unpleasantness.

A couple of days later Ad heard a knock at the door.

'Come in.'

It was John Casson with the transfer order to move Ad to the hospital for POWs at Bad Sulza near Weimar.

'Let me take you outside on your wheelchair.'

'Look, I don't really need it, I'm on crutches now.'

Something was wrong. The movement outside beyond the range of the hidden microphone was more urgent than usual.

'Listen, Adlam, something really bad has happened. All of us have to brace ourselves for something the Germans are cooking up.'

'What the hell is going on?'

'The Kommandant has gone away for a few days. The underlings have started roasting prisoners in cells in the main camp. They put them into tiny rooms then turn up the heaters so that the metal beds are too hot to touch. They close all the ventilation ports so that men have had to lie on the floor and suck air from underneath the door. They also refuse to give men water and refuse them medical treatment.'

'Christ, when did they start doing this?'

'A couple of days ago. They have done six blokes already and they are in such a bad way that they will be coming up to the clinic later on today. Please let all the other men know and tell them that "forewarned is forearmed". Squadron Leader Elliott has sent a letter of complaint to the protecting power but that could take weeks to get there and we don't know if it will be successful anyway.'

So, things were turning nasty. Would he be able to hold out if they tried it with him? How long could he stand the heat treatment? He was learning now how information could be elicited. He might not have anything important himself, but he might have a semi-important morsel that could be put together with someone else's semi-important morsel.

CHAPTER 19

If they came for him there was only one thing to do. It was the 'name, rank and number' game. That was all he could do.

Suddenly there was a new adjutant. John Casson had been transferred without warning to a new camp at Sagan, which was known as Stalag Luft III. Whether he had asked to be removed because of the increasingly bitter rows with Freeman or whether the Kommandant had had him moved for other reasons remained unclear.

The Kommandant had, however, returned from an absence and stopped the heat torture immediately.

In the face of all of this storm, stress and aggravation there was only one thing to do: write to Miranda and try to enter a world where things were better.

Kriegsgefangenenlager   Date 16. 5. 43

From 626241 Sgt Adlam

To Mrs M. A. Adlam

Gloucester

13 Millbrook St

England

My own dear wife,

Here I am, dear, writing from the hospital where I am, and I hope that you are well and cheered up a lot now that you know I am OK. I am nearly better and am trying to get up and stay up. Well, dear, five of us got out of our machine and it's a good job my parachute worked. Believe it or not I landed in water and got soaked. However, that is all over now and we must both wait patiently for the end of all this. It won't be long. My pay will be saved for me and we will have a nest egg for my return. I hope the other allowance is through and you can manage. If not, write to RAF accounts and they may let you have some of my pay.

BOMBS AND BARBED WIRE

I'm afraid you won't be able to write until I get to a prison camp but cheer up Anne, dear.

Look after my fishing rod, won't you? Tell Mum and Dad I am OK. Remember that I love you and always will and you are everything that I have to come back to. Don't worry about me, I wasn't hurt much and will be walking around soon. Am being well looked after and have bacca to smoke. Would love to clean my teeth, they are very dirty.

All my love, keep smiling, will write soon.

Your loving husband

Ad xxxxx

The next day the word went around from whoever it was that was running the secret radio. The RAF had bombed three dams in the Ruhr Valley and put two of them out of action. The men from Bomber Command could not understand how this was possible. The biggest imaginable bomb was a 4000-pound (2200 kilogram) cookie, which would bring tears to the eyes of anyone underneath it but would never bring a dam down.

'But the BBC never lies,' someone is bound to have said.

'They lied about the Dieppe Raid,' Ad is bound to have thought. If so, he was now smart enough not to voice this opinion.

Ad awaited his transport to Bad Sulza, near Weimar. Ad had to laugh. Weimar had been the seat of German government in the 1920s. It had been the failure of the Weimar Republic which had seen Hitler come to power. On 22 May, after two weeks at the Hohemark clinic, Ad was moved to Bad Sulza.

Casson had been right. The hospital at Bad Sulza was not good. It was a converted youth hostel which had been built for the Hitler Youth. The place was unsanitary and overrun by enormous rats that fed royally, courtesy of the plentiful supply of corpses. Nevertheless, the medical staff did what they could for the enemy forces. The place had about 800 inmates crowded into narrow barrack huts. The majority were British forces who had been severely injured at Dunkirk three years previously.

CHAPTER 19

He looked for the rest of the crew there. It was in vain. He knew it was impossible that Johnny Lennox and Bernard Moody had survived. There was no way of knowing. He could only hope. Of the others who had been sighted at Dulag Luft there was no sign either.

Ad was there for – how long? He was losing count of days and weeks. Nevertheless, his wounds, especially the severe one in his leg, had healed. On 11 July orders came through to move to Spangenberg camp near Kassel. It was squalid, overcrowded and foul. Would he really be stuck here for years? It was a sinister prospect.

After some ten weeks came an order that he was to go somewhere to the east. The next day he entered a railway freight van with 30 or 40 others.

Ad was now less in agony from his recuperating wounds but more in agony that Miranda might not know of his fate. He did not know when, or even if, his letters would be delivered at all. In far-off Gloucester something had happened, which was quite odd. Actually, it was very odd.

One morning Miranda heard a letter drop onto the linoleum behind the front door in the tiny terraced house in Millbrook Steet, Gloucester.

'Letter!' announced her landlady. Could it be from him? Miranda felt a sharp pang of disappointment. It was not on any official stationery. It was postmarked Grimsby in Lincolnshire; she didn't even know where that was. The letter was addressed personally to Miranda but in an unknown hand. What she read astonished her.

May 24th 1943   *Mrs Markham*
24 Ayscough Street
West Marsh

BOMBS AND BARBED WIRE

Grimsby

Dear Madam,

Just a few lines hoping you are not offended at me writing to you. I am a mother with three sons and a son-in-law serving in the forces. I write down prisoners of war names when I listen to the wireless. I thought I would like to let you know that either your son or husband is a prisoner of war. I do hope this war will soon be over and the loved ones return home safe and well. Although there will be a lot of sad hearts. I write to several people and it is impossible to write to everyone and had some nice letters back. I write down prisoner of war names in a book so if there is anyone who is missing or you have not heard from I will be only too pleased to let anyone know if I have their names down. I don't always get the right name and address as the German man does not always give them out right as I have had several letters returned. I do hope this finds you alright. Although you might have heard by the time you get this letter. I hope so. Your husband or son's number was given as 626241 today at 2.30 o'clock. Well, I think I will soon close so I will say good afternoon.

From a friend

Mrs Markham

The 'German man' was William Joyce – the infamous 'Lord Haw Haw'. He was a traitor who had left England at the start of the war and was making propaganda broadcasts for the Germans. Each day he would read out a long list of shot-down airmen. This guaranteed a huge radio audience. When he made his daily calls, which began with his own peculiar intonation – 'Jarmany calling, Jarmany calling' – his listenership outnumbered those of the BBC.

Most people in wartime Britain would happily have pulled the lever to hang Lord Haw Haw but, after his capture, this delight was reserved for the official hangman.

CHAPTER 20

WELCOME TO STALAG LUFT III!

1 OCTOBER 1943

'Oy! Wake up!'

Oh, no! He was still in the same dark, dismal railway truck with straw on the floor and a foul-smelling latrine bucket in the corner. The 'puff – puff – puff' of the locomotive was clearly slowing. Brakes screamed. Buffers clattered as couplings slackened.

'Have we got to Blackpool yet?'

'Well, we've certainly arrived somewhere. The train of railway trucks clanked to a halt. The steam locomotive hissed and relaxed and was now, in RAF terms, standing at ease. They looked over the top of the crude wooden boards on the side and through the barbed wire which had been crudely nailed to discourage escape.

In the goods yard two dozen guards, two with barking German Shepherd dogs, were standing nonchalantly, rifles over their shoulders, waiting for the cattle truck doors to open.

'What colour are those uniforms?' A bearded Kriegie behind him asked the question with some urgency.

'Sort of bluey-grey, looks like the Luftwaffe to me.'

'Thank Christ for that!'

'What do you mean?'

'Well, if they were grey-green they would be SS. That means that they're not going to shoot us or at least not yet.'

BOMBS AND BARBED WIRE

Jumping down from the train was painful. God, that wound in his leg still bloody hurt and it was nearly five months since he had been shot.

After a brief roll call, the Luftwaffe detail marched them out of the goods yard towards a dense pine forest. Over his shoulder he could see a small and rather sad, dejected-looking town. It was an industrial place that resembled some of the scruffier Welsh mining towns which were not too far from his native Gloucester. A guard said, 'Welcome to Sagan'. They were somewhere to the far east of Germany.

Some older civilians passed them by: a man and two women. Ad noted that you never saw younger civilians in Germany. Presumably they were too busy being shot on the eastern front for Adolf's greater glory. He waited for the inevitable.

'*Mörder! Verbrecher! Kindermörder!*' They shook their fists, hate in their eyes, sparkling spittle spuming from lips drawn back in canine spleen.

'*Genug! Haut mal ab!*' the nearest guard snarled at them.

He was actually starting to understand a little German now. In essence, the guard had said, 'Enough, bugger off.'

'I am glad to see that our efforts are not entirely in vain.'

The man beside him smiled.

'*Schweige!*' shouted the guard. '*Halt's Maul!*' Shut up! They complied more out of exhaustion and hunger than from any great respect for the master race. They trudged on in silence along a rough track which took them deeper into the pine forest. After 20 minutes the column of dejected RAF men came across a clearing. It was not just any clearing: it was big. As Ad saw more and more of it he realised that it was huge. In fact, it was vast! It was the largest POW camp that any of them had ever seen. It could have accommodated several football pitches. There were guard towers – 'goon boxes' – every hundred yards. There were high barbed wire fences. There were searchlights.

A guard creaked opened a large gate, which led them into the first compound. This had several buildings, one of which flew a Red Cross flag and was presumably a hospital. He was to learn that this was the Vorlager or outer compound. He did not see any Kriegies hanging

CHAPTER 20

around in this area, only some Luftwaffe men plus some civilians, possibly men from the local town.

The guard opened a second gate which took him into the vast compound. This contained two dozen or so wooden huts, each laid out in a pattern with commendable Teutonic efficiency and accuracy. It was all very definitely 'in Ordnung'. As far as he could tell, looking through the high barbed wire fences, there were several other such compounds. Each compound had a large parade ground or 'Appelplatz' as he would come to know it. There were additional buildings; one was large and looked like a theatre. In the middle of the Appelplatz there were football goalposts. There was the smell of fresh wood. Every hut was brand new. Apparently, this entire compound had just been built and he was among the first prisoners sent to enjoy its delights.

In this compound there were several dozen Kriegies who looked with a blend of mild interest and boredom at the column of 'new boys' as they filed in. Many of the Kriegies had beards. Many had shaved heads. Some had RAF uniforms; some had uniforms from some other air forces. What on earth were those uniforms? Polish? Czech? Ruritanian? Some wore civilian trousers, jackets or pullovers. The most ominous factor, however, was that some looked as though they had been there for years and had the apathetic look of men who had lost any aspiration of seeing the outside world again. Ad made a mental note that that was not going to happen to him.

He began to search faces. Lennox? Was it possible that he had survived? Was he there? What about Knight, Graham or Roberts? How about? His first job was to find them. Just to find that they had survived would be a major morale boost for him. There had been a hint at Dulag Luft that Knight, Graham, Prieur and Roberts had been alive but none at all at the intermediary camps at Bad Sulza or Spangenberg. Of Lennox and Moody there had been no sign at all. There could be no question about it; they were dead.

There were so many RAF men in German hands that finding them was a 'needle and haystack' proposition. His surviving crew mates could be at Barth or Lamsdorf or Heydekrug or dozens of other places where the Germans held prisoners. In a back-handed way that was good; it gave an illusion of hope that they may still be alive.

'*Achtung! Stillstanden!*' shouted the Feldwebel.

The column shuffled to a decidedly unmilitary halt and came to a grudging and desultory 'attention'. They were outside of the large building. The Feldwebel saluted smartly to a British officer whose rank badges betokened that he was a squadron leader and the German escort party dismissed.

'OK, chaps!' said the squadron leader. 'Into the theatre if you would be so kind. Just leave any personal effects or bags outside.' He added drily, 'No-one is going to steal them.'

This brought a laugh from those still alive enough to laugh. The train journey had taken a couple of days; they had had no food and water had been in short supply.

The inside of the theatre reminded Ad of a somewhat primitive version of the briefing room at Gransden Lodge. There was no map of Europe but there were the serried ranks of assorted airmen plus that same sense of tense expectation. The similarity was taken further when the senior British officer (SBO for short) walked down the central aisle with a small retinue of two squadron leaders. Every airman stood up without thinking. One of the squadron leaders was very striking: tall, rather theatrical looking, somewhat charismatic and very sure of himself. He had the kind of self-confidence that was either bred in over generations or the result of a more recently acquired personality disorder. Either way, Ad would never forget his first sight of Roger Bushell. He had heard that name before, but where?

'Call the men to order if you would, Squadron Leader.'

'Parade… Parade, attention! Parade… stand easy!'

They clattered into the 'easy' position.

'I know that bloke over there,' Ad said to himself. 'I would not be surprised if it was that bloke from Dulag Luft, the adjutant, Casson.' He had disappeared suddenly after reported rows with Freeman, the Mosleyite. Ad was sure it was him. Then the man was gone.

'Parade… parade, be seated.'

CHAPTER 20

They sat down. The squadron leader saluted the group captain.

'Well, chaps, welcome, if that is the word, to Stalag Luft III. My name is Group Captain Massey. I am the senior British officer; the other senior officers here are Squadron Leader Jennens, who is my adjutant; Squadron Leaders Day and Bushell. Now, I know that you have all had a rotten journey from wherever you have come from, so I will be brief.

'This place is Sagan, which is just inside Germany on the eastern side. We are 100 miles south-east of Berlin; a similar distance north of Prague and about twice that far from the Baltic Sea at Stettin. Poland, or what used to be Poland, starts a few miles to the east. We are a very long way away from anywhere. This compound is the North Compound and has kindly been built by the Germans as luxury accommodation for us.'

After his brief but intensely unpleasant sojourns at Bad Sulza and Spangenberg, Ad did not even respond to the implied irony of that statement. This accommodation was not bad.

'Now, there are just three points of issue with which I need to acquaint you. Firstly, you are still very much in the Royal Air Force or any other force to which you owe allegiance.'

Ad wondered if this applied to the Ruritanians he had seen outside. Presumably it did. Were they under RAF command as well?

Massey proceeded. 'That means that you are under military discipline and everything that that entails. It also means that you extend to the Luftwaffe officers the same respect as you would to an RAF officer. What I mean is all of the courtesies such as saluting and standing up when they enter the room. You address them as "Herr Hauptmann" or "Herr Major" or whatever. You'll soon get the hang of the names if you haven't already.

'Secondly, I have to draw your attention to the somewhat prep-school practice of 'goon baiting'. It's not done, chaps! We have had some fellows sent to the cooler for indulging in it, great fun though it may be. More urgently, the Germans have the whip hand over us in one vital aspect of our existence. They take delivery of the Red Cross parcels. Without them we should be quite badly off.'

BOMBS AND BARBED WIRE

Ad thought of the men that he had seen as they walked through the camp. They all looked half-starved and many looked positively ill. Could it get much worse?

'There is also a fundamental difference between us and our German captors.'

This brought a muffled giggle around the hall.

'Settle down, there's good chaps!' hissed Jennens.

'We do not want to be here, but the German guards very much want to be here.' He paused for effect. 'As you will know, the Germans have suffered massive defeats at Stalingrad, Kursk. The bombing war on the Ruhr and Hamburg has caused mass devastation.'

This brought a cheer from the ranks.

The adjutant, Jennens stood up from his seat. 'Gentlemen, the SBO has not finished, please pay attention, it is very important.'

'Italy has changed sides; North Africa is lost to them; British and American forces have forged through Sicily and up to Naples. The Russians are killing Germans by the tens of thousands.' Again, he paused for effect. This time there was silence, but the body language bore witness that this last feature was a very good thing indeed.

'Therefore, it follows that the guards, goons or whatever you want to call them, are very happy here. They don't get much more to eat than we do; in fact, with the Red Cross parcels we probably eat better than they do. They are, however, happy that they have not got some crazy bloody Russian running them over in a tank. 'Incidentally, that is what happens to German service personnel who mess up in any way. They are sent eastwards and I understand that few ever return.

'You can be polite to the guards but remember: there is a war on. They will have been briefed to pick up any information they can. This is especially so for anyone who has flown on a high-profile raid such as the dams raid or anyone who has flown in photographic reconnaissance in Mosquitoes. There has also been a raid on a place called Peenemünde. If any of you have been on that raid, please keep it very close to yourself. We do not know what that raid was about, but the Germans are mad keen to isolate anyone who might have flown in it.

CHAPTER 20

'They are keen to glean anything they can from those of you flying Mosquitoes or Mustangs. They are keen for information on Pathfinders; they are keen to find navigators who have been using recent technology developments. At the moment, all the guards know is your name, rank and number. Keep it that way. Be Like Dad, Keep Mum, but also remember, unhappy goons are dangerous goons.

'Would those with injuries please raise their hands? You will accompany Flight Lieutenant McAlpine to the hospital for a checkup with the MO. Fall out over here to my right if you would. Now, before I finally let you go to your huts there is just one formality which we need to observe.'

'Oh, God,' thought Ad, 'please let it be quick and please just let me sleep.'

'We have caught a number of intruders in our ranks. They were working for the Germans, sent here to spy on us. They were nasty types, Mosley's people mainly, but also a couple of Irish republican troublemakers. We caught them, took off their RAF uniforms, which they were not fit to wear, and handed them back to the goons stark bollock naked and with the odd black eye to adorn their nakedness. As a result of this, it is my requirement that each one of you must be vouched for by two members from the RAF station from which you made your last takeoff.'

Weary, sleepy and exhausted, Ad hardly noticed this decree but just went to pick up his bag, which contained pitifully little. He joined the queue at the medical officer's hut.

The MO appeared to have very little equipment, medicines or even sticking plasters. He did, at least, appear to be a qualified doctor from a British university: another civvy in uniform.

'Well, whoever patched this leg up did a good job. Jerry chap, was he?'

'Yes, sir, well, sort of. Polish born but said he was German.'

'Whatever he was he's done a good job. I'm passing you as fit so after you leave here pop over to see the intelligence officer if you would be so good.'

'Good morning,' said the flight lieutenant. 'Have a seat, please, Sergeant...' he looked at some notes on a clipboard in front of him, '... er, Adlam is it?'

'Yes, sir.'

'My name is Crawley, but you may call me Aidan; we don't stand too much on ceremony here'.

'Right, sir, that is, Aidan.'

The room had been cleared of its occupants to allow these debriefs of new arrivals to take place. Ad had found it slightly odd that in his new accommodation a man had been deputed to accompany him everywhere. The man had been pleasant enough. 'Do you have to follow me even to the bloody latrine?' Ad had asked.

'Yes,' the man had said. He was a flight sergeant from 106 Squadron, shot down over Essen. The man had accompanied him to this interrogation room. It was all so very odd. It was very similar to the atmosphere at Dulag Luft when the assorted interrogators had pumped him for information.

'Now, Adlam, what squadron are you from?'

'405 Squadron.'

'And where was your home station?'

'Gransden Lodge outside Cambridge.' Ad was starting not to like this man. He had the firm jaw of a toff and an accent to match; his lips were thin and without generosity and his eyes were hooded as if they were hiding furtively in his skull.

Crawley looked at a list.

'Don't think so, old man, 405 is a Canadian outfit but they're not at Gransden. Want to have another go?'

'We were at Leeming, 6 Group RCAF, but we were transferred to 8 Group at Gransden.'

He was starting to like this man even less. He had not said the purpose of the interview or what his role was. He was an Intelligence Officer and, as such, reminiscent of his interrogators at Dulag Luft more than an RAF man who was on the same side as himself.

'The squadron was transferred to Pathfinders, sir.'

'If you're in Pathfinders, where's your Pathfinder badge?'

CHAPTER 20

'I was shot down before I finished Pathfinder training, so I don't have one. Anyway, Pathfinders don't wear the badge when they're on ops in case they are shot down and the Germans take too much interest in them.' He might have added 'as you well know'.

'When were you shot down?'

'On 4 May on Dortmund.'

'Did you complete the operation?'

'No, a nightfighter got us before we arrived there.'

The manner in which this somewhat ugly man pressed him was even more intrusive than and at least as unpleasant as that of the interrogators at Dulag Luft. Would they put him into solitary if he did not talk? Most of all he wondered why on earth this procedure had to be done at all. There had been nothing like it at Bad Sulza or even Dulag Luft.

'Is that your own tunic that you are wearing?'

'Yes.' This at least was a reasonable question. Many Kriegies wore uniforms which they had picked up since capture. He had noticed that Squadron Leader Bushell, who had the air of a rather rakish pilot, wore the tunic of a navigator. There were RAF men in Fleet Air Arm uniforms and vice versa.

'So, you are a flight engineer?'

'What OTU were you at?'

'Honeybourne in Worcestershire.'

'What was the number of your OTU?'

'Twenty-four'.

'How many hangars are there at RAF Honeybourne?'

'Five, from memory. One "J" type and four "T2" types. Well, I think that's right. I'm sure you can always check.'

Crawley smiled. He was going to check all right!

Christ almighty! This was becoming tedious. The questions droned on.

What were the names of the pubs? Where was the nearest cinema? How did you get there? What were the colour of the buses? How much was the bus fare?

After a quarter of an hour or so Crawley paused.

'That is all for now, Sergeant Adlam, you are dismissed. But you have to be here at this room at 1000 hours tomorrow morning. Flight!'

He called in the flight sergeant to continue with the surveillance.

They walked around the compound. After the previous accommodation in the Third Reich this was vast.

'How many in this compound?' he asked the flight sergeant.

'Well, this is the North Compound and its brand new as you can see. There's about 2500 I would say. There's about another 800 or so in the East Compound; that one is chockers, which is why they have built this one. Then there is the South Compound and the Central Compound, which is where the yanks are.'

A German in a boiler suit came towards them. Ad was to learn that this was Gefreiter (Corporal) Karl Griese, known universally as 'Rubberneck'.

'That is our chief ferret,' said the flight sergeant.

'What on earth is that?'

'He spends all his time looking for evidence of escapes. Well, you see those metal rods that he is carrying?'

'Well, they press them into the ground all the time looking for tunnels.'

'Why the boiler suits?'

'They go around the camp prying and poking into everything and they have to be ready to descend into tunnels or anything else at a moment's notice. Oh, and we've caught them in the ceiling space in huts, as well, listening in to our conversations.'

'WHAT?'

'The best thing with the ferrets is to give them as wide a berth as possible.'

As they walked around the camp the flight sergeant showed him a football pitch, a theatre which the Kriegies were just completing building, a golf course (albeit rather narrow) and the inevitable Appelplatz, which is where roll calls were held.

At the appointed hour the flight sergeant delivered him back to Crawley.

As Crawley invited him to take a seat, Ad found that he was in the company of four other men.

CHAPTER 20

'Sergeant Adlam, let me introduce you to Flight Lieutenant Lago, Flight Lieutenant Colwell, Flying Officer Hoddinott and Flight Lieutenant Murphy. Now, these gentlemen are all from 405 Squadron. Gentlemen, can you identify Sergeant Adlam for me?'

They looked at him. They all shook their heads. His morale plummeted.

A Bomber Command station with three flights might have some 300–400 airmen and several times as many erks. A station such as Leeming or Gransden Lodge, which also housed a Heavy Conversion Unit, would have half as many again or even double. If you were one of 800 airmen, you were not going to stand out. Ad had been on 405 Squadron for less than three months. There was a characteristic of Bomber Command stations that crews would stick closely together and also stay close to their erks. Crews typically did not associate with other crews. It was to be expected that these men would not recognise him.

'When were you shot down?' asked Hoddinott in that familiar Canadian accent, so similar to Johnny's.

'On 4 May on Dortmund, how about you?'

'Fourth of April on Kiel.'

'Hey! That was my second op. I was on that raid.'

'What was the sky like?'

'Terrible, there was 10/10 cloud cover for most of it.'

Hoddinott nodded at Crawley.

'What was your first raid with 405?'

'St Nazaire two nights before.'

Again, Hoddinott nodded at Crawley.

'Thank you, gentlemen, you can leave us now.'

That was it, then. Ad had been vouched for and could now be accepted for what he was.

Crawley looked at him gravely.

'Sergeant Adlam, I am sorry to tell you that you do not meet our criteria for identification. As heartening as that short encounter was, four airmen from 405 Squadron have failed to recognise you. That means that you must continue to be accompanied everywhere unless and until you find someone who can vouch for you or you prove to be a German plant. If that were to be the case, we will kick the living daylights out of you and you can go back to your German masters.'

'Are you off your bloody rocker? Are you calling me a German stool pigeon?'

'I am calling you someone who has not met our criteria for identification. We have caught German plants in this camp and we will continue to catch them. I would imagine that you might have met one or two people of that nature at Dulag Luft?'

Ad nodded. 'Yes, admittedly there were two really nasty guys who were on the other side.'

'Let's hope you find someone to vouch for you, old boy, eh?'

He and the flight sergeant walked out. Ad was approaching despondency. He had wanted to drop bombs on Nazis and had done so with great gusto. He had been shot down by a nightfighter and shot up by ground forces. He had been in – how many? – four prisoner of war camps and now this posh and rather creepy man was telling him he might be a German plant. The promised 'kicking' did not worry him that much. If he were not accepted as an airman, what would it do for the supply of letters from Miranda? That was the worst bit.

There was nothing for it; he would just write to her again. The letters took him out of the POW camps with their air of misery, fug of cigarettes and all-pervading smell of drying washing and boiled cabbage.

'Come on,' said the flight sergeant, 'let's go and have a look at the theatre.'

As they walked Ad said, 'Can I ask you a question?'

'Ask away, old boy, but I can't guarantee to answer it.'

'Well, in my hut they were telling me about… Oh, I'm sure they were shooting a line.'

'About what?'

'Well, it was about a squadron leader who was here. He is supposed to have had false legs and…'

'Oh, Squadron Leader Bader. What a laugh that was!'

'You mean it's true?' asked Ad.

'What did they tell you?'

CHAPTER 20

'The story goes he had lost both of his legs but was still an incredibly good pilot. They said that he was an absolute bloody nuisance and the Germans were going to transfer him to some inescapable castle.'

'That's right, that's Colditz. It's where they send the naughty boys and people who might be bargaining chips, like Churchill's nephew. Well, they said he refused to go and the Germans were getting into all sorts of bad temper. Poor old Kommandant Lindeiner looked like he was going to burst a blood vessel.'

'What happened?'

The flight sergeant continued. 'Harry Day had known Bader from their time in 23 Squadron together. He persuaded Bader that it could all turn very nasty and Bader piped down and agreed to go. Well, sort of.' He laughed uproariously.

'What do you mean "sort of"?'

'Well, Von Lindeiner arranged for a guard escort for Bader, about ten big Luftwaffe chaps in full combat kit and rifles. Bloody terrifying if you ask me,' said the flight sergeant.

'You saw it?'

'The whole North Compound did. These Luftwaffe chaps all lined up and then Bader walked along the line and began to inspect them.'

They both laughed involuntarily.

'He told one chap his cap badge was filthy and to report to him in the morning. Von Lindeiner was beside himself in rage. The Luftwaffe wallahs were totally embarrassed and had nowhere to look and Kriegies were literally falling around in laughter.'

They both fell into more uncontrollable laughter, drawing attention from other prisoners walking around the compounds and the guards in the nearest tower.

'Steady on, old chap, doesn't do to attract the goons' attention too much; they might get nervy.'

The laughter stopped. The Bader story had been a welcome distraction, but now reality crashed in on him again.

He looked around the compound. All around were double barbed wire walls over 4 metres high, 3 metres apart and with notices warning about mines. Every hundred yards or so he saw a goon box:

the wooden observation points on stilts. Out of each goon box there poked a sinister black slotted gun barrel: MG34s. They had twice the rate of fire of British Bren guns and could cut a man in half.

'Oh,' said the flight sergeant, 'you see that wire there?'

He pointed to a single wire which ran parallel to the barbed wire wall and about 30 feet inside it.

'Yes?'

'If you cross that they shoot. Best not to push your luck. They do not shout warnings first. Christ Almighty!' the flight sergeant suddenly exclaimed. 'Adlam, don't look, just act normal.'

'What on earth is it?'

'Be very careful how you look but you see those bushes at ten o'clock?'

'Erm, those dark green ones?'

'Yes, just look in the middle, can you see something glinting in there?'

'Yes, what on earth is it?'

'It's Rubberneck or one of his little mates snooping on us. They are looking for any signs of an escape attempt.'

'Well, is there an escape attempt?'

The flight sergeant suddenly became more circumspect.

'You're still on probation, my old China, you can't ask questions like that.'

As they approached the theatre, they passed a man in the dark blue uniform of the Fleet Air Arm. Somehow, he looked familiar. Ad was unsure of the beard, though. The face certainly rang a bell with him. The man was carrying a lectern, presumably a stage prop, into the theatre door. He showed no sign of recognising Ad. And yet…

''Scuse me, haven't we met before?'

The man rested the lectern on the ground.

'Hang on,' said Ad, 'You were at Dulag Luft. You visited me in the Hohemark clinic.'

'Oh God!' said the man and offered a handshake.

'You were in bed with, er, a nasty piece of shrapnel in the back…'

'In the neck, actually.'

CHAPTER 20

'And you had a bullet in the leg. That's right, that new chap Ittershagen wanted to chop your leg off but the old Polish chap stopped him. I remember that. Well, welcome to Stalag Luft III.'

The man who was organising the theatre was, indeed, Lieutenant Commander John Casson, who had been the adjutant at Dulag Luft and whose job it had been to look after wounded airmen – including Ad – at the clinic. A quick visit to Crawley, with the flight sergeant in tow for the last time, sorted out Ad's bona fides. Ad was in. He was accepted as a genuine Kriegie. That meant that he lost his escort of the flight sergeant but also that his letters to and from Miranda were now guaranteed.

'Look, Adlam,' said Casson conspiratorially, 'I want you to settle in and then come and see me. I won't be far away. There's a chap that I would like you to meet.'

As the excitement of the entry to the camp gradually subsided, a pain began to ache within Ad's soul. He had not yet had a letter from Miranda. It was understandable that letters could not easily have found him at Dulag Luft, Bad Sulza or Spangenberg but now he had a stable address, how long would it be before he heard from her? Would she be all right? Yes, she was capable beyond her 19 years; she could look after herself. How would she be getting on with the family? Would the job be working out for her? Would she be settling down into British life and the British climate after the warmth of South Africa? Oh! What was going on? He would have given a month's Red Cross parcels just for one letter.

CHAPTER 21
A PENGUIN ONCE AGAIN

5 OCTOBER 1943

'Hello, old boy, settling in?'

Ad looked up from his washing.

'Hello, John. As well as can be expected, I suppose.'

'Find any livestock in your trousers?'

'No, thank Christ, I was expecting to be crawling after that last train trip.'

'Let me get to the point, would you like a job?'

'Might be, what sort of job?'

He stopped scrubbing and looked up with the intense interest of a man who was suddenly offered relief from the endless boredom to come.

'Would you be interested in a job that had to do with the war effort?'

'In that case definitely. What do I have to do?'

'Could you come to hut 117 at 1030?'

'I'll be there with bells on.'

CHAPTER 21

That sounded like a pleasant prospect. He had now been through three prisoner of war camps and this was his fourth. He had settled into the routine fairly quickly. He got himself allocated a bunk, met the cohabiters of his hut, set up his meagre personal possessions in the small space available, and generally got on with life.

The routine began with Appel (parade) in the morning followed by a brisk walk around the compound before breakfast. The weather was becoming cold now, and he was having to wear whatever warmer clothing he could scrounge. After breakfast came the daily routine of playing cards, playing chess and physical jerks.

Then he hoped to find a letter from Miranda. None came. Perhaps the system had not caught up with his new address yet. God! Those letters were important!

Casson's approach, however, put a different spin on events. Do something for the war effort? Now that was enticing and alluring!

Settling down into Stalag Luft III had been an odd business compared to other camps. There was a theatre, lots of sport activities and a chap could sign up for classes in virtually everything. Immediately on passing the security clearance he had signed up to learn Afrikaans with a view to returning to South Africa with Miranda. There were several South Africans among the prisoners who could offer classes.

The chaps in his hut had seemed friendly enough. Flight Lieutenant Moran seemed to be leader of the hut. Quite whether this was because he was the ranking officer or because he was a large dominating figure with red hair and a ready wit remained unclear. He had already discovered that every closed community produced its natural leaders. The rest of them were a friendly bunch and had given him cigarettes and offered congratulations on passing the security clearance. There it was! That bloody security clearance again. There was one chap he did not take to: Visser was a Dutchman, grey of face, with rather slitted eyes and probably best described as having a remote personality. There was always one! Also, in the camps, you did not know what horrors men had endured when they were shot down. You did not know, either, what had happened to men if the civilian population had got to them before the Luftwaffe or civil police picked them up.

'So,' said Ad, dragging on a social cigarette with his new hut mates, 'what happens when they find a German plant in the camp?'

This raised a gale of laughter. It was clear that finding a stool pigeon was a game that everyone enjoyed.

'Well, it depends,' said a slight, red-haired man with a Liverpool accent and mischievous eye. 'If we're in a bad mood there are a couple of big Afrikaaners in hut 119 who will happily take a man behind a hut and break a few ribs.'

'And if you're in a good mood?'

The question brought a heavy bout of laughter from a Scotsman who rejoiced in the name of Archie Ainsley. His accent said 'north of the border'. He was from Edinburgh.

'I was over in the East Compound before they moved us over here. We found a guy called – was it Norris? Yes! He had been one of Mosley's fascists before the war. Christ knows what he was doing in the RAF. He should have been in the Luftwaffe. Anyway, Little X…'

The hut went quiet.

Moran broke in with his booming voice, 'Get to the point, Archie! The upshot was that someone gave him duff gen (incorrect intelligence) about a non-existent tunnel. The ferrets did a raid that night. They didn't find a tunnel, but we knew that the info had come from Norris.'

'What happened with you in a good mood?' asked Ad quizzically. Instinct told him not to ask who Little X was.

Archie took up the narrative again. 'Aw, we stripped him naked, painted his balls bright red…'

'… With very nasty oil paint of course,' added Moran, 'and marched him around the camp until the goons came and took him off us.'

Archie added, 'And we all sang "Do You Know the Muffin Man?" as we paraded him around.

Ad joined in the general laughter but had to reflect for a moment. The war was a deadly business. This war was carried on in the cat and mouse game of espionage between two groups of people (the Luftwaffe and the RAF) who, oddly enough, got on quite well together in daily dealings. Schoolboy pranks were very common. Ad wondered if this

CHAPTER 21

was because so many of the prisoners, especially the pilots, had come straight from private schools or university into the air force.

'Tell you what, though,' Archie added, 'the Germans have no respect for stool pigeons. Even Rubberneck told me he thought it was funny afterwards. Incidentally, watch out for that bugger. Griese will pump you for information. If he thinks you know something, he'll recommend to the Kommandant that a few days in the cooler will loosen your tongue.'

Later that morning, Ad ambled over to hut 117. He was surprised to find that it was packed.

'Settle down if you would, chaps, and please stand easy.'

The RAF squadron leader who he had seen at the induction took centre stage; the rest of them sat on bunks or lined the walls. A blue haze of cigarette smoke wended its lazy way to the ceiling. There was the distinctive smell of male sweat in the barrack and the ever-present festoon of drying underpants, but that was his new normality. Casson was there, having apparently invited several of the participants.

'My name is Harry Day and for some reason everyone calls me "Wings".' Everyone laughed. 'Wings Day' was the most significant event in the Royal Air Force calendar: the anniversary of its foundation.

There was something on Ad's mind. Where had he heard of Harry Day before? It came to him immediately. John Casson had talked about him at Dulag Luft: Day had had his photo on the front of the Luftwaffe's *Der Adler* magazine and was potentially on a treason charge when he returned home. Yes, and Day had also been involved in planning escapes from Dulag Luft.

Day proceeded. 'Now, I know that you all have urgent work to be getting on with.' Again, a ripple of laughter. 'But you have been invited here for a purpose.'

He looked around for effect.

'Now you are all new boys in the camp and have also passed through security clearance. We assume you are loyal to the British Empire and His Majesty?'

They nodded general assent. 'Our talent spotter, Lieutenant Commander Casson, has also identified you as keen types who might be interested in carrying on the war and, well, rather getting involved in things.'

Most nodded. Some were non-committal. Some shrugged.

'I see there are a couple of you who do not seem very keen. Look, I do know that every one of you has had a rough time of it. If you just want to sit the war out that is perfectly understandable.'

'Sorry, sir, 28 ops, shot down twice and a prang when an engine failed. I've really had enough.'

'That's OK, pilot officer, no-one will think any the worse of you; you may dismiss if you would.'

Two others went with him.

He spoke very pointedly after they had left the room. 'These men do not lack moral fibre; they are brave men who have done their bit for King and Country and you are to treat them as such. Is that clear?'

Day took up his narrative again.

'Let me start with a question. Is it true, or is it not, that every one of you is lucky to be alive?'

They all nodded or muttered 'very much so' or words to that effect.

'You have all jumped out of burning aircraft and, for a few seconds at least, you thought you were going to die.'

Ad, together with all the others, nodded.

'I would also guess that if you felt that you were giving up your life you were quite happy to do so. Such a sacrifice would mean that you had played your part in winning the war against the Nazis?' There was general agreement. Giving your life to help beat the Nazis was as natural as breathing, walking or going to the lav.

Ad noticed that, while the majority were taking 'Wings' Day very seriously, two were looking idly out of the window. Clearly, they were lookouts.

'So, now in captivity you cannot do anything more to beat the Nazis? You are just stuck here passively? You are safe but impotent?'

Day's speech was clearly prepared; Ad was curious to see where the logic was leading.

'Let me put something to you. If you had the chance to carry on the war effort, would you take it?'

CHAPTER 21

'Too bloody true!'

'Let me tell you a story. At Dulag Luft, Squadron Leader Bushell, Lieutenant Commander Fanshawe, myself and some 20 others escaped through a tunnel.'

Day first looked pointedly at the tall, imposing squadron leader who Ad had seen at the initial welcome. Day also looked pointedly at Fanshawe, who was easy to recognise in the dark blue uniform of the Fleet Air Arm with impressive gold ribbons around the cuffs. Where had he heard the name 'Fanshawe' before?

'The Germans estimated that 50,000 men were engaged in the hunt for us. Later, at the camp at Szubin, Bushell, Fanshawe, myself and some 25 others escaped, and some 300,000 Germans were in the hunt.' He had their full attention.

'Now, at Stalag Luft III we intend to get 200 out.'

He paused for effect. There was a stunned silence followed by wolf whistles and a chorus of 'bloody hell'.

'Does anyone have any idea how many Germans that will tie down?'

There was silence.

'Well, quite frankly neither do I.' This was met with knowing smiles and suppressed laughter.

'But it is a lot.' Day was serious now. 'A big escape will tie down an awful, awful lot of Germans.'

'Ferret in the compound!' shouted a lookout. 'Ferret just signing in at the main gate. It's bloody Griese and his little mate Keen-Type.'

'Taffy!' shouted Day.

A slightly rotund flight lieutenant came to the fore. Ad mused that he had obviously flown in a Halifax becase he would have stuck in the narrower escape hatch of a Lancaster.

'OK, everyone with me...' And he led them in an impromptu chorus of 'White Cliffs of Dover'. Ad joined in. Five minutes later a tall gangly figure appeared in the doorway. He was dressed in the blue boiler suit of the ferrets and carried the inevitable iron rod. He was an unpleasant looking man with a characteristic long neck which reminded Ad of a Christmas turkey.

'Rubberneck,' whispered a voice.

BOMBS AND BARBED WIRE

'*Guten Morgen,* Gefreiter Griese. Do you want to join us?' asked Taffy with a cheeky grin.

'Only if you sing "Lili Marlene",' he replied with the air of a man demonstrating his natural superiority and added, '… in German.'

They all laughed.

Taffy carried on. 'OK everybody… There'll be blue skies over…'

Half an hour later Rubberneck was still poking about the compound.

'Meeting dismissed,' said Day with an air of resignation. He pulled himself to his full height. 'Those of you who want in on the project meet back here tomorrow at the same time.'

Ad ambled back to his hut, catching up with Casson as he did so.

'Why did the meeting have to stop?' he asked.

'Standing orders, old man. There is never any activity if there is a goon in the compound. It's one of Big X's rules.'

Big X? Little X? What on earth was this about? The project, whatever it was, had infrastructure, planning and thought about it. Ad certainly wanted to be in on it whatever it was. He resolved to return the next day.

'John, that bloke Fanshawe, did you mention him to me when we met at Dulag Luft?

'Well remembered! He was my navigator when we were shot down. I was overjoyed to find him here.'

'So, it is possible to reunite with a lost crew.'

'It's possible, old man, but don't get your hopes up, needles and haystacks and all that. See you at 1030 tomorrow?'

'I'll be there.'

'Thank you, everyone, settle down if you would.' 'Wings' Day brought the assembly, informal and rag-tag though it was, to order.

'Right, well, we seem to have lost about a third of our group yesterday, which is about par for the course. Let me carry on from where we were when we were so rudely interrupted. The project is to get 200 men out of the camp and into the German countryside.'

This was met with wolf whistles and expressions of general astonishment.

CHAPTER 21

'How many do we expect to make it home?' asked a voice.

To Ad's surprise, Day's answer was, 'We don't know and we're not bothered. It is essential to understand that the objective is to cause inconvenience to the Germans in the numbers of troops that they will need to hunt us down. If no-one makes it home but we tie down 100,000 Germans, then we are successful.'

'Think of Von Clausewitz's first principle of war,' said the tall, rather imposing figure of Squadron Leader Bushell. 'The master principle in waging war is the selection and maintenance of the aim.' He had only seen Bushell a couple of times but there was something about him that compelled attention. Was it the slightly sinister face? Bushell had a scar over his left eye, which gave him the air of an attractive-but-ugly film star such as James Mason or Peter Lorre. Was it the slight South African accent? Was it the air of magisterial pomp learned at the bar during his short but successful time as a barrister before the war?

Bushell was a man who had that rare commodity: charisma. He was well aware of it and clearly intended to use it to its full advantage. At any rate, Roger Bushell was not the sort of character that Ad commonly encountered in Gloucester's murky back streets. He was manifestly someone born to lead. Most were happy to be led by him.

'Now,' said Day, taking back the initiative of the meeting. 'I am assuming that all of you wish to take part in one way or another?'

There were nods of assent.

'Let me tell you what we need,' Day continued.

He ran through a list of required skills: tailors, map makers, engineers, compass manufacturers, and people with an artistic bent for forgery. As each group raised their hands in the air they were assigned to the head of that particular specialism. This was clearly a very well-planned operation.

'Next, we need diggers. Firstly, are there any men who were wounded in being shot down or who have any other wounds or disabilities?'

Ad, with the neckwound and legwound raised his arm, as did several others.

'Right, well, you chaps are excused from digging.'

BOMBS AND BARBED WIRE

Ad's heart sank. His wounds had healed but still gave some discomfort. He did not fancy digging with that bullet wound. On the other hand, he did not wish to miss out and he wished that very earnestly.

Day selected about a dozen men as diggers and allocated them to Flight Lieutenant Floody, who was, it seemed, in charge of digging.

The remainder were divided into two groups.

'You chaps, from here to here,' Day drew a partition with his arm, 'you wallahs to the left, go with Flight Lieutenant Harsh on security and the rest of you with Lieutenant Commander Fanshawe as penguins.'

'WHAT?' thought Ad. What on earth are penguins? He had worked long and hard to leave behind the world of penguins: airmen who did not fly. Now, it seemed, he was to be a penguin again – but what sort?

'Now, before I send you off for your briefings, we have some standing orders to attend to. You see before you a number of officers who are organising various functions in the operation. Unless you are introduced to them in some other way you are not to greet them or talk to them. You are not to acknowledge them in any way. Rubberneck has got his ferrets looking out for unusual contacts between people; he also has his hidey holes outside of the barbed wire perimeter and watches with eagle eye for any sort of observation of that sort. In particular, you do not acknowledge Squadron Leader Bushell.'

That told Ad that Bushell was the ringleader. Bushell was Big X. 'Now some of you will come across Squadron Leader Bushell through the camp theatre where he is currently rehearsing the role of Professor Higgins in *Pygmalion*. Let me lay it on thick. If you work in the theatre and therefore you have been introduced to and have met Squadron Leader Bushell you may talk to him. If you have no other means of knowing him, you do not.'

He looked around for assent. All heads nodded.

'Lookouts, are there any signs of our Teutonic friends out there?'

'All clear, sir.'

'Right, well, as we part, let me remind you of what Mr Churchill said. "Let us therefore brace ourselves to our duties, and so bear

CHAPTER 21

ourselves, that if the British Empire and its Commonwealth last for a thousand years, men will still say, "This was their finest hour." Because if, or when, we pull this off it will be the finest hour for all of us. Parade! Parade, dismiss.'

'Penguins, come with me if you would,' said Lieutenant Commander Fanshawe.

The newly arrived Kriegies were already learning how to move around the compound in numbers that would not alert the guards looking down with bored eyes from their goon boxes. They did not move as a crowd from one hut to another. Griese or one of his minions would pick that up immediately. They took circuitous routes in twos or threes, many going to other huts first before assembling in Fanshawe's hut.

Ad would never forget the briefing which he then received. Knowing that Fanshawe was his new boss, he now observed him more closely. He was impressed that Fanshawe had been shot down divebombing the Scharnhorst. He was something of an old-fashioned navy man. He was not someone who would hob-nob with other ranks. He was a man who clearly lived in a world where everything was 'ship shape and Bristol fashion' or, as Ad was learning, 'in Ordnung'. This led to his nickname of 'Hornblower', which betokened his talent for military propriety at all times. He was always 'sir' to other ranks and not someone to be called by his first name, whatever that might be.

'Lookouts in position?'

'Aye, aye, sir.'

'Right, chaps, this is how it works,' said Fanshawe. 'You wear a greatcoat such as this one. You go to one of the huts where digging takes place and you put this apparatus under your coat.'

He pulled a strange double-sausage contraption from its hiding place beneath a bunk. It was fashioned from a pair of men's long johns. 'You put the strap around your neck, you fill the top of the long johns with earth – both sides – and then you put your hands in your pockets. You will find that the pockets have been removed, which gives you access to two draw strings.'

He looked around to see that everyone followed him.

BOMBS AND BARBED WIRE

'Then you walk away and around the compound; when you think no-one is looking you pull the draw strings and the earth gradually falls out the bottom of the long Johns. You walk around to flatten the earth in and Bob's your uncle.'

Ad was in awe; it was so simple yet so effective.

'Now, there is one snag to which I do need to alert you. The topsoil here is grey as you can see. The soil underneath is yellow. If the Germans notice too much yellow soil on the top they will put two and two together very quickly indeed. If you are dumping yellow soil it is vital that you camouflage it as well as ever you can: the success of the mission depends upon that small but vital detail. Any questions?'

Ad asked, 'Has the decision been taken who will escape?'

'It has most definitely not, but the policy is "officers only" so I'm afraid you will miss out, Sergeant.' Fanshawe was not the most gracious. Anyway, there was a war on and Ad now had a chance to do his bit, so he may as well get on with it, even if he would have preferred to say or do something very unpleasant to this rather cold fish.

'When will the escape take place?'

'Well, we have winter coming up now so not until the new escaping season, which is likely to be around Easter time next year. The tunnels are not yet ready and, even if they were, the conditions are too cold to send men out.'

'Have the Germans got any idea that an escape is being planned?'

'They are not stupid. That is why the ferrets go around with their metal rods looking for tunnels. There have been about 50 tunnels in the past and every one was an amateurish shamble. This time we want to be more professional. Look, that's enough questions, go over to hut 104 and we'll get you started.'

They all kept on the greatcoats which they had been given. As they approached hut 104 all was quiet. One or two men read novels or played chess outside. There was nothing to suggest anything out of the ordinary. They approached the door. Inside was the sound of men working: a lot of men.

A man on the door asked them their business.

CHAPTER 21

'Penguins,' said one. 'Hornblower sent us.' They were getting the hang of this place very quickly.

The crucible of industry inside the door belied the easy, bored aspect of outside.

A large stove had been moved; it was still burning and wisps of blue-grey smoke found their way into the chilly morning air.

Then came the first curious discovery. Where the stove had stood was a hole, about 1 metre across, leading down into a sheer, vertical shaft. Ad looked down. The interior of the shaft was lit with very bright lights. He could see that the shaft was 10 metres deep. At the bottom a man, naked to the waist, operated a large primitive concertina device of some kind. It appeared to be a pump, which pushed air into a horizontal shaft. Empty Klim condensed milk cans were connected end to end to form a primitive but effective air duct.

Another man stood at the top of the shaft and was pulling up a heavy rope. As the end of the rope came to the top, Ad saw that it pulled up a pair of long johns filled with earth.

'Right, lads, who's the first for penguin duty?'

Ad stood at the edge of the shaft and had, in effect, placed himself at the front of the queue.

'Right,' said the man. 'Take off the greatcoat. That's it. Put the strap around your neck so that the long johns hang down your body. That's it.'

Ad staggered momentarily under the weight. Hornblower had not mentioned how heavy these things would be when they were full.

'Put your greatcoat back on and put your hands in your pockets. Can you feel the draw strings through the pocket? Now, all you have to do is to walk across the compound, several of you together and preferably a long way from here, and gradually pull the draw strings letting out the soil. Then you tread it in and bring back the empty long johns. Couldn't be easier, eh?'

Now Ad discovered why the soil distributors were so called: with the heavy weight around their neck they waddled and wobbled in an ungainly vertical manner just like penguins. As the compound was about half a mile wide, there was a lot of space in which to wander and make the soil disappear. On the other hand, a long walk with this weight was heavy work. But to Ambrose Adlam and the hundreds of other men engaged in any heavy work that would make life difficult for the enemy it was light work; very light work indeed.

The strap pulled painfully against the shrapnel wound in his neck. He had to put that out of his mind and compose his next letter to Miranda.

Just as he had experienced 'Alice in Wonderland' moments at Dulag Luft, so it was here at Stalag Luft III. Moran, it was revealed, was indeed, Little X. That meant that he was the hut representative to the escape committee. He took decisions as to who worked on what part of the project. He was the person to whom to go with questions. He was also the person who solved issues so that the main organisers were never crowded around with airmen asking questions: the Germans would have noticed it in seconds. He was also the man who organised rations from Red Cross parcels so that the diggers 10 metres underground would be given more rations than people on less physically demanding duties.

Visser turned out to be Little S: he was the hut representative for security. He had the 'say-so' on when and if a man was accepted into the hut. He must have had discussions with Crawley as to Ad's trustworthiness. Ad did have to wonder what would have happened if he had not bumped into Casson who was able to vouch for him.

It was also Visser's task to report any security risks to Day. He also had the contacts with the men who had the radios. Wireless operators from bomber crews were the men who could build and operate a radio. You never quite knew which ones, however, and you never, ever found out where the radios were. The word-of-mouth system did, however, work so efficiently that prisoners always knew of events in the wider war before the guards did.

The guards, and even Rubberneck, knew that clandestine radios were operating in defiance of Kommandant Von Lindeiner's specific orders. However, the information from the BBC was much more trustworthy than what they heard from the official Deutschland Sender. The war was reaching a critical stage now. The overweening self-confidence of the Germans after Dunkirk and Operation Barbarossa was fading.

CHAPTER 21

Italy had changed sides and declared war on Germany. The bomber war in Germany was reaching new crescendos. Firestorms on Kassel and Hamburg had burned the cities to the ground. The fires went on for seven days. Waffen SS troops had carried out massacres in Italy and Greece in addition to the routine massacres in Russia.

The news from Russia was by far the most worrying of all from the German point of view. Since the vast tank battle at Kursk in July, a few weeks ago, the German army had not been able to hold back the Soviets. Now the Soviets had taken the crucially important city of Smolensk. They were inching westwards. The German propaganda was upbeat and with lots of jolly marching music. But too many regiments and even complete divisions were not coming home. Too many of the guards had brothers, cousins or friends who had disappeared with no known fate. Ad had fretted about Johnny and Bernard Moody. The guards were fretting about a lot more than two men each.

Visser was the man to whom all of this was passed on by the radio operators, whoever they were. He would then repeat it.

'It's all a bit like the Freemasons,' said Archie breezily. 'Once you have been initiated all these secrets become yours for the taking. My dad was in it, but he would never tell me what the secrets were.'

'Don't they do things with goats?' Moran interrupted.

'I don't know but he did become very excited when we used to go past this very expensive grocers in Edinburgh that sold goats milk cheese.'

'There you are, you see, told you so!' opined Moran with an air of magisterial finality.

'Food,' said a voice. 'When are the next Red Cross parcels due?'

'Tomorrow morning after Appel.'

'Roll on, tomorrow bloody morning.'

There was still no letter from Miranda. That thought was with him when he woke up, when he had breakfast, when he 'penguined' his way across the compound in the forenoon, when he had lunch and when he penguined in the afternoon. The thoughts of Miranda and her letters and how she was going back in Gloucester crowded his every moment. He had not brought a photo with him. Damn! Damn and bugger it!

Griese had come around the hut again and tried to engage Ad in conversation. What did he know about radios? It probably interested Griese that Ad did not take on the 'beaten' stance of a long-time prisoner. What was the secret of his high morale? What was he involved in? Who were his friends?

Ad, like the other Kriegies, learned quickly to avoid Griese and not fall into conversation with him. It would be too easy to give something away.

Moran was to confide something even stranger to Ad and the other new penguins on the block.

There had been another tunnel. It was known as Tom but had been found by the Germans and filled with water. The tunnel on which they were working was known as Harry and was the one which was now the great hope for escape.

'Just one thing,' Moran had said, 'you cannot use the word "Harry" unless you are speaking about an identifiable person. The goons have been known to use microphones to listen in to us.'

'Wilco.'

'Over and out.'

'Moran, what about Dick?'

'Who's Dick?'

'Well, if there is a Tom and a Harry it stands to reason that there must be a Dick.'

'Sorry, old chap, no idea what you're on about.' That seemed very strange indeed, but he let it pass.

Harry, the brainchild of Roger Bushell, was a brilliant idea. It gave the men purpose. It was doing something for the war effort. It alleviated the awful boredom.

Ad's life now had three singular and separate driving forces. The most pressing was food: how to get it, how to eat it and how to share it. The notion of taking more than a fair share was looked on as very bad form. 'Not done, old boy!' he had seen one miscreant admonished.

His second driving force was the tunnel. After the soul-numbing inactivity of the previous camps this was wonderful, and he loved Roger

CHAPTER 21

Bushell for his project. For the men captivity meant there was no light in their lives, but Bushell had turned that light on for all of them.

His third driving force was the letters from Miranda, or the lack of them. Each day he attended the post distribution. Each day there was nothing. He rationalised the difficulty of post tracking him through the different camps and pacified himself with the thought.

It did not work. If he received letters he would have felt himself in limbo from the world. Without them he was in hell.

CHAPTER 22
THAT BITTER SWEET WINTER OF '43

JANUARY 1944

It seemed that Griese was never out of the huts. He or his team were always tapping walls, looking under floor boards, searching for clues or engaging men in conversation. The reason for the pleasant conversations with Griese was always clear: he was pumping them for information. The slightest nod might betray knowledge about escapes. God! They hated him! In the normal run of events most of the Kriegies would afford him the credit that he was doing his job. With Griese they perceived that miserable and misanthropic attitude found in the most assiduous and detestable traffic policeman. They hated him even more!

'Just doing my job, sir.' You could almost hear Griese saying it. As with a traffic policeman it did not do to antagonise, it was best to cajole them and try to get the best – or least bad – deal available.

One day a bored, jaded Kriegie asked, 'Corporal Griese, what is that song that I hear the Luftwaffe men sing? It goes….' He hummed it.

'*Ich hatte einen Kameraden*,' replied Griese with a true sadness on his face. 'I had a comrade. We sing it in the honour of a colleague who has died.'

'But no-one is dying here.'

'Many of the guards are from the German army and are on relief from the front or lightly injured. Then they go back to the front.' Griese left.

CHAPTER 22

'You know,' said Archie, 'Griese looked almost human then. The Jerries must be dropping like flies on the Russian front. They're singing that song all the flipping time.'

'Griese, human?' asked Ad.

'No, not really, not really at all.' They laughed.

If any of them had been posed the question 'was the 1943 winter bitter or sweet?' they would all have said 'bitter'. Their prime reason for existing was to win the war but they had all been sitting it out for months. All of them were cut off from home.

But then, unexpectedly and unforewarned came the big day. A small flimsy blue piece of paper arrived in the camp. It was addressed to him. He thought his heart would burst. The actual wording merely said that she was well and looking forward to seeing him. Small it was, flimsy it was but he read it and read it and read it. It had come from Gloucester, from England and most of all, it came from her. She knew he was alive! He was not an emotional man who wore his heart on his sleeve but he would probably have admitted, had anyone asked him, that the tears were welling up inside. He read it again just to be sure.

Ad did eventually receive more letters from Miranda but that said more about the postal service than it did about her frequency of writing. The bitterness of his ongoing existence manifested itself in the cold as well. Sagan was in the far east of Germany. Ad was starting to understand that winters there were freezing. Then there was the food. Thank goodness for the Red Cross parcels!

These might contain:
- 1/4 lb packet of tea or tin of coffee powder
- Bar of milk or plain chocolate (often Cadbury's fruit and nut chocolate, or something similar)
- Tinned pudding
- Tin of meat roll (spam)
- Tin of processed cheese
- Klim – a Canadian form of instant milk – (or Carnation or Nestle brand)
- Tin of dried eggs

- Tin of sardines or herrings
- Tin of preserve
- Tin of margarine
- Tin of sugar
- Tin of vegetables
- Tin of biscuits
- Bar of soap
- Tin of 50 cigarettes or tobacco (sent separately—usually Player's brand cigarettes, or Digger flake pipe tobacco).

Of all of these ingredients, the Klim was the most important. This was for a very particular reason as Ad was just about to discover.

When Ad had first looked down the tunnel shaft in hut 104 he had seen a half-naked man operating some kind of air pump. The Klim tins were fashioned in their hundreds, arranged end to end to form a long pipe line which extended from the pump to the far end of the tunnel. Klim tins were therefore kept, washed out and hoarded until someone came around to collect them.

True to form, Griese asked, 'We never see any Klim tins in the rubbish, why is that, Sergeant Adlam?'

'We're so hungry, we just eat them.'

'I don't think so, Sergeant Adlam, I don't think so at all.'

Griese was irritating. The worst thing about him was that he was not stupid: not stupid at all.

The best laid schemes do often go wrong. This was certainly true for Ad in his role as penguin. The amount of yellow subsoil was now proving to be of much greater volume than the grey topsoil. The volume of yellow subsoil which they were taking out of the tunnel was proving too great to make disappear. The 'big four' – Bushell, Floody, Clarke and Fanshawe – had put a hold on digging until a solution could be found. This involved Day as the effective senior British officer. Bushell proposed that the large space below the seats in the new theatre could be used for disposal. Fanshawe had pointed out that the tools to build the theatre were given 'on parole', with

CHAPTER 22

the promise that they would not be used for escape purposes. The RAF prisoners had actually respected this to the spirit and letter. No building tools had been used for escape.

It was Bushell, the ingenious barrister, who came up with the answer. 'The space under the seats isn't on parole. We can do with it as we like.' They had found another place to dispose of the vast amounts of yellow subsoil out of the view of the ferrets. Ad was then intrigued to find that there was yet another abandoned tunnel: Dick. So, Ad had been right. There was a 'Dick' after all.

'Why not use Dick to dispose of soil?' asked one Kriegie. Dick became another hidden space which proved very useful in the invisible soil disposal industry within Stalag Luft III.

Then, on that unforgettable morning, Ad and the other men in the hut heard the noise.

'What is that for an excitement?' asked Visser slowly emerging from his bunk. Now that Ad knew Visser better he did not seem so sinister any more, just a stolid Nederlander but really, at heart, a good type.

From the East Compound a noise was expanding like a football crowd in full roar.

Ad's cohabiters dressed and ran over to the barbed wire where the North Compound met the East Compound. Other men were running over as well. They knew they could not go beyond the 'wire of death' and saw very clearly that the goon in the goon box was fully alert. The menacing slotted barrel of his MG34 machine gun stood at the ready.

Over in the East Compound German officers were running around; ferrets were running around; staff cars appeared in the compound and disgorged more German officers who also ran around.

'What the hell is going on?' shouted one airman.

From the East Compound came the reply, 'We've got three blokes out! Three blokes have made an escape last night and got clean away.'

The roar from the Kriegies in the East Compound was taken up by the Kriegies in the North Compound. Hands were clapped, backs were slapped, laughter reigned all around.

'OK, chaps,' said Day, 'we don't want to upset our hosts too much, back to barracks. I think that gentleman up in the goon box would like to shoot the lot of us.'

They looked up at him. He looked down at them over the sights of his machine gun. Yes, he would like to shoot the lot of them.

They dutifully returned. The story found its way across the wire very quickly that three RAF flight lieutenants, Williams, Codner and a Canadian called Philpott, had made the most astonishing escape. Ad and the other prisoners had noticed that the prisoners in that compound were strangely keen on their gym horse. They spent hours every day vaulting over it. As it turned out, while they were vaulting the three flight lieutenants had been underneath it. They had constructed a tunnel to the outside world. It quickly became known as 'The Wooden Horse Escape'. This truly astonishing feat was of inestimable value to the morale of the prisoners; less so for the German officers, guards and ferrets.

'We will catch them,' said Rubberneck with a perfectly straight face and hint of malice as to what might befall them when they were caught.

Meanwhile, it was back to the task at hand.

And so it came to pass that Ad penguined his way into the theatre to drop his load and return for more.

John Casson was there together with Bushell directing a rehearsal for the upcoming production of George Bernard Shaw's *Pygmalion*. Ad had never seen a rehearsal of a play before; in fact, he had rarely seen a play. He stood fascinated and no-one seemed to mind him being there.

'Hold it there, if you would, Roger. Now when Professor Higgins says, "The great secret, Eliza, is not having bad manners or good manners or any other particular sort of manners," what is going through his mind?'

'I suppose he is telling her how to behave like a lady,' said Bushell.

'There is something else as well which is really important. He is starting to fall in love with her and Higgins needs to express that when he is delivering that line.'

CHAPTER 22

'How the hell do you know that?' Roger Bushell demanded the satisfaction of an answer in the best traditions of the Old Bailey. 'It's a bit bloody far-fetched if you ask me.'

'George Bernard Shaw told that to my mother when they were in rehearsals and he wrote the play,' said Casson without a hint of ego, bombast or (sin of sins to an airman) 'shooting a line'.

'Anyway,' he continued, 'the important thing is to remember that Shaw's female leads are always brighter than his male leads: think of Major Barbara, St Joan or Candida.'

'Miranda?' thought Ad. 'Did he say Miranda?' No, he hadn't, but the misheard name brought him back to reality. He was becoming desperate to hear from her. He had been at this camp for weeks now. The letters had been really heartening but the numbers arriving were just a trickle. He needed a flood of letters from her just to remain sane.

He was starting to lose count of how long he had been there. That was what a prisoner must not do. However, he reasoned that he would wait two more weeks and then get five letters all at once. That was the normal pattern. Oh God! He was cold, hungry and deprived of the woman he loved. Was there no end to this bloody awful war? His despair might have been tempered had he known that he was about to meet another quite remarkable character.

The problem for Ad working as a penguin was the weight on the neck. There was still one residual and rather sharp piece of shrapnel in his neck muscle. The pressure of the back strap on the wound, although healed, caused more pain than he really wanted to bear. He went to see Moran in his clandestine guise of Little X.

'That's no problem, old boy. Go and see George Harsh. He'll be able to fix you up with alternative employment.'

Flight Lieutenant George Harsh was one of the most remarkable men in Stalag Luft III or, indeed, anywhere in the British armed forces. He was an American who spoke with the Rhett Butler tones of Atlanta, Georgia. He was the scion of a rich Georgia family who had inherited the inconceivable sum of half million dollars in his early twenties.

Work was optional for George Harsh and although he was nominally enrolled as a medical student, the curriculum was mainly a bore. He really was looking for the brilliant electric current of excitement. Any old lark would do. One of his rich and indolent friends proposed that it would be a really good idea to hold up a small shop at gun point. It was really just a prank. They didn't need the money but they were lusting for the adrenaline thrill that went with a real-life robbery.

Unfortunately for all concerned, the proprietor pulled a handgun from under the counter and, in an exchange of fire, Harsh shot him. A maid at his residence found Harsh's bloodstained clothing and called the police.

The jury took 15 minutes to find Harsh and his friends guilty and recommended the death penalty with no reservations. Fortunately for George, his family was able to spend tens of thousands of dollars in legal advice. They were able to avail themselves of the best justice that money could buy. His death sentence was commuted to life on the chain gang. The case against Harsh was proven clear and most would have gone to the electric chair. The chain gang was the best that he could expect.

During a violent break from the chain gang, Harsh refused to join in but stayed to help a guard who had been wounded. This earned him a semi-pardon and he was transferred to a regular prison. Then Harsh was the beneficiary of a large dollop of outrageously good fortune: a prisoner developed severe appendicitis. It was the middle of the night. No doctor was available. Harsh performed the appendectomy and saved the man's life. This earned him a pardon.

By now he had spent 12 years in jail and World War II was starting. Harsh travelled immediately to Canada to join up with the Royal Canadian Air Force as a gunner. He duly found himself posted to 102 Squadron at Topcliffe, Yorkshire. From the exotic steamy climate of Georgia, the 'thin winds', incessant rain and 'Wuthering Heights' nature of North Yorkshire could only have been purgatory for him. At any rate he took part in the three initial thousand bomber raids on Cologne, Essen and Bremen in 1942. Then he was on the major offensives on Hamburg, the Ruhr and Berlin. Having survived almost two years in combat he was shot down on a raid on Cologne shortly

CHAPTER 22

before finishing a tour of duty which would have seen him classified as 'expired'. Instead, he found himself at Stalag Luft III, a major participant in the escape project as security officer.

'I'm looking for Flight Lieutenant Harsh.'

'Harsh here, what can I do for you?'

'I'm Adlam. Flight Lieutenant Moran sent me over; he said you might have a job for me.'

'Perfect, Sergeant Adlam! I am, as it happens, short of a duty pilot this morning and you are just the man I need.' He pronounced the word 'man' as 'may-un'. That drawl was something that Ad had only ever come across when he heard two Americans on that initial train journey to Honeybourne. God! That seemed decades ago!

'What does a duty pilot do?'

'It's dead easy,' said Harsh, 'but it's also very, very important. Now what you do is to sit on a chair by a table at the gate to the compound. When a goon comes in you get him to sign a form giving time of entry and time of exit. Oh, and the goon has to salute you as well so you will need a hat. Look, here's an officer's cap that will do. He ain't going to know if you're a sergeant or an air vice marshal.'

'Sorry to be slow but why is this important?'

'Well, this is how it works, Adlam. When you get the goon to sign the form you do your level best to slow him down. When you stand to take his salute someone else will be watching and they will pass a message to the digging team for digging to stop. Standing orders: no digging while a goon is in the compound. Oh, and take a book to read, otherwise it gets a bit boring.'

For the first hour no-one came. Archie had recommended *Redgauntlet* by Sir Walter Scott from the camp library.

'Oh, come on, this is a great read, this is the one for you. I couldn't put it down when I read it.'

Archie appeared by the gate. 'How do you like the book?'

'Well, it's OK. Look, honestly, Archie, it would probably have appealed more when I was about 15.'

'That's an interesting thing to say, right enough.'

'Why's that?'

BOMBS AND BARBED WIRE

'I was 15 when I read it. Anyway, it'll pass the time. Look out, here's Rubberneck.'

'Good morning!' The ferret came to a smart salute.

'Good morning, Gefreiter Griese, and how are you today?'

Griese put down his metal rod, which, for the ferrets, amounted to a badge of office.

'Very well thank you.'

Griese was in a relaxed mood this morning. He asked about the book. Archie said very proudly that it was a Scottish classic. Griese said there was a lot of mutual respect between Germany and Scotland.

'Our famous composer Max Bruch loved Scotland and wrote music in a Scottish style.'

Ad and Archie exchanged glances. They were being buttered up. Griese was up to something.

'You know, if you were to help me I could probably find some ways to help you.'

'Such as?'

'Well, the mail has been a little slow of late.'

Ad bristled. Archie tensed. Griese noted how his well-aimed barbs had gone home.

'The mail could be speeded up if it were in the interests of one person or another.' He smiled.

'And the price?'

'Hardly anything, hardly anything at all. Just tell me where the Klim cans go.'

'No idea what you mean, Gefreiter Griese,' said Ad.

'I don't see what you're driving at, Gefreiter Griese,' said Archie. 'When the Klim cans are empty we just put them in the bin.'

'Well, Flight Lieutenant Ainsley, there are no Klim cans in the bin. They disappear into thin air. Now, if you could just give me a hint where they go perhaps I can help you in return.'

'I've no idea, Archie, have you?'

'Search me; no idea at all.'

'We Germans are not as stupid as you would like to believe.' Griese smiled and moved on, metal rod clasped firmly under his arm.

CHAPTER 22

'The trouble is,' said Ad, 'he's right.'

'*Dinnae fash yersel*; he hasn't a clue.'

'But he knows that something is going on and that the Klim cans are involved in it somehow.

God! Griese was clever! He knew that something was going on as was demonstrated by his endless searches of huts, of barrack rooms, of latrines. He knew that somehow or other the missing Klim cans were significant. It was just that he could not put the missing piece into the jigsaw puzzle. The secret of the tunnel remained unsolved. The major problem was that the Germans knew that something was afoot but could not find it.

They laughed like schoolboys at the notion of 'getting one over' on the goons. If this thing worked and 200 men got out it would be wonderful, absolutely wonderful. It would be worth all the hunger, all the cold, all the boredom, all the isolation from Miranda, all the sheer bloody inconvenience of war and even the bullet and the piece of shrapnel, which was starting to play up again.

Then a flood of letters arrived from her! There were several of them, all with postmarks of some weeks or months ago. That bastard Griese had not lied: the letters were being kept as hostages against 'good behaviour'. Presumably the gentlemanly Kommandant Von Lindeiner must have stepped in and told Griese he took a particularly dim view of this sort of behaviour.

Ad forgot *Redgauntlet* and devoured the letters one by one. They were short on detail but said the two things that were the most important to him in his own world. She was all right and she missed him.

He read the letters over and over and over and over. He wrote back straightaway.

My own dear wife, I received a few letters from you a few days ago and I am very glad that you are well as I am always thinking of you and wondering how you are getting on. I am very well and I love you more than anything else in the world, Anne sweetheart. Every day I seem to miss you more and more if it is possible to do so. However, my darling, I am confident that we shall not be apart much longer and that I can come back and love you as you deserve to be loved, which is more than the whole world. Keep smiling my dear as you say, our good days lie in the future. I know you will always be true to me, Anne darling. As regards settling down, where you want to go is where I want to go. I know that South Africa is where you want to be and that goes for me. I am surprised that your mum has a daughter. Congratulate her for me but don't forget to tell her that I already have got the best one for a wife.

I also remember our sweet moments, darling. There will be many more. Glad you are happy where you are and hope it will always be a decent place for you while I'm away. Keep smiling dear heart. I love you and always will. Remember that it will soon be over and we will have our home and our children.

God bless you and keep you safe for me. Goodbye for now, will write again soon. All my love and kisses,

The letter to his Miranda / Anne most definitely did not tell her of the great drama unfolding around her husband.

'Hello, old boy,' said Casson poking his head around the hut door. 'Are you on your own?'

'Yes,' said Ad, 'they're all off watching the grand hockey match. I'm just writing a letter home.'

'Bang on, old chap. Well, confidentially, that is what I would like to talk to you about. Mind if I help myself to a brew-up?'

'No, help yourself,' said Ad placing his pencil aside. 'You have the air of a man who wants a favour.'

'In a manner of speaking, yes. It has to do with that letter that you are writing. Now, what I am about to ask you has to be in the strictest confidence and I mean that you cannot tell anyone, even in this hut, is that agreeable?'

'I suppose so, yes,' said Ad sitting up to his full height. 'What on earth do you want me to do?'

CHAPTER 22

'Well, firstly, you have to give me your undertaking that you will not ask any questions. You know there are all of those signs around England saying, "Be Like Dad, Keep Mum"?'

'Yes.'

'That is what I am asking you to do.'

'OK, how can I help you?'

'Well, you can help me by finishing that letter. I assume it is going back to Blighty?'

'Yes, it's to my wife in Gloucester.'

When it is finished, give it to me without sealing it. I will give you the letter back transposed in my own handwriting. All you have to do is to copy exactly what I have written but in your own handwriting. Then send it off.'

'Your timing is bang on, it's nearly finished, there you are… "Your ever-loving husband, Ad".'

'Back in half a jiffy!'

Casson returned to the hut about half an hour later. The grand exhibition hockey match was, by now, at a crucial stage and the roars could be heard across the vastness of the camp.

'Right, now copy this out.'

'This is exactly what I wrote except for a couple of words here and there and these few squiggles. Christ! You're sending information back to England, aren't you?'

'Do you remember that bit about being like Dad?'

'Yes, don't worry, I'll keep Mum.'

'Let me see you do it. That's it, perfect. When you get a reply will you let me see it?'

'Of course, I'll just get this over to the post box.'

It was known to the senior British officer and very few others in Stalag Luft III that Lieutenant Commander John Casson was an agent for MI9, a top-secret wing of British military intelligence which dealt with communication with prisoners. He was sending back information about the camp, about German morale and miscellaneous information. Had the Germans found out he would have been handed over to the Gestapo, tortured brutally and finally, if he was lucky, shot. The German authorities never suspected that any such communication was going on. It was a secret at Stalag Luft III, which was even deeper than that of the escape project. No book has ever been written about it.

Some small sign on the outside of the envelope gave indication that this was an information carrying letter. The prisoners' postal service in the UK would have isolated the letter and placed it in a letterbox to an unknown destination. This was MI9. The information was noted, the letter resealed, and the recipient would receive the letter some days late. Given the general slowness of the postal service the delayed letter was not noticeable.

The recipient would, of course, have no idea the part they had played in relaying top-secret information from inside the Third Reich to whoever the clandestine people were who decoded it.

CHAPTER 23
EXTORTION AND TWO EARTHQUAKES

FEBRUARY 1944

There was a respectful knock on the hut door.

'Yeah, come in.' It was Griese. Why was he respectful? Why did he not just barge in as he normally did? What was he up to?

'Sergeant Adlam [he pronounced it 'Etlem'], I have a question for you. It is not important but just an amusing little item perhaps.'

When Griese thought of an amusing little item he was definitely up to something.

'Why do you prisoners call us Germans "goons"?'

Ad smiled blandly. The senior British officer had issued a standing order for just this eventuality: to answer the inevitable question in a non-goon-baiting way. 'It stands for German Officer or Non-Commissioned Officer.' To his amazement he kept a straight face.

The German sense of humour did not resemble the British sense of humour in any way. Griese appeared satisfied. He had not come into the hut just to ask that. Griese affected a grotesquely unconvincing nonchalance as he walked around the barrack room, looking at half-read books and half-played chess games.

Where did Ad come from? What was his job in Civvy Street?

'I, too, was bored with my job but was called up into the Luftwaffe. I would have preferred to have just worked as a carpenter. You know, you and I have more in common than we have against each other.'

'Oh really?' Griese was up to something!

'You know, there are some surplus spam tins in the Red Cross storeroom. I would be happy to get half a dozen of them for you if…'

'If what, Gefreiter Griese?'

'All you have to do is give me a clue as to what happens to the Klim tins. It is not important, but I would just be interested to…'

'Raus!' Get out!

'What is the mystery, Sergeant Adlam?'

'There is no mystery with bloody Klim tins and I cannot imagine why you are even asking the question. Please just get out unless you are on official business. *Komm, raus mit dir!*'

Griese was getting too close to the truth. Ad would have to report it to Harsh or McGill, who were in charge of security.

Ad never ceased to be utterly impressed that the breakout from Stalag Luft III involved some 600 men. That required numbers equivalent to those at his former place of work, the Gloucester Oil Mills. The tunnel was the biggest project in which Ad had yet worked. As with any large and complex organisation (for such it was) it displayed a sophisticated command and control structure, well thought through division of labour and used its employees' talents to the full. It was a model capitalist enterprise except that it did not make money.

As a general member of the team – one without specific talents such as forgery, map making or compass manufacture – Ad would expect to cycle through the non-specialist tasks. He had already sampled 'penguining', acting as lookout and manning the gate as 'duty pilot'. More was to eventuate.

'I'm glad to be doing my bit,' he might well have said to Moran, the Little X of his hut. 'Have you got any more interesting jobs, though?'

'Perfect timing!' boomed Moran. 'I was talking to Tim Valenn this morning and he is experiencing some difficulties. Do you know Valenn?'

'Is that the bloke with the bushy ginger moustache who looks like a caricature of what civvies think an RAF man looks like?'

'Well, he runs Dean and Dawson, if you don't know him I suspect you are just about to. Leave it with me.'

CHAPTER 23

Ad had heard of Dean and Dawson in the organisation but didn't quite know what it did. It was not done to be too inquisitive about parts of the organisation, in which you did not have a personal involvement. He would learn that it was the department that specialised in forgery of vital documents. The name came from a well-known travel agency in London.

Valenn was exactly the right man in exactly the right place. By inclination he was a graphic artist and had designed wallpaper and fabrics for his uncle's design studio. By a sad misfortune his father had persuaded him into the dark night of the soul that is banking. Fortunately for Valenn, Adolf Hitler had entered the world arena. The resulting opportunity to risk his life in a Hurricane fighter had saved him from a grisly fate among balance sheets, dusty ledger books and an early morning commute from East Grinstead or somewhere similar. For a creative person like Valenn, such an existence was a fate considerably worse than death itself. For Tim Valenn, the really important point was that at Stalag Luft III he could really put his talents to use.

'Come in, old boy,' said Valenn. 'You're Sergeant Adlam are you? I'm Tim Valenn and this is Marcel Zillesen.'

Zillesen proved to be yet another of those interesting and fascinating people that Ad was destined to meet. He was born in leafy Northamptonshire in middle England to German parents. He was educated at the upper-crust Gresham's school but also, crucially, in Berlin. He spoke fluent upper-crust Hochdeutsch like a genuine Prussian officer. He spent much of his time translating the German poet Rainer Maria Rilke into English.

Zillesen was one of only a handful of Englishmen who had attended a Nazi rally in Nürnberg and had actually seen Adolf Hitler speak. He would say quite openly that if he had stayed longer in Germany, he could quite easily have fallen under the Nazis' spell. In the event, his exposure to National Socialism had demonstrated to him the conviction of its septic nature. He had emerged from Germany as one who loved the traditional German culture but hated Nazism to the bottom of his soul.

BOMBS AND BARBED WIRE

In the camp, Zillesen offered two major skills to the X committee. Firstly, his fluent German meant that he could talk to officers, guards and ferrets alike – and gain their confidence. Secondly, despite his privileged education, he was a born scrounger.

Two other Kriegies joined them. Valenn was clearly in the chair. There were five of them in the room, the others having been requested in a very polite manner to go for a walk.

'Hello there, Thommo!' Valenn shouted down the corridor. 'Is the coast clear?'

'You're OK, Tim, there's no goons on the compound.'

'Right, gentlemen, welcome to Dean and Dawson.' He passed a list to each of the three new recruits to that august organisation. 'Gentlemen, as you know, we intend to spring 200 people out of the camp. As you will all have noticed from your sojourn in the Third Reich, the Germans are somewhat obsessed with paperwork, ID cards and the like. The list in front of you represents the most common ones; in all there are 80. We don't really need such things as Hitler Youth Passes. The X committee also takes the view that ID cards for the Federation of German Girls are also a bit superfluous.'

'Depends on your disguise, though, doesn't it?' said a sergeant whose name was Alan and who spoke with a strong Merseyside accent. They all laughed.

'Well, most of our disguises have got to do with foreign workers,' said Valenn. 'That covers the dodgy spoken German and also makes it more likely that you would be travelling. We also have a few travelling salesmen, one or two fancy their chances in German uniforms, and one or two as bombing victims, members of trades and guilds and even a few as Nazi party members. Our job is to get hold of the documents to forge.'

Marcel Zillesen spoke. 'You get hold of the documents and Tim's forgers will do the necessary. What you have to do is to borrow the document for a day or two.'

They looked at the list. Each man gave a long whistle in a very low register.

CHAPTER 23

Document Name in German	Significance
Personalausweis	Personal identity card: similar to that used in Britain in World War II. Had to be carried by everyone and subject to arbitrary checks on trains, in shops or even in the street
Vorläufiger Ausweis	Temporary identity card
Kennkarte	Another form of identity card
Carte d'identité	Personal identity card used in France
Soldbuch	Soldier's pay book – used also as an identity check for military personnel.
Polizeiliche Bescheinigung	Pass for foreign workers to work in Germany
Urlaubsschein	Holiday pass for foreign workers
Rückkehrsschein	Pass to allow a foreign worker to return to Germany
Dienstausweis	A pass to allow foreign workers to be on Wehrmacht property
Arbeitsbuch	Employment ID card
Arbeitsbuch für Ausländer	Foreigners' employment ID card
Reisepass	Travel permit
Grenzausweis	Border pass
Gewerbelegitimationskarte	Commercial traveller's ID card
Ausweis Ämtlicher Gewerberollen	Company representative's ID card
Handwerkskarte Handwerkskammer	Guild ID card
Ahnenpas	Family tree document, Aryan.
Fremdenpass, Deutsches Reich	Passport for foreign workers to work in Germany
Bombenpass	Bomb victim's pass
Mitgliedskarte NSDAP	Nazi Party Membership Card
Pass, Reichsarbeitsdienst	State labour service pass

'You want us to get hold of all this lot?' said Alan with total incredulity on his face. 'You're not asking for much then?' In the Merseyside accent it sounded more like 'Yernorraskingformuchden?'

Valenn smiled. 'Marcel will tell you how the scheme operates.'

'Right,' said Zillesen, 'You're just joining Dean and Dawson, so we'll give you a couple of easy ones. Now, there is something that you need to know. I have been chatting to the goons ever since I got here a few months ago and I have found which ones are likely to be co-operative. Now, Alan, what I want you to do is to talk to Hauptmann Pieber. Chat him up over a few days and then borrow his Leica camera. Tell him, oh, you know, Kriegies want to take photos to send home to their families.'

'Is he going to believe that?'

'Probably not, but he can't stand bloody Hitler and he just wants the Third Reich over and done with. The goons know we are up to something but I'm taking the bet that Pieber will not rat on us even if he suspects something. Now, this chappie here, what's your name?'

'Laurie.'

'Right, Laurie, your job is to get over to the Vorlager (the outer compound) on some pretext and swipe half a dozen bottles of ink and some pens to go with them. The photos, obviously, are for passes and the ink is for writing on them.'

'Do I ask anyone?'

'No, just steal them.'

'What about the rubber stamps that the Germans like so much?'

'We have loads of them made from rubber boot heels. And we also need someone who can write Sütterlin script; I don't suppose any of you can manage that?'

'What the hell is that?' asked the Merseyside accent.

'Is that that funny joined-up writing that the Germans use?' asked Laurie. Zillesen nodded.

'All of the passes have to be in that handwriting. If you write as if you went to school in Liverpool and not Lübeck the goons are going to pick it up in seconds.'

'Birkenhead, actually.'

'And finally, Ad. I have a job for you as well. I would like you to get hold of a *Gewerbelegitimationskarte*.'

'I can't even say it, how the hell do I get hold of one of those?'

'Talk to Feldwebel Ulrich, you may find he can be very forthcoming.'

CHAPTER 23

'What? The Hundenführer? The sergeant with the slavering Alsatians?'

'That's the bloke. I mean don't go at it like a bull at the proverbial gate. What you need to do is to admire his dogs and get chatting with him. His English isn't bad. Then, when you think you've got his confidence ask him for it point blank.'

'That sounds like a one-way trip to the Gestapo. That's far too bloody dangerous.'

'Ah, well, I did say I had been chatting. Now, as it turns out Ulrich's brother was actually in Gestapo hands. It was a complete mistake of identity. They kept him a week without telling anyone they had arrested him and now he cannot have children. You may therefore find Ulrich rather forthcoming. Ask him for what you want. It is up to him to decide how to do it. Oh, it's a commercial traveller's permit, by the way. But you must learn to say it in German.'

'I'll start chatting to him and get practising.'

'Good man.' The slow painstaking process of ingratiation, infiltration and confidence-building began.

A few days later came an earthquake.

'Christ almighty!' shouted Archie Ainsley bursting into the hut.

'What's up, old boy?' asked Moran looking up from washing his socks. 'Is there a busload of randy nurses outside?'

'Hey, Moran, this is serious,' he insisted in his polished Edinburgh tones. 'I've just heard the mother and father of a row in Harry Day's room. I mean a real bloody row.'

'Who was he arguing with?' asked Ad.

'Well, it was Day and Bushell having a barney with Bill Jennens and John Casson.'

'I say, you weren't eavesdropping, old man?'

'I would have needed to be deaf not to eavesdrop; they were going at it hammer and tongs.'

'What was it all about?'

By this time the half dozen or so men in the hut, also variously washing, reading, smoking and playing chess, took an interest.

'Jennens told Day to abandon the escape and Casson agreed with him.'

'What? I can't believe it!'

'Well, seemingly Jennens had been called over to Von Lindeiner's office on some pretext and Von Lindeiner had very pointedly gone out of the room. On the table there was an official order. It was clear that Von Lindeiner wanted Jennens to read the paper while he was conveniently out.'

'Does Jennens speak German?'

'*Und zwar ganz fliessend!*' said a voice in affirmation.

'Jennens said that the order was headed Geheime Staatspolizei – the Gestapo.'

'Sounds bloody ominous.'

'It was bloody ominous; the advisory notice said that if any of us escape, British and Americans are to be held by the Gestapo until a decision has been made about them. Any non-British or non-American escaper was to be shot out of hand.'

'They wouldn't,' said Moran. 'The Luftwaffe are too civilised a bunch for that.'

'That is what Day said,' said Ainsley. 'But Jennens said that the whole point was that it would not be a Luftwaffe matter anymore. It would be out of their hands. Most of the Luftwaffe blokes are all right but this is the bloody Gestapo and they are not all right. Actually, I don't think the Luftwaffe like them any more than we do.'

'So, the Kommandant just left Jennens in the office to read the order? Sounds like a put-up job to me,' opined Moran dismissively. 'Von Lindeiner has been making these sorts of noises for weeks now. I reckon he knows there's something going on; he is worried he will be in trouble if there is an escape and he wants to dissuade us.'

'Christ, this is bloody déjà vu!' said Archie. 'That is exactly what Day said. But Casson backed him up. Casson is friendly with quite a few of the officers and especially the security boss, Eberhardt. He said that Eberhardt had told him something similar but Casson didn't know whether to believe it.'

'So, what happened next?' asked Ad.

'Well, Casson said, "You had better believe it, Harry, it really looks as if we are sending men to their deaths if the escape goes ahead." Day had a really interesting response, he said that every man in the camp

CHAPTER 23

was on borrowed time anyway. We had all been shot down and in the normal run of events every one of us would have been killed. Anyway, it was our duty to the Royal Air Force and His Majesty to escape and cause the Germans as much trouble as possible.

'Jennens pleaded with him and said, "The Russians are just about to retake Leningrad, the Germans are losing in Italy if we ever get past bloody Cassino; the flippin' war can't last that much longer. It is just not worth risking men's lives." That is when Bushell weighed in.'

'I can imagine what Big X said.'

'Yes, it was rather predictable. It was all, "Come on, you types, this is our chance to give the goons a biff on the chin; we are still on active service and we have to do what we can for King and Country."'

'Quite honestly,' said Moran, 'I sometimes think this is just a new kind of sport for Roger now that he can't go skiing or pleading cases at the bar or whatever exciting things he did before the war.'

Archie went on. 'Anyway, then Roger said, "Listen, you blokes, I don't want to be offensive, but I think you just lack the courage to do what is necessary. Harry has escaped three times. I've been out twice. Neither of you have been out at all. I'm sorry but I think you're both just guilty of rank cowardice." There was a stunned silence in the room and I waited for the sound of knuckles on nose.'

'Then what?'

'Day said, "I do hate to mention this, Roger, but Casson actually dive-bombed the Scharnhorst with Fanshawe. Jennens is a wing commander and didn't get there by rank cowardice. Would you care to take that back?" Roger took it back straightaway. He said, "Oh look, you chaps, I'm sorry but you know what I mean." Casson said, "No, Roger, I don't know what you mean. The escape is not going to stop the German war effort enough to get 200 men shot."

'Roger said, "You blokes just don't understand, do you? When we got out last time we tied down tens of thousands of goons. Tens of bloody thousands. That's what it's all about!"

'Casson said, "No, Roger, 200 men dead, that's what it's all about." Anyway, Day called it to a halt and said we were going around in circles. He said he would think about it. Bushell reminded Casson there was a rehearsal of *Pygmalion* at 3.30. Casson said he expected Bushell to come without his script. They agreed but they also agreed not to mention any of the discussion outside the four of them.'

'Except there was an eavesdropper.'

'I say,' said Ainsley, 'I was hardly an eavesdropper, I…'

'Thank God there was,' said Moran. 'Thank God there was!'

Of the altercation there was no more heard. Bushell did indeed come to rehearsal without his script and was word perfect or nearly so. That meant that the production was getting closer, and also the breakout. The tunnel had been closed over the harshest of the winter period because the ground was too hard to dig. Now the new year of 1944 was three months in, the tunnel was reopened.

'Not bad!' said the first man down. 'There are some palings that need to be replaced but not that many.' Remedial work took only a couple of days and digging resumed. Meanwhile the production of civilian clothing carried on unabated as did the production of documents, compasses, maps and all of the other logistical necessities.

If there was one truly great aspect to Bushell's 'Great Escape' project, it was that it gave purpose to the lives of the hundreds of men involved in it. Many, such as Day, Fanshawe and Casson, had been prisoners of war for four years. At first there had been no end in sight, now there really was an end in sight as the Russians drove inexorably closer. The Third Reich shrivelled by the day like a dying poisonous plant. It was true that there was a lot of distance to cover until the Russian tanks were grinding down Unter den Linden in Berlin. Nevertheless, the sense of inevitable catastrophe grew day by day like a cancer in the German soul. Both Kriegies and captors knew it.

It was March now and the X committee were finalising the date for the breakout itself. The night of March 24/25 looked good. It was destined to be a moonless night; the digging would have to speed up but that was achievable. Best of all, Corporal Griese, Rubberneck,

CHAPTER 23

was going for two weeks' leave. The ferrets were known to be sick of his assiduous searches and would most probably slacken off while he was away.

For Ad, the task of obtaining documents proceeded with gusto. He was greatly amused to find how easy it was to bribe the guards. Chocolate, coffee and tins of spam were high-value items as the death throes of the Third Reich were beginning and, beyond the barbed wire gates, supplies of food were starting to dry up.

Zillesen gave him the task of sourcing a Polizeiliche Bescheinigung. This was the pass that a foreign worker needed to work in Germany. Checks and controls in the street were frequent, random and usually carried out by the police or officials with great efficiency. An escaper could not pass himself off as a foreign worker without one. The methodology for obtaining one was amusing in its simplicity.

'Morning, Corporal Mohren, what are you doing this morning?'

'Same as every bloody morning! God! I will be glad when this is all over.'

'Yes, I hear the Russians are approaching the Polish border now.'

There was a silence. The implication remained unspoken: it was only a matter of time before the Russians were at the gates of Stalag Luft III. It might happen a year away or possibly sooner.

'Oh look, don't worry about that, how is your girlfriend?'

'Oh, Irmgard is very well, we hope we will get married next year.'

The whole of Germany, apart from their leader, had expected since the debacle at Stalingrad, a year ago, that Germany was going to lose the war. The only question was how painful it was going to be for those unfortunate to survive. Again, there was a silence. Both men knew that 'next year' meant 'if we are still alive'.

'Oh, look on the bright side,' said Ad. 'Enjoy the war because the peace is going to be awful.' It was a common saying and, in its way, quite funny. Neither man laughed.

'Well, how can we enjoy the war? We haven't even seen chocolate or real coffee outside of the wire for three, no four years. I tell you, Sergeant Adlam, you are eating better in here than we are out there. The Red Cross parcels are keeping you prisoners in luxury.'

'Would you like a bar of soap to give to Irmgard? Or possibly some chocolate? We might have some coffee powder to spare. I could ask around. The lads know that you are a decent man and I am sure they would like to help.'

'If that were possible Irmgard and her parents would be very grateful.'

'By the way, have you tried the Cadbury's chocolate with fruit and nuts? It is absolutely delicious.'

'You are truly a man with a great heart, Sergeant Adlam.'

'Well, almost with a great heart but there is a small favour that you could do for me.'

'Ah! I thought that might be the case.'

'Get me a Polizeiliche Bescheinigung. I just want to keep it for one day. To me in the morning and to you in the evening with a tin of coffee and a bar of chocolate. Sind wir uns einig?'

'If I get caught they will send me to the Eastern Front. Men are not coming back from there.'

'Tuesday morning after Appel?'

A silence.

'Meet me behind the theatre; I will see what I can do.'

Ad had to be careful. Clearly this tack could not be tried with convinced Nazis, men who were fearful, or men with no useful contacts. Happily, a considerable number were content to be corrupted if there was something in it for them. The ultimate bait was the offer of a handwritten letter identifying the guards saying that the guard was innocent of any atrocities. These were the holy grail of inducements and only for the most deserving – and most 'helpful' – cases.

Ad found it beyond credibility when Zillesen told him it was normal practice to get the guards to sign a form for the coffee, chocolate and cigarettes given to them. The Germans had it in their DNA that everything had to be 'In Ordnung'. Very few refused to sign. This was useful: it provided very effective leverage for further favours of information or documentation out of them.

'Bloody good, Ad,' said Zillesen. 'This Bescheinigung is from a French foreign worker, which is exactly what we need and it's in great condition as well. Tim Valens's forgers will love it.'

CHAPTER 23

'Look, Zillesen, Mohren talks to a lot of these foreign workers who are working outside the camp and he comes across them in the admin office. But you give it back at 5.30, OK?'

'Admin office, eh? That's wizard, old boy. Oh, and give Mohren a bonus packet of Senior Service cigarettes but make sure that he signs for it. I have another job for you in a couple of days' time.'

Once again Ad and Mohren fell into talking. Irmgard's parents were less than convinced that Mohren was the man for their daughter. He was only a lowly corporal and might not be alive in a few months' time. The inducements from the Red Cross parcels were helping to change their minds, however.

Once again, Ad was able to offer things for Irmgard's parents' table in the most literal of senses. Tin of ham? Marmalade – the good stuff from Dundee not the revolting German 'ersatz' version? English cream biscuits?

'How about more soap?' Mohren volunteered. 'Irmgard likes the soap.'

'I need an embossing machine from the admin office, the kind that embosses photos on identity cards.'

'*Was denn? Bist du ganz verrückt?* Are you completely mad? That is completely impossible. I cannot do it. I am sorry.' He turned and walked away.

'Oh, that's a shame,' said Zillesen. Ad had thought that he would show some frustration, irritation or some other sign of defeat. 'Not to worry, old tin-pan-lids, here's what we do…'

A day later Ad fell into conversation with Mohren again.

'Gefreiter Mohren, do you want to pop into hut 119? There's a couple of chaps having coffee and biscuits.'

'I suppose you want to persuade me to get you an embossing machine? Well, I cannot; it is not possible. Do you understand this, Sergeant Adlam?'

'Coffee and biscuits?'

'As long as you understand my position.'

Hut 119 was unaccountably empty. That was odd because at this time of day, mid-morning, the hut was normally full of bored, thin men playing the inevitable chess, washing the inevitable socks or, equally inevitably, talking of life after the war. Today there were only two. They looked as if they meant business. Ad closed the door before Mohren could escape.

'Have a seat, Corporal Mohren. Do have some coffee and biscuits. These are English custard creams and quite delicious.'

Mohren looked uneasy.

'It would be best if you sat down,' said one of the men.

'Corporal Mohren, I want to introduce you to Flight Lieutenant Zakasziewski and Pilot Officer Budnik.'

'So, Corporal Mohren, I understand that you have some difficulty in finding an embossing machine for us?'

'I have already explained to Sergeant Adlam that it is quite impossible. If that is all I am here for please, gentlemen, keep your coffee and biscuits and I will get on with my duties.'

'SIT DOWN!' insisted Zakasziewski. I want you to look at this paper.' It was a list showing all of the Red Cross food which Mohren had accepted.

'We have the originals, Corporal Mohren. Your signature is against all of them. You have really accepted quite a lot of hospitality from the Royal Air Force.'

'If you use that against me,' spluttered Mohren, 'you will go to the cooler for one week or even two weeks; how will you like that?' Mohren's face was red; his breath came short and sharp. He was beginning to look like a cornered animal.

'That is very possibly true,' said Budnik. 'And where will you go, Corporal Mohren?'

'Let me tell you quite clearly,'continued Zakasziewski. 'If it had been just one or two tins of Plumrose ham they would have sent you to the Eastern Front. For this lot, what do you suppose they will do?'

Mohren was silent.

'You will stand against a wall and a firing squad will shoot you,' smiled Budnik. 'Have you heard of the guilt-by-association laws that that nice Mr Himmler has introduced? This lot represents black market dealing at a serious level. The Gestapo will hold your family guilty as well and they are likely to find themselves somewhere very

CHAPTER 23

unpleasant. Corporal Mohren, the sad reality is that if you choose to be non-co-operative your family could be in one of your government's slave camps. I understand the life expectancy is about two months. It would be on your conscience for the rest of your life, mind you, in two months' time you may or may not still have a life.'

Budkin looked at Mohren with epic seriousness.

'Where are you from, Corporal Mohren?'

'Elsass Lothringen,' said Mohren nervously.

'If you are from there you will have heard of the camp at Natzweiler-Stuthof? Have you heard of the rumours that they make lampshades out of dead prisoners' tattoos there?'

'Who has not heard those rumours? I do not believe them anyway.'

'Well, your family will find out for certain if the authorities see the extent of the largesse which you have received, not to mention the documents that you gave us to copy. How many brothers do you have? How many sisters? Do you know what the SS do with women in concentration camps?'

'They would work in the SS brothel until they were of no further use,' said Zakasziewski.

'I cannot believe that men would be so vile as to engage in blackmail such as this,' said Mohren. 'What harm have I ever done to you?'

'Don't talk to us about harm,' said Budkin. 'Do you see that badge on your tunic?'

He pointed to the German eagle with Swastika.

'Do you remember the first of September 1939, the Golden Polish Autumn? Hmm? Do you?'

Mohren was silent.

'My father was a school teacher. They took him away. We never saw him again and according to the rumours he was taken to Auschwitz Main Camp, but we never really found out. At any rate he never came back. A week after that my brother was accused of anti-German agitation. They put him against the wall in the town square and shot him with 20 others. They forced the mothers into the best seats – on chairs in the front row – and they had to watch as their children were shot. They screamed and screamed and screamed.'

'That was nothing to do with me,' Mohren said, grasping what high moral ground he was able.

'Do you see that badge on your tunic?' asked Zakasziewski. 'The one with the swastika on it?'

Mohren nodded.

'So do we.' There was silence in the room. Somewhere in the distance they heard the sounds of choir practice. No-one spoke.

'Oh, jolly good show,' said Zillesen a day later as Ad passed over the embossing machine.

'It's got to be back in the office by tomorrow or they will miss it.'

'That's a bit tight on time but we'll see what we can do. You know, it never ceases to astonish me what amazing things you can get hold of in this world if only you know the right people.'

'Quite so,' said Ad, beaming. 'Quite so!'

Hardly had this taken place when the second earthquake made itself felt.

'They've done what? They've done bloody what? They can't bloody do that!' shouted Moran in utter incredulity at Ainsley. 'Well, let me talk to them before they go.'

'Well, they've bloody done it and they've gone,' said Ainsley. 'You know how some names were read out at Appel this morning and to go to the admin office in the Vorlager?'

'I wondered what that was about.'

'Well, in effect, the guards arrested them and marched them off to the subcamp 10 miles (16 kilometres) away at Bellario. They didn't have time to pack up their gear, the guards came around afterwards and packed up all their belongings.'

CHAPTER 23

'Hello, you blokes,' said Ad cheerfully. 'What's all going on? There seems to be some sort of flap on.'

'They've taken 19 of the top escapers to Bellario,' said Ainsley in his most lugubrious Scottish tones. 'Floody, Fanshawe, Stanford-Tuck and Harsh have all gone. It was an ambush. The Kommandant is not bloody stupid. That is why we had all those searches; he knew there was something going on but just could not find out what it was.'

'So, the escape is off, then? There's no leadership left. This looks like a very dicey do to me if all the leadership is gone,' said Ad ruefully. 'All that bloody work for months and it's all down the drain.'

There was silence in the hut. Outside they could hear the sound of a football match somewhere across the compound.

The door burst open.

'Roger!' shouted Moran.

'Hello, you types,' said Bushell with his pipe clenched between his teeth and a piratical glint in his eye.

'I suppose you have heard about the deportations. You've got to hand it to the Kommandant. He could have called the SS in, but he found a humane but effective military solution to his problem. Send the ringleaders off to Bellario and all will be well. I've also heard a rumour around the compound that the escape is off. Well, I'm here to tell you all that that is completely duff gen. The escape is very much on.'

The reappearance of Bushell had brought back Moran's customary booming personality.

'Well, the goons have sent 19 off; we have 600 men working on this project. Almost every one of the deportees has a deputy who can take over immediately. So that is what the deputies do. They take over now, this morning, and the show goes on.'

'The escape is still on?' asked Ad in wonderment.

'Mm, of course it's still on, old boy,' said Bushell with his favourite barrister's mock supercilious grin. 'Must dash, I have to spread the word to the other huts.'

'Well, I've got a rather juicy Arbeitsbuch für Ausländer [workpass for foreigners] for Zillesen,' added Ad. He felt rather proud of the way that that German expression just rolled off his tongue. The wonderfully named document was an additional passport that non-German workers had to carry at all times during their employment in the Third Reich.

'In that case, I suggest you give it to him post haste; he wants all of those things yesterday. Oh, I forgot to mention, the Kommandant thought I was not involved and didn't think "Wings" Day was involved either. That's the Boche for you, though. They get all the small things right and all the big things wrong. Anyway, must dash to pass the good news on. Toodle pip!'

And so saying, Bushell left as quickly as he had appeared.

CHAPTER 24
I SEE YOU STAND LIKE GREYHOUNDS IN THE SLIPS

1 MARCH 1943

'The Sturmbannführer Brunner has arrived, Herr Oberst.'

'Thank you, Dietrich, please make sure that he has everything that he requires and assure him courteously that I will be with him directly.'

Gott im Himmel! Das is doch eine lauter Schande! That is absolutely shameful! Earthquakes of rage and injustice clattered and stuttered through Kommandant Von Lindeiner's heart, mind and soul like a railway train derailed in a narrow tunnel. As a Prussian Junker and member of the officer corps it was a matter of pride and class that he should not let it show. He, a colonel in the German Wehrmacht, would have to kow-tow to this arrogant SS pig.

Moreover, Von Lindeiner nominally outranked Brunner who was of mere major rank in the General SS. It pained Von Lindeiner, this having to say 'Heil Hitler' and treat with fawning respect a man whose grandfather might have polished the boots of his own grandfather. He had met the man before; he had the manner and style of a Bavarian farm boy. Von Lindeiner was, however, quite clear as to the rules of engagement with such creatures as this. If he did not give 'the German greeting' or did not give it enthusiastically enough, then he and his entire family could see the inside of one of those places, to which the SS sent recalcitrants for re-education.

'*Heil Hitler, Herr Sturmbannführer, Willkommen in Stalag Luft III.* Can I offer you a coffee perhaps? I am afraid we only have Ersatzkaffee, but I do find that one can develop a taste for it after a time.'

An orderly took the Sturmbannführer's heavy black leather coat. The man's grey-green uniform with its black collar patches and cuff patch were immaculate; Von Lindeiner would have to give him credit for that, or, at least, give credit to his batman. The gleaming silver death's-head motif on his elegant cap sent shivers of terror through Von Lindeiner, which is exactly what it was supposed to do.

'Ach, gut, Herr Oberst, perhaps I can come directly to the purpose of this visit.'

The man's rural accent stank of the cowshed. How dare this jumped-up oaf speak before being spoken to in the presence of a member of the landed gentry? What sort of degraded country was Adolf Hitler delivering in his Thousand Year Reich?

Von Lindeiner held his seething emotions in check; he smiled graciously, charmingly even. 'I would, indeed, be glad if you would do so.' The orderly offered the Sturmbannführer a cigarette from a polished silver cigarette box. Von Lindeiner declined the offer with a regal motion of his hand. He addressed Brunner with the formal 'Sie'. Normally, with caps off and with a cup of coffee – even the vile Ersatzkaffee – in their hand two middle-ranking officers would address each other by the more familiar 'du' form. It was a calculated insult which remained delicately just outside the point where an SS man might reasonably take offence. Both men knew it.

'Herr Oberst, our intelligence tells us that a prison break is imminent in this camp. Higher authority requires me to ask you for a situation report and to know what steps you are taking to counter this.'

Brunner had countered the colonel's calculated insult with another. It was clear to both men that 'intelligence' meant that the SS had informers among Von Lindeiner's staff in the camp. This was not a surprise to the colonel, who knew perfectly well how the cancerous infiltration of the Third Reich insinuated, metastasised and operated.

CHAPTER 24

Neither did he blame the informers whoever they were. He knew how the system could browbeat and terrorise little men whose cousin, perhaps, had muttered darkly in a drunken stupor that Germany might not win the war and therefore brought excruciating SS pressure on the entire family. To inform on others was the best insurance policy to ingratiate that poor little man with those whose power encompassed life and death. The trouble was that in these awful days of the SS ascendancy everyone was a little man: including Luftwaffe colonels.

'The Herr Sturmbannführer is well informed. It is absolutely true. We have definite concerns about a possible breakout. Three things have led to this. Firstly, my guards report seeing trails of yellow soil on the surface of the ground. This soil is clearly from underground and is being distributed as the tunnel is being dug.'

'Is this so in all five compounds, Herr Oberst?'

'No, only the North Compound, which is the larger British compound. We have watched the other four compounds carefully but there is nothing comparable.'

'And secondly?'

'We have caught guards with materials from Red Cross parcels: coffee, British cigarettes, chocolate. Under questioning they have sworn on their mothers' graves that they were presents. The amounts of this contraband were large.'

'How interesting it is, Herr Oberst, that these terror-fliers have real coffee and decent Germans have to drink this fucking pigswill.' He nodded at the cup of Ersatzkaffee with disdain. The room was silent. Von Lindeiner was not going to be drawn into uttering the insults which coursed through his brain.

'The British are a very generous people, Herr Oberst, but perhaps even they are not that generous. Please give me the personnel involved. We in the SS have places where the truth can always be persuaded out of people.'

'I have had every one of them transferred to the army and sent to the Eastern Front, Herr Sturmbannführer.'

This was not strictly true, but it would take too much time and effort for Brunner to challenge it.

Von Lindeiner continued. 'The amount of contraband that we have found suggests a concerted effort on behalf of some of the prisoners to extract favours of one sort or another out of the guards. We do not know what those favours are, but it certainly arouses suspicions.'

'And thirdly?' The man looked at him now with the cold, reptilian eyes of some slithery creature in a jungle about to strike its prey.

'Morale is noticeably much higher in the North Compound than other compounds. In the other compounds there is a sullen acceptance of indefinite imprisonment. You can see it in the men's bearing, in their sloppy uniforms and in their eyes.'

'And in the North Compound?'

'The eyes say "bravado"; "no surrender" and "we are up to something". Uniforms are more military. The walk around the Appelplatz is quicker. The bearing is of military men and not lost souls.'

Brunner was silent.

'Let me explain what steps we have taken to enable you to make the appropriate report to higher authority.' He thought but did not add, 'Whoever your vile higher SS authority might be.'

The reptile eyes were on him again; Von Lindeiner began to feel very hot inside his Wehrmacht uniform.

'Well, I have identified 19 men whom the guards reported as most likely to escape. I isolated them after Appel and marched them off to the subcamp at Bellario without even going back to their barracks.'

The reptile eyes in the reptile head nodded at him silently.

'I have authorised repeated snap-Appels to catch out any men who might be underground, for instance engaged in tunnel digging.'

Again, the dead eyes nodded at him.

'We have caught no-one. I have repeatedly run heavy trucks over the ground between the Appelplatz and the perimeter fence to crumble any tunnel. We did this in the past and discovered perhaps 20 such attempts, all of them amateur. Then we found a large and much better tunnel last year and filled it with water. In the last six months we have found none.'

'Which means that they are either giving up tunnelling or have got better at it. But you said, yourself, Herr Oberst, that your men were

CHAPTER 24

finding trails of yellow soil in the compound. So, the inference is that they are becoming more professional.'

'That would appear to be the case.'

'What else have you done?'

'My men have advised which huts are the most likely ones to be the starting point of a tunnel. We have repeatedly marched the inmates outside and ripped the walls and floors apart. There was just one thing that we found.'

'What was that?' Those snake eyes were on him again.

'A note saying, "you're too late". It sounds like a childish joke but when you put it together with the other evidence it sounds like silly children knowing a secret and being clever, too clever, perhaps. I would have to say that the British are somewhat given to schoolboy pranks; they are very different to the Americans in that sense.'

'What other evidence?'

'The censors report a large number of letters from the North Compound including such sentiments as "we'll be home soon" or "the beers are on me sooner than you think" and that sort of thing. That is not happening in the other compounds. The guards also report that bed boards and other timber is disappearing in the North Compound. Now, possibly, they may have been burning them in stoves.'

'Are bed boards disappearing in the other compounds?'

'Yes, but only to a small degree, nothing like in the North Compound. When you put the evidence together it forms a consistent broad logic: they are planning to escape.'

'And if there were to be a breakout, Herr Oberst, when do you consider it most likely?'

'We think the third week in April. At the moment it is too cold; the ground is too solid for digging and anyone escaping is likely to freeze to death. As the temperature warms up and digging becomes less difficult the first available moonless nights are about 20 April.'

'I see. And what of Squadron Leader Bushell? Is he one of your 19? He has already escaped twice.'

'My advice is that he has settled down and is directing plays. I saw him in *Treasure Island*; I would have to say it was delightful.' The colonel realised that to a man such as Brunner the refined delights of Robert Louis Stevenson were irrelevant at best and poison at worst.

The orderly removed the half-drunk coffee cups. Von Lindeiner hoped that the torturous interview with Brunner was at an end.

'Finally, Herr Oberst, I am to reiterate orders to you in person. You were sent a written order last month. My orders from the Reichssicherheithauptamt [the main Reich Security Office] are to ensure that you have received the order and are quite clear as to its intent.

'Essentially, any men who escape from Luftwaffe or Army custody and who are not British or American are to be given immediately to the SS or Gestapo to deal with. British and American escapers are to be held in custody and the SS or Gestapo informed. The local unit will decide what to do with them on a case by case basis. I can also tell you verbally that if Squadron Leader Bushell is captured escaping he is to be given to the SS immediately for extraordinary treatment.'

The nature of the extraordinary treatment was clear in principle if not in detail.

'I must remind the Sturmbannführer that Germany is a signatory of the Geneva Convention regarding the treatment of prisoners of war,' cautioned Kommandant Von Lindeiner carefully.

The snake eyes now glistened with that peculiar glint of the coarse-grained functionary upon whom Adolf Hitler had bestowed a power beyond expectation, reason or limitation.

'I am also to tell you that you are specifically ordered not to communicate any of this to any of the prisoners including the senior British officer, padre or medical officer. I am sure the order is quite clear. Orders are orders, Herr Oberst, and I am sure that as a German officer you would see it as your duty to support that principle wholeheartedly.'

Von Lindeiner seethed! This ill-bred Bavarian oaf was lecturing a Junker about duty!

He smiled ingratiatingly. 'Of course, Herr Sturmbannführer, of course. Let me see you to your car.'

He was going to have to say 'Heil Hitler' again, which disgusted him to the depths of his well-bred soul. The alternative to saying it was

CHAPTER 24

worse, much worse. As they parted, both men knew the subtext of the meeting. If there was to be a breakout then Von Lindeiner's fate was a foregone conclusion as was that of any men falling into the hands of the SS or Gestapo butchers.

'Ad, are you ready?' It was Archie Ainsley. 'The briefing is in hut 117. The lookouts are posted and we have to be there in five minutes.'

'Oh bugger! I'm just halfway through washing my underpants.'

'Well, laddie, bring them with you, I'm sure Big X will not worry about you scrubbing your unmentionables.'

The hut was filled with some 30 men. Squadron Leader Day was to open proceedings; Ker-Ramsay, as the newly appointed chief tunnel engineer, was to give the first main talk.

'Gentlemen, I am about to tell you something quite remarkable, but I do assure you it is pukka gen. In the last two weeks since the Germans moved our 19 chaps out of the main camp, our productivity has, in general terms, doubled.' He paused and took his applause. 'In two or three days we will be in a position to make the breakthrough into the fresh air.'

This brought about even louder cheering.

'Shut up, you silly bastards, do you want to bring the Germans around?'

Their nemesis among the ferrets, 'Rubberneck' Griese, was on leave but there were plenty more to take his place.

'Those of you who have been penguins will run out of work in the next five days or so. You will now wait to be stood down from that task. Squadron Leader Bushell, however, has something else lined up for you.'

Roger Bushell took up the address with his Oxbridge barrister's South African accent.

'Right, you types, I asked for volunteers among the penguins for a new task and you lot have drawn the short straw. Now, just to be clear on this, none of you will escape. We have had 510 applications to join the escape. We offered the top 30 places to those who have the best chance of a home run and have made the greatest contribution. We chose the next 70 out of those who made a big contribution and balloted the remaining 100. We intend to get 200 out and before you start all that silly cheering again please do not do so because you will be turning our beautiful project into a very shaky do.'

The room was full of very controlled airmen who smiled broadly. Some clenched their fists in joy. Some punched the air. Some slapped their friend on the back.

'I can now reveal that the job for which you foolishly volunteered is that of escape marshal. It is a vital role.'

Bushell outlined the two major tasks which were required of the marshals. Ad looked at Archie. They shrugged at each other. The job was simple enough but vital to the success of the venture.

'Now,' said Bushell as he finished the short explanation, 'any questions?'

'When does the breakout happen?'

'It needs to be on 24 March. That is two weeks from now. Ker-Ramsey tells me he can finish the tunnel in about two or three days' time then it will be sealed until the big night.'

He looked around to ensure that everyone had understood.

'That means it is still going to be very cold when we escape, but we are bound to do it then if we are going to do it. If we lose our chance the whole op goes for a Burton.'

'Why is that, Roger?' asked a voice. 'Why not leave it until the weather has warmed up a bit. It's bloody parky out there.'

'There are three reasons which force our hand. Firstly, the increase of Appels and searches and so forth tell us that the Germans know we are up to something. The activity is so frequent that we have to go sooner rather than later.' He looked around again. The frequency of the Appels was not lost on anyone, nor the significance.

'Secondly, if we wait for better weather the ice in the ground will doubtlessly melt.' He looked at Ker-Ramsey who took up the narrative.

'At the moment Harry is stable: tunnel Harry, that is, not Harry Day.' He looked around to take his silent applause from the indulgent

CHAPTER 24

smiles. 'Those of you who have been down there can attest to that. If there is a sudden thaw there is a clear danger that Harry will flood and possibly collapse completely. We just don't know but we cannot risk waiting for the thaw to see what happens.'

And the third reason?

Squadron Leader Day took up the address.

'Well, when Roger and I were at Dulag Luft, we got out and a dozen or so escapers tied down some hundreds of Jerries looking for us. When we were at Barth, Roger and I got out with 20 or so chaps and there were thousands of Jerries looking for us. If we can get 200 out, we will have hundreds of thousands looking for us.'

There were wolf whistles all around the hut.

'Look at it this way, chaps. The Russians have just lifted the siege of Leningrad. The Red Army is into Poland already and almost into Rumania and Hungary. The British and American armies are halfway up Italy and heading northwards all the time. They are still bogged down at the monastery at Cassino but once that is gone, Rome falls. The Royal Air Force and USAAF are bombing Germany virtually every night. If there is one thing that the Germans cannot afford it is manpower. If our breakout ties down hundreds of thousands – and we will – we are doing what we are supposed to be doing: hitting the Germans bloody hard and taking the war to the Boche! Any questions?'

Sidney Dowse spoke. 'Sir, I am very friendly with one of the orderlies in the Kommandant's office. He says there was an SS type in the Kommandant's office yesterday and that the SS bloke said that any escaping prisoners were to be handed over to them. Is that something we should worry about?'

'Well, Pilot Officer Dowse, if they did hand the escapers over to the SS they would doubtlessly shoot the lot of us. But let's think about it. Every man in this room – and in this camp – has jumped out of a burning plane. Hardly any of us got out with all of our crew. In some cases, we are sole survivors from crews. We are all on borrowed time anyway. Let us use that borrowed time well.'

The hut was silent. They knew that Day was right. They had all put their lives in jeopardy to fly over the Third Reich. But for a finely tuned twist of luck every one of them would have been dead. Ad looked at Archie. Archie looked at Ad. The risks to the escapers were formidable. There was nothing to say.

'However, I have known the Luftwaffe chaps for four years now. They are more like us than either we or they would admit to and the majority are honourable. I cannot see them passing our chaps over to the SS. Any further questions?'

'Roger, if, for any reason we cannot go on the 24th of March can we postpone a day if we have to?'

'No, sorry, Tim, we absolutely cannot postpone. The 25th of March is a Saturday, which would leave our chaps taking trains early on Sunday morning. Sunday morning trains are rare beasts and we know from the guards that they are often postponed or run late. By Monday we will have lost the advantage of the moonless night.'

'What happens if we wait a month until late April?'

'The Germans will probably have found the tunnel.' There was silence.

There was tension in the room. Bushell's King's Counsel brain had clearly thought through all of the angles. His case was irresistible.

'Gentlemen,' said Bushell as if addressing a jury in the summing of a murder trial, 'we either go on the 24th or we give up.'

The marshals' first task began that day.

Like the other marshals, Ad was given an allocation of ten men to put through the process. It was crucial that he did now know them personally. Given that there were now around 10,000 men in the camp and some 3000 in the North Compound this was not difficult. The interviews were carried out in rooms which were cleared of other Kriegies during the afternoon. As ever, a whole superstructure of lookouts, signals, nods and winks was in operation. This extended from the camp gate to the empty room in which he found himself.

'Right, bring the first one in.'

Another Kriegie, also taking the role of a Wehrmacht NCO, ushered the man in.

'Your name?'

The man said nothing.

CHAPTER 24

'I repeat, what is your name?'

As with all the prisoners who had been through the clearing camp at Dulag Luft, Ad had seen the German style of interrogation at first hand.

There was silence.

'I Boshidarov,' said the man, attempting to look as stupid as possible.

He was dressed in poor workman's clothes; he looked unshaven and rather pitiful. The pitifulness was clearly his preferred method of getting his captors to dismiss him as worthless.

'*Geben Sie mir Ihren Personalausweis, Polizeiliche Bescheinigung und Reisepass.*'

The man looked even more stupid than ever.

'*Nix verstenn, Meister, nix verstenn. Ik Bulgaria. Ik Plovdiv.*'

Ad stood up and calmly walked up to the man. Without warning he smashed him across the face with the flat of his hand.

'Ouch! What the flippin' heck do you think you're doing?'

'I'm breaking your ridiculous bloody cover. This flannel will not work. You have been in this room for 30 seconds and already your disguise is blown. Bloody Bulgarian? That accent sounds like it comes from Birmingham.'

'West Bromwich actually. I'll have to brush up on this disguise a bit, though, won't I?' Out of role, the man stood like an RAF officer.

'It's ridiculous. How much Bulgarian does someone from West Bromwich speak?'

'As much as a German speaks – none.'

'Oh God! Please go and talk to whoever is organising these disguises and get a better one. This will just not do at all. Right, let's have the next one in.'

The next man was brought in by the 'Wehrmacht NCO'.

'Name?'

'Van Heusen.'

'Ah, so you will have some nice shirts?'

'Oh, I'm not related to them.'

'But you are in disguise and on the run? Van Heusen is an American brand and not a Dutch brand and you have just fallen for it.'

'I say, that's not cricket.'

'The Wehrmacht and the SS are not going to play cricket, go back and come in again.'

'Name?'

'Van Heusen.'

'Ah, so you will have some nice shirts?'

'I'm sorry, I don't understand.'

'*Geben Sie mir Ihren Personalausweis, Ihre Polizeiliche Bescheinigung und Ihren Reisepass.*'

The man gave him the three documents without any difficulty.

'What is your business in the Reich?'

'I was called into the Reichsarbeitdienst to work in a factory.'

'What does the factory make?'

'Military uniforms, mainly for the SS.'

'How many pips does an SS Obersturmführer have on his collar tab?'

'Three silver pips, centred with a silver stripe around the outside.'

'Where is the factory?'

'Limburg an der Lahn.'

'You have seen the cathedral in Limburg an der Lahn?'

'Of course, Herr Feldwebel, it dominates the town.'

'How many towers does it have?'

'Five.'

Ad looked at the briefing sheet. That was the correct answer; the man had done his homework.

He looked at the Personalausweis, the identity card. He looked closely at the card and closely at the man.

'*Ja, alles in Ordnung.*'

'*Danke.*'

'*Bitte.*'

The man was keeping in character to the end.

Ad made a note on the control sheet. 'Possibly OK'.

He did not have a sufficient command of German to interrogate him to any length. That did not matter; the man was unlikely to speak German well enough to be convincing in a sustained interrogation.

'Next.'

CHAPTER 24

So it was that the marshals performed mock interrogations to test credibility. Then came the disguise to end all disguises: Harry Day.

'Next.'

The 'Wehrmacht NCO' brought in Harry Day wearing the full resplendent uniform of a British colonel. With him was Pavel Tobolski, a Pole.

'Name?'

'My name is Colonel Day, formerly of the Royal Inniskilling Fusiliers.'

Ad had to fight to keep a straight face.

'*Und Sie?*' he asked the 'escort'.

'*Ich bin Unterfeldwebel Krauss, vom 278ten Infantrieregiment, ein Teil des 95ten Volksgrenadierdivisions. Meine Pflicht ist als Begleit mit diesem Offizer nach dem Oberkommando der Wehrmacht in Berlin.*'

Well, he was not going to shake this man's spoken German. It sounded convincing to Ad and, as far as he could tell, to any German who might interrogate him.

'*Personalausweis bitte.*'

'*Der Oberst hat keinen Personalausweis sondern einen Vorläufigen Ausweis. Bitte.*'

And so saying, he handed the temporary pass to Wehrmacht Feldwebel Adlam.

The pass looked very official, except that it did not yet have its final touch: the date stamp.

'And why are you going to OKW Berlin, Herr Oberst?'

'I am Irish not British, and my loyalty has always been to an phoblacht eireann.'

'To what?'

'To the Irish Republic, the land of my ancestors. I propose to meet with senior officers in the Oberkommando, Wehrmacht and give them vital information to help the German war effort. Beyond that I cannot answer any questions.'

'*Alles in Ordnung, abtreten.*' Everything is in order. Dismissed.

'I say,' said Day, 'I'm not sure a sergeant can dismiss a colonel.'

'Point taken, sir. Actually though, I'm not sure a colonel would answer questions put to him by a mere sergeant and I would suggest that a German sergeant would not have the cheek to ask questions of a colonel, even an enemy colonel.'

'Hmm, I'm inclined to agree. If I get asked any questions, I will just use that phrase that they always using when they are in high dudgeon, what is it again?'

'*Das ist eine Frechheit!*' chimed in Tobolski. 'I think Adlam is right, sir. If a colonel answered questions to a sergeant, it would not look convincing.'

At the end of his first task as a marshal the prognosis was desperately clear. Virtually all reports going back to Bushell said the same thing: the man was likely to come through only the simplest of interrogations. With almost all of them, the best chance was to remain unseen and unnoticed.

The word went through the compound like a forest fire. Next Friday was the day for the escape: 24 March. 'Harry' was closed down and all work had ceased now. All diggers and penguins were stood down. Tim Valens's forgers produced their final documents. Tommy Guest's tailors produced their last suits, hats and coats. Des Plunkett's team printed off their final maps. Al Hake's compass manufacturers delivered their last compasses, each bearing the minute lettering 'Made in Stalag Luft III'. Zillesen's scrounging came to an end.

So then, this was it. For some men it had been four years of waiting, of deprivation and of longing for home and family and a beer down the pub and Saturday night up the West End in London or Manchester Piccadilly or Lime Street in Liverpool. The boredom and the cold and the estrangement had worn some down. The escape was their way back to self-belief, self-confidence and, if they were lucky, their way back to Blighty.

There had been that visit by an SS Sturmbannführer some days ago. What was the purpose of that? Sidney Dowse had previously seen orders on the Kommandant's desk and had had that confirmed by his friendly mole that the SS man had told the Kommandant

CHAPTER 24

that prisoners were to be handed over to the SS butchers for special treatment. There was little doubt as to what that meant.

No! You could not think that way. There was a war on, too many people had put too much effort, too much 'blood, toil, tears and sweat' into this to stop it now, whatever the consequences. Roger Bushell had an understudy for his role as Professor Higgins in *Pygmalion*. His understudy had been told, quietly, to be ready to tread the boards. The show would go on.

CHAPTER 25
THE GREAT ESCAPE – THE MOMENT OF TRUTH

24 MARCH 1944

So that was it, then! The decisions were taken. The die was cast. The wheel was in spin. Bushell had quietly announced that his understudy, Flight Lieutenant Ian Marshall, would be treading the boards in the upcoming production of Shaw's *Pygmalion*; Bushell would be elsewhere. Bushell, meanwhile, had managed a quick and furtive conversation through the barbed wire with Bub Clarke, the senior American officer in the South Compound. 'We're going out tonight; don't do anything to screw us up.'

'We have nothing planned, Roger. Good luck.'

Ad had interrogated his ten men. Their chances were not good. If they stayed out of sight they might make it, otherwise they were almost certain to be arrested. Nevertheless, he had to admit that other aspects were well done. The clothes were convincing. The vital travel

CHAPTER 25

documents were works of art. At least half of the documents would survive even a detailed examination. The railway timetables were up to date. The maps were excellent.

Another issue arose: Paul Brickhill, whom Bushell had chosen as one of the escapers, had now seen the inside of the tunnel. His claustrophobia made him seek a meeting with Bushell. He could not do it. 'Thank you for being so frank, Paul.' They did not know it at the time but Paul Brickhill was destined to bring the story of the great escape to world-wide prominence. It was he who coined the expression 'The Great Escape' in the title of his book some six years later.

Despite all his various roles, Ad had still not been down the tunnel. This was a mark of Bushell's professionalism. Chaps who did the digging or shoring up and were involved in excavation or ventilation were allowed down that hole. To others it was strictly out of bounds. 'We're waging war; we're not running a bloody tourist attraction,' Bushell might have pontificated.

Ad could not imagine what it would be like to drop 10 yards into the ground, trundle for 100 yards on a trolley in a space less than one yard wide and then ascend another 8 yards beyond the wire. In any event he was not to have the dubious luxury of finding out. The escape was an 'officers only' affair. It was true that two sergeants – Bergland and Esplid – had been selected. They were both Norwegian, but their excellent command of German gave them a 'high chance' rating as they were likely to succeed. Ad's Kriegiedeutsch would not put him in that category.

There was still that old, old feeling though. In Merry England there was always 'them' and 'us' and if you were not one of 'them', old boy, then you just were not the right sort of chap.

The camp was covered in a blanket of heavy snow. The senior British officer had given strict orders: do what you normally do. Don't bait the goons. Don't draw attention to yourself. The tension mounted. Ad had that feeling that every young boy has before he does his first dive into a swimming pool: will it be alright?

Then came the bombshell. Bushell and Day had approached Len Hall for advice. Hall was an oddity in Stalag Luft III. He was probably the only prisoner who had not been shot down in action but had been torpedoed in the middle of the ocean. His main claim to fame in the escape, however, was that he was from the RAF Meteorological Branch. In these very challenging weather conditions that meant he was a key player.

He advised that the weather was going to remain very cold for the next few days – painfully cold with frost, snow, ice, the chance of frostbite, hypothermia and all the other dire consequences that flow from those dreadful conditions. He also advised that the nights were going to be dark because of the cloud cover and the lack of moonlight.

This provoked an impassioned debate in the committee. One proposal was that the train travellers should break out first to give them the chance to get away. The remainder, known as the 'hard-arsers', who would improvise their way across country, should break out a month later when the weather was better. Bushell reiterated that this would not work. Once the Germans knew for certain that a tunnel existed they would find it very quickly; it was also possible that the SS Sturmbannführer would return, bringing firing squads and worse in his wake.

As a compromise, they decided to give double rations to the hard-arsers to see them through. It was accepted as general truth that the hard-arsers were very unlikely to make it. Bushell had told them quite clearly: if the cold is too much then just give yourself up and they'll bring you back here.

Lieutenant Commander Casson still counselled against the entire venture.

'No, Roger, if men give themselves up or are recaptured, the Luftwaffe will not bring them back here. The Gestapo or SS will get hold of them and that means certain death. For Christ's sake, this scheme is getting sillier by the day. The goons have told us that German civvies are hanging aircrews from trees. We know that the Nazi government is actually allowing civilians to lynch shot-down airmen. We know that the SS is trying to get hold of all of the POW camps and we also know that if they do then they will shoot the bloody

CHAPTER 25

lot of us. The war is coming to an end anyway – what the hell do you hope to achieve from all of this?'

'Oh, for Christ's sake, John, we have had 600 men working on this for over a year. Do you want us just to sit down like tame Labradors and say, "Sorry, chaps, it's all off?" It's not on, old boy, it won't work.'

'Roger, I am perfectly aware how much effort has gone into this...'

'John, for Christ's sake, man, you were one of our strongest supporters when we started. Look, we have had a lot to do with the Luftwaffe and we know that by and large they are decent men.'

'For the umpteenth time, Roger, it's not the bloody Luftwaffe that we have to worry about, it's the SS.'

'I'm sorry, John, but we can't stop now. Even if the SS did get us, at least we are going down fighting and not just sitting on our backsides and doing nothing.'

'Well, I hope you realise that you could be condemning 200 men to death. I would hate those lives to be sacrificed because of your damned ego.'

'My damned ego? You shouldn't be called bloody Casson, you should be called bloody Cassandra.' Both men looked at each other.

'Oh, look, John, I'm sorry. I take that back unreservedly. Look, we made the original offer of escape to 30 of our best workers on the project and you were one of those 30. That offer is still open if you want to take it up. Think about it, eh?'

'No, Roger, what you are planning is brilliant, but it is not just an escape; it is a bloody escapade and it is going to end in tears. You are going to get men killed.'

'This conversation is at an end, John. I'm sorry. We have nothing more to say. Good morning.'

In the narrowly confined Kriegie world any angry exchange was inevitably overheard, repeated and amplified. Casson would normally have been branded 'defeatist', but no-one had any time to dwell on it.

BOMBS AND BARBED WIRE

Bushell spoke to Day. Tonight was going to be cold – intensely cold – and posed an extraordinary risk. Len Hall's advice was that tomorrow night might not be so bad. They were going to have to do it. 'We'll go tomorrow night whatever happens. Make sense to you, Harry?'

'Yes, I think we have to. Tell you what, Roger, it feels bloody good to be taking the war back to the Boche.'

'Doesn't it, though? Doesn't it?'

The news of the postponement brought a sense of anticlimax across the camp. Bushell gave the marshals orders to get around their men and make sure they kept their bloody chins up. 'Tomorrow night is definitely on come hell or high Wehrmacht command.'

The marshals had a further task: identify the men from hut 104 who were not on the breakout list. Make billeting arrangements for them in other huts. It was one of those small, detailed but very important niceties which separate the good projects from the bad. If the goers and the non-goers were all to be in hut 104 then the hut was going to explode with the number of people in it.

'C'mon, chaps, just be normal. Do the things you would normally do.'

It was the marshals' jobs to make sure that everyone washed their socks or walked around the perimeter or played cards or did whatever they did. They specifically looked out for groups of men who stood around talking too earnestly. In the world of the Kriegie, conversations were commonly at a low volume with a vaguely disinterested sometimes even bored look on the men's faces. Any discussion group that looked too purposeful was going to attract the goons' attention.

Rehearsals had to go on for the play. The odd snowball fight was arranged. The odd snowman built.

The afternoon wore on and the tension built. The light faded. Outwardly the camp had its normal sad landscape: bored prisoners, little activity, and bored and freezing Wehrmacht soldiers in the goon boxes. Lights came on in the huts, one by one. It was time for the marshals' final task.

They were to stand at strategic points across the Appelplatz and leading to hut 104. They stood in twos or threes quietly talking

CHAPTER 25

about something or other or, given the fact that Bushell had theatrical leanings, may just have done what actors do on stage: said 'rhubarb, rhubarb'. As a single man or group passed by they would say 'go left', 'go right' or 'pass straight on'.

Thus it was that 200 would-be escapers were surrounded by a couple of hundred more non-escapers performing apparently random movements and patterns and swirls to sweep the escapers surreptitiously into hut 104. The goons had spotted nothing. Nothing!

The word was certainly out that John Casson had had another row with Bushell, but there was too much else to think about. Anyway, Casson was out of circulation, being over at the theatre directing the dress rehearsal for *Pygmalion* in Bushell's absence.

Ad walked past hut 104 for the last time before the breakout. Oh HELL! There were so many men inside the hut that there was steam issuing forth out of the windows. The whole hut looked like one of those engine sheds where the Great Western Railway serviced its steam locomotives in Gloucester. Surely the goons would think it odd that so many windows were open on a freezing night, which they had to be for ventilation. Surely the goons would notice the clouds of white steam billowing forth into the freezing night air. Apparently, they did not.

At the appointed hour the goons came and put the bars across the doors to keep the prisoners in. They had not noticed anything whatsoever. Thank goodness Rubberneck was on leave. He would have picked up on the slightest clue and those clouds of steam would never have escaped his rapt attention. The countdown began.

Afterwards, Ad was vague on times but he remembered the events very clearly. He remembered the silence in his hut. No-one played chess. No-one did washing. No-one studied homework from the Afrikaans language lessons. The tension made the cold air as thick as the miasma in a jungle up the Congo River. The silence, the lack of conversation and the tension continued until someone said, 'They'll be moving the stove now.'

Five minutes later another voice said, 'They'll be opening the trap now.'

Then 'the railway travellers will be entering the tunnel'. The railway travellers had to go first because – rather obviously – they had trains to catch. There will be ten out by now. Ad's hut was silent. Outside they could hear the patrolling goons, still unaware of the dramatic developments taking place below their feet. The Hundenführer patrolled with his dogs but their sensitive noses noticed nothing amiss. The tunnel was too deep. The searchlights meandered in their lazy, bored arcs. Outside, in the compound, it seemed just another night.

There would be 20 out by now. They could hear the barking of the German Shepherd dog recede into the distance.

'The time to worry is when that dog doesn't bark,' said a voice.

'That's been done.'

'What has?'

'The dog that didn't bark in the night. Sherlock Holmes I think.'

'Put a sock in it, you two! This is a bit more bloody serious than Sherlock bloody Holmes.'

There will be 40 out by now.

There was more silence. 'The hard-arsers will be going into the tunnel now.'

More silence. The silence seemed to go on for hours.

There will be 60 out by now.

'Turn the light out or it will look suspicious.'

More silence. The more religiously-inclined prayed. The others just hoped as, perhaps, they had never hoped in their lives. Just let them get back to Blighty in one piece.

One by one the men dozed off. The silence persisted.

Crack, crack!

Oh Christ, no! Those were rifle shots.

Ad thought of how he had heard that sound a split second before the searing pain in his leg. He looked at his watch; it was shortly after five on a cold freezing morning. Those who were dozing awoke and looked out of the window. There was nothing unusual to be seen. Then they heard a commotion over at the guardhouse. A blaze of light as the door opened and the sound of German military boots clattering over the paths that led to that point in the wood where the tunnel emerged. The tunnel had been found.

From hut 104 they could see a pall of smoke arise.

CHAPTER 25

'They're burning the incriminating evidence,' said a voice.

'God, there's no bloody shortage of that.'

The Hundenführer with his dog ran over to hut 104. The door was barred from inside. He banged on the door and shouted. There was silence for some considerable time. 'What the hell is going on? It's all too quiet.'

The speaker had spoken too soon. Several personnel carriers appeared filled with Luftwaffe guards in full battle order with rapid-fire Schmeisser machine guns. The Luftwaffe personnel surrounded hut 104 and set up a light machine gun at each corner of the block.

'Christ almighty! They're not going to shoot them?'

Shortly after that, Colonel von Lindeiner appeared with Captain Pieber. They could hear the Kommandant shouting. 'You do not know what you have done!' They heard that plainly. What could it mean? The Kommandant was shouting and screaming like a man out of his mind. This was all very odd because the entire impression of the colonel was that he was old-school and gentlemanly. Most Kriegies actually liked him and had respect for him. But the tirade continued. 'You fools, you imbeciles, you have no idea what you have done. You do not know what is going to happen!'

The door to hut 104 opened slowly and gingerly.

Then the Kommandant ordered all of the men out of the hut and to strip to their underwear. A snowstorm was developing; this situation was becoming unpleasant. A couple of the airmen made a joke about the situation and were put into the charge of one of the guards, who looked as though he would quite happily shoot them on the spot. In the event he took them to the cooler, which in these severe conditions was a heavy enough punishment.

Then there was heavy knocking at the door of Ad's hut. They heard the wooden outside bar being withdrawn. Two guards entered with Schmeisser machine guns at the ready. The look in their eye said that even the usual wisecrack would give enough excuse for a trigger to be pulled and men splattered into pieces.

'You lot, just shut up! You take your clothes off, all of them and form up outside the barrack. If there is one word from any of you, we pull the trigger and if you don't believe us please just let us show you.'

The snow was becoming worse. Ad felt a level of cold that he had never experienced in his life. He shivered, he trembled. The cold was not like cold that he had experienced before. This was so cold that it was painful. He had not suffered from frost bite but knew that it was very bad and that he might now be on his way to enduring its excruciating touch. He stood there not daring to talk or look at the man beside him or look at the guards. Oh God! He trembled, he shivered, he ached with the cold that went deep into his inner being so much that he could think of little else.

After a painful half hour, one of the administration staff appeared with boxes of photos and checked off each man in turn until the full extent of the breakout was understood.

The next day, on the Sunday, the Kriegies were to learn that 76 had got out.

There was still tension in the air. The Kommandant had been heard screaming during the day. The mood had changed. The Kriegies were kept locked in their huts. They did not wash socks or play chess. They smoked cigarettes in silence. There was no appetite to talk. The guards' behaviour had changed from 'we're all in this together' to 'we will shoot you given half a chance'. The entire guard detachment on Stalag Luft III were likely to be sent to the Eastern Front. That meant death.

There was only one thing for it. Ad wrote to Miranda.

CHAPTER 26
REALITY DAWNS

25 MARCH 1944

Before lunchtime on the Sunday morning the first escapers were recaptured. All prisoners still remained confined to barracks, but the word went from hut to hut that the first half dozen or so were in the guardhouse. This led to a wave of cheering and clapping. '*Halt's verfluchte Maul!*' shouted a stentorian voice from outside and there was silence.

For Ad, for the rest of the men in that hut and for the men in all the huts, the morning of 25 March was sweet. Ad had been a prisoner for almost a year; some had been there for four years since Dunkirk or even the ill-fated British invasion of Norway. They had sat, they had whinged, they had washed socks and tended gardens but now they had really done something. Morale was high. After the first terrified shock of the Germans' response a swift thaw set in. Laughter was in the air. By common consent it was better not to be too triumphal about this victory. For victory it was!

'This probably means that *Pygmalion* is postponed. I was so looking forward to that,' said a voice and the hut burst into irreverent laughter.

The words of the Kommandant still echoed around their minds: 'You do not know what you have done!' What did that mean? For the moment, at least, that morning was a time to savour success. That morning was a time to reflect. 'Kriegies? Yes! But we still keep fighting against Hitler!' That morning was a time for smirks, for smiles, for giggles and for a certain national pride: the kind that only comes from victory. Victory! They savoured the word like a glass of rare and precious wine, not that most of them had ever tasted such a thing.

Huts remained sealed and under guard. Even so, the whispers passed through the ether. The German civil police had ordered a Kriegfahndung. 'What on earth is one of those?' Ad asked.

'It's a general alert,' said Archie. 'There will be every soldier, policeman, Hitler Youth boy and Home Guard geezer pulled out of bed in a huge radius to look for Roger and his mates.'

'And every Gestapo and SS man?' asked Ad. There was silence. They both knew that any escaper falling into their hands was in for broken bones, rifle butts and possible death. The unheeded warning from John Casson was now causing the men in the camp to reflect more earnestly. Had they taken part in a huge prank just to get men killed?

For the moment there was nothing for it. They made breakfast from Red Cross parcels. There was silence.

The camp was still on high alert. Over at hut 104 more and more staff cars congregated with officers, guards with dogs and a very gratifying hullabaloo.

'Can you see anything, Archie?'

'Not really and I'm not really game to go outside; it looks as though the goons would be quite happy to shoot us.'

Ad finished writing a letter. He would offer it to John Casson later for coding purposes, but goodness knows when he would see John Casson.

Silence.

25 March 1944

Stalag Luft III

My own dear wife

Received a letter from you today. Glad you are well, sweetheart as I am fine. I see you have moved, dear. Hope you like your new lodgings. Glad you are cycling around and keeping fit. No photo yet, sweetheart. Don't forget to send Afrikaans books. Keep

CHAPTER 26

smiling, dear, and keep on loving me as I love you dearly and think of you always. Keep smiling, Anne dear. Soon we will be together for always.

All my love. God bless you, your ever-loving husband,

Ad

On the face of it this is a routine epistle from a prisoner of war to his wife. The calm, unhurried prose covers over the boiling turmoil which Ad must have felt when he was writing it.

'Well, we got 70-odd out; it was short of 200 but not a bad effort for all that,' said Ad to his bunkmates in the hut.

'The trouble is, what happens now?'

The first consequence bordered on comedy. Captain Pieber had arrived at the cooler to find that the Kommandant had sent twice as many men there as the cooler could actually hold. What was intended as cells for solitary confinement was more like a social club. The surplus was returned to barracks. At least they were not being shot out of hand.

The second consequence did not involve the RAF men but did rather worry them. Some four days later an official Luftwaffe car arrived at the camp. Two senior Luftwaffe officers served a writ on Colonel Von Lindeiner to advise that he was to be court-martialled. This led to the Kommandant experiencing severe heart palpitations. Colonel Von Braune replaced Colonel Von Lindeiner. The Kriegies were genuinely sorry for Colonel Von Lindeiner, who had tried to be fair and decent in difficult circumstances. There were many questions to the guards as to his health.

The third consequence did not involve RAF men but did not worry them. The appalling Rubberneck returned from leave, was arrested immediately and removed from the camp pending a court-martial. By common consent, both RAF and Luftwaffe men agreed that this was a good thing. He was not heard of again.

Sooner or later there were going to be consequences for the escapers, if not those remaining. They waited to see what events would unfold.

BOMBS AND BARBED WIRE

The hut went back to doing what it always did. Men washed flipping socks. Men played flipping chess. Men played flipping cards or read or learned their lines for the now-postponed *Pygmalion*. Every so often another staff car would roar through the compound going to hut 104. This would result in an outburst of clapping, cat calls and general irreverent jeering until inevitably a loud voice shouted '*Schweigen Sie!*' It was all very pleasant indeed, if also slightly threatening.

Gradually the camp slid back into its normal routine. After a day or so they were allowed out again onto the Appelplatz and Ad could post his letter to Miranda. The new Luftwaffe regime headed by Colonel Von Braune held a roll call with great efficiency twice a day. It was all too late. The horses, 76 of them, had bolted. Hut 104 continued to hold a fascination for Luftwaffe officers. It seemed that dozens of them had come from the surrounding area to visit its wonders. The new Kommandant still looked very unamused by events – as well he might.

It may have been five or possibly six days before the next batch of escapers was brought back. Green and Poynter were brought back through the gates and taken straight to the cooler. The entire camp joined a chorus of 'For They Are Jolly Good Fellows'. Even the loud, menacing '*Schweigen Sie*' failed to dampen the singing.

John Casson had been very friendly with Eberhardt, one of the Luftwaffe officers. This man had said, 'I am very glad it is not you. Some very bad things are going to happen.' He would not say more. This story went around the camp. The mood changed. There was still the joy of winning but also the realisation of risk: very great risk. They waited with great joy tinged with great apprehension.

And so it was, that a week after the breakout, a few escapers had drifted under heavy guard back to camp, although in numbers rather less than expected. Still, it was too early to see any pattern to the unfolding events. The guards were not quite as unamused as a few days previously. A couple of guards, who had seen the entrance to the tunnel, had even, and very confidentially, expressed a grudging admiration. Initially, no Luftwaffe guard would venture down the

CHAPTER 26

tunnel for fear of a booby trap. Eventually, one brave guard chanced his luck and had duly popped out on the other side of the fence.

'The tunnel has a railway in it,' he reported. 'It is all very professionally propped up. It is well made and even has two staging points halfway along. There is a system to blow fresh air through pipes made up of Klim cans.'

'You know what?' Archie said to Ad. 'Young Mr Griese will understand now where all those Klim cans went. You remember how he was always asking where they disappeared to?'

The barrack laughed uproariously. Griese was gone forever. The guards thought he was probably sent to the Eastern front to fight the Russians. It is unlikely that he came back.

'Best of all,' said Ad, 'he knew he was on the right track; there really was a breakout on but he just couldn't fathom the connection.'

For the new Kommandant and senior officers, the problems arose in direct proportion to the excellence of the tunnel. How had the guards not followed up the very obvious clue that the disappearance of the Klim cans was so significant? How had thousands of bed boards disappeared and no-one had undertaken an investigation? How had the guards not noticed the disposal of hundreds of tons of yellow sand? Well, that had been noted but not acted on effectively. Perhaps most sinister of all, if the men could stay at large for this length of time they must have had documents: how had these been procured? For the senior staff the writing, in heavy German gothic script, was starting to appear on the wall in menacing black ink.

A few more escapers dribbled back to camp at gunpoint: Bethel, Broderick, Churchill, Marshall, Ogilvie, Royle, Shand and Thompson. That, at least, was reassuring. The cooler was, once again, so full that most new arrivals were returned immediately to barracks. For them, at least, there was a brief period of celebrity. 'What had they seen outside?' 'How far did they get?' 'How were they caught?' 'What were the interrogations like?'

By now the prisoners knew for certain that the total who had escaped was 76. Thirteen had been brought back so perhaps all 76 would trickle back over the next days and weeks. Some ten days after

BOMBS AND BARBED WIRE

the escape the new Kommandant, Colonel Von Braune, called Group Captain Massey to his office. Massey had been the official senior British officer for some years but complications from a leg wound had made his life extremely difficult. 'Wings' Day had fulfilled the role for most practical purposes. Now Day himself had disappeared with the rest of them. This summons sounded ominous.

Massey asked Squadron Leader Murray to accompany him as interpreter. On entering the Kommandant's office Massey was quite unsure what to expect, but common sense told him to be prepared mentally for bad news. He could never have predicted what he was about to hear.

There were no formalities.

'*Setzen Sie sich.*' Oberst Von Braune invited Group Captain Massey to be seated. His face was grim.

Major Simoleit, the Kommandant's adjutant, stood beside the colonel. His face was grave. Both British officers noticed that neither Von Braune or Simoleit would look them in the eye.

The colonel spoke mechanically, as if the words were being spoken by some other person. Murray translated. 'Oberkommandowehrmacht armed forces high command have ordered me to inform you as follows. Forty-one of the escapers were shot trying to escape.' The group captain registered a mixture of surprise, horror and impotent, sudden rage.

'Ask him how many men were wounded,' he snapped at Murray.

'*Keine.*'

Murray was silent for a moment and looked at Massey. He translated the colonel's reply: 'None.'

There was silence. Von Braune and Simoleit looked profoundly uncomfortable. Massey repeated himself: 'Ask him again how many were wounded.' Murray translated.

'Oberkommandowehrmacht has ordered that I am only permitted to tell you that 41 men were shot while resisting arrest.'

Massey persisted. 'Ask him again how many were wounded.'

'I am only permitted to read to you from the communiqué.'

Massey was beside himself with anger.

CHAPTER 26

'I want a list of the men who were shot.'

Colonel von Braune nodded in silence. They did not speak further. Von Braune looked profoundly uncomfortable. Massey was livid beyond speech.

He left and Murray followed him out. The word went around from hut to hut. Forty-one were dead. Murdered. There was the comforting fact that there was a war on and that they were all doing their duty. Nevertheless, this was different to dropping 4000-pound bombs, impersonally, from 17,000 feet. This was personal and the feeling could not be easily reconciled. Some days later the figure of murdered men rose to 50.

The mood in the camp had now progressed from the apathy of the pre-breakout days to the tension of the breakout itself to the euphoria of success to the dreadful realisation of the murders. Had it been worth it?

Yes. Most felt that it had definitely been worth it.

A week later the Kommandant had a list of murdered RAF men posted on the camp noticeboard.

Rank	Name	Service
Flying Officer	Henry Birkland	RCAF
Flight Lieutenant	Edward Gordon Brettell DFC	RAF
Flight Lieutenant	Leslie George Bull DFC	RAF
Squadron Leader	Roger Joyce Bushell	RAF
Flight Lieutenant	Michael James Casey	RAF
Squadron Leader	James Catanach DFC	RAAF
Flight Lieutenant	Arnold George Christensen	RNZAF
Flying Officer	Dennis Herbert Cochran	RAF
Squadron Leader	Ian Kingston Pembroke Cross DFC	RAF
Sergeant	Halldor Espelid	RAF
Flight Lieutenant	Brian Herbert Evans	RAF
Lieutenant	Nils Jørgen Fuglesang	RAF
Lieutenant	Johannes Gouws	SAAF
Flight Lieutenant	William Jack Grisman	RAF
Flight Lieutenant	Alistair Donald Mackintosh Gunn	RAF

BOMBS AND BARBED WIRE

Rank	Name	Service
Warrant Officer	Albert Horace Hake	RAAF
Flight Lieutenant	Charles Piers Hall	RAF
Flight Lieutenant	Anthony Ross Henzell Hayter	RAF
Flight Lieutenant	Edgar Spottiswoode Humphreys	RAF
Flying Officer	Gordon Arthur Kidder	RCAF
Flight Lieutenant	Reginald Kierath	RAAF
Flight Lieutenant	Antoni Kiewnarski	RAF
Squadron Leader	Thomas Gresham Kirby-Green	RAF
Flying Officer	Wlodzimierz A Kolanowski	PAF
Flying Officer	Stanislaw Z Krol	RAF
Flight Lieutenant	Patrick Wilson Langford	RCAF
Flight Lieutenant	Thomas Barker Leigh	RAF
Flight Lieutenant	James Leslie Robert Long	RAF
Flight Lieutenant	Romas Marcinkus	RAF
Lieutenant	Clement Aldwyn Neville McGarr	SAAF
Flight Lieutenant	George Edward McGill	RCAF
Flight Lieutenant	Harold John Milford	RAF
Flying Officer	Jerzy T Mondschein	RAF
Flying Officer	Kazimierz Pawluk	RAF
Flight Lieutenant	Henri Albert Picard	RAF
Flying Officer	Porokoru Patapu Pohe	RNZAF
Lieutenant	Bernard W M Scheidhauer	FFAF
Pilot Officer	Sotiris Skanzikas	RHAF
Lieutenant	Rupert J Stevens	SAAF
Flying Officer	Robert Campbell Stewart	RAF
Flying Officer	John Gifford Stower	RAF
Flying Officer	Denys Oliver Street	RAF
Flight Lieutenant	Cyril Douglas Swain	RAF
Flight Lieutenant	Alfred B Thompson	RCAF
Flying Officer	Pawel Tobolski	PAF
Flight Lieutenant	Ivo P Tonder	RAF
Squadron Leader	Leonard Henry Trent	RNZAF
Flight Lieutenant	Arnost Valenta	RAF

CHAPTER 26

Rank	Name	Service
Flight Lieutenant	Gilbert William Walenn	RAF
Flight Lieutenant	James Chrystall Wernham	RCAF
Flight Lieutenant	George William Wiley	RCAF
Squadron Leader	John Edwin Ashley Williams DFC	RAAF
Flight Lieutenant	John Francis Williams	RAF
Flight Lieutenant	Raymond L N van Wymeersch	RAF

For Ad and the men crowded around him as they looked at the list the document was one of horror. These were friends that they had known. They were men that they had laughed with and worked with and walked around the compound with. A few more men had trickled in, but the flow had, effectively, stopped. Only some 20-odd returned.

This led to speculation. They knew who was killed. They knew who was back. There were six names not accounted for. There was no Day, there was no James and there was no Dowse. Could it possibly be that they had made it? Day was such an iconic character that if he alone had made his home run then that, at least, was some kind of victory. They were to discover from a camp guard that Day, James and Dowse were in Sachsenhausen concentration camp. That was a fate worse than anyone could imagine. Why take them there? Why not just shoot them? There were three other names not accounted for: Bergsland, Müller and Van Der Stock. Could it be? Could it possibly be that they had made it?

The atmosphere in the camp changed to one of intense depression. It went through Ad's mind time and time again: '50 men killed'. *Pygmalion* went ahead under a dark cloud. They did not invite the Kommandant or other senior German officers to the performance, probably to their shamefaced relief.

The relationship between the Kriegies and the guards now progressed to a new level of irony. Up until now there had been some mutual respect. The guards had respect for men who had jumped out of burning aeroplanes. The Kriegies respected that the guards, for the most part, were professional. Most guards acted within the confines of the Geneva Convention and several friendships had even blossomed.

BOMBS AND BARBED WIRE

Now, the guards represented a regime which had murdered 50 of their friends. It was nevertheless clear that the majority of the guards had negative feelings about the crime as much as the prisoners. They were not to blame and the prisoners did not hold them guilty, but the buggers still wore that Swastika on their uniform. Nevertheless, they knew that if a guard was found commiserating with the prisoners then that guard would be transferred to an effective death sentence on the Eastern Front without delay.

And still the feeling persisted. It was a feeling of death, a feeling of murder. Ad tried to put the pictures out of his mind. There was not enough activity in the camp to stop it. The Afrikaans lessons could not erase the pictures of men being shot in cold blood. The jovial sing-songs could not take away the vision of SS or Gestapo men cocking their weapons in full consciousness and then pulling the trigger. The earnest debates in the debating society could not lessen the pain, the grief, the outrage. Bushell, Marcinkus, 'Cookie' Long and all the others, all with their brains blown out and lying in some sordid cell or country back road. It made him want to vomit.

The previous Kommandant, Von Lindeiner, had said, 'You do not know what you have done!' He had clearly been told what would happen to prisoners. They could not say they had not been warned. John Casson had tried to persuade Bushell to drop the escape and had clearly been warned about 'consequences' even if the precise consequences were not spelled out.

The remaining days in Stalag Luft III were dark, shot through with sadness and powerless rage. Prisoners and guards alike were morose and depressed. Would this bloody war never end? Would he never get back to Miranda?

If there was a crumb of comfort it was in the eyewitness sightings from those prisoners who had returned. Berlin was a wasteland. 'There is not a window left in the entire city,' reported the returnees. Half of the city was a wasteland. There were hundreds of buildings just left as rubble, without the streets even being cleared. There were banners everywhere with slogans such as '*Der Sieg wird unser sein*' (Victory will

CHAPTER 26

be ours) and '*Unsere Maure brechen, unsere Herzen nicht*' (Our walls may break but not our hearts).

'Oh, and the only people in Germany with anything to eat is us. The food situation is so bad that Germans would kill for a Red Cross parcel.' It occurred to Ad and the other prisoners that that might actually be literally true.

The new Kommandant had 'Harry' filled with raw sewage and the entry and exit tunnels filled with concrete. 'Poor old Harry,' said Ad. They had to laugh, though; the Germans had still never found Dick! That was another small but piquant victory!

Meanwhile, the Eastern Front – and the Russian army – was getting closer and closer by the day. It was only a matter of months or even weeks before the Russians would be at Sagan. What would happen to the prisoners? Would the SS get them first? What would the Russians do when they arrived? As conversations between enemies resumed quietly, the guards' advice was clear: 'You don't want to fall into the hands of the Russians. They are animals.' Life was becoming more uncomfortable by the day.

Some weeks later at Appel, Group Captain Massey called the men to stand easy before he had them dismissed.

'Chaps, I do know that letters are getting through now less and less frequently, but I thought I might share one with you that I have received this morning. It reads "The pints are on us down the West End on Saturday night. From your pals Wilson, Keppel and Betty".'

There was silence. What on earth did that mean? Wilson, Keppel and Betty were a popular comedy team in variety shows throughout Britain.

'It's Van Der Stock, Müller and Bergland!' shouted a voice. 'They've bloody made a home run.'

'Parade, atten-shun. Par-ade, dis-miss.'

The men snapped to attention, performed a right turn as they were long accustomed to doing and broke into complete pandemonium. Men jumped for joy. Ad embraced Archie. Men shook hands and shouted and men waved triumphantly at the guards. The scene was extremely un-British. The only stiff upper lips in sight were those of the Germans, who maintained discipline but looked outraged and humiliated and profoundly unamused.

'Adjutant, for God's sake get these men back to barracks before the goons start shooting.'

Three home runs was a victory. A victory!

A message reached the camp via John Casson's clandestine contact with MI9, wherever that might be. 'No more escapes' was the order. Despite years of inactivity in a prison camp, the military discipline and command structure of the RAF was still in good health.

CHAPTER 27

FALLINGBOSTEL: THE THREE REALITIES AND W/O DEANS

JUNE 1944

After the escape at Stalag Luft III and the murderous aftermath, life dropped sadly and sharply back into a lower gear. The escape had given so many of them a reason to live. It had been a partial success and the men felt they had at least achieved something. The 'no escape' order meant that they would just have to sit out the rest of the war in passive, sullen hunger, anger and frustration. Perhaps greater than any of these was the incessant nagging fear of being handed over to the SS for summary execution. That could happen next week, or tomorrow, or this afternoon. The word came through the secret radio, wherever it might be, that the Allies had landed in Normandy but were bogged down in establishing a foothold. Normandy! It was so far away it might as well have been the moon.

The weeks and months and hunger and fear dragged on after the ripples from the escape had died down. One morning they were summoned to Appel. Group Captain Massey announced a move of all non-officer ranks to another camp at Thorn. This was very odd because the Russian advance was from the east, yet they were being sent further eastwards.

BOMBS AND BARBED WIRE

'Oh well, as long as we get fed.'

An endless train journey with 80 men crammed into a goods van took them to their new abode. The camp at Thorn was a series of old decrepit fortresses built to protect the Austro-Hungarian Empire from a possible attack by the Russians. Conditions were poor. The men were packed into the barracks, some sleeping on floors. Food became scarcer. The supply of Red Cross parcels began to falter. Hitler's Thousand Year Reich was starting to fall apart and, in the prison camps as out in the streets of Germany itself, it was being felt.

After one month (or was it two?) the word went around the camp. 'Listen, you lot, there is going to be an announcement at Appel this morning. The SBO has given an order. When he makes the announcement no-one is to say anything. Apparently, this is very important. No-one is to say anything, is that clear? There is to be no repeat of any of the letting off steam we have seen recently, as understandable as it may be.'

They nodded in sullen assent.

After Appel they noticed that the German officers dismissed the guards' detachment before the announcement. Something was going on. An immediate fear chilled him to the bone: were they to be given to the SS?

'Gentlemen, I think you have all heard my express order regarding this announcement?'

He looked at the serried ranks and for their compliance: from his demeanour it was clear that compliance was demanded and was important.

'We have heard from a BBC broadcast that a bomb has exploded at Adolf Hitler's headquarters at Rastenburg on the Eastern Front.'

He looked around the parade. Discipline held. There was not a murmur. Men looked at each other. They grinned in utter delight. They exploded with silent laughter.

'It is not clear at this stage whether Hitler is alive or dead. Clearly the answer to this question has potentially got very big implications for us. It also has implications for the German military and civilians as well. When more is learned I will share it with you further. I order

CHAPTER 27

you not to refer to this in any letters home as we do not know what reprisals such a statement might trigger off. I order you all, also, not to bait or taunt the guards. That is likely to result in one or more of them letting fly with their rifle. If there are any questions the adjutant will be available.'

'Parade! Parade, DIS… MISS.'

What could it mean? The end of the war? If Hitler were dead, then Germany might just throw in the towel and accept the inevitable. On the other hand, they might just throw prisoners to the SS butchers in an orgy of revenge. Or would they keep on fighting? Looking around at the guards in the next couple of days told them that the majority of their captors would be perfectly happy if the nightmare were over – and preferably without the Russians visiting their own particular brand of slaughter and bestiality on the country. A few were certainly die-hard Nazis who would fight. Most were clearly not.

If Hitler were not dead, then there was bound to be a witch hunt for anyone involved. Inevitably, furtive discussions with friendly guards took place. Most seemed as happy as the Kriegies to hear that Hitler might be dead. The friendly Germans warned which guards were the Nazis, with whom they should never discuss this.

From the miserable confines of their dank and dismal fortress they could hear the hiss and see the steam as trains passed along. Several times a day they saw or heard trains moving ever eastwards to shore up the front against the oncoming and unstoppable Russians. The procession of troop trains appeared to be without end. But still, on the radio and now barely concealed at all, the news was inevitable and monotonous. 'The Russian army continues to press into Poland.'

A quick calculation showed that at the rate of the Russian advance, they could be on German territory within six weeks.

In the first week of August the senior British officer called an extra Appel.

'We have received orders that this camp is to be evacuated.'

He waited until the inevitable chorus of 'Oh gawd! Not again' to die away.

'We leave at 0800 hours tomorrow. Pack up your gear and be ready to leave. The entire camp is being moved Westwards to a place north of Hannover.'

'Oh Christ!' Ad thought. Another of those nightmare journeys in the bloody cattle trucks.

The camp was subdued that night.

'Everyone ready?' asked the adjutant brightly as he came in at first light to do a final check. 'Oh, this place is being turned over to a German Landwehr (Home Guard) unit who are arriving here in a couple of days' time. Be sure to leave it in good order for them.'

So, stopping only to smash up every bed, break every window, wreck any single device which could be of use to the middle-aged members of the Landwehr – and, giving special attention to rendering every toilet unusable – they formed up in ranks once again on the Appelplatz. There was a definite jauntiness in the snap to attention and the 'stand easy'.

The guards, for whatever reason, reacted to this outbreak of vandalism with conspicuous apathy. Men staring starkly into the face of national defeat, humiliation and possible death find, perhaps, that broken toilets are not of great importance.

'There's good chaps,' said the SBO drily as the water forced its way out of smashed water pipes resembling the fountains which gurgle and chortle in impressive display in Trafalgar Square, London.

'Our train has, indeed, arrived at the station,' the SBO informed them. 'Unfortunately, no locomotive is available to take us for some hours. Now, I need ten men to volunteer for a task which is really important. Oh, come on, you dozy lot, let's see some hands!'

'What's the job, sir?'

'I need men to climb on top of the carriages and paint "RAF POW" in very large yellow letters on the roofs. There have been some similar trains strafed by our own fighters in the last few days, or so I am reliably informed by the Kommandant.'

Their new abode was to be Fallingbostel. The camp was unbelievably vast, maybe six times the size of Stalag Luft III. Now Ad could see the extent to which the war had progressed. The number

CHAPTER 27

of RAF and American aircrew members was in the tens of thousands or so it seemed.

The camp at Fallingbostel proved to be similar to that at Thorn in one vital respect: he had to draw a mattress from the store and find a spare piece of floor in a corridor on which to place it. The huts were designed for 150 but held 400. Now he was to find a new kind of prisoner: RAF men who had been shot down not flying from England to Germany but flying from airfields in France to hit targets within France or Germany. The Normandy landings had taken place some two months previously. Talking to men who had been involved in the invasion had been wonderful for morale. The foothold had been gained on the first day; Caen was the strategic objective but after the advance was held up for two months. The Germans were nevertheless being pushed back inexorably, day by day. Each mile of land gained meant a day or so closer to the end of the war.

Ad hoped that his brother Bill had been at D Day; he was born for it and would have loved it! The hunger reminded him that it was still there, gnawing at his innards.

This brought Ad to contemplate the three realities of his life at Fallingbostel.

The first reality was the endless holy trinity of hunger, isolation and depression. The visible slowing down of Red Cross parcels after the move to Thorn had now slowed to a trickle at Falllingbostel. To go along with this, letters from home had effectively stopped. His morale was plummeting. He still wrote his two letters and four postcards a month but had no idea if they were finding their way home. Some guards were becoming noticeably ingratiating and asked for letters certifying that they had not taken part in atrocities. Some guards were becoming nastier in their desperation.

'I hope your wife is enjoying her black American boyfriend; I bet he is enjoying her.'

'Don't react to it! Don't react!'

His second reality was the fantasy world into which he climbed to escape. He sought out men in the dark brown uniforms of the South African Air Force.

BOMBS AND BARBED WIRE

'*Goeie môre, my naam is Adlam. Ek probeer om Afrikaans te leer en ek sal dankbaar wees as jy my sou help?*' (Good morning, I'm called Adlam. I want to learn Afrikaans and would be grateful if you would help me.)

'*Hoekom wil jy Afrikaans te leer?*' (Why do you want to learn Afrikaans?)

'*My vrou is van Oos-Londen in Kaapprovinsie en ek wil om daar te woon na die oorlog.*' (My wife is from East London in Cape Province and I want to live there after the war.)

It gave both the various South Africans and Ad a mission to accomplish and gave a veneer of reality to the fantasy. Then, within his fantasy world, he would take Miranda on a trip to Devon; they would have a small house and two children called Paul and Pat. The culmination of the fantasy was when his train would pull into Gloucester Central railway station; he would open the carriage door before the train stopped and run down the platform and hold her in his arms. He replayed that fantasy in his head a dozen times; a thousand times; a million times.

The third reality was the one which was the darkest. The secret radios confirmed day by day that the Allies were winning across all fronts and every day. German counterattacks on all fronts had finished. Now the Germans were merely fighting to stave off the inevitable catastrophic defeat.

The Kriegies had heard the thunder of Russian artillery in the far distance before they left Stalag Luft III. Now, north of Hannover they could hear the massive RAF armadas, 600, 700, 800 Lancaster and Halifax bombers which shook the huts and rattled the windows as they passed overhead to hit Berlin, Stettin, Leipzig, Chemnitz, Königsberg. By day, they could see the condensation trails of the United States Air Force Flying Fortresses and Liberators. It all had to end somewhere: what would the end be?

Some guards had told them that the plan was to hand them all over to the SS. That meant death. What would happen if the Russians got them first? Stories abounded of Russian atrocities. The extent to which the British and Americans were on the same side as the Russians was in doubt. Word had got out that the Russians had murdered thousands of Polish officers in the early part of the war.

CHAPTER 27

The Russians had also stopped outside Warsaw and let the Germans finish off the Polish resistance before moving in to finish off the Germans. What utter bastards!

He had to retreat to his fantasy world: East London; Devon; Gloucester Central station. The depression became worse. The hunger became worse. He would give anything, anything just not to feel hungry.

Ad and some of the others had asked the guards what they knew of some strange trains that passed by on the railway just outside the camp. The trains were made of cattle trucks but were apparently full of civilians being moved eastwards under SS guards. The guards shrugged their shoulders; they had no idea either. 'Outside these walls you do not ask questions. No-one seems to know what these trains are but if you ask questions about those trains you could find yourself inside one of them. Whatever it is, it is not going to be good.'

After a month or so, the camp was besieged with a huge influx of new Kriegies. Many were in the khaki of the British army, some were in the uniforms of American troops, some were in RAF blue-grey, and some in the similar colour of the USAAF. Each was sent into their own appropriate compound. These were the men who had been taken prisoner at the failed operation at Arnhem.

At around the same time there appeared a man who had done the rounds of the Stalag-Luft accommodation at Barth, Sagan, Heydekrug and Thorn. He was a tough, uncompromising Glaswegian and natural leader of men: Warrant Officer James 'Dixie' Deans. Deans had been a pilot in a Whitley Bomber from 77 Squadron, RAF, and had been shot down in an attack on Bremen in 1940. At Fallingbostel, in the sergeants' compound, he was to find himself the highest ranked. He was therefore the senior British officer (SBO). That was odd. At Sagan there had been a group captain and several wing commanders and squadron leaders. Why was a warrant officer the highest ranked RAF member? The officers had clearly been sent somewhere else. Ad and the other Kriegies could only hope they were still alive.

Deans had found the compound much as Ad had been seeing it for the last month: dreary, dirty and despairing. Deans saw to it that the Kommandant, Oberst Hermann Ostmann, accepted him as SBO and called a parade of all ranks. He brought them to attention and dressed them down for being a load of scruffy, dirty bastards. He informed them that this sloppiness was stopping forthwith. Each man was going to wash and shave every day. Apparently, he did not spell out any punishments for non-compliance; he was in charge and that was how it was going to be.

The men responded at once and favourably. Deans instituted a regime of regular exercise and daily parades. Uniforms became smarter and washed more frequently; men stood more rigidly to attention; drill improved from sloppy on day one to an acceptable standard a week later. Morale went up.

Deans also did some other things of which the Germans were not aware. Firstly, he found out where the clandestine radios were and organised a word-of-mouth news service across the whole of the camp. This would bring much-valued news of the war to the Kriegies. Now, everyone knew how close the Russians were coming to them and also of progress on the Western Front after the disaster at Arnhem. The news service was also known to the Germans. Unlike the situation in other camps, the Germans did not try to close the radios down. They preferred to ask the Kriegies about progress in the war because their own radio station, Reichsender Hamburg, was known to tell lies, subservient to the dying authority of the German Nazi party.

Deans also immediately organised a trading and bribery market within the camp. He took a levy on the cigarette rations, which he used to compromise the guards. A guard, once compromised, could be persuaded to do anything required. This resulted in additional

CHAPTER 27

supplies of food at a time when Red Cross parcels were not coming through. It resulted in the provision of medicines at a time when the Third Reich had little left for its own people. It also resulted in improvements in accommodation and the provisions of more mattresses and blankets.

According to those who knew, Deans was said to have a secret store of several million cigarettes with which to bribe guards, but this remained unconfirmed.

Deans was also working for MI9. This he would have hidden from even the other prisoners. As with John Casson at Stalag Luft III, he was sending coded messages home. The code was based on a particular edition of a German–English dictionary. He had sent home details of the location of the V-weapons factory at Peenemünde, which he had learned from some guards who spoke carelessly. Deans also sent back relocations of factories and details of the Mark VI Tiger tank. Quite how the code worked remains a mystery.

Deans' efforts started almost immediately to have an effect on the psychology of the camp. Although the British, Americans and Canadians were prisoners, they were on the side that was winning the war and they were starting to look like it. It was now the German guards who looked sloppy and dispirited. Conversations between prisoners and guards now began to dwell on such topics as whether Britain had signed the Geneva Convention. Yes, they had. 'Did the British treat their prisoners well?' Yes, as far as anyone knew they were fair to their prisoners. 'What were the most important things to take into captivity with you?'

By now the Red Cross parcels had stopped altogether. Ad had not seen a letter from Miranda for months. That made him very unsettled. At least he was not alone. The lack of her letters was a terrible deprivation but at least the failure in delivery indicated yet another failure in the dying Third Reich. That had to be good.

BOMBS AND BARBED WIRE

And the hunger went on and on. The rations were now down to one loaf of bread between ten men per day. The half pint of thin soup made of cabbage or turnips or potato peelings held body and soul together but not much more. Ambrose Adlam looked like a skeleton. His ribs stuck out. His arms were like sticks with little muscle left on them. He could not bear to look at his face in the shaving mirror; his eyes looked enormous in his head, the skull just covered with paper-thin flesh. Miranda would be horrified when, and if, she eventually got to see him.

After Christmas more men piled into the camp. These were primarily Americans, thousands of them, who had been taken prisoner after the Battle of the Bulge between Belgium and Germany. The newcomers were sent into a different compound and put up in a tented camp. Given that night-time temperatures were dropping well below zero this was a misfortune in the extreme. Cases of frostbite increased in number. Ad was glad to be in the first-class accommodation, sleeping in the corridor of a hut in a mattress on the floor. He just wanted to be out of there and never to have to think about it in the whole of his life again.

Then came the bombshell!

Kommandant Ostmann called Appel. Some two dozen guards entered the huts. They could hear the sound of breaking wood. Several trucks appeared in the compound. The guards were loading all of the mattresses onto the trucks and also the wooden slats which held the mattresses.

'So, gentlemen, you will be asking yourselves what is going on. Let me clear up matters for you. Higher authority has ordered me to remove all of your bedding.'

This led to murmuring and complaining in the ranks.

'Parade! Parade, attent-ion!' shouted Deans. There was silence.

'This is in retaliation. It has come to the attention of higher authority that your own people have treated Luftwaffe personnel very

CHAPTER 27

badly in one of your camps in Egypt. Your own people have denied Luftwaffe personnel sleeping measures and therefore you are to be treated in the same way. Thank you, Mr Deans, please dismiss your men.'

When they returned to the barracks every mattress, every pillow, every sheet and every bed board had been removed.

Deans marched purposefully towards the sentry on the gate.

'*Oberfeldwebel Deans will sich beim Kommandant melden.*' Warrant Officer Deans wishes to speak with the Kommandant. Fluent German was one of Deans' talents. It was to serve him well.

What Deans actually said to the Kommandant remains unknown and there were no minutes from the meeting. It is most likely to have been on the lines of 'What are you most worried about? A possible court-martial from the Oberkommando Wehrmacht for disobeying an order or a war crimes trial in a few months' time?'

The bedding was restored.

After some more time, black time, dead time, time which hung like corpses on the gallows, could it have been four months, five months, six months... came another daytime Appel.

'Gentlemen,' said Deans, 'we are to leave this camp. The British have crossed the Rhein.' This was punctuated by massive cheering. 'And I might add that the Black Watch were the first unit to cross. But also we are to leave this camp. We are to move in a northerly direction towards Lübeck. We do not appear to have a clear destination. Nor do we have transport.'

So, then, the mighty Third Reich had now decayed internally to the point where its entire infrastructure was on the point of collapsing – or had already collapsed.

'We will form up on the Appelplatz in two hours' time; bring with you only what you can carry.'

Ad packed his few belongings in silence. His possessions at this time consisted of little more than his letters from Miranda. He was well aware that the next episode in his life could end in one sort of tragedy or another.

CHAPTER 28
THE LONG MARCH

22 APRIL 1945

And so it was that Ad formed up with 12,000 other airmen to march 'towards Lübeck'. Lübeck was 150 miles (250 kilometres) to the north-east. No-one seemed to know if they were to go to Lübeck itself, to a camp near Lübeck or if Lübeck were just a staging post to somewhere else. No-one seemed to have any clear orders, least of all the German escort.

The mood was sombre. The prisoners' narrow aspirations were to survive, to find something to eat and not to fall into the hands of the SS or the Russians. The German guards' aspirations were similar. In one of those odd quirks of fortune which occurs in wartime, British prisoners and German guards shared the same objective: just to get to the end of this total mess. They were now all on the same side.

For the prisoners, 'Dixie' Deans was clearly in charge. On the German side it was no longer clear who was in charge. The Kommandant was most certainly in attendance somewhere nearby but appeared to give no orders whatsoever, his authority much diminished. There were one or two junior officers and some non-commissioned officers. Who was running the show remained uncertain.

Deans spoke to the senior non-commissioned officers. 'It is completely unclear where they are sending us. They don't know where we are heading for today. They don't know if there are any billets for us. They don't know if there is any food laid on. All we can do is to assume the worst.'

CHAPTER 28

He let the message sink in. 'Assume we have to forage for food. Assume you will have to make your own arrangements for billets and assume the locals will be hostile. There is one other thing, though, lads. You can assume we have won the war and when you're on that road and you see any German civvies or, especially, a man in uniform you can walk with your heads held high.'

They formed into six columns, each 2000 strong and each with an escort of guards. The guards, by this time, were drawn from the ranks of the war-wounded, the more-than-middle-aged and the 'unfit for duty' brigade. The German guards did not have transport, any more than the prisoners. The German soldiers, Landwehr men and men from the Reich work service walked alongside them. The fire-breathing Nazis of a couple of years ago had all but disappeared. Now Germany was made up of a population which was as hungry as the prisoners, depressed and just waiting for the war to end.

Ad did not look back. The camp at Fallingbostel was an experience to forget. They all just wanted the overcrowding, the overflowing latrines and the gnawing of the hunger out of their minds. Now they were awaiting another gauntlet from the civvies as they passed through villages.

'If one of those Hitler Youth creeps shouts something at me, I will kick his arse so hard it will split his lederhosen into six different pieces,' said a voice behind him.

Then came the surprise. As they walked along, the civilians, old men, old women, the disabled and the war-wounded looked at them with mild interest, but no-one said anything. They looked down at the street.

Ad walked along with a guard with whom he had had some conversations.

'What's going on, Dieter? There's something funny about the place. Where are all the Hitler Youth idiots?'

'Sergeant Adlam, terrible things are coming to light. Did you know that there was a camp, Stalag XIC, on the other side of the training area eastwards of the Fallingbostel?'

'There were so many camps I have no idea where they were.'

BOMBS AND BARBED WIRE

'This one was about 30 kilometres south-east. It is at a village called Bergen-Belsen. British troops moved in there four days ago. It has not been mentioned on the radio, but local people have been talking about it.' The British soldiers found tens of thousands of dead and dying people.

'Kriegies?'

'No, they were German civilians: Jews and other civilians from across Europe. It is terrible.'

'Oh my God! But why are these people looking so glum?'

'They are worried what the British and Americans will do to them. They are also running out of food. You have not had much to eat; the local population has little more than you have.'

'Where are all the nasty little Hitler Youth boys? We're missing their happy smiling faces.'

'They were taken away for training to defend Berlin.'

'WHAT? They were putting 13-and 14-year-olds in against the bloody Russians?'

'Yes.' He looked glum. 'Our leaders have taken 14-year-old boys. They trained them to fight on bicycles against Russian tanks.'

'What? Really?'

'Really, Sergeant Adlam.'

Ad and the guard walked on in silence. The Hitler Youth boys had been horrible little pests but not even the most irritated Kriegie could wish that on them.

The guard broke the silence. 'I expect those boys are all dead.' There was another silence as they trudged along. 'What do you think your soldiers will do to the civilians?' There was fear in his voice. 'Will they send them away?'

Ad had heard this before. Germans always seemed to worry about being sent 'away' wherever that may be.

'Look, I don't know. I don't know where "away" is, but I doubt it very much. These are just old people and war-wounded. I don't think anything will happen to them.'

They walked along in silence.

'Everything OK, boys?' said a cheery Glasgow accent from behind him. 'Dixie' Deans had availed himself of a bicycle and was riding up

CHAPTER 28

and down the column asking if everyone was all right. To all intents the role of Deans now resembled that of a leader of a weekend walking group who set direction, decided when to stop and when to start up again. It was clear that he had enough psychological advantage that the guards were not going to stop him.

'OK, lads, there's a village up ahead so we might stop there for a bite to eat.'

So saying, he cycled off to the head of the column, which promptly stopped. They had only travelled about 4 miles but in their emaciated state were in desperate need of a rest. A village pump provided water. The locals were happy to bargain for cigarettes. Raw potatoes, cabbages and turnips were not haute cuisine but were perfectly adequate for keeping body and soul together.

One or two of the Kriegies who had built up a reserve of Reichsmarks discovered that they were no longer in demand.

The old men of the village were quite clear. 'We don't want paper money; we can't spend it. We want cigarettes. We can buy anything with cigarettes.'

The Third Reich had come to this: the currency had failed, and it was now in total collapse.

On leaving the village someone let out a gasp. Hanging from a tree was a man, a woman and two young girls. They were swinging gently in the light breeze, their strangled faces only too visible in the midday light.

'Oh my Christ!' said someone.

'It is the SS,' said Dieter. 'Look, there is a placard around the man's neck: *Ich glaubte nicht am endlichen Sieg*. I did not believe in final victory.'

Deans came along on his bicycle and ordered half a dozen men to cut them down.

'Treat them with respect, boys. We've had it bad but they've had it worse.'

They ascertained from the villagers that an SS unit had been there the previous afternoon, but they did not know where they went.

They passed through more villages. There was more barter. Then they found a column of refugees heading westwards. A short conversation with a woman ascertained that they were from East Prussia, an area which the Russians had overrun.

'If you think the Russians will get this far west, you should just leave your homes and go. They are animals.' She told of a village called Nemmersdorf in East Prussia. The Russians had taken it; the Germans counterattacked and retook it. The Russian soldiers had butchered several hundred German civilians. Women had been crucified on barn doors and raped. Several hundred French and Italian prisoners of war had been systematically murdered.

The guards confirmed the story. 'There is film of this,' the guards had said. 'If the Russians get you before the British or Americans, we do not know what will happen to you.'

'We're on the same side as the Russians.'

'You might think so, but the Russians might not. Everything we hear about them says they are inhuman beasts.'

The woman said no more. That drawn face showed the horror she had seen. The refugees moved westwards to an unknown destination. Many of the people in the village packed what they could and headed westwards along with the prisoners.

At night they found yet another similar village. Deans once more came along on his bicycle rather like a solicitous border collie looking after his sheep.

'Just as we thought, boys, there are no billets, there's no rations. We're getting good at this, though. Just move into the village and see what you can arrange with the locals.'

Some bought a bed, or a floor for the night with cigarettes. Some moved into barns or sheds. Some moved into the local church. Some moved into farmyards, garages or anything with a roof. Fortunately, it was chilly but not freezing.

The farms afforded more vegetables, a little bread and water from the pumps. The farmers had little to offer. They themselves had little left.

The next day they pressed on. The older guards were beginning to show signs of fatigue. The prisoners carried their rifles and packs. No-one tried to escape. There was nowhere to escape to and, anyway, if a man on the run fell in among an SS unit their fate was fairly clear.

CHAPTER 28

A pattern emerged. You would wake up in the morning and shave in a stream or in the water of an ice-cold farmyard pump. Breakfast was a luxury but sometimes cigarette barter was able to achieve it. You would form up into columns and head north or north-east. West was not possible: the vast Lüneberger Heide area was like the North Yorkshire Moors – relatively uninhabited and hostile to humans without the means of support.

They passed through a number of sullen, depressed villages. The villages were not ravaged by war, or at least not yet. Two aspects became clear very quickly. The entire civilian populationwas as badly off as the prisoners. The Nazis had confiscated almost all of their food, their animals and their means of livelihood such as vehicles or wagons. Anyone who had protested had been hanged from a tree opposite their house. A suitable placard around their neck pointed out how unpatriotic they were. The other aspect was that the farming population were as happy to trade with the prisoners as the prisoners were with them. In the final analysis, neither had much and bartering was down to a minimum. A stop, even in the middle of the day, meant an instant sleep, no matter where they were or what the weather was like.

As they headed north, they came across several more sad processions of refugees. From time to time they came across lines of refugees heading eastwards to escape the fighting as the British army pressed into North Germany. They met the other lines of refugees heading westwards to escape the Russians. The refugees in both lines were defeated, exhausted, demoralised. There was nothing that could be done for them, not until the war ended, whenever that might be.

In the afternoon they would come across a village and the same procedure would carry on. The guards now walked with the prisoners as friends more than jailers. In the evening they would find a village, find a barn, a shed or a wall and doss down. No-one asked any more where they might be heading.

To the east they could hear the soft rumbling of artillery, lots of it. The Russians were getting closer.

The whole numbing routine carried on, day after day, for about a week. No-one asked how far they had travelled: apathy was setting in.

In fact, they were averaging 10 miles (16 kilometres) a day but in their debilitated state it felt like 70.

When a break in the routine happened it was for the worse: much worse.

Ad had observed that they had not seen or heard any bombers passing overhead for the last couple of weeks. There were no Luftwaffe aircraft and no RAF or USAAF aircraft to be seen. It was clear that something was happening but what?

'Hey, lads, there's a flight of fighters up there. They're RAF Typhoons.'

The flight turned towards them and came to a lower altitude, apparently to have a look at what they might be. The leader winged-over and began to fly towards them. Ad saw the twinkling of lights sparking from the wings of the lead aeroplane. Someone yelled out, 'Take cover! For God's sake, take cover!' Ad dived into a ditch and lay with his hands over his head. The first rounds struck the road. Ad realised these were not just bullets: they were cannon shells which would rip a man apart if they hit him. The cannon shells from the lead aeroplane raked the road from one side to the other.

He heard the 'pop-pop-pop' of the explosion as they hit the road surface.

Someone was screaming, 'We're British, you bastards! We're bloody British!'

The 'pop-pop-pop' noise expanded until it became a hail of explosions all around him. Above the melee of exploding shells he could hear screams; they were the blood-curdling screams of men who were being torn limb from limb by the explosions of the cannon shells. The Typhoon leader passed over them and the explosions stopped. He put his head out of the ditch. Men were looking at the stump where a leg had been severed and were screaming in abject fear. One or two were already dead.

More explosions began: a second Typhoon was on his run-in. Ad hunkered down in the ditch and put his hands over his head. Once again, the maelstrom of high explosive boiled and shattered only a few feet from where he lay. He knew that if a single one of those shells

CHAPTER 28

were to find him then he was dead meat: and meat in the most literal sense of the word.

The explosions stopped but then started again and again as nine Typhoons, one after the other, cold bloodedly targeted the column, aimed towards it and fired their cannon shells into the quivering mass of humanity below. The attack lasted perhaps two minutes, but it must have been the most terrifying two minutes of his life: much worse than being shot down on the way to Dortmund.

Deans rode along on his bicycle. He organised the wounded men to lie as comfortably as possible on the side of the road. It was already clear that many were dead and others were dying as they lay bleeding or their organs were shattered by shell fire. There were no medical supplies, no medical orderlies. One or two men had done first aid training and did what they could. It was very little. An hour later it was clear that 50 men were dead and another ten were likely to die soon. Around 200 were wounded – about half were walking-wounded but half were not able to move.

The column marched on. Deans left a detachment of men to look after the wounded and dying but with little hope of finding any medical help for them.

The next day the column marched to yet another village. They learned that the Elbe was just ahead. The Elbe nears its estuary at Hamburg at this point. It is very wide. Passage without boats was impossible. The column still didn't know where it was supposed to be heading.

'Where to now, Dixie?' asked a wag. 'That is a very good question, if I might say so.'

As they marched, or rather trudged, into the village one of the local inhabitants ran into the street. Ad saw him say something to the men at the head of the column. This resulted in an explosion of cheering. The explosion of cheering moved rapidly backwards. What on earth was it?

'Hitler's dead! He's shot himself.'

No football cup final or cricket match or any other sporting occasion ever saw cheering and dancing and embracing and clapping and jumping for joy such as that village saw. Afterwards, Ad would have had no idea where the village was or what it was called. It was just 'the place where everyone went completely crazy.'

The guards clearly felt they should not cheer but looked for guidance towards their officers, who did not look too displeased. It meant it was nearly over, the nightmare was nearly over. But that in itself caused a problem. Where the hell were they supposed to go?

Deans asked to speak to the Kommandant, who had reappeared and was walking along with them.

'Oberst Ostmann, can you please advise me, as senior British officer, where this column is heading for?'

'No, Herr Oberfeldwebel, I cannot. My orders were to bring you to the Lübeck area, but I have received nothing more definite than that.'

'Well, do you know if your command structure is still operating?'

'No, Herr Oberfeldwebel, I do not. I have heard nothing from my command for some two weeks now.'

'Might I have permission to make a suggestion, sir?'

'Well, Herr Oberfeldwebel?'

'We have the Elbe ahead of us and no obvious means of crossing it, so we cannot go to Lübeck. We have heard the Russian guns to the east every day for a week now. I propose, sir, that you should take the view that the German command structure no longer operates and decide whether you want to surrender to the British or to the Russians. Both options appear to be very available.'

Oberst Ostmann considered for a moment. 'What do you propose?'

'I propose that you authorise me to travel under close escort to the west to make contact with the forward units of the British army. We don't know where they are, but they cannot be far away now. I will return with an officer of sufficient rank to whom you and your men can surrender.'

'What do you suppose will happen to my men if we surrender, Herr Oberfeldwebel?'

'The British are signatories of the Geneva Convention. I cannot pretend to know in any detail as to your treatment. I would remind you, though, that the Russians are not signatories of the Geneva Convention. We know from refugees that many of their units are not

CHAPTER 28

taking prisoners at all. Under British captivity I imagine you would be treated much as we were, but you will receive a lot more rations.'

Oberst Ostmann gave an order to his adjutant. Fifteen minutes later the adjutant drove up in a rather comfortable Mercedes saloon car, which had apparently belonged to a Nazi official who had recently left the village in a hurry.

'Take two officers with you. We will await your return at this village.'

'Very good, sir, I will bring up what medical help I can for the men wounded in the last village.'

The column halted. The men fell out, fell down and fell into a deep, deep sleep. Those who could did what was possible for the wounded. Some more died. They bartered more food from the locals. Now the population was down to what they had grown in their gardens. All they could do was wait. After a day they worried that he might have been killed by a trigger-happy forward patrol. After two days this was beginning to seem more likely.

Around 48 hours later there was a stir at the head of the column.

'Dixie's back!'

The Mercedes with Deans and the two German officers pulled up beside the Kommandant's billet. Behind him was a scout car containing a British major in full combat order carrying a German Schmeisser machine gun. Behind them were two ambulances which were sent immediately to the casualties at the last village and bringing up the rear were two trucks carrying loaves of bread.

Ad watched as the major stepped forward to the Kommandant and saluted smartly.

'Major Henry, sir, British Sixth Parachute Division representing Lieutenant General Baker. The general apologises for not being here personally but he has some rather urgent business to attend to on the riverbank.' Ostmann smiled.

'Very well, Major Henry, I surrender myself and my men and trust you will treat us in accordance with the Geneva Convention.' Ostmann handed his service pistol to the major with a '*bitte schön*'.

'Now,' said Henry, addressing a group of men who had gathered around him, 'have any of these blokes given you any trouble in captivity?'

'Yes,' said one Kriegie – or former Kriegie – 'there was one bastard who was always telling us that the SS were going to hang us all and that our wives were all being screwed by black Americans.'

'All yours,' said Henry and gave him the Kommandant's pistol. 'Go and sort him out.'

The man walked off with the pistol. A minute or so later two sharp cracks were heard. The man returned the pistol.

'Yes, Herr Oberst, from this point, you will be treated according to the Geneva Convention.'

They all knew that they should not have laughed. They all did.

At three o'clock the next afternoon the column, now walking with great purpose and preceded by a man with a Union Jack, approached the British lines. All of the Germans had surrendered their weapons, which were being carried by RAF men. But where were the British lines? They walked along a road just like the roads they had been walking on for the last 12 days. There was no difference.

Without warning, a British soldier in heavy camouflage order appeared out of a hedgerow pointing a machine pistol forward. His uniform was the same colour as the soil of the countryside – his uniform was totally impregnated with it. He looked uncompromising; it was the look of a man who could no longer remember how long he had been in combat but did not necessarily want it to come to an end. He was one of those soldiers to whom the war was an adventure sport.

'You the Brylcreem Boys; POWs?'

'That's us,' said Deans.

'Walk along the road and you'll find the adjutant about a mile down the road. Just tell the Herrenvolk not to make any sudden moves or my men may get jumpy.'

Deans brought the Germans to a position inside the ranks of the RAF men protecting them from the sights of any snipers who might be in the trees.

'Just walk along with us, take your caps off and you'll be all right. They'll find something to eat for all of us.'

CHAPTER 28

Ad looked at the Germans. He knew that this would be the last he would see of them. If anything, they were grateful that the war was over. Most of them were just blokes like him and he hoped they would not have too hard a time in the days and years to come.

As they walked along the road Ad could see that in the bushes, the hedgerows and the copses of trees there were hundreds of British uniforms, thousands of them, heavily armed and dangerous. It was over. It was all over.

He fell into conversation with a lieutenant.

'How long were you in captivity, old boy?'

'Actually, I don't know. What's the date?'

'It's 3 May, old boy.'

Ad laughed. 'Two years: it's almost my anniversary. I took off on 4 May 1943 to bomb Dortmund and never got back. I do hope the raid was worth it.'

'Not really, we still had to fight for every inch to get from Normandy to here.'

The most important thing was food. British army trucks brought forward enough for everyone including the guards. The meagre field diet of spam and self-heating cans of soup was the most delicious meal that he had had in his life. Two days after living in an impromptu tented camp a truck took him on an eight-hour drive through smashed villages, mined roads and ruined farms. He jumped out of the truck in Brussels, where they were all given new uniforms, a shower in a mobile unit and a couple of days' leave until transport could be arranged back to the UK. In Brussels there was beer; there were no Appels; he was free! He was bloody free!

As his aeroplane touched down, back in England's green and pleasant land, the news came through that Admiral Dönitz had surrendered the Axis forces to General Montgomery on Lüneberger Heide, very close to where he had just walked, or trekked or stumbled for two dreadful weeks.

It was all over. In Trafalgar Square, in London, crowds danced in a frenzied and hilariously un-British way. Winston Churchill appeared on the balcony of Buckingham Palace to tumultuous, ecstatic homage from a vast, packed crowd. The blackout ended. There were lights in the streets again. Ad just wanted to be on the train back to Gloucester and Miranda.

At last, it was all over.

It was all over.

CHAPTER 29

THE 1219 FROM PADDINGTON TO GLOUCESTER (CENTRAL)

12 MAY 1945

> *The train now standing at platform 5 is the 1219 to Cheltenham Spa calling at Reading General, Swindon, Gloucester Central and Cheltenham Spa.*

Ah! That was OK; he had a half-hour until it went. He smiled as he caught sight of himself in the glass window outside the station bar. This is what Miranda would see in a couple of hours' time. He had been well fed by the NAAFI since liberation a week ago. He still hadn't fattened up, but he found it so wonderful that he could smile again. He felt resplendent in his brand-new uniform, with his sergeant's stripes and his flight engineer brevet. He really did like that brevet!

This was the first time he had been alone since being liberated somewhere in northern Germany. Then it struck him: it was the first time he had been alone with his own thoughts since he had been in the hospital ward at Dulag Luft. It also struck him that the last time he had been on Paddington station was when he had left to join 405 Squadron. He had known, of course, that he was unlikely to complete the tour of 30 operations and had wondered at the time if he would see Paddington station again. Here he was, nevertheless; he had survived and thousands of others had not.

Perhaps he would treat himself to a half pint of bitter in celebration of his lucky survival. Perhaps not. He had learned in the last couple of days that people always saw the flight engineer brevet on his uniform: that meant aircrew and that drew people to you.

It catapulted an otherwise ordinary man to the status of hero. That was not really what he wanted. Ad was a private man. He had done what he felt he had to do but had no desire to have any attention drawn to himself. He would have liked a drink with Johnny or Bernie, but they were dead and in a grave somewhere in Germany. He would have liked a pint with the other crew members, but they had disappeared into the void somewhere.

Anyway, strangers buying you drinks always wanted to know what you had done. He could not talk about dropping 1000-pound high explosive bombs, knowing he had personally been responsible for the deaths of hundreds of women and children. He could not talk about jumping out of a burning plane. The memory was still too psychologically raw. He could not talk about being shot by the Luftwaffe. He could not talk of the 50 men shot at Sagan or how he had been involved in their deaths. He could not talk of the cold and hunger. He could not talk of the idiotic march across northern Germany or the men shot up by their own planes. He could not talk of his proximity to the transit camp of Belsen, whose horrors were now emblazoned across the papers.

The few people that he had talked to back in Blighty demanded stories of the German beasts and the levels of depravity which he had seen. It just wasn't true! A vast majority of the Luftwaffe personnel had been decent blokes that you would have shared a pint with in different circumstances. The SS and Gestapo certainly operated at an extreme level of savagery, but he had hardly seen them. He could even

CHAPTER 29

feel some sympathy with the older civilians who had screamed at the RAF uniforms in the street. They were terrified of what was going to happen and terrified with good reason. The nasty little Hitler Youth boys were just dupes who had been told lies about the glory of the Third Reich. They were doubtlessly proud to die for the Führer. At Lauenberg, the first town he had seen after liberation, he had learned that a whole generation had vanished. All the Hitler Youth boys had indeed been taken away to defend Berlin. None had come back. Their parents feared the worst. So did Ad. It meant that tens of thousands of young teenage boys had been taken away to be summarily massacred by the Russians. He could not talk about that either.

He could not talk about the starving population in Germany, he could not talk about the bodies he had seen swinging in the breeze. He could not talk about the women who would sell themselves for ten cigarettes, or five if the competition was hot.

Oh God! He just needed it all out of his head. And so, after the first couple of encounters in pubs he had just said that he had not been really a hero who had been in aircrew, he had just flown a desk and pushed a pen in a place outside Cambridge. They looked disappointed, but it kept those thoughts away from his head.

However, for the family, he was destined to be a hero of a different sort. He had packets of Gold Leaf cigarettes for all the family in Gloucester. For the kids he had sixpenny bars of Cadbury's chocolate. He could buy them cheaply in the NAAFI, but he knew that out in the land of civilians these were luxuries. He also had two pairs of nylon stockings for Miranda. He had bought them off a spiv but in those days of austerity it was poor etiquette to ask where someone had purchased something. It was even worse etiquette to tell them. He decided to walk through the arch into the street outside. This was better; in fact, it was wonderful. He walked outside the huge Paddington station and walked down Praed Street. There was no guard on the gate to shoot him. He could just walk and walk if he wanted to.

A policeman shared a joke with a taxi driver. 'So my inspector said…' Ad didn't catch the rest of it but the cabbie laughed out loud. Nurses, looking very professional in red-lined dark blue capes, walked off shift from St Mary's Hospital across the road. A railway lorry drove out through the arch with a load of parcels. Red buses drove purposefully to Maida Vale, Willesden Junction and East Acton. It was all so normal, so free, there were no more goon boxes, carnivorous Alsatian dogs and men with firearms. His eyes filled. A more emotional man might have burst into tears at the sheer joy and delicate beauty of freedom. The first thing was to get back with Miranda and the family. His job in the Gloucester Oil Mills was held open for him by law. Was that what he really wanted? No, he did not think so. He had telephoned friends back in Gloucester who had told him a rumour about his brother Bill. He had been blown up by a landmine some two months after D Day, somewhere in northern France. He was wounded and had been in and out of hospital. He was in a bad way. He had heard that the army had tried to keep Bill on, but the wounds were severe and his future was uncertain.

At least Bill was alive. At least he was still walking on two legs. At least as far as anyone knew.

'Do you mind if I stand beside the window, sir?' The train clattered out of Paddington station and up the bank towards the imperiously huge locomotive sheds at Old Oak Common.

'Yes, certainly, lad, I'm not a "sir", though, I'm a sergeant'. He smiled at the boy's dad.

Oh no! He knew what was coming next.

'You've got an "E" brevet, you're a flight engineer.'

'Oh, I just flew a typewriter in a place outside Cambridge.'

'Don't ask so many questions, Edwin. Look, here's Old Oak Common.'

He broke off the conversation with a polite smile and buried himself in the newspaper. The boy looked at the dozens of steam locomotives in the yard outside the engine sheds. 'Oh look, Dad, there's three Kings over there and at least four Castles.'

'Gosh! Those are smashers!' said his dad with magnificently feigned parental enthusiasm.

That is what 14-year-old boys are supposed to do, Ad thought. They are supposed to be boys and interested in railway locomotives.

CHAPTER 29

He had seen hundreds of the little sods in Germany dressed up in Hitler Youth uniforms and taunting the prisoners. Now all those boys had been packed off to Berlin to their deaths as meat underneath a Russian tank. He knew that it was very important to get these thoughts out of his head.

After liberation, he had been kept at his squadron base, Gransden Lodge, longer than he had hoped. It had been good to see that the windmill was still there. That horrible little man, Junge, at Dulag Luft had asked him about the windmill. He had wondered how Junge had known. That had really bothered him. Now it simply did not matter. He smiled that the erstwhile mystery was of no interest either to him or anyone else on earth.

He had been given two or three medical assessments which had pronounced him chronically thin. He had actually suspected that this might be the case due to his ribs standing out like a xylophone. Fortunately, there was nothing worse to concern the medical officers. Then he had been debriefed by various officers on his time in imprisonment.

Then came the very detailed and very searching debriefs on the escape from Stalag Luft III. Military men in civilian clothes asked him about these. An RAF officer would be seated at the table but would not speak. He had no idea who these men were, and they never introduced themselves. Later, someone would suggest they were MI5, but you never quite knew. They wanted to know all about the officers; all about the guards; all about the living conditions; all about the escape. What did he know of Bushell, of Floody, of Day, of Fanshawe or any of the other leaders? How had the German guards reacted to the escape and then to the murders?

They were interestingly different to the Luftwaffe interrogators. The Luftwaffe men had been sophisticated academics, who were clearly civilians in uniform and who had subtle techniques to persuade a man to open up. These men were rough, tough military men in civilian clothes who just came out and asked a very direct question, looking for a very direct answer.

Had he ever suspected any collaboration between RAF personnel and the Luftwaffe? Had he ever seen these men? They showed him photographs. He shook his head. What did he know of the man called Rubberneck? Of Rudi? 'Rudi? Never heard of him'. Of the friendly Hundenführer with his dogs? They had debriefed him several times. He had asked the reason. The officer had told him they were putting together a picture of the escape to pursue the people who were responsible. They were going after anyone with any culpability whatsoever. When they got them there was going to be retribution.

'Why are they talking to me so much, sir?'

'You wrote a letter home on the day of the Great Escape, didn't you? It intrigued them that you would do that rather than spend all day talking about the escape.'

'How the hell did they know that?'

'I don't know, Adlam. Anyway, you're finished, so ask the adjutant to draw you up a railway warrant and I suggest you pop off and see your family before any silly clot dreams up more questions for you.'

He turned the paper. The pictures from Bergen Belsen had been headline news for days now. He caught a glimpse of the emaciated, white, living corpses. He had to fold up the paper quickly. For a moment he remembered that stomach-curdling stench when the wind blew from the south-east. He had to get out of the compartment.

'Is the buffet car to the left or the right, can you remember?'

The boy's father looked at him in politely muted amazement.

'Buffet car? We haven't seen a buffet car on this line since hostilities started. There's a war on. At least there was a war on. Where have you been?'

'Excuse me, I must just pop out.'

He stood in the corridor with his thoughts. As the train slowed down for the approach into Reading General station, he caught sight of the jail: Victorian, red and grim. For a second, he felt empathy with the people in it. They could not walk through the railway arch at Paddington station as he had done. They could not buy packets

CHAPTER 29

of cigarettes from the NAAFI or nylons from spivs or do any of the normal things that people did. Then it hit him. It wasn't the same thing at all.

The blokes in Reading gaol were there because they had pulled a swifty for self-gratification. The Kriegies had been in gaol because they had put their lives on the line to put the Third Reich and all of its disgusting works out of business.

As the train stopped the family eased politely past him.

'Bye, Sergeant,' said the dad. 'But with a flight engineer brevet I don't think you flew a typewriter near Cambridge. Anyway, I just want to say thanks for all you did and please accept these from us.'

He pressed a packet of 20 Player's Navy Cut cigarettes into his hand, descended to the platform and slammed the door.

He had the compartment to himself. He looked at his new watch, which had cost ten Capstan cigarettes from a grateful old man in Lauenberg. It was now only 90 minutes until he would see her again. He had sent a telegram and hoped that she had received it.

Now, he had to get his mind into gear. First thing was to see Miranda. The thought sent a frisson of electricity through him. It had been over two years since he had seen her. They had to think about what they were going to do in the post–war world. Oh God! How was he to tell her that he was only on leave and not demobilised? The new wing commander at Gransden Lodge had told them all that they were still service personnel. The war was still going on in the east and it was completely possible that the squadron would be sent to the east to fight the Japs.

She would want to know about what had happened to him. She would have known that the breezy, brittle optimism which had always been in his letters was fake and that he must have known very, very bad times. She might ask if he had been mistreated or might quietly look at his body for any signs of scars. Apart from the bullet and shrapnel wounds there were none.

Then there were the things that she did not know. What would he tell her about those? He decided to confess that the hunger pangs were so bad that they were even worse than the pangs from being away from her. This would let her be magnanimous and earn him some much-desired cuddles. He knew that it would not lead to her cooking him enormous meals. Food rationing now was even more severe than he had known in 1943. There was something else about that confession. It might take the focus onto matters that he could control and away from the things that he just did not want to talk about.

Swindon! Closer now! He buried himself in the crossword to avoid the newcomers in the compartment asking about that 'E' brevet.

He had a week at home and needed to plan it out. There was the family to see: that was paramount. He was especially worried about Bill. Then he wanted to go and have a pint in his local pub and then… just walk along the Severn with Miranda and talk about the future. Yes! The most important thing for him was to forget Sagan and Fallingbostel and Thorn and just think of what was going to be. They wanted a family. They wanted a nice house somewhere. That was the thing to focus on.

Fallingbostel? It was only 20 days ago but seemed like years. The hunger, the deprivation and the overcrowding were already half out of his mind. He wanted it all the way out. He would never forget Dixie Deans though.

He glimpsed a name on a signal box as the train clattered past it: Kemble! Only 20 minutes! He decided to give her the nylons when they were home. It would be crowded on the bus, especially with his heavy kitbag. He hoped that when he got there only he and she would be there. He could see the family later in the evening. He searched his mind for what he really wanted. It was nothing exotic. He just wanted to have a cup of tea and a biscuit with her, hold her hand and put some music on the BBC Light Service. When he had been at Sagan, if he could have achieved that, he would have thought he was the King of bloody England.

Sagan! That was already – he was losing track – it was months ago. He would have to map it all out when he got home. No, he wouldn't. He just wanted Sagan in its rightful place: outside of his head. The Russians would have had Sagan for some weeks now. God knows how many civilians they would have shot. He just wanted Sagan out of his

CHAPTER 29

head.

Stonehouse! Only ten minutes. Inside, he giggled a private giggle. He was only ten minutes away from seeing her. Even as a quiet and reserved man his heart was racing. The intensity of anticipation made the train, which was travelling at 60 miles an hour, seem as if it were travelling at five miles an hour or even going backwards.

It reminded him of the train from Stalag Luft III to Thorn. That really had gone at five miles an hour and really had gone backwards. Stalag Luft III was the one that he wanted out of his head the most. The murder of those 50 men showed how the Nazis were capable of reaching the depths of depravity. He had done his bit for those escapers but that, in turn, meant he had an unwitting involvement in their death. Would he have done it again? Yes, he would! Would he have got into that Halifax bomber knowing that it would be shot down before he got to Dortmund? Yes, without hesitation! There was a job to be done and there was no option available to him to say that he could not take part.

The train slowed. His heart raced. God! He hoped that the telegram boy had delivered it to the right house. He hoped that she would not have been out doing the shopping or on some other errand and failed to receive the telegram. The train slowly pulled into Gloucester (Central) station. He pulled down the window and put his head out. He searched the platform. He could not see her. His moment of panic reminded him of that moment of panic before jumping out of the plane.

Behind the ticket barrier an arm waved. Someone in a beige coat – a woman – was waving. He looked closer. The train ground to a sudden halt. It was her! It was her! The carriage door seemed to open itself; he grabbed his kitbag and ran down the platform with it on his shoulder. She stood at the barrier. She ran through the barrier, her eyes on him; his eyes were on her.

'Madam, you will need a platform ticket!' shouted a ticket inspector in a large black-peaked cap.

She was only three yards away, her eyes already moist with emotion. He wanted to shout her name but could not get the word 'Miranda' out.

He put out his hand towards her as she raced towards him. She put her hand out to him. They were now almost touching, their fingers touched …

THE END

APPENDIX 1

WHAT BECAME OF THE PEOPLE IN THE STORY?

Name	Role in Story	What Happened Later?
Adlam, Bill, Captain	Ad's elder brother who was at Dunkirk, Dieppe and D Day	Survived the war but suffered through war wounds. Migrated to Australia in 1960. Died 1980.
Adlam, Miranda	Ad's wife, whom he married in South Africa	Stayed in Gloucester, remained there until she died in 2012.
Adlam, Ambrose A, Sergeant	Central character	Returned to Gloucester and married life with Miranda. Became a postman. Died on 17 April 1962 after a very short illness. The cause of death was a sudden and very aggressive abscess in the brain which is believed to have been a late reaction to the piece of flak which wounded him when shot down.
Ainsley, Archie, Flight Lt	Fellow inmate at Stalag Luft III	Returned to native Edinburgh pursued an otherwise normal life. He was highly amused – and delighted – to see that fellow inmate Rupert Davies became a successful actor in the 1960s.
Bauer – Schlichtegroll, Gustav, Leutnant	Interrogator at Dulag Luft	Prosecuted at a British war crimes trial at Wuppertal for torture by overheating cells. Acquitted.

BOMBS AND BARBED WIRE

Name	Role in Story	What Happened Later?
Freeman, Pilot Officer Benson	British fascist sympathiser at Dulag Luft	Joined the Waffen SS in 1943 as Untersturmführer (Second Lieutenant). Captured at war's end and given ten years in jail in the UK.
Brickhill, Paul	Refused to escape through the tunnel on grounds of claustrophobia	Wrote classic war stories: *The Dam Busters*, *Reach for the Sky*, *The Great Escape* and *Escape or Die*.
Casson, John, Lt Commander	Adjutant at Dulag Luft; worked on the escape but later counselled against it. Agent for MI9	Returned to the UK but found his peer group were all promoted several ranks higher. Left the navy and went into theatrical production in Glasgow. Emigrated to Australia.
Crawley, Aidan	Chief interrogator for RAF prisoners arriving at Stalag Luft III. It was his job to identify Luftwaffe 'plants'	Became a Labour MP 1945 – 51 and a Conservative MP 1962 – 67. Also became a TV personality on current affairs programs. His book *Escape from Germany* is a major source of information for this book.
Day, Harry, Squadron Leader	Effective Senior British Officer at Stalag Luft III	After the escape was held in Flossenberg, Dachau and Sachsenhausen concentration camps where he was chained to the floor. Promoted to Group Captain on liberation. Was technical adviser to the films *Reach for the Sky* and *The Great Escape* in both of which he is depicted.
Deans, 'Dixie', Warrant Officer	Senior British officer at Fallingbostel and leader during the long march	Returned to England and found work as executive officer at London School of Economics.
Eberhardt, Heinrich Leutnant	Interrogator at Dulag Luft	Prosecuted at a British war crimes trial at Wuppertal for torture by overheating cells. Committed to three years' jail.
Fanshawe, Lt Commander	Organiser of the 'Penguins' at Stalag Luft III	Remained in the navy after the war and later transferred to the Royal Australian Navy where he met John Casson's son, Tony who was on national service.

APPENDIX 1

Name	Role in Story	What Happened Later?
Fauquier, Wing Commander Johnny	Ad's commanding officer at 405 Squadron	Completed two tours of duty: 50 operations. Became commanding officer of 617 squadron after the death of Guy Gibson. Returned to private business in Canada after the war.
Graham, Sergeant	Bomb aimer	Not known
Griese, Corporal Karl	Chief 'ferret' at Stalag Luft III	His fate is unclear. He does, however, disappear from the narratives of all accounts of the great escape. We could theorise that he was court-martialled and sent to the Eastern Front.
Junge, Major	Interrogator at Dulag Luft	Prosecuted at a British war crimes trial at Wuppertal for torture by overheating cells. Committed to five years' jail.
Killinger, Oberstleutnant	Kommandant at Dulag Luft	Prosecuted at a British war crimes trial at Wuppertal for torture by overheating cells. Committed to five years' jail.
Knight, Sergeant A.T.	Navigator in Lennox's crew	Not known
Lennox, John	Ad's pilot	Interred at Reichswald Forest War Cemetery, Germany: grave 15. F. 14.
Moody, Bernard	Rear gunner in Lennox's crew	Interred at Reichswald Forest War Cemetery, Germany: grave 15. F. 16.
Prieur, Jacques, Sgt	Mid-upper Gunner in Lennox's crew	Not known
Roberts, Sergeant	Wireless operator in Lennox's crew	Not known
Thimmig, Wolfgang, Oberleutnant	Luftwaffe pilot who shot down Lennox's crew including Ambrose	Shot down 24 allied aircraft. Reached the rank of Oberstleutnant and was Geschwaderkommodore for NJG2. Joined the reformed Luftwaffe after World War II. He became German military attaché to Sweden and later helped to create the post-imperial air force in Nigeria.

BOMBS AND BARBED WIRE

Name	Role in Story	What Happened Later?
Von Lindeiner, Colonel	Kommandant of Stalag Luft III during Ad's time there.	After his arrest he feigned insanity to avoid court-martial. Was later second in command of an army unit fighting against the Russians. Spent two years in British captivity. Was spared further severe punishment due to the evidence of many former inmates that he was innocent of any criminal activity against prisoners.

APPENDIX 2
AMBROSE'S ODYSSEY

Camp Name	Camp Location	Entry Dates
Auswertestelle West (Dulag Luft)	Oberursel near Frankfurt	7 May 1943
Stalag IXC (Hospital)	Bad Sulza, near Weimar	22 May 1943
Stalag IXAH	Spangenberg, near Kassel	11 July 1943
Stalag Luft III	Sagan, near Breslau (modern Żagań, Poland)	1 October 1943
Stalag XXA (357)	Thorn, near Posen (modern Toruń, Poland)	1 July 1944
Stalag 357	Fallingbostel, near Hannover	August 1944
March from Fallingbostel to Lübeck area		April – May 1945

BOMBS AND BARBED WIRE

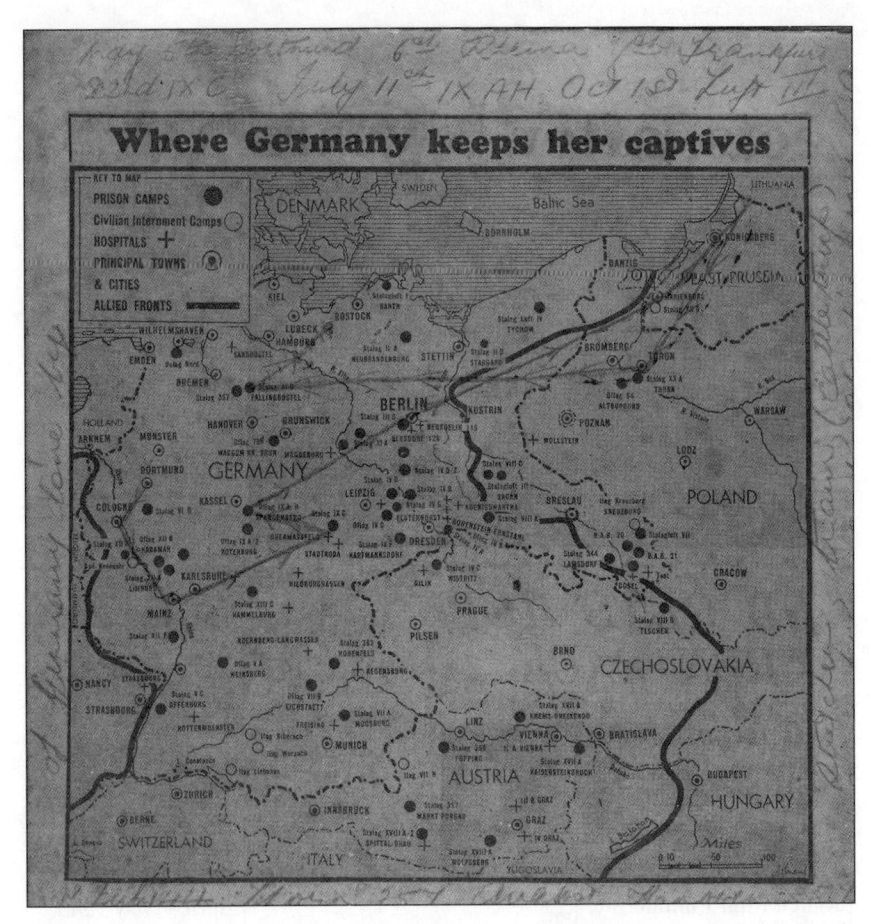

Ad's tour of Germany. Ambrose drew on this map for his children to show his travels through Germany as a prisoner. Interestingly he has placed Stalag Luft III some 200 kilometres to the north east of the actual location (Adlam Family Collection).

SELECT BIBLIOGRAPHY

Books

Bellamy, C. 2009, *Absolute War*, Pan Military Classics
Burt, K. Leasor, J. 1956, *The One That Got Away*, Fontana Books, London
Brickhill, P. 1950, *The Great Escape*, Faber, London
Brickhill, P. 1957, *Reach for the Sky*, Fontana Books, London and Glasgow
Bushby, J. 1972, *Gunner's Moon*, Futura Publications, London
Carroll, T. 2004, *The Great Escape from Stalag Luft III*, Pocket Books, London,
Chorlton, M. 2012, *The RAF Pathfinders*, Countryside Books (GB)
Charlwood, D. 1956, *No Moon Tonight*, Angus & Robertson, Australia
Cheshire, L. 1955, *Bomber Pilot*, Arrow Books (UK)
Constable, T.J. & Toliver, R.F. 1986, *Das Waren die Deutschen Fliegerasse 1939 – 1945* Motorverlag, Stuttgart
Cooper, A. 2013, *Air Battle of the Ruhr*, Pen and Sword Aviation, Barnsley UK
Crawley, A. 1956, *Escape from Germany*, Fontana Books, London and Glasgow
Dear, I.C.B and Foot, M.R.D. 1995, *The Oxford Companion to the Second World War* Oxford University Press
Eriksson, P. 2017, Alarmstart: *The German Fighter Pilot's Exerience in the Second World War* Amberley Publishing, UK
Freeman, R. 1993, *The Royal Air Force of World War Two in Colour*, Brockhampton Press, London
Falconer, J. 1998, *Bomber Command Handbook 1939–1945*, Sutton Publishing, UK
Feast, S. 1992, *The Pathfinder Companion*, Grub Street Press, London
Hastings, M. 1979, *Bomber Command*, Pan MacMillan, London
Halfpenny, B.B. 2004, *Bomber Aircrew in World War Two*, Pen and Sword Aviation, Barnsley, South Yorkshire

Irving, D. 1964, *Und Deuschlands Städte Starben Nicht*, Schweizer Druck und Verlagshaus AG, Zürich
Murray, W. 1988, *Luftwaffe*, Grafton Publishing, London
Neillands, R. 2004, *The Bomber War*, John Murray, London
Pearson, S. 2013, *The Great Escaper*, Hodder & Stoughton, London
Richards, D. 2001, *RAF Bomber Command in the Second World War*, Penguin, London
Terraine, J. 2010, *The Right of the Line*, Pen and Sword Military, Barnsley, South Yorkshire
Williams, E. 1953, *The Wooden Horse*, Fontana Books, London and Glasgow
Wilson, K. 2019 *Men of Air*, Simon and Schuster

Journals
Rollings C, 'Dulag Luft' *After the Battle* No 106 1999 pp3-27

UK National Archives
RAF Operational Record Books ref AIR/27/1788
Royal Air Force personell record of 626241 Sergeant Adlam, A.A

Selected Websites
Bomber Command Museum, Canada
https://www.bombercommandmuseum.ca/bomber-command/bomber-command-no-405-vancouver-squadron/

405 Squadron Association
http://www.405sqn.com/history.html

RAF Pathfinders Archive
https://raf-pathfinders.com/405-squadron/

No 10 Squadron RAF
https://en.wikipedia.org/wiki/No._10_Squadron_RAF

Aircrew Remembered
http://aircrewremembered.com

An Airman's Letter to his Mother
https://en.wikipedia.org/wiki/An_Airman%27s_Letter_to_His_Mother

38 Squadron RAF
https://en.wikipedia.org/wiki/No._38_Squadron_RAF

SELECT BIBLIOGRAPHY

Ken Fenton's War
https://kenfentonswar.com/dulag-luft/

The Real Great Escape
http://therealgreatescape.com/stalag-luft-iii/

Stalag Luft III Prison Camp Musuem
https://www.atlasobscura.com/places/great-escape-prisoner-camp-museum-stalag-luft-3

The True Story of the Great Escape
https://www.history.co.uk/article/the-true-story-of-the-great-escape

Australian War Memorial
https://www.awm.gov.au/visit/exhibitions/stolenyears/ww2/germany/story5

Stalag XIb Fallingbostel
https://www.google.com/search?client=firefox-b-d&q=fallingbostel

ACKNOWLEDGEMENTS

When I first started on this journey I needed luck. The project started life with a reasonable narrative. If it was to develop to a really good read it was essential that I have a breakthrough or two. There were, indeed, breakthroughs at hand. I would like to acknowledge the people who helped that journey along.

Firstly, I would like to acknowledge the late Mrs Miranda (Anne) Adlam of Gloucester, England. She kept the wartime letters from Ambrose (Ad) her husband, which proved what no one in the family had even guessed: he had been in Stalag Luft III at the time of the great escape. Fortunately her request to destroy the letters was not acted on by her children. This would have killed the story for ever.

Secondly, I wish to acknowledge the late Mr Tony Casson of Melbourne, Australia, son of Lieutenant Commander John Casson. John Casson was at Dulag Luft, the interrogation centre for newly shot-down airmen. Later he was heavily involved in the Great Escape from Stalag Luft III. He had, fortunately talked about it in detail to his son. In the research phase, Tony gave of his time to me generously and, crucially, provided some aspects of the Great Escape, which have remained hidden from other researchers into that astonishing event.

I must also acknowledge my co-writer Michael Adlam, Ambrose' son. Mike initially requested the project, provided photographs and details of his father's life and carefully vetted the developing drafts. He was a joy to work with, throughout.

I would also like to pay tribute to the Royal Australian Air Force History and Heritage Branch who together with the Royal Canadian Air Force History and Heritage Office have provided valuable documents and guidance.

ACKNOWLEDGMENTS

I particularly wish to acknowledge the United Kingdom National Archives at Kew for the now-declassified records relating to all aspects of Royal Air Force operations in World War II. The operational records books were vital in piecing together Ambrose Adlam's story.

I would also like to acknowledge the other authors who have written about RAF Bomber Command; life in German prisoner of war camps, especially those of Dulag Luft; Stalag Luft III and, especially, the Great Escape itself.

I must pay tribute to Denny Neave and Allison Paterson of Big Sky Publishing for their enthusiasm, encouragement and belief in the project and their managerial skill in turning the project into a book.

I would especially like to acknowledge the following men who flew in RAF Bomber Command. I had drawn heavily on their experience for a previous project. Between them they gave me a vast canvas of Royal Air Force life on which to draw for this project. This ranged across operational detail; nomenclature; air force life and culture; anecdotes of facts, feelings and faults.

- Sergant Frank Walshaw, 44 Squadron, Wireless Operator;
- Pilot Office Peter Langdon, 44 Squadron, Flight Engineer; 227 Squadron, Pilot;
- Pilot Officer Colin Watt DFM, 44 Squadron, Pilot;
- Flying Officer Don Charlwood, 103 Squadron, Navigator;
- Warrant Officer Bert Dowty, 44 Squadron, Front Gunner;
- Warrant Officer Dennis Over, 106 and 227 Squadron, Rear Gunner;
- Sergeant Charles Churchill DFM, 44 Squadron, Wireless Operator.

Finally, I wish to pay tribute to the 185,000 men who flew in RAF Bomber Command for their determination, their modest courage and their acceptance that their own life may have to be given to rid the world of an evil. Almost all of the stories are lost.

At least not this one!

Jeff Steel
Melbourne, Australia,
January 2021.

ABOUT THE AUTHORS

JEFF STEEL

My interest in Hitler's war started dramatically. At age seven, with my parents, I emerged from Euston Station in London. The immediate area resembled a smoke-blackened Pompeii. 'There was a terrible war' my parents told me. Their house in Coventry had been bombed: their sole remaining possession was a large mirror. The world had gone mad. This triggered a strong desire to understand the craziness.

The result of this seminal event was a lifetime of intense curiosity on all aspects of the war. As a student I had worked in Germany on the site of the Battle of the Bulge. I found many artefacts; fortunately none of them exploded. During my professional life in Information Technology, I visited many World War II sites. These range from Pearl Harbour, Dresden and the Burma Railway. I not only met and gathered the stories from men who had fought for the Allied side, but also the veterans of Stalingrad and the Siege of Leningrad.

Over time one paramount feature distilled its way to prominence. *In the crucible of war ordinary men do extraordinary things.*

My breakthrough in writing was to ghost-write 'No Heil Hitler' for my friend Paul Cieslar, which won a Pulitzer prize and is now published in four countries.

This success led to other assignments. And so it is with 'Bombs and Barbed Wire'. For the Adlam family, their father had missing years in his life. He was an ordinary, decent, undramatic man. The key to the secret of his extraordinary wartime adventures had lain hidden for sixty years in a chocolate box. The family had never thought about it ... *then we found the story!*

ABOUT THE AUTHORS

MIKE ADLAM

Dad never spoke much about the war, and as I was only 11-years old when he died. I never really knew anything about what he did, although I had picked up little snippets that stuck with me for a lifetime. Mum never mentioned what he (and she) had done in the war; after he died she was too consumed with grief and the bringing up of four young children to have time for that.

The years rolled on, I first worked in pharmaceuticals in the United Kingdom before starting my own company in 2008. It wasn't until Mum died in 2012 that my thoughts returned to those snippets I had heard as a young boy. By then I had also inherited a chocolate box full of letters that Dad had written to Mum from the prisoner of war camps he had been in.

It was those letters which took me on this amazing journey, first to Germany on the 70th anniversary of Dad being shot down. We laid wreaths on the graves of the two crew members who died as my father bailed out of the burning plane. Then through a family member I was introduced to Jeff Steel who offered to take a look at the letters. What Jeff discovered in those letters, that had been in that Black Magic chocolate box for over 60 years, amazed me and my family. My father's very simple wartime communication not only resulted in this book, but brought me closer than I had ever been to Dad, a father I had never really known.

More books from Big Sky Publishing

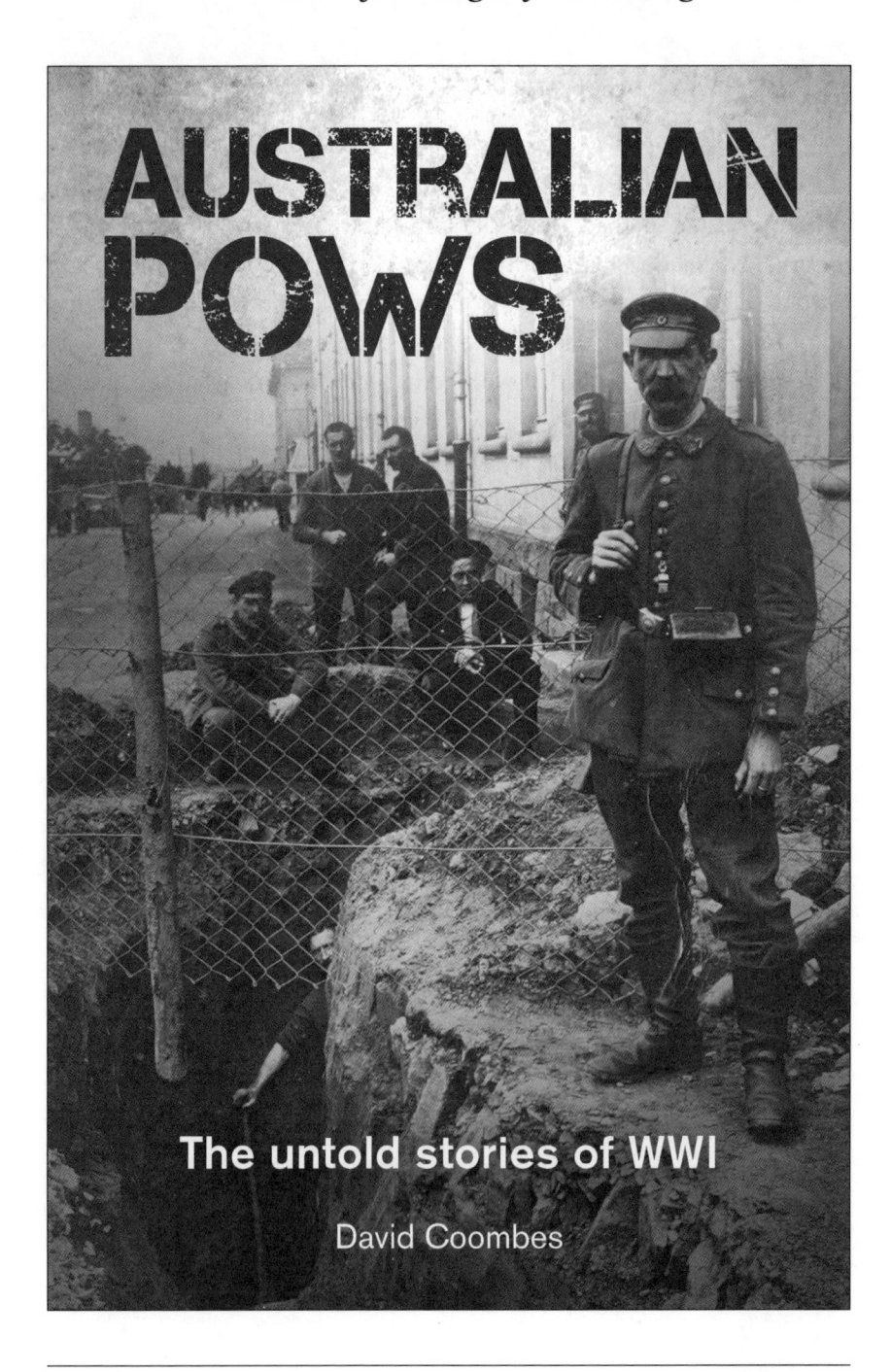

AUSTRALIAN POWS

The untold stories of WWI

David Coombes

View sample pages, reviews and information on this book and other titles at
www.bigskypublishing.com.au

BIG SKY PUBLISHING

More books from Big Sky Publishing

"an incredible true story"

THE MUSIC MAKER OF AUSCHWITZ IV

JACI BYRNE

View sample pages, reviews and information on this book and other titles at
www.bigskypublishing.com.au

BIG SKY PUBLISHING

For more great titles visit
www.bigskypublishing.com.au